The Stuart Editions

AN ANTHOLOGY OF JACOBEAN DRAMA

VOLUME II

RICHARD C. HARRIER is Chairman of the English Department of Washington Square College, New York University. An authority on the manuscripts and poetry of Sir Thomas Wyatt, Professor Harrier has been awarded a Folger Library study grant and a research grant from The American Philosophical Society.

The Stuart Editions

J. Max Patrick, *series editor*

ALREADY PUBLISHED

An Anthology
of
JACOBEAN DRAMA

Volume II

EDITED

WITH AN INTRODUCTION, NOTES, AND VARIANTS

BY

RICHARD C. HARRIER

New York University Press
1963

This book was first published in 1963 in the
Doubleday Anchor Seventeenth-Century Series.
Library of Congress Catalog Card No. 63-8749
Copyright © 1963 by Doubleday & Company, Inc.
All Rights Reserved
Printed in the United States of America

CONTENTS

INTRODUCTION

The four plays brought together here are engaging examples of dramatic sensibility. They are not offered particularly for the study of tragedy, satire, or comedy, although that approach may also be profitable, especially in connection with the accompanying volume. Each play is strikingly individual; and the range of temperaments is large, even when similar kinds of experience are represented. Together they describe the arc of theatrical spirit from the century's first decade to the eve of the civil war—raging, exploring, soaring, and breaking into cruder elements.[1]

The Changeling, one of the greatest English plays, is a work of collaboration between Thomas Middleton and William Rowley. The more distinguished of the two, Thomas Middleton, was born in London in 1580. He was educated at Queen's College, Oxford, but did not take a degree, probably because of financial difficulties resulting from his mother's second marriage. Returning to London, he began a literary career with fashionable pieces of morality and satire, *The Wisdom of Solomon Paraphrased* (1597)[2] and *Micro-cynicon, Six Snarling Satires* (1599). Throughout his career, he continued to produce a variety of popular forms, realistic prose pamphlets, moral and elegiac verse, masques, and pageants. After 1613 he designed many of the annual pageants in honor of each Lord Mayor of London; and this city connection was

[1] My adjectives refer to Tourneur, Middleton-Rowley, Ford, and Shirley respectively. I have placed Tourneur's play second, although it is the earliest, because it is better to begin with work whose authorship has not been disputed.

[2] Dates given in parentheses are dates of publication. For additional information see the Chronology.

made official in 1620, when he became City Chronologer, a position he held until his death in 1627. He was followed in that office by Ben Jonson.

The first phase of Middleton's work includes some memorable scenes of London life. In *The Family of Love* he portrays those familiar grotesques of the day, the lecherous courtier, the pandering citizen, and the Puritan. Using the disguised-prince plot in *The Phoenix*, the kingdom's vicious humours are displayed and censured before the prince closes the play with appropriate punishments. Two more plays written before 1606 complete a survey of city types, *Your Five Gallants* and *Michaelmas Term*. Also about this time, Middleton wrote *A Trick to Catch the Old One*, which Philip Massinger paralleled some fifteen years later in *A New Way to Pay Old Debts*.

The most sensational event in Middleton's theatrical career occurred in August 1624, when the King's Men performed *A Game at Chess*. This play had—so far as is known—the longest opening run of any between *Tamberlaine* and the closing of the theatres, drawing in thousands a day for about nine days. But it is hardly a play at all. Rather, it is a spectacle of the political chess game then going on between Gondomar, the Spanish ambassador in London, and the royal family. The actual checkmate which Protestant London feared would have been a marriage between Prince Charles and the Spanish infanta. The prince had, in fact, run off with the Duke of Buckingham—like two knights in a medieval romance—to have a look at the girl. But both the play and the adventure turned out well for England. As a finale, Middleton had Gondomar and his men driven down Hell-mouth; and after a boring sojourn, Charles returned uncommitted. Knowing that they were inviting the wrath of the Privy Council, the players had chosen a time when the king was away. Within a short time, however, they were summoned, forbidden to play, and Middleton was imprisoned.

In the genre of tragedy Middleton wrote only one other play, *Women Beware Women*, which may be dated about 1621. Like *The Changeling*, it is a study in "the progressive deterioration of character,[3] based on the life of Bianca Capello, paramour of Francesco de' Medici, Duke of Florence. The chess game in this play was transformed by T. S. Eliot into a scene symbolic of the modern wasteland.[4]

Virtually nothing is known of the early life of William Rowley, who may have been born about 1585. He began his career as an actor in the Duke of York's company (later the Prince's Men) in 1608. He was one of its leading members until 1617, when A Fair Quarrel was published, apparently his first collaboration with Middleton. The sort of role Rowley specialized in is represented by Jacques, "a simple clownish Gentleman," in his own play All's Lost by Lust, and the Fat Bishop in Middleton's A Game at Chess. In the new license given to the King's Men in 1625, Rowley's name occurs, supporting other evidence that he ended his career with that troupe. He died in 1626.

His own plays are A Shoemaker a Gentleman, written about 1608, A New Wonder, A Woman Never Vexed, about 1610, All's Lost by Lust, about 1619, and A Match at Midnight, about 1622. His earliest collaboration, in 1607, was The Travels of the Three English Brothers, with John Day and George Wilkins. His collaborations with Middleton include The Old Law, about 1615, in which Philip Massinger also had a hand. With Middleton as the only other writer, he did A Fair Quarrel in 1617, The World Tossed at Tennis, 1620, The Changeling, 1622, and The Spanish Gypsy in 1623. But Rowley also accommodated his genial style to those of several other writers. With Thomas Dekker and John Ford he wrote The Witch of Edmonton in 1621, with John Fletcher The Maid of the Mill, 1623, and with John Webster A Cure for a Cuckold, 1625.[5]

[3] The phrase of M. C. Bradbrook quoted in Samuel Schoenbaum, Middleton's Tragedies (New York, 1955), p. 102.

[4] See The Wasteland, Section II and notes. The reader may recall that Vittoria Accoramboni (the White Devil), mistress of the Duke of Bracciano, is sometimes confused with Bianca Capello.

[5] See D. M. Robb, "The Canon of William Rowley's Plays," MLi., XLV (April 1950), 129–41.

According to a note by Edmond Malone in his copy of the
1653 Quarto of *The Changeling*, the play was licensed by Sir
Henry Herbert, Master of Revels, in 1622. It was performed
at court in January 1624 by the reorganized Lady Elizabeth's
Men; but its control was vested in the person of Christopher
Beeston, owner of the Phoenix. *The Changeling* remained a
popular play until the close of the theatres in 1642, being
performed by Queen Henrietta's Men at the Salisbury Court
Theatre under Christopher Beeston, and by the troupe of boys
under his son William. Its popularity, however, was largely
due to the role of the Changeling Antonio as done by the two
outstanding comedians of Queen Henrietta's company, William Robbins and Timothy Reade. After the Restoration it was
revived, with Thomas Betterton acting Deflores and Thomas
Sheppy triumphing as Antonio. The 1668 Quarto of the play
mentions that it was performed at the theatre in Lincoln's
Inn Fields by the Duke of York's Men, the troupe led by Sir
William Davenant.

One source of the main plot in *The Changeling* is John
Reynolds' *The Triumphs of God's Revenge Against the Crying and Execrable Sin of Murther*, a collection of thirty tales
illustrating the title without psychological subtlety but with
considerable edifying comment. The first book of the collection, containing the source of the play, was published in 1621.

In Reynolds' story, Deflores is an attractive gallant who
murders Alonzo for Beatrice after she has fallen in love with
Alsemero in church. Deflores does not demand her virginity
as the price of the crime, being content with a few kisses.
Sometime after Beatrice is married to Alsemero, Alsemero
becomes violently jealous—for no good reason—and in revenge
Beatrice comes to accept Deflores as her lover. Differing completely from the character in the play, Alsemero more than
matches the adulterers in villainy. Becoming suspicious, he
traps them and murders them. Still later, Tomazo challenges
Alsemero to a duel, believing him to be responsible for the
death of Alonzo. Instead of meeting the challenge honorably,
Alsemero kills Tomazo with a trick and flees; but he is
caught, confesses, and is executed. God's revenge is com-
pleted when the corpse of Alsemero is thrown into the sea,

and those of Beatrice and Deflores are exhumed and burned.[6]

There are many versions in folk tales of the bed trick by which Diaphanta is substituted for Beatrice, but the immediate source of that plot is probably Leonard Digges's *Gerardo, the Unfortunate Spaniard,* entered for publication in March 1622. In Digges's novel, itself a translation from a Spanish tale, Isdaura (Beatrice) is left in the care of an old servant while her father voyages to the new world. On his return the father decides to marry Isdaura to Roberto, son of an old friend, unaware that the servant has been madly in love with the girl all the while and had hoped to win her. One evening just before the wedding, the old servant goes to Isdaura's room, threatens to kill her if she will not promise to marry him instead, and finally ravishes her. When he is asleep Isdaura stabs him and leaves his body in the street, escaping all suspicion of the act. Then, being in the position of Beatrice on her wedding night, she must contrive to use her maid Julia as Diaphanta is used.[7] It has also been argued that the old servant, ugly and unwanted, is a source for the figure of Deflores, in addition to the more obvious influence of Shakespeare's Iago and Richard III.

N. W. Bawcutt has pointed out that Middleton and Rowley were stimulated by these sources because they had already used similar episodes in earlier works. Rowley did a version of the murdered-substitute plot in *All's Lost by Lust* (III. iii; IV. ii), and the Rowley-Middleton play *A Fair Quarrel* included an episode similar to Deflores' demand of Beatrice after the murder (III. ii. 29–141). Middleton's own *The Family of Love* is a source for the sub-plot in the relations of Lipsalve, Gudgeon, and Dr. Glister. The doctor is enlisted by Lipsalve and Gudgeon in their courtship of Mistress Purge; but they are duped into beating one another, since he is their secret rival in love. Intending to cuckold him in revenge, Lip-

---

[6] For further details and excerpts from Reynolds' book, see the edition of N. W. Bawcutt, introduction and appendix. Also, *The Anchor Anthology of Short Fiction of the Seventeenth Century,* edited by Charles C. Mish, Doubleday Anchor Books, 1963.

[7] See E. G. Mathews, "The Murdered Substitute Tale," *MLQ,* VI (June 1945), 187–95.

salve and Gudgeon gain entrance into the doctor's house as
patients; but he penetrates their disguise and foils them. This
sequence suggests much of the Antonio and Franciscus sub-
plot, including the duel which never comes about. The house
of Alibius, in which it occurs, has a general similarity to the
Bethlehem Hospital (Bedlam) of Jacobean London.[8]

Editors and students of *The Changeling* have shown a re-
markable consistency in dividing the work of the two dramatists. Rowley is usually given the opening and close of the
play, I. i.–ii. and V. iii. In addition, Rowley is thought to
have done III. iii. and IV. iii. These scenes make up the comic
sub-plot and material in the popular moral tradition. To Middleton are assigned the more sophisticated and ironic scenes :
II. i–ii; III. i–ii, iv; IV. i–ii; V. i–ii. Despite the unanimity of
the scholars, it is well to keep in mind "that curious law (of
undeniable operation in Jacobean drama) by which the result of collaboration of any two or three men is not the sum-
mation of their qualities, but often some rather different
product."[9]

Very little is known about the life of Cyril Tourneur (or
Turnor). He may be related to the Richard Turnor who held
English offices in the Netherlands, including the lieutenancy
of Brill from 1585 to 1596. Tourneur seems to have abandoned the stage in 1613 after a very brief career. The latter
part of his life was spent overseas in the foreign service, first
in the lowlands and then at Cadiz. He died in Ireland in 1626.

His first work was a political satire called *The Transformed
Metamorphosis* (1600), anticipating a revival of the Golden
Age under the monarch who would follow Elizabeth.
Tourneur's prophetic utterance proved all too mistaken,
but it secured his political connections. His one undoubted
play is *The Atheist's Tragedy, or the Honest Man's Revenge*
(1611). He is also the author of a lost tragi-comedy called
The Nobleman, entered for publication in 1612.

[8] See Robert Reed, *Bedlam on the Jacobean Stage* (Cambridge,
Mass., 1952), pp. 34 ff.

[9] Una M. Ellis-Fermor, *The Jacobean Drama, An Interpretation*
(London, 1936), p. xi.

The Revenger's Tragedy was entered in the Stationers' Register, together with Middleton's *A Trick to Catch the Old One*, in 1607. The first quarto appeared in the same year without an author's name on the title page. A half century later the play was attributed to Tourneur, and until the twentieth century his authorship remained unquestioned. Among the reasons for doubting Tourneur's right to the play are the erratic nature of seventeenth-century catalogues and lists and the contrasting nature of *The Atheist's Tragedy.* But disputes about authorship are usually motivated by the wish to add a good play to a favorite author's list, or by the wish to remove a bad one. In the case of *The Revenger's Tragedy*, a number of dissenters have wished to give the play to Middleton, and some of his mannerisms have been found in its text.[10] The majority of scholars, however, prefer to leave it to the credit of Tourneur, and so do I. The reader may begin his study of the problem by comparing its nature with the Middleton portions of *The Changeling.* He must keep in mind, however, that *The Revenger's Tragedy* was written some fifteen years earlier, and that Middleton's early comedies are probably more relevant, despite the difference in genre. If at times the play is reminiscent of Webster's *The White Devil,* the reader need not be surprised. John Webster has also been proposed as the author.

The dramatist whose name may well follow in honor after those of Shakespeare, Marlowe, and Jonson is John Ford. He is the last of undoubted genius, and of that peculiar quality one associates with the age of Sidney, Ralegh, Essex, and Shakespeare. Ford, a younger son of an old Devonshire family, was born in 1586. His mother was the niece of Lord Chief Justice Popham; and he was intended for the legal profession, being admitted to the Middle Temple in 1602. Ford never became a barrister, however, and the small legacy left him by his father may reflect family disapproval.

[10] See the review of arguments in Samuel Schoenbaum, *Middleton's Tragedies.* More recently, an anti-Middleton argument is well made by Inga-Stina Ekeblad, "On the Authorship of *The Revenger's Tragedy,*" *English Studies* XLI (1960), 225–40.

His spirit was no doubt too Platonic for legal affairs, a fact evident from his first work, *Fame's Memorial* (1606), an elegy on the death of the Earl of Devonshire. Dedicated to the Countess Penelope, who was earlier Sidney's Stella and Lady Rich, the poem celebrates the cult of romantic love. Similarly, in his best work as a dramatist, Ford was deeply committed to situations of passion—sometimes unnatural passion—frustrated by the demands of honor. And he writes with such intensity of conviction that the fictional experience has the illusion of personal participation. His motto was *Fide Honor*, "By Faith—Honor," an anagram of his name.

We do not know anything definite about Ford's beginning in the theatre. Little is clear before 1621, when he wrote *The Witch of Edmonton* with Thomas Dekker and William Rowley. He continued to collaborate with Dekker in four additional plays, but after 1624 he began to work alone. Ford's major works, all written between 1627 and 1632 are: *The Lover's Melancholy, Love's Sacrifice, The Broken Heart*, and *'Tis Pity She's a Whore*. These four plays were published in 1633. In the following year, Ford added a fine historical play, *The Chronicle History of Perkin Warbeck, A Strange Truth*, based in part on Bacon's *History of the Reign of Henry VII* (1622). His last independent work was *The Lady's Trial*, licensed in 1638, but the date of his death is unknown.

Ford owes much to his study of Robert Burton's *Anatomy of Melancholy* (1621), an infinitely richer collection of psychological lore than was available to Shakespeare.[11] Burton's work stimulated the dramatist's analysis of the passions, their hidden ways and inevitable dominance of the whole personality. And if the remarks of a therapist like Tecnicus do not embody the art his name implies, they reflect on victims of unforgettable power and beauty. Bassanes, Orgilus, Penthea, and Calantha are a timeless monument of human involvement and isolation.

The comment of Una Ellis-Fermor on *The Broken Heart*

[11] See Blaine S. Ewing, *Burtonian Melancholy in the Plays of John Ford* (Princeton, 1940); and George F. Sensabaugh, *The Tragic Muse of John Ford* (Stanford and London, 1944).

as it was illuminated on a modern stage is particularly worth noting.

> *The Broken Heart* is, to most of Ford's readers, the su-
> preme reach of his genius. If the comic plot were excised,
> and we have the evidence of Maeterlinck's translation
> and Marcel Schwob's comment upon the acting version
> thus obtained to show us that nothing is lost and much
> is gained by excising it, a play is left which for sim-
> plicity and compactness of line, for dignity and for com-
> pression of emotion, thought and phrase is unsurpassed
> in Jacobean drama.[12]

This play—and Ford's genius in general—seems to have taken strength from the situation which was weakening the English stage, namely, its ever closer relation to the court.

The court of Henrietta Maria, the French Catholic—and half Medici—Queen of Charles I, was the focus of Ford's interest in aristocratic sensibility. There is no evidence of a direct and personal connection between the dramatist and the court, but he was close to men like Richard Crashaw and James Shirley, who—as Catholics—were familiar with the queen and those around her. Henrietta Maria was a striking combination of religious piety and innocent paganism, finding an outlet for the latter impulse in the traditions of pastoralism and Platonic love. No event in her life better illustrates this fact than her acting in a production of Walter Montague's *The Shepherd's Paradise*, late in 1632. The participation of the queen and her maids of honor in a theatrical was of course unprecedented, and it soon became the center of the long national dispute about the morality of the stage. For William Prynne in particular, who had been collecting over nine years the furious assaults of Puritanism on the stage, the queen's adventure was the opening of a tragedy. When Prynne's *Histriomastix* appeared in the winter of 1632 (dated 1633), his attacks were interpreted by Archbishop Laud as aimed at the queen, and even the king. After some litigation, Prynne was deprived of his university honors, pilloried, had

[12] *The Jacobean Drama*, p. 232. See also the remarks of Charles Lamb quoted at the end of my notes to the play.

his ears cut off, and was imprisoned for life. Meanwhile, the gentlemen of London vied in displaying their devotion to theatricals.

Another production favored by the queen was William Davenant's masque *The Temple of Love,* which tableaued the planting of love's true religion in a "dull northern isle." A comment on this affair occurs in one of James Howell's letters dated June 3, 1634.

> The Court affords little News at present, but that there is a Love call'd Platonick Love, which much sways there of late; it is a Love abstracted from all corporeal gross Impressions and sensual Appetite, but consists in Contemplations and Ideas of the Mind, not in any carnal Fruition. This Love sets the Wits of the Town on work; and they say there will be a Mask shortly of it, whereof Her Majesty and her Maids of Honour will be part.[13]

The language of courtly love, derived chiefly from Petrarch's sonnets and the poems of the French Pleiade, was surely well known to English courtiers long before the arrival of Henrietta Maria in 1625. Stated briefly, the religion of love required a worship of beauty and took as axiomatic the equation of beauty with virtue. Its practice took two directions. One, represented by Cardinal Bembo's discourse in Castiglione's *The Courtier,* limited lovers to a kiss and the feasting of eyes, while the mind soared toward mystical union. Another, illustrated in Ford's *'Tis Pity She's a Whore,* acted on the principle that love should be restrained by no law or approved experience, and dared to assert the purity of incest. But Ford is not doctrinaire. He is the creator of some of the greatest designs in the logic of passion, whether it is turned inward upon itself or flows outward with the senses into the other infinite.

James Shirley is the only major dramatist who was born an Elizabethan (1596) and died a witness of the Restoration

---

[13] Joseph Jacobs, ed., *The Familiar Letters of James Howell* (London, 1890), pp. 317–18.

(1666). He followed Philip Massinger and William Shakespeare as leading writer for the King's Men, and after the
Restoration at least eighteen of his plays were revived. *The
Lady of Pleasure,* however, does not appear to have been
one of those.

Shirley was born of a London family and entered the Merchant Taylor's School in 1608. According to Anthony Wood,
he spent several years at Oxford before matriculating in St.
Catharine's College, Cambridge, in 1615. After his M.A. degree Shirley entered the Anglican Church and went to St.
Albans, Hertfordshire, where he taught in the grammar school
and soon became its master. He married Elizabeth Gilmet,
daughter of a family which included two mayors of St. Albans.

In 1624 Shirley left his position as head of the grammar
school and settled in London. The reason was probably his
conversion to Catholicism. He immediately began writing
two plays a year for the company at the Cockpit (Phoenix) in
Drury Lane; and he continued that practice with only one
short break until 1636, when he departed for Ireland. Shirley's first play was *Love Tricks, or the School of Compliment.*

When the London theatres closed under the threat of
plague on May 12, 1636, Shirley went to Dublin, where he
wrote for the Irish company organized by John Ogilby.
Among his efforts for that group are *The Royal Master, St.
Patrick for Ireland,* and a revision of Middleton's *No Wit No
Help Like a Woman's.*

On his return to London in April 1640, Shirley became
dramatist for the King's Men, Philip Massinger having died a
month earlier. After the closing of the theatres in September
of 1642, he joined the royalist forces under William Cavendish, Earl of Newcastle; but he did not follow his patron to
Paris after the royalist defeat. Instead, Shirley returned to
London, took up his old profession of teaching, and found aid
as well as companionship in the household of Thomas Stanley
the classicist.[14] In 1646 Shirley published his non-dramatic

[14] See Galbraith Miller Crump, ed., *The Poems and Translations
of Thomas Stanley* (Oxford, 1962), p. xxv. This volume includes
Stanley's translation of Pico's *Platonicke Discourse of Love.*

verse, and in 1647 he furnished commendatory verses for the
Beaumont and Fletcher folio. There is no definite evidence,
however, that he was an editor of the folio. Throughout the
years of the Commonwealth, Shirley seems to have lived com-
fortably, and he died—as Anthony Wood put it—from "af-
frightments, disconsolations, and other miseries" of the great
fire of London, 1666.

The Lady of Pleasure was written for Queen Henrietta's
Men in 1635. Several years earlier Shirley had become a
Valet of the Royal Chamber, and his compliment to the "two
royall luminaries" (IV. iii. 175) is based on personal observa-
tion. The play as a whole—one that Shirley thought among
his best—contrasts with Ford's use of similar material. Shirley
writes as both professional dramatist and courtier, limited by
social awareness and pragmatic spirit. Therefore, his play is
not simply a comedy of manners or a tribute to Platonic love
but an uncertain mixture of both. It is no doubt a failure but
an interesting one. The lady of pleasure herself, Aretina Bornwell, is a Jonsonian humour running to breathless horror and
reform; while Celestina employs a worldly wisdom in the
pursuit of honorable love, another kind of pleasure. Shirley
offers a definition of the good and noble life which is primarily
negative, and he does it with an air of superiority not soundly
based on genuine literary accomplishment. But he has the
merit of sincere good sense trying to accommodate itself to
historical realities. His failure was the failure of the culture
he lived for, and he was fortunate enough to see that culture
reborn with new power and brilliance.

The texts of the plays are in the spelling of the original
quartos, with the exception of *i, j, u,* and *v,* which are used
in the modern fashion. The purpose of this editorial policy is
to take the student forcibly back into the language of the
period in which the works were written. Since the moderniza-
tion of Shakespeare's texts became fashionable, many editions
of Tudor and Stuart plays have been produced in modern
spelling. The result has been a loss of comprehension, despite
the proliferation of glosses and notes. Modernized texts en-

courage the ignoring of glosses and eliminate the rich context of verbal association which illuminated the originals.

Some consistent alteration has been made in order to focus the student's eye on the language of the play. Titles and names of characters have been regularized or modernized; but in one notable instance, that of Sentlove (Scentlove) in *The Lady of Pleasure*, I have returned to the quarto spelling. Abbreviations have been silently expanded. Stage directions are placed and phrased for the most part in modern style; but I have made no attempt to locate any scene, since the dramatists did not concern themselves with the matter. Punctuation has sometimes been altered for sense without notation in the variants, but the seventeenth-century uses of the period and colon have been preserved wherever possible. Capitals have been added, but no capital has been removed from a word meant to be set off within the line. Wherever the apostrophe occurs it has been kept but placed where a modern writer would place it. The apostrophes added have been necessary to distinguish contractions from possessives. Occasional changes in spelling and emendations are recorded in the variants.

There follows a table of events in which the careers of Middleton, Rowley, Tourneur, Ford, and Shirley are outlined against the major events of the age. Since Shakespeare's career is most frequently described, it is represented here at only a few major points. I have made a particular effort to present a list of dramatic publications during the Commonwealth, since these items seem to be available only in the most complex bibliographies or specialized studies. The authorities for dating are W. W. Greg, G. E. Bentley, E. K. Chambers, A. Harbage, C. S. Lewis, and D. Bush.

The editor wishes to express his deep appreciation to the directors of the Houghton Library, the Folger Shakespeare Library, and the Pierpont Morgan Library for permission to print the works in these two volumes. He also wishes to thank them for use of their libraries' resources.

A Note on Footnotes

There are three sets of footnotes for the text in this edition, all numbered by scenes:

(a) footnotes, or glosses, to difficult or obscure words, indicated in the text by a superscript number, as, for example, [1,2,3,] etc., are to be found on the bottom of the page in which the relevant text appears;

(b) variants, or alternate manuscript versions, designated in the text by a superscript number in *brackets*, as, for example, [1],[2],[3], etc., are to be found in the back of the book;

(c) explanatory notes, or more extended commentary, designated by a superscript number in *parentheses* in the text, as, for example, (1),(2),(3), etc., are to be found also in the back of the book.

CHRONOLOGY

1558   Elizabeth I accedes to the throne.
Robert Greene born.

1559   George Chapman born in Hitchin, Hertfordshire.
Matthew Parker becomes Archbishop of Canterbury.
A Mirror for Magistrates published.
Jasper Heywood's translation of Seneca's *Troas* published.
Gammer Gurton's Needle probably written for performance at Christ's College, Cambridge.

1560   Jasper Heywood's translation of Seneca's *Thyestes* published.
Geneva Bible .published.

1561   *Gorboduc* acted at Christmas in the great hall of the Inner Temple before Queen Elizabeth.
Jasper Heywood's translation of Seneca's *Hercules Furens* published.
Francis Bacon born.
Sir Thomas Hoby translates Castiglione's *Book of the Courtier*.

1562   Civil War in France; Elizabeth makes a secret treaty with the Huguenots.
Arthur Brooke's *Romeus and Juliet* published.
Lope de Vega born.

1563   John Foxe's *Acts and Monuments* (*Book of Martyrs*) published.
The Thirty-nine Articles define the national church.
Plague in London.

1564   Shakespeare, Christopher Marlowe, and Galileo born.
John Calvin, Michelangelo, and Vesalius die.
Flemish Protestant refugees come to England.

1566   George Gascoigne's *Supposes* probably acted at Christmas in Gray's Inn.
John Studley's translation of Seneca's *Agamemnon* and *Medea* published.

Gismonde of Salerne acted before the queen.

James (later James I) born.

1567   Revolt in the Netherlands.

1568   Mary Queen of Scots flees to England.

1569   Rebellion of Norfolk and northern earls crushed.

1570   Pope Pius V excommunicates Elizabeth.

1571   Battle of Lepanto.

1572   Ben Jonson born in or near London.

John Donne born.

Massacre of St. Bartholomew.

Statute against vagabonds, including actors without patrons.

1576   John Marston born at Wardington.

The Theatre is built in London.

Blackfriars Theatre opened.

1577   The Curtain Theatre is built.

Robert Burton born.

Francis Drake begins his voyage around the world.

1578   John Lyly's *Euphues* published.

1579   John Fletcher born.

Stephen Gosson attacks plays in *The School of Abuse*.

Spenser's *The Shepherd's Calendar* published.

Sir Thomas North's translation of Plutarch's *Lives* published.

Negotiations opened for marriage of Elizabeth to Alençon, Duke of Anjou.

1580   Thomas Middleton born in London. Approximate date of John Webster's birth.

1581   Seneca's *Ten Tragedies* published.

Alençon (Monsieur) in England, courting Elizabeth.

1582   Plague in London.

1583   Philip Massinger born.

The Queen's Players are formed.

John Whitgift becomes Archbishop of Canterbury.

1584   Francis Beaumont born.

John Lyly's *Campaspe* and *Sapho and Phao* played before the queen by the boys of the Royal Chapel and St. Paul's.

George Peele's *Arraignment of Paris* acted before the queen by the Chapel children.

William of Orange is assassinated.

1585   Approximate date of William Rowley's birth.

Expedition to the Netherlands under the Earl of Leicester.

Cardinal Montalto becomes Sixtus V.

Ronsard dies.

1586   John Ford born.

Probable date for performance of Thomas Kyd's *Spanish Tragedy* (if not earlier).

Sir Philip Sidney dies from wounds after the Battle of Zutphen.

Trial of Mary Queen of Scots.

1587   Marlowe's *Tamburlaine* Part I acted.

Greene's *Alphonsus King of Aragon* acted.

Holinshed's *Chronicles* (2nd ed.) published.

Mary Queen of Scots executed.

Pope Sixtus V proclaims crusade against England.

1588   Defeat of the Armada.

Marlowe's *Tamburlaine* Part II acted.

John Lyly's *Galathea* and *Endimion* acted before the queen at Greenwich.

The Misfortunes of Arthur acted before the queen, with dumb shows by Francis Bacon.

1589   Marlowe's *Jew of Malta* acted.

1590   John Lyly's *Midas* acted.

Sidney's *Arcadia* (I, II, part of III) published.

Spenser's *Faerie Queene* (I–III) published.

Approximate date of Shakespeare's Henry VI plays, through 1592.

1591   Robert Greene's *Orlando Furioso* acted.

Sidney's *Astrophel and Stella* (bad text) published.

Spenser's *Complaints, Daphnaida* published.

English forces aid Henri IV in France.

1592   Robert Greene dies, having attacked Shakespeare as an "upstart crow" in his *Groatsworth of Wit*.

Plague in London.

Montaigne dies.

1593   Theatres closed by plague.

Marlowe slain by Ingram Frizer at Deptford.

Shakespeare's *Venus and Adonis* published.

Sidney's *Arcadia* (I–V) published.

Henri IV is converted to Catholicism.

1594   George Chapman's *Shadow of Night* published.

Shakespeare's *Rape of Lucrece* published.

Thomas Kyd dies.

1595   Shakespeare's *Midsummer-Night's Dream* and *Richard II*
        probably acted; Shakespeare paid as Chamberlain's man,
        with Richard Burbage and Will Kempe.

        Sidney's *Defense of Poesy* published.

        Spenser's *Colin Clout, Amoretti,* and *Epithalamion* pub-
        lished.

1596   James Shirley born. George Peele dies.

        Chapman's *Blind Beggar of Alexandria* acted by Admiral's
        Men.

        Spenser's *Faerie Queene* (I–VI) published, also *Four
        Hymns* and *Prothalamion.*

1597   Chapman's *An Humourous Day's Mirth* acted by Admiral's
        Men.

        Lost play *The Isle of Dogs* by Jonson and Thomas Nashe
        acted; Jonson imprisoned, and theatres closed.

        Shakespeare's *Henry IV* probably acted.

1598   Middleton matriculates at Queen's College, Oxford.

        Jonson's *Every Man in his Humour* acted.

        Chapman's *Achilles Shield, Iliad* (I–VII) published.

        Marston's *Metamorphosis of Pygmalion's Image* published
        with *Certain Satires,* also his *Scourge of Villainy.*

        Sidney's *Arcadia, Lady of May, Certain Sonnets,* and
        Astrophel published.

        Francis Meres, in *Palladis Tamia,* commends Shakespeare,
        Jonson, and Chapman.

        Jonson kills Gabriel Spencer in a duel.

1599   The Globe Theatre is opened.

        Jonson's *Every Man Out of his Humour* acted at the Globe.

        Marston's *Antonio and Mellida* (Part I) probably acted,
        also his revision of *Histriomastix.*

        Shakespeare's *Henry V* acted.

        Thomas Dekker's *Shoemaker's Holiday* acted.

        Spenser dies.

        Elizabeth sends Essex to Ireland; he returns and is im-
        prisoned.

        The Archbishop of Canterbury publicly burns satires and
        pamphlets.

1600   The Fortune Theatre is built.

        Cyril Tourneur's *Transformed Metamorphosis* published.

        Jonson's *Cynthia's Revels* acted and *Every Man Out of his
        Humour* published.

1601   Jonson's *Poetaster* acted, *Every Man in his Humour* pub-
           lished.
         Marston's *What You Will* probably acted.
         Dekker and Marston's *Satiromastix* acted at the Globe.
         Essex attempts revolt, is executed.
1602   Middleton writes *Blurt, Master Constable.*
         Chapman's *Gentleman Usher* and *May Day* probably acted.
1603   Elizabeth dies; James I accedes. Plague.
         Jonson's *Sejanus* acted at the Globe by the new King's
           Men.
         Marston's *Dutch Courtesan* probably acted.
         Shakespeare's *Hamlet* (first quarto) published.
         John Florio's translation of Montaigne's *Essays* published.
1604   Marston's *Malcontent* acted.
         Chapman's *Bussy D'Ambois* probably acted.
         Jonson's *Entertainment at Highgate* performed.
         Hamlet (second quarto) published.
         Hampton Court Conference.
         Bancroft becomes Archbishop of Canterbury.
1605   Jonson, Chapman, and Marston collaborate on *Eastward
           Ho!;* all three are imprisoned.
         Marston's *The Fawne* probably acted.
         Jonson's *Masque of Blackness* performed at Whitehall.
         Bacon's *Advancement of Learning* published.
         Gunpowder Plot.
1606   John Ford's *Fame's Memorial* and *Honour Triumphant*
           published.
         Jonson's *Volpone* acted at the Globe, Cambridge and Ox-
           ford.
         Marston's *Sophonisba* published.
         John Lyly dies.
1607   Middleton's *The Phoenix* and *Michaelmas Term* published.
         William Rowley's name first appears in the epistle prefaced
           to *Travels of the Three English Brothers.*
         Jonson's *Theobald's Entertainment* performed.
1608   Middleton's *Trick to Catch the Old One; A Mad World,
           My Masters; The Family of Love* published. *Your Five
           Gallants* entered for publication.
         Chapman's *Charles Duke of Byron* acted.
         John Fletcher's *Faithful Shepherdess* acted.
         Jonson's *Masque of Beauty* probably performed.

Marston is imprisoned in Newgate for an offensive play at
  Blackfriars.

1609   Jonson's *Epicoene* acted; also his *Masque of Queens*.

Beaumont and Fletcher's *Philaster* acted.

John Marston enters the Anglican Church.

1610   Jonson's *The Alchemist* acted.

Chapman's *Revenge of Bussy D'Ambois* probably acted.

Cyril Tourneur's *Atheist's Tragedy* probably acted.

1611   Cyril Tourneur's *Atheist's Tragedy* published.

Jonson's *Catiline* acted; also his masques, *Oberon* and *Love
  Freed from Ignorance and Folly*.

Beaumont and Fletcher's *King and No King* and *Maid's
  Tragedy* acted.

Shakespeare's *The Tempest* acted.

Abbot becomes Archbishop of Canterbury.

Parliament dissolved.

The King James Bible published.

1612   Cyril Tourneur's lost play *The Nobleman* entered.

John Webster's *The White Devil* acted.

Jonson quarrels with Inigo Jones, accompanies the son of
  Sir Walter Raleigh to France as tutor.

Thomas Shelton's translation of *Don Quixote* (I) published.

Prince Henry dies.

Lancashire witches hanged.

1613   Middleton's *Running Stream* and *Triumph of Truth* entertainments performed.

Jonson returns to England.

Chapman's *Tragedy of Chabot* probably acted.

Marston's *Insatiate Countess* published.

The Globe burns down at a performance of *Henry VIII*.

Princess Elizabeth is married to the Elector Palatine.

Webster publishes *A Monumental Column*, with other
  elegies for Prince Henry by Chapman, Heywood, Tourneur, Donne, Herbert, Campion, *et al.*

Sir Thomas Overbury dies in the Tower.

1614   Webster's *Duchess of Malfi* is probably acted.

Jonson's *Bartholomew Fair* acted.

Sir Thomas Overbury's *Characters* published.

1615   Jonson's masque *Mercury Vindicated* performed.

Trial of Sir Thomas Overbury's murderers.

1616   Shakespeare and Francis Beaumont die.

Middleton's *Civitatis Amor* performed.

Jonson's *The Devil is an Ass* acted, also his masque *The Golden Age Restored.*

Chapman's translations *The Whole Works of Homer* and *The Divine Poem of Musaeus* published.

Jonson's *Works* published, including the revised *Every Man in his Humour;* he receives a royal pension.

1617   Jonson's masque *A Vision of Delight* performed.

1618   Jonson travels to Scotland, converses with Drummond of Hawthornden; Jonson's masque *Pleasure Reconciled to Virtue* performed.

Chapman's translation of Hesiod published.

Sir Walter Raleigh is executed.

The Thirty Years War begins in Germany.

1619   Middleton's *Inner Temple Masque* published.

John Fletcher's *Humourous Lieutenant* acted.

Jonson made M.A. of Oxford, meets with the Tribe of Ben in the Apollo Room, Devil's Head Tavern.

Nathan Field dies.

Ten Shakespeare quartos are published in a collection.

Queen Anne dies.

1620   Middleton is made City Chronologer.

Webster's *The Devil's Law Case* probably acted.

Thomas Shelton's translation of *Don Quixote* (II) published.

1621   Jonson's masques, *News from the New World Discovered in the Moon* and *Metamorphosed Gypsies* performed.

Robert Burton's *Anatomy of Melancholy* published (revised editions 1624, 1628, 1632, 1638, 1651).

1622   Jonson's *Masque of Augurs* performed.

Thomas Middleton and William Rowley's *The Changeling* acted.

1623   The Shakespeare First Folio is published.

Webster's *Monuments of Honour* (Mayor's pageant) published.

Jonson's manuscripts destroyed by fire; his masque *Time Vindicated* performed.

Philip Massinger's *The Bondman* acted.

Prince Charles and the Duke of Buckingham go to Madrid.

1624   Middleton's *A Game at Chess* acted.

Middleton and Rowley's *The Changeling* acted at Whitehall.

Shirley moves from St. Albans to London, writes *The School of Compliment*.

Jonson's masques, *Neptune's Triumph* and *Pan's Anniversary* performed.

Marriage between Prince Charles and Henrietta Maria arranged.

1625 James I dies; Charles I accedes and marries.
Jonson's masque *The Fortunate Isles* performed.
Massinger's *New Way to Pay Old Debts* acted.
John Fletcher dies.
Plague in London.

1626 William Rowley dies. Cyril Tourneur dies.
Shirley's *The Wedding* acted.
Jonson's *Staple of News* acted.
Massinger's *Roman Actor* acted.
Francis Bacon and Lancelot Andrewes die.

1627 Thomas Middleton dies.
William Davenant's *The Cruel Brother* acted.

1628 Jonson suffers a paralytic stroke, succeeds Middleton as City Chronologer.
John Ford's *The Lover's Melancholy* acted.
Richard Brome's *The City Wit* acted.

1629 Ford's *The Lover's Melancholy* published.
Shirley's *The Wedding* published.
Jonson pensioned by Charles I, his *New Inn* acted.
Brome's *The Northern Lass* acted.

1630 Middleton's *A Chaste Maid in Cheapside* published.
Shirley's *Grateful Servant* published.
Arthur Wilson's *Inconstant Lady* probably acted.
Charles II born.

1631 Shirley's *The Traitor* acted, *School of Compliment* published.
Massinger's *Believe as You List* acted.
John Donne dies. John Dryden born.

1632 The Shakespeare Second Folio is published.
Shirley's *The Changes* published.
John Lyly's *Six Court Comedies* published.
Jonson's *Magnetic Lady* acted.
Queen Henrietta Maria acts in Walter Montague's *The Shepherd's Paradise* as William Prynne publishes *Histriomastix* (dated 1633).
Thomas Dekker dies.

1633 Ford's *'Tis Pity She's a Whore, The Broken Heart,* and
        Love's Sacrifice published.
     Shirley's *Bird in a Cage* and *Witty Fair One* published, his
        Gamester and *The Young Admiral* acted.
     Rowley's *All's Lost by Lust* published.
     Marston's *Tragedies and Comedies* published.
     William Laud becomes Archbishop of Canterbury.
1634 George Chapman and John Marston die.
     Ingio Jones and James Shirley's *Masque of Peace* performed
        by Inns of Court.
     William Prynne is pilloried and imprisoned until 1637.
     Richard Brome and Thomas Heywood's *The Late Lanca-
        shire Witches* acted.
     Milton's *Masque (Comus)* performed.
1635 Shirley's *Lady of Pleasure* acted, his *Traitor* published.
     John Greene sees *The Changeling* and *The Inconstant Lady*
        acted.
     Davenant's *News from Plymouth, Temple of Love,* and
        The Platonic Lover acted and performed.
     Thomas Cartwright's *The Ordinary* acted.
     Jonson's son dies.
1636 Shirley goes to Ireland.
     Cartwright's *The Royal Slave* acted.
     Davenant's *Triumphs of the Prince D'Amour* performed.
     Massinger's *The Bashful Lover* acted.
     The theatres close for about seventeen months.
1637 Ben Jonson dies.
     Shirley's *Lady of Pleasure, The Example, The Gamester,
        Hyde Park,* and *The Young Admiral* published.
     Milton's *Masque (Comus)* published.
     John Suckling's *Aglaura* acted.
1638 John Webster dies. Christopher Beeston dies.
     Shirley's *A Royal Master* and *The Duke's Mistress* published.
     Ford's *The Lady's Trial* and *The Fancies Chaste and Noble*
        published.
     Jonsonius Virbius published (33 memorial poems).
     Davenant is pensioned as assumed poet laureate.
1639 Shirley's *The Politician* acted; *The Ball* and *The Maid's
        Revenge* published; *The Gentleman of Venice* entered.
     Chapman and Shirley's *Chabot* published.
     Davenant's *The Spanish Lovers* acted.
     War with Scotland. Treaty of Berwick.

1640   Shirley's St. *Patrick for Ireland, Love's Cruelty, The Opportunity, The Constant Maid,* and *The Humourous Courtier* published. *The Doubtful Heir* entered. His (?) *Arcadia* published.

Jonson's *Works* (II) published (later plays, masques, verse, and prose).

Francis Beaumont's *Poems* published.

Philip Massinger and Robert Burton die.

The Long Parliament impeaches Strafford and Laud.

1641   Shirley's *The Cardinal* acted.

Brome's *A Jovial Crew* acted.

Thomas Heywood dies. William Wycherley born.

Parliament orders dismissal of the queen's Catholic attendants. Army Plot. Trial of Strafford (March).

Marriage of Princess Mary and Prince William of Orange (May). Execution of Strafford (May).

1642   Shirley's *The Sisters* acted.

Abraham Cowley's *The Guardian* acted.

John Denham's tragedy *The Sophy* published.

Denham's *Cooper's Hill* published.

Sir John Suckling dies and Thomas Shadwell is born.

Sir Isaac Newton born.

Cardinal Richelieu dies.

The king attempts to arrest Parliamentary leaders and flees Whitehall (January). Queen sails for Holland (February). Royal standard raised at Nottingham (August) and king goes to Oxford. Theatres close on September 2nd. Battle of Edgehill (October).

1643   Davenant's *Unfortunate Lovers* published.

William Cartwright dies and Lord Falkland is killed.

The queen lands at Bridlington and is impeached for treason (February–May).

1644   Royalists ejected from Cambridge. Battle of Marston Moor (July). The queen sails from Falmouth.

1645   Milton's *Poems* published, including *Arcades*.

James Howell's *Epistolae* (I) published.

Archbishop Laud executed (January). Battle of Naseby (June).

1646   James Shirley's *Poems* published.

Crashaw's *Steps to the Temple* and Vaughan's *Poems* published.

Suckling's *Fragmenta Aurea* published.

Robert Cox, actor and maker of drolls, begins his career
with *The Merry Conceits of Bottom the Weaver.*

The king surrenders to the Scots army. Prince of Wales flees
to Paris. Oxford surrenders.

1647   Beaumont and Fletcher folio published.

Sir Richard Fanshawe's translation of Guarini's *Il Pastor
Fido* published.

Parliamentary ordinances suppress plays.

The king is delivered to Parliament, is seized by the army,
and escapes to Isle of Wight.

1648   Jasper Mayne's tragicomedy *The Amorous War* published.

Sir Edward Sherburne's translation of Seneca's *Medea* published.

Crafty Cromwell (I & II) published.

Army seizes King Charles and enters London.

1649   King Charles I tried and executed (January 30).

Charles II proclaimed king in Scotland. Commonwealth
proclaimed in England. Cromwell in Ireland.

Davenant's *Love and Honour* published.

William Cavendish's *The Country Captain* and *Variety*
published.

John Ogilby's translation of Virgil published.

Richard Crashaw dies.

1650   Davenant's *Gondibert* published.

Abraham Cowley's *The Guardian* (*Cutter of Coleman
Street*) published.

Thomas May dies and Jeremy Collier is born.

Charles II arrives in Scotland (June). Battle of Dunbar
(September). William of Orange born.

1651   William Cartwright's *Comedies, Tragi-comedies, with Other
Poems* published: *The Lady Errant, The Ordinary,* and
The Siege, or Love's Convert.

Edmund Prestwich's translation of Seneca's *Hippolytus*
published.

Charles II crowned at Scone (January). Battle of Worcester
(September). Charles flees to Fécamp.

1652   Beaumont and Fletcher's *Wild-Goose Chase* published.

Richard Brome's *A Jovial Crew* published.

The Widow published, with names of Jonson, Fletcher, and
Middleton on the title-page.

Hugo Grotius' *Sophompaneas, or Joseph, A Tragedy* published.

End of war in Ireland.

1653   James Shirley's *Six New Plays* published: *The Brothers,
       The Sisters, The Doubtfull Heir, The Imposture, The
       Cardinal,* and *The Court Secret.*

       Richard Brome's *Five New Plays* published: *A Mad Couple
       Well Matched, The Novella, The Court Beggar, The City
       Wit,* and *The Damoiselle.*

       Middleton and Rowley's *The Changeling* and *The Spanish
       Gipsy* published.

       William Heming's *The Fatal Contract* published.

       Margaret Cavendish's *Poems and Fancies* published.

       Walton's *Complete Angler* published.

       Sir Thomas Urquhart's translation of Rabelais (I & II)
       published.

       Parliament expelled by Cromwell. Protectorate established.

1654   Chapman's *Alphonsus of Germany* and *Revenge for Honour*
       published.

       Webster's *Appius and Virginia* published.

       Alexander Brome's *The Cunning Lovers* published.

       Richard Flecknoe's *Ariadne Deserted by Theseus* (drama
       with recitative music) and *Love's Dominion* published.

       T. R.'s translation of Corneille's *Extravagant Shepherd*
       published.

       John Selden and William Habington die.

       Parliament acts against plays. Treaty with Holland.

       Charles II leaves France.

1655   Shirley's *The Gentleman of Venice* and *The Politician*
       published.

       Heywood and Rowley's *Fortune by Land and Sea* pub-
       lished.

       Robert Daborne's *The Poor Man's Comfort* published.

       Robert Davenport's *King John and Matilda* published.

       Thomas Stanley's translation of Aristophanes' *The Clouds*
       published.

       Sir William Lower's translation of Corneille's *Polyeuctes*
       published.

       William Strode's *The Floating Island* published.

       Robert Cox's *Actaeon and Diana* collection published.

       Philip Massinger's *Three New Plays* published: *The Bash-
       ful Lover, The Guardian,* and *A Very Woman.*

       War with Spain. Treaty with France.

1656 Middleton, Rowley, and Massinger's *The Old Law* published.

Ford and Dekker's *The Sun's Darling* published.

Davenant's *The Siege of Rhodes* (I) acted at Rutland House and published (perspective scenes and recitative music).

Sir William Lower's translation of Corneille's *Horatius* published.

Gerard Langbaine the younger born.

Parliament of the Second Protectorate opens.

1657 Middleton's *No Wit Like a Woman's* published.

Middleton's *Two New Plays* published: *More Dissemblers Besides Women,* and *Women Beware Women.*

Lodowick Carlell's *Two New Plays* published: *The Fool,* and *Osmond the Great Turk.*

Richard Brome's *The Queen's Exchange* published.

Sir Aston Cokayn's *The Obstinate Lady* published.

Lust's Dominion published, attributed to Marlowe.

John Dennis and Thomas Killigrew the younger born.

Cromwell refuses the crown, is established as Protector by Parliament. Alliance with France against Spain.

1658 Cromwell dies on September 3rd. Richard Cromwell becomes Protector.

Rowley, Dekker, and Ford's *Witch of Edmonton* published.

Massinger's *City Madam* published.

Davenant's *The Cruelty of the Spaniards in Peru* published.

Thomas May's *The Old Couple* published.

Sir William Lower's *The Enchanted Lovers* printed in The Hague.

William Chamberlayne's *Love's Victory* published.

Sir Aston Cokayn's *A Chain of Golden Poems* published: *Masque at Bretby,* and *Trappolin Supposed a Prince.*

1659 Walter Montague's *The Shepherd's Paradise* published.

Davenant's *Sir Francis Drake* published.

John Day's *The Blind Beggar of Bednal Green* published.

Lady Alimony published.

Richard Flecknoe's *The Marriage of Oceanus and Britannia* published.

Sir William Lower's *The Noble Ingratitude* printed in The Hague.

H. H.'s translation of Aristophanes' *The World's Idol, Plutus* published.

Richard Brome's *Five New Plays* published: *The English Moor, The Lovesick Court, The Weeding of the Covent Garden, The New Academy,* and *The Queen and Concubine.*

Sir John Suckling's *Last Remains* published, including *The Sad One, A Tragedy.*

General Monk leads the army from Scotland.

1660   The new Parliament recalls Charles II, who enters London on May 29th. Theatre patents are granted Thomas Killigrew the elder and Sir William Davenant. The Royal Society is organized. The Duke of York marries Anne Hyde (September). Henrietta Maria arrives in England (November).

John Dancer's translation of Tasso's *Aminta* published.

Sir William Lower's *The Amorous Fantasm* printed in The Hague.

1661   Middleton's *Mayor of Queenborough* published.

Webster and Rowley's *A Cure for a Cuckold* published.

Pepys sees a performance of *The Changeling* (on February 23rd) and likes it.

1662   Middleton's *Anything for a Quiet Life* published.

Rowley's *The Birth of Merlin* published.

Princess Mary, daughter of the Duke of York and later Queen Mary, born. Charles II marries Catherine of Braganza.

1663   Davenant's *The Siege of Rhodes* (II) published.

1664   Killigrew's *Comedies and Tragedies* published: *The Princess* and *The Parson's Wedding.*

1665   Princess Anne, daughter of the Duke of York and later Queen Anne, born.

1666   Great fire of London.

James Shirley dies.

THE CHANGELING

BY

THOMAS MIDDLETON

AND

WILLIAM ROWLEY

THE

CHANGELING:

As it was Acted (with great Applause)
at the Privat house in D r u r y-L a n e,
and *Salisbury Court.*

Written by ⎨ *THOMAS MIDLETON,* ⎬ Gent'.
         ⎨   and   ⎬
         ⎨ *WILLIAM ROWLEY.* ⎬

Never Printed before.

LONDON,
Printed for H u m p h r e y M o s e l e y, and are to
be sold at his shop at the sign of the *Princes-Arms*
in St. *Pauls* Church-yard, 1 6 5 3.

DRAMATIS PERSONAE

VERMANDERO,	*Father to Beatrice.*
TOMAZO DE PIRACQUO,	*A Noble Lord.*
ALONZO DE PIRACQUO,	*His brother, Suitor to Beatrice.*
ALSEMERO,	*A Nobleman, afterwards married to Beatrice.*
JASPERINO,	*His Friend.*
ALIBIUS,*[1]*	*A jealous Doctor.*
LOLLIO,	*His man.*
PEDRO,	*Friend to Antonio.*
ANTONIO,	*The Changeling.*
FRANCISCUS,	*The Counterfeit Madman.*
DEFLORES,	*Servant to Vermandero.*
MADMEN.	
SERVANTS.	
BEATRICE[—JOANNA],	*Daughter to Vermandero.*
DIAPHANTA,	*Her Wayting-woman.*
ISABELLA,	*Wife to Alibius.*

THE SCENE

ALICANT.[2]

Actus primus. [Scena prima.]

Enter ALSEMERO.

[ALSEMERO.] Twas in the Temple where I first beheld
      her,
  And now agen the same; what *Omen* yet
  Follows of that? None but imaginary;
  Why should my hopes or fate be timerous?
  The place is holy, so is my intent :   5
  I love her beauties to the holy purpose,[1]
  And that (me thinks) admits comparison
  With mans first creation, the place blest,[2]
  And is his right home back[(1)] (if he atchieve it).
  The Church hath first begun our interview   10
  And that's the place must joyn us into one,
  So there's beginning and perfection too.

          Enter JASPERINO.

JASPERINO. O Sir, are you here? Come, the wind's fair
      with you,
  Y'are like to have a swift and pleasant passage.
ALSEMERO. Sure y'are deceived, friend, 'tis contrary   15
  In my best judgement.
JASPERINO. What, for *Malta?*
  If you could buy[(2)] a gale amongst the Witches,
  They could not serve you such a lucky penyworth
  As comes a' Gods Name.[3]
ALSEMERO.   Even now I observ'd
  The temples Vane to turn full in my face,   20
  I know 'tis against me.
JASPERINO.   Against you?
  Then you know not where you are.
ALSEMERO.   Not well indeed.
JASPERINO. Are you not well, sir?
ALSEMERO.   Yes, Jasperino.
  Unless there be some hidden malady

ACT I. SCENE I.   of Eden.
[1] *purpose :* marriage.   [3] *a' Gods Name :* for nothing,
[2] *the place blest :* the Garden   gratis.

Within me, that I understand not.

JASPERINO.   And that   25
    I begin to doubt,[4] sir; I never knew
    Your inclinations to travels at a pause
    With any cause to hinder it, till now.
    Ashore you were wont to call your servants up,
    And help to trap your Horses for the speed.[5]   30
    At sea I have seen you weigh the anchor with 'em,
    Hoyst sails for fear to lose the formost breath,
    Be in continuall prayers for fair winds,
    And have you chang'd your orizons?[(3)]

ALSEMERO.   No, friend,
    I keep the same church, same devotion.   35

JASPERINO. Lover I'm sure y'are none, the Stoick
    Was found in you long agoe; your mother
    Nor best friends, who have set snares of beauty, I,
    And choyce ones too, could never trap you that way.
    What might be the cause?

ALSEMERO.   Lord, how violent   40
    Thou art; I was but meditating of
    Somewhat I heard within the temple.

JASPERINO. Is this violence? 'tis but idleness
    Compar'd with your hast yesterday.

ALSEMERO. I'm all this while a-going, man.   45

Enter Servants.

JASPERINO. Backwards, I think, sir. Look, your servants.

1 SERVANT. The sea-men call; shall we Boord your
    trunks?

ALSEMERO. No, not today.

JASPERINO. Tis the criticall[6] day, it seems, and the signe
    in *Aquarius*.   50

2 SERVANT. We must not to sea today; this smoke will
    bring forth fire.

ALSEMERO. Keep all on shore; I doe not know the end
    (Which needs I must do) of an affair in hand
    Ere I can go to sea.   55

[4] *doubt :* fear.
[5] *to trap your horses for the speed :* to speed arrangements.
[6] *criticall :* propitious for sailing.

1 SERVANT. Well, your pleasure.

2 SERVANT. Let him e'n take his leasure too; we are
safer on land.   *Exeunt Servants.*

Enter BEATRICE-JOANNA, DIAPHANTA, *and Servants;*[1]
      [ALSEMERO *greets and kisses* BEATRICE.]

JASPERINO. [*Aside.*] How now! The Laws of the *Medes*
are chang'd sure; salute a woman? He kisses too :   60
wonderfull! Where learnt he this? And does it perfectly too; in my conscience[7] he nere rehearst it before. Nay, goe on, this will be stranger and better
news at *Valentia,*(4) then if he had ransom'd half
Greece from the *Turk.*

BEATRICE. You are a Scholar, sir.   65

ALSEMERO.   A weak one, Lady.

BEATRICE. Which of the Sciences is this love you speak
                              of?

ALSEMERO. From your tongue I take it to be musick.

BEATRICE. You are skilfull in't, can sing at first sight.[8], (5)

ALSEMERO. And I have shew'd you all my skil at once.
I want more words to express me further,   70
And must be forc'd to repetition :
I love you dearly.

BEATRICE.   Be better advis'd, sir :
Our eyes are Centinels unto our judgements,
And should give certain judgement what they see;
But they are rash sometimes, and tell us wonders   75
Of common things, which when our judgements find,
They can check the eyes, and cal them blind.

ALSEMERO. But I am further, Lady; yesterday
Was mine eyes imployment, and hither now
They brought my judgement, where are both agreed.   80
Both Houses then consenting, 'tis agreed;
Onely there wants the confirmation
By the hand Royall, that's your part, Lady.[9]

---

[7] *in my conscience :* I could
swear.

[8] *can sing at first sight :* can
sight-read music.

[9] The king's signature confirms
a bill approved by both houses
of Parliament (*eyes* and
judgement).

BEATRICE. Oh, there's one above me, sir.[10] [*Aside.*] For
            five dayes past[(6)]
  To be recal'd! Sure, mine eyes were mistaken;   85
  This was the man was meant me. That he should
            come
  So neer his time, and miss it!
JASPERINO. [*Aside.*] We might have come by the
  Carriers from *Valentia,* I see, and sav'd all our sea-
  provision : we are at farthest,[11] sure. Methinks I   90
  should doe something too.
  I meant to be a venturer[12] in this voyage.
  Yonder's another Vessell, I'le board her,
  If she be lawfull prize, down goes her top-sail.[13]
                [*He greets* DIAPHANTA.]
        Enter DEFLORES.
DEFLORES. Lady, your father—
BEATRICE.   Is in health, I hope.   95
DEFLORES. Your eye shall instantly instruct you, Lady.
  He's coming hitherward.
BEATRICE.   What needed then
  Your dutious preface? I had rather
  He had come unexpected; you must stall[14]
  A good presence with unnecessary blabbing :   100
  And how welcome for your part you are,
  I'm sure you know.
DEFLORES. [*Aside.*] Wilt never mend this scorn
  One side nor other? Must I be enjoyn'd
  To follow still[15] whilst she flies from me? Well,
  Fates do your worst, I'le please my self with sight   105
  Of her, at all opportunities,
  If but to spite her anger; I know she had
  Rather see me dead then living, and yet
  She knows no cause for't, but a peevish will.

---

[10] *Oh, there's . . . sir :* her father above her, and God
  over the king.
[11] *at farthest :* desperately off
  course.
[12] *venturer :* commercial in-
vestor.
[13] *down . . . top-sail :* a sign of
  surrender.
[14] *stall :* forestall.
[15] *still :* continually.

ALSEMERO. You seem'd displeas'd, Lady, on the sudden.   110
BEATRICE. Your pardon, Sir, 'tis my infirmity,
    Nor can I other reason render you,
    Then his or hers, [of][2] some particular thing
    They must abandon as a deadly poyson,
    Which to a thousand other tasts were wholsome;
    Such to mine eyes is that same fellow there,   115
    The same that report speaks of the Basilisk.[16, (7)]
ALSEMERO. This is a frequent frailty in our nature;
    There's scarce a man amongst a thousand sound,[3]
    But hath his imperfection : one distastes
    The sent of Roses, which to infinites   120
    Most pleasing is, and odoriferous;
    One oyle, the enemy of poyson;
    Another Wine, the cheerer of the heart,
    And lively refresher of the countenance.
    Indeed this fault (if so it be) is generall;   125
    There's scarce a thing but is both lov'd and loath'd,
    My self (I must confesse) have the same frailty.
BEATRICE. And what may[4] be your poyson, sir? I am
        bold with you.
ALSEMERO. What might be your desire, perhaps, a
        cherry.
BEATRICE. I am no enemy to any creature   130
    My memory has, but yon Gentleman.
ALSEMERO. He does ill to tempt your sight, if he knew it.
BEATRICE. He cannot be ignorant of that, Sir,
    I have not spar'd to tell him so; and I want[17]
    To help my self, since he's a Gentleman   135
    In good respect with my father, and follows him.
ALSEMERO. He's out of his place then now.
                     [They talk apart.]
JASPERINO. I am a mad Wag, wench.
DIAPHANTA. So me thinks; but for your comfort I can
    tell you, we have a Doctor[18] in the Citie that   140
    undertakes the cure of such.

16 *Basilisk :* a mythical beast   17 *want :* lack means.
    that killed with its glance.   18 *Doctor :* Alibius.

JASPERINO. Tush, I know what Physick is best for the
state of mine own body.

DIAPHANTA. 'Tis scarce a well govern'd state, I beleeve.

JASPERINO. I could shew thee such a thing with an
Ingredian[t][5] that we two would compound to-   145
gether, and if it did not tame the maddest blood i'th
town for two hours after, Ile nere profess Physick
agen.

DIAPHANTA. A little poppy,[8] Sir, were good to cause
you sleep.

JASPERINO. Poppy? I'le give thee a pop i'th lips for
that first, and begin there: [*kisses her*] Poppy is one   150
simple[19] indeed, and Cuckow[20] (what you call't)
another : I'le discover[9] no more now, another time
I'le shew thee all.

BEATRICE. My Father, Sir.

> *Enter* VERMANDERO *and servants.*

VERMANDERO. Oh, Joanna, I came to meet thee,
Your devotion's ended?

BEATRICE.   For this time, Sir.   155
[*Aside.*] I shall change[10] my Saint, I fear me; I
                                    find
A giddy turning in me; [*to* VERMANDERO] Sir, this
                                    while
I am beholding to this Gentleman,
Who left his own way to keep me company,
And in discourse I find him much desirous   160
To see your castle : He hath deserv'd it, Sir,
If ye please to grant it.

VERMANDERO.   With all my heart, Sir.
Yet ther's an article between,[21] I must know
Your countrey; we use not to give survey
Of our chief strengths to strangers; our citadels   165
Are plac'd conspicuous to outward view,
On Promonts tops; but within are secrets.

ALSEMERO. A *Valentian*, Sir.

---

[19] *simple :* herb medicine.

[20] *Cuckow :* Wake-robin, an
elongated plant.

[21] *article between :* condition to
be settled.

VERMANDERO.   A *Valentian?*
That's native, Sir; of what name, I beseech you?
ALSEMERO. Alsemero, Sir.
VERMANDERO.   Alsemero; not the son   170
Of John de Alsemero?
ALSEMERO.   The same; Sir.
VERMANDERO. My best love bids you welcome.
BEATRICE. [*Aside.*]   He was
                    wont
To call me so,(11) and then he speaks a most
Unfeigned truth.22
VERMANDERO.   Oh, Sir, I knew your father;
We two were in acquaintance long agoe,   175
Before our chins were worth Iulan[6], (12) down,23
And so continued till the stamp of time
Had coin'd us into silver : Well, he's gone,
A good Souldier went with him.
ALSEMERO. You went together in that, Sir.   180
VERMANDERO. No, by Saint Jaques,(13) I came behind
                    him.
Yet I have done somewhat too; an unhappy day
Swallowed him at last at *Gibralter*(14)
In fight with those rebellious *Hollanders*,
Was it not so?
ALSEMERO.   Whose death I had reveng'd,   185
Or followed him in Fate, had not the late League
Prevented me.
VERMANDERO.   I, I, 'twas time to breath :
Oh, Joanna, I should ha told thee news,
I saw Piracquo lately.
BEATRICE. [*Aside.*]   That's ill news.
VERMANDERO. He's hot preparing for this day of   190
                    triumph,
Thou must be a Bride within this sevenight.
ALSEMERO. [*Aside.*]   Ha!
BEATRICE. Nay, good Sir, be not so violent, with speed

22 *He was . . . truth :* since she   23 *Iulan down :* first growth of
welcomes Alsemero pas-   beard. See note.
sionately.

I cannot render satisfaction
Unto the dear companion of my soule,
Virginity (whom I thus long have liv'd with)   195
And part with it so rude and suddenly;
Can such friends divide, never to meet agen,
Without a solemne farewell?
VERMANDERO.   Tush, tush, there's a toy.
ALSEMERO. [*Aside.*] I must now part, and never meet
                        agen
With any joy on earth; [*to* VERMANDERO.] Sir, your   200
                        pardon,
My affairs call on me.
VERMANDERO.   How, Sir? by no means;
Not chang'd so soon, I hope! You must see my castle,
And her best entertainment ere we part;
I shall think my self unkindly us'd else.
Come, come, let's on, I had good hope your stay   205
Had been a while with us in Alicant;[7]
I might have bid you to my daughters wedding.
ALSEMERO. [*Aside.*] He means to feast me, and poysons
                        me before hand;
[*To* VERMANDERO.] I should be dearly glad to be
                        there, sir,
Did my occasions suit as I could wish.   210
BEATRICE. I shall be sorry if you be not there
When it is done, sir—but not so suddenly.
VERMANDERO. I tell you, sir, the Gentleman's compleat,
A Courtier and a Gallant, enricht
With many fair and noble ornaments;   215
I would not change him for a son-in-law
For any he in Spain, the proudest he,
And we have great ones, that you know.
ALSEMERO.   He's much
Bound to you, sir.
VERMANDERO.   He shall be bound to me,
As fast as this tie can hold him; I'le want[24]   220
My will else.

24 *want :* fail to get.

BEATRICE. [*Aside.*] I shall want mine if you do it.

VERMANDERO. But come, by the way I'le tell you more
of him :

ALSEMERO. [*Aside.*] How shall I dare to venture in his
castle,
When he discharges murderers²⁵ at the gate?
But I must on, for back I cannot goe.⁽¹⁵⁾   225

BEATRICE. [*Aside.*] Not this Serpent⁽¹⁶⁾ gone yet?
[*Drops a glove.*]

VERMANDERO.   Look, Girle, thy
glove's faln;
[ALSEMERO *moves to pick it up.*]
Stay, stay,—Deflores, help a little.
[*Exeunt* VERMANDERO, ALSEMERO, JASPERINO,
and Servants.]

DEFLORES. [*Offering the glove.*]   Here, Lady.

BEATRICE. Mischief on your officious forwardness!
Who bade you stoop? They touch my hand no more :
There, for t'others sake I part with this;   230
[*She takes off and throws down the other glove.*]
Take 'um and draw thine own skin off with 'um.
Exeunt [*all but* DEFLORES.]

DEFLORES. Here's a favour come—with a mischief!
Now⁽¹⁷⁾
I know she had rather wear my pelt tan'd in a pair
Of dancing pumps, then I should thrust my fingers
Into her sockets here; I know she hates me,   235
Yet cannot chuse but love her :
No matter,—if but to vex her, I'le haunt her still,
Though I get nothing else, I'le have my will.   *Exit.*

[ACTUS PRIMUS. SCENA SECUNDA.]

Enter ALIBIUS *and* LOLLIO.

ALIBIUS. Lollio, I must trust thee with a secret,
But thou must keep it.

²⁵ *murderers :* scatter-shot
cannon.

LOLLIO. I was ever close to a secret, Sir.

ALIBIUS. The diligence that I have found in thee,
   The care and industry already past,   5
   Assures me of thy good continuance.
   Lollio, I have a wife.

LOLLIO. Fie, sir, 'tis too late to keep her secret, she's
   known to be married all the town and countrey over.

ALIBIUS. Thou goest too fast, my Lollio, that knowledge   10
   I allow no man can be bar'd it;
   But there is a knowledge which is neerer,
   Deeper and sweeter, Lollio.

LOLLIO. Well, sir, let us handle that between you and I.

ALIBIUS. 'Tis that I go about, man; Lollio,   15
   My wife is young.

LOLLIO. So much the worse to be kept secret, sir.

ALIBIUS. Why now thou meet'st the substance of the
   point, I am old, Lollio.

LOLLIO. No, sir, 'tis I am old Lollio.   20

ALIBIUS. Yet why may not this concord and sympathize?
   Old trees and young plants often grow together,
   Well enough agreeing.

LOLLIO. I, sir, but the old trees raise themselves higher
   and broader than the young plants.   25

ALIBIUS. Shrewd application : there's the fear, man![1]
   I would wear my ring[(1)] on my own finger;
   Whilst it is borrowed it is none of mine,
   But his that useth it.

LOLLIO. You must keep it on still then; if it but lye by,   30
   one or other wil be thrusting into't.

ALIBIUS. Thou conceiv'st me, Lollio; here thy watchful
        eye
   Must have imployment, I cannot alwayes be
   At home.

LOLLIO. I dare swear you cannot.   35

ALIBIUS. I must look out.

   Act I. Scene ii.
[1] The spreading tree suggests
the horns of a cuckold.

LOLLIO. I know't, you must look out, 'tis every mans
           case.
ALIBIUS. Here I doe say must thy imployment be,
    To watch her treadings, and in my absence
    Supply my place.   40
LOLLIO. I'le do my best, Sir, yet surely I cannot see who
    you should have cause to be jealous of.
ALIBIUS. Thy reason for that, Lollio? 'Tis
    A comfortable question.
LOLLIO. We have but two sorts of people in the house,   45
    and both under the whip, that's fools and mad-men;
    the one has not wit enough to be knaves, and the
    other not knavery enough to be fools.
ALIBIUS. I, those are all my Patients, Lollio.
    I do profess the cure of either sort :   50
    My trade, my living 'tis, I thrive by it;
    But here's the care that mixes with my thrift,[2]
    The daily Visitants,[3] that come to see
    My brainsick Patients, I would not have
    To see my wife : Gallants I do observe   55
    Of quick entising eyes, rich in habits,[2]
    Of stature and proportion very comely :
    These are most shrewd temptations, Lollio.
LOLLIO. They may be easily answered, Sir; if they come
    to see the Fools and Mad-men, you and I may serve   60
    the turn, and let my Mistress alone, she's of neither
    sort.
ALIBIUS. 'Tis a good ward,[3] indeed come they to see
    Our Mad-men or our Fools, let 'um see no more
    Then what they come for; by that consequent
    They must not see her, I'm sure she's no fool.   65
LOLLIO. And I'm sure she's no mad-man.
ALIBIUS. Hold that Buckler[4] fast, Lollio; my trust
    Is on thee, and I account it firm and strong.
    What hour is't, Lollio?
LOLLIO. Towards belly-hour, Sir.   70

---

2 *habits :* dress.   4 *Buckler :* Shield.
3 *ward :* defense, answer.

ALIBIUS. Dinner time? Thou mean'st twelve a'clock.

LOLLIO. Yes, Sir, for every part has his hour; we wake at
six and look about us, that's eye-hour; at seven we
should pray, that's knee-hour; at eight walk, that's
leg-hour; at nine gather flowers, and pluck a Rose,[5]   75
that's nose-hour; at ten we drink, that's mouth-hour;
at eleven lay about us for victuals, that's hand-hour;
at twelve go to dinner, that's belly-hour.

ALIBIUS. Profoundly, Lollio! It wil be long
Ere all thy Scholars learn this Lesson, and   80
I did look to have a new one entred;—stay,
I think my expectation is come home.
        Enter PEDRO *and* ANTONIO *like an Idiot.*[(4)]

PEDRO. Save you, sir, my business speaks it self,
This sight takes off the labour of my tongue.

ALIBIUS. I, I, Sir, 'tis plain enough you mean   85
Him for my patient.

PEDRO. And if your pains prove but commodious, to
give but some little strength to his sick and weak part
of Nature in him, these [*gives him money*] are but
patterns to shew you of the whole pieces that will   90
follow to you, beside the charge of diet, washing, and
other necessaries fully defrayed.[1]

ALIBIUS. Believe it, sir, there shall no care be wanting.

LOLLIO. Sir, an officer in this place may deserve som-
thing; the trouble will pass through my hands.[2]

PEDRO. 'Tis fit something should come to your hands   95
then, sir.   [*Gives him money.*]

LOLLIO. Yes, sir, 'tis I must keep him sweet, and read to
him; what is his name?

PEDRO. His name is Antonio; marry,[6] we use but half to
him, onely Tonie.[(5)]   100

LOLLIO. Tonie, Tonie, 'tis enough, and a very good name
for a fool; what's your name, Tonie?

ANTONIO. He, he, he! well, I thank you, cousin, he, he,
he!

[5] *pluck a Rose :* urinate.   [6] *marry :* common exclamation
                                        from "by Mary."

LOLLIO. Good Boy! hold up your head : he can laugh,
    I perceive by that he is no beast.[6]   105
PEDRO. Well, sir,
    If you can raise him but to any height,
    Any degree of wit, might he attain
    (As I might say) to creep but on all four
    Towards the chair of wit, or walk on crutches,   110
    'Twould add an honour to your worthy pains,
    And a great family might pray for you,
    To which he should be heire, had he discretion
    To claim and guide his own; assure you, sir,
    He is a Gentleman.   115
LOLLIO. Nay, there's no body doubted that; at first
    sight[7] I knew him for a Gentleman, he looks no
    other yet.
PEDRO. Let him have good attendance and sweet
    lodging.
LOLLIO. As good as my Mistress lies in, sir, and as you
    allow us time and means, we can raise him to the   120
    higher degree of discretion.
PEDRO. Nay, there shall no cost want, sir.
LOLLIO. He will hardly be stretcht up to the wit of a
    Magnifico.⁷
PEDRO. Oh no, that's not to be expected, far shorter will   125
    be enough.
LOLLIO. I'le warrant you [I'le] make[3] him fit to
    bear office in five weeks; I'le undertake to wind him
    up[8] to the wit of Constable.
PEDRO. If it be lower then that it might serve turn.   130
LOLLIO. No, fie, to levell him with a Headborough,
    Beadle, or Watchman, were but little better then he
    is; Constable I'le able him : if he do come to be a
    Justice afterwards, let him thank the Keeper. Or I'le
    go further with you, say I do bring him up to my   135
    own pitch, say I make him as wise as my self.
PEDRO. Why, there I would have it.

⁷ *Magnifico :* Noble, Grandee.

LOLLIO. Well, go to, either I'le be as errant a fool as he,
   or he shall be as wise as I, and then I think 'twill
   serve his turn.   140
PEDRO. Nay, I doe like thy wit passing well.
LOLLIO. Yes, you may, yet if I had not been a fool, I
   had had more wit then I have too; remember what
   state[8] you find me in.
PEDRO. I wil, and so leave you : your best cares, I 145
   beseech you.
ALIBIUS. Take you none with you, leave 'um all with us.
                                  Exit PEDRO.
ANTONIO. Oh, my cousin's gone, cousin, cousin, oh!
LOLLIO. Peace, Peace, Tony, you must not cry, child,
   you must be whipt if you do; your cousin is here 150
   still, I am your cousin, Tony.
ANTONIO. He, he, then I'le not cry, if thou bee'st my
   cousin, he, he, he.
LOLLIO. I were best try his wit a little, that I may know
   what Form[9] to place him in.   155
ALIBIUS. I, doe Lollio, doe.
LOLLIO. I must ask him easie questions at first; Tony,
   how many true fingers has a Taylor on his right hand?
ANTONIO. As many as on his left, cousin.
LOLLIO. Good, and how many on both?   160
ANTONIO. Two less then a Dewce, cousin.[10]
LOLLIO. Very well answered; I come to you agen, cousin
   Tony : How many fools goes to a wise man?
ANTONIO. Fourty in a day sometimes, cousin.
LOLLIO. Fourty in a day? How prove you that?   165
ANTONIO. All that fall out amongst themselves, and go
   to[11] a Lawyer to be made friends.
LOLLIO. A parlous[12] fool! He must sit in the fourth

---

[8] *state :* keeper in a madhouse.
[9] *Form :* Grade.
[10] *Two less . . . cousin :* None,
   because tailors were thought
   dishonest (untrue).

[11] Antonio has interpreted *go to*
   as "visit." Lollio meant it to
   mean "constitute."
[12] *parlous :* sharp, shrewd.

Form at least, I perceive that : I come again, Tony :
How many knaves make an honest man?   170
ANTONIO. I know not that, cousin.
LOLLIO. No, the question is too hard for you : I'le tell
    you, cousin, there's three knaves may make an
    honest man, a Sergeant, a Jaylor, and a Beadle; the
    Sergeant catches him, the Jaylor holds him, and the   175
    Beadle lashes him; and if he be not honest then, the
    Hangman must cure him.
ANTONIO. Ha, ha, ha! that's fine sport, cousin.
ALIBIUS. This was too deep a question for the fool,
    Lollio.
LOLLIO. Yes, this might have serv'd your self, tho I say't;
    once more, and you shall goe play, Tony.[4]   180
ANTONIO. I, play at push-pin,[9] cousin, ha, he.
LOLLIO. So thou shalt; say how many fools are here—
ANTONIO. Two, cousin, thou and I.
LOLLIO. Nay, y'are too forward there; Tony, mark my
    question : how many fools and knaves are here? A   185
    fool before a knave, a fool behind a knave, between
    every two fools a knave; how many fools, how many
    knaves?
ANTONIO. I never learnt so far, cousin.
ALIBIUS. Thou putst too hard questions to him, Lollio.
LOLLIO. I'le make him understand it easily; cousin, stand 190
    there.[10]
ANTONIO. I, cousin.
LOLLIO. Master, stand you next the fool.
ALIBIUS. Well, Lollio.
LOLLIO. Here's my place : mark now, Tony, there a fool   195
    before a knave.
ANTONIO. That's I, cousin.
LOLLIO. Here's a fool behind a knave, that's I, and be-
    tween us two fools there is a knave, that's my Master;
    'tis but we three, that's all.   200
ANTONIO. We three, we three,[11] cousin.
                                            Mad-men within.
1 WITHIN. Put's head i'th pillory, the bread's too little.
2 WITHIN. Fly, fly, and he catches the swallow.

3 WITHIN. Give her more onion, or the Divell put the
    rope[12] about her cragg.[13]   205
LOLLIO. You may hear what time of day it is, the Chimes
    of Bedlam goes.
ALIBIUS. Peace, peace, or the wyer[14] comes!
3 WITHIN. Cat whore, Cat whore, her permasant,
    her[13] permasant.[15]
ALIBIUS. Peace, I say! Their hour's come, they must be   210
    fed, Lollio.
LOLLIO. There's no hope of recovery of that Welsh mad-
    man, was undone by a Mouse, that spoild him a Per-
    masant; lost his wits for't.[5]
ALIBIUS. Go to your charge, Lollio, I'le to mine.   215
LOLLIO. Goe to your mad-mens Ward, let me alone with
    your fools.
ALIBIUS. And remember my last charge, Lollio.   *Exit.*
LOLLIO. Of which your Patients do you think I am?
    Come, Tony, you must amongst your School-fellows   220
    now; there's pretty Scholars amongst 'um, I can tell
    you; there's some of 'em at *stultus, stulta, stultum.*[16]
ANTONIO. I would see the mad-men, cousin, if they
    would not bite me.
LOLLIO. No, they shall not bite thee, Tony.   225
ANTONIO. They bite when they are at dinner, do they
    not, cuz?
LOLLIO. They bite at dinner indeed, Tony; well, I hope
    to get credit by thee; I like thee the best of all the
    Scholars that ever I brought up, and thou shalt prove
    a wise man, or I'le prove a fool my selfe.   *Exeunt.* 230

[13] *cragg :* neck.
[14] *wyer :* whip.
[15] *permasant :* Parmesan
    cheese.

[16] *there's some . . . stultum :*
    They can decline the Latin
    for "foolish."

ACTUS SECUNDUS. [SCENA PRIMA.]

Enter BEATRICE *and* JASPERINO *severally.*
BEATRICE. Oh, Sir, I'm ready now for that fair service,
   Which makes the name of friend sit glorious on you.
   Good Angels and this conduct be your guide,
                  [*Gives him a paper.*]
   Fitness of time and place is there set down, sir.
JASPERINO. The joy I shall return rewards my service.   5
                              Exit.

BEATRICE. How wise is Alsemero in his friend!
   It is a sign he makes his choyce with judgement.
   Then I appear in nothing more approv'd,
   Then making choyce of him;
   For 'tis a Principle, he that can chuse   10
   That bosome well, who of his thoughts partakes,
   Proves most discreet in every choyce he makes.
   Me thinks I love now with the eyes[1] of judgement.
   And see the way to merit, clearly see it.
   A true deserver like a Diamond[2] sparkles,   15
   In darkness you may see him, that's in absence,
   Which is the greatest darkness falls on love;
   Yet is he best discern'd then
   With intellectuall eye-sight; what's Piracquo
   My Father spends his breath for? And his blessing   20
   Is onely mine, as I regard his name,[1]
   Else it goes from me, and turns head against me,
   Transform'd into a Curse; some speedy way
   Must be remembred; he's so forward too,
   So urgent that way, scarce allows me breath   25
   To speak to my new comforts.
             Enter DEFLORES.
DEFLORES. [*Aside.*]   Yonder's she.
   What ever ails me, now a' late especially,

ACT II. SCENE I.
[1] *And his . . . name:* He will
bless her only if she obeys.

I can as well be hang'd as refrain seeing her;
Some twenty times a day, nay, not so little,
Doe I force errands, frame wayes and excuses   30
To come into her sight, and I have small reason for't,
And less incouragement; for she baits me still
Every time worse then other, does profess herself
The cruellest enemy to my face, in town,
At no hand² can abide the sight of me,(3)   35
As if danger, or ill luck hung in my looks.
I must confess my face is bad enough,
But I know far worse has better fortune,
And not endur'd alone, but doted on,
And yet such pickhaird faces, chins like Witches,   40
Here and there five hairs, whispering in a corner,
As if they grew in fear one of another,
Wrinkles like troughs, where swine deformity swils
The tears of perjury that lie there like wash
Fallen from the slimy and dishonest eye,   45
Yet such a one pluckt sweets without restraint,
And has the grace of beauty to his sweet.³
Though my hard fate has thrust me out to servitude,
I tumbled into th'world a Gentleman.
She turns her blessed eye upon me now,   50
And I'le indure all storms before I part with't.
BEATRICE. [*Aside.*] Again!
This ominous ill-fac'd fellow more disturbs me,
Then all my other passions.
DEFLORES. [*Aside.*]   Now't begins agen,
I'le stand this storm of hail though the stones pelt me. 55
BEATRICE. Thy business? What's thy business?
DEFLORES. [*Aside.*]   Soft and
                    fair,
I cannot part so soon now.
BEATRICE. [*Aside.*]   The villain's fixt—
[*To* DEFLORES.] Thou standing toad-pool!
DEFLORES. [*Aside.*]   The showre
                    falls amain now.

---

² *At no hand :* On no account.   ³ *sweet :* sweetheart.

BEATRICE. Who sent thee? What's thy errand? Leave
                  my sight.

DEFLORES. My Lord your father charg'd me to deliver   60
   A message to you.

BEATRICE.   What, another since?
   Do't and be hang'd then; let me be rid of thee.

DEFLORES. True service merits mercy.

BEATRICE.   What's thy message?

DEFLORES. Let beauty settle but in patience,
   You shall hear all.

BEATRICE.   A dallying, trifling torment!   65

DEFLORES. Signior Alonzo de Piracquo, Lady,
   Sole brother to Tomazo de Piracquo,—

BEATRICE. Slave, when wil't make an end?

DEFLORES. [*Aside.*]   Too soon I
               shall.

BEATRICE. What all this while of him?

DEFLORES.   The said Alonzo,
   With the foresaid Tomazo—

BEATRICE.   Yet agen?   70

DEFLORES. Is new alighted.

BEATRICE.   Vengeance strike the news!
   Thou thing most loath'd, what cause was there in this
   To bring thee to my sight?

DEFLORES.   My Lord your father
   Charg'd me to seek you out.

BEATRICE.   Is there no other
   To send his errand by?

DEFLORES.   It seems 'tis my luck   75
   To be i'th way still.

BEATRICE.   Get thee from me.

DEFLORES.   So.
   [*Aside.*] Why, am not I an Asse to devise wayes
   Thus to be raild at? I must see her still.
   I shall have a mad qualm within this houre agen,
   I know't, and like a Common Garden Bull,(4)   80
   I doe but take breath to be lug'd⁴ agen.

---

4 *lug'd :* baited.

What this may bode I know not; I'le despair the less,
Because ther's daily presidents of bad faces
Belov'd beyond all reason; these foul chops
May come into favour one day, 'mongst his fellows :   85
Wrangling has prov'd the mistress of good pastime,
As children cry themselves asleep, I ha' seen
Women have chid themselves abed to men.
                                    Exit DEFLORES.
BEATRICE. I never see this fellow, but I think
    Of some harm towards me; danger's in my mind still,   90
    I scarce leave trembling of an hour after.
    The next good mood I find my father in,
    I'le get him quite discarded : oh, I was
    Lost in this small disturbance and forgot
    Afflictions fiercer torrent that now comes,   95
    To beare down all my comforts.
        Enter VERMANDERO, ALONZO, [*and*] TOMAZO.
VERMANDERO.   Y'are both welcome,
    But an especiall one belongs to you, sir,
    To whose most noble name our love presents
    The addition of a son, our son Alonzo.
ALONZO. The treasury of honor cannot bring forth   100
    A Title I should more rejoyce in, sir.
VERMANDERO. You have improv'd it well; daughter,
                                    prepare,
    The day will steal upon thee suddenly.
BEATRICE. [*Aside.*] Howe'er, I will be sure to keep[5, (5)]
                                    the night,
    If it should come so neer me.
            [BEATRICE *and* VERMANDERO *talk apart.*]
TOMAZO.   Alonzo.
ALONZO.   Brother?   105
TOMAZO. In troth I see small welcome in her eye.
ALONZO. Fie, you are too severe a censurer
    Of love in all points, there's no bringing on you.[6]
    If Lovers should mark every thing a fault,

---

[5] *keep :* guard against.   ing you a suitable actor in a
[6] *no bringing on you :* no mak-   love scene.

Affection would be like an ill set book,   110
Whose faults might prove as big as half the volume.
BEATRICE. That's all I do intreat.
VERMANDERO.   It is but reasonable;
  I'le see what my son sayes too't : Son Alonzo,
  Here's a motion made but to reprieve
  A Maidenhead three dayes longer; the request   115
  Is not far out of reason, for indeed
  The former time is pinching.
ALONZO.   Though my joyes
  Be set back so much time as I could wish
  They had been forward, yet since she desires it,
  The time is set as pleasing as before,   120
  I find no gladness wanting.
VERMANDERO. May I ever meet it in that poynt still :
  Y'are nobly welcome, sirs.
                    Exeunt VERMANDERO *and* BEATRICE.
TOMAZO. So, did you mark the dulness of her parting
  now?
ALONZO. What dulness? Thou art so exceptious still.   125
TOMAZO. Why, let it goe then, I am but a fool
  To mark your harms so heedfully.
ALONZO.   Where's the over-
            sight?
TOMAZO. Come, your faith's cousened[7] in her, strongly
            cousened;
  Unsettle your affection with all speed
  Wisdome can bring it too, your peace is ruin'd else.   130
  Think what a torment 'tis to marry one
  Whose heart is leapt into anothers bosome :
  If ever pleasure she receive from thee,
  It comes not in thy name, or of thy gift;
  She lies but with another in thine arms,   135
  He the half father unto all thy children
  In the conception; if he get 'em not,
  She helps to get 'em for him, in his passions, [1], (6)
            and how dangerous

---

[7] *cousened :* deceived.

And shamefull her restraint may goe in time to,
It is not to be thought on without sufferings.   140
ALONZO. You speak as if she lov'd some other, then.
TOMAZO. Do you apprehend so slowly?
ALONZO.   Nay, and[8] that
    Be your fear onely, I am safe enough;
    Preserve your friendship and your counsel, brother,
    For times of more distress; I should depart   145
    An enemy, a dangerous, deadly one
    To any but thy self, that should but think
    She knew the meaning of inconstancy,
    Much less the use and practice; yet w'are[2] friends.
    Pray let no more be urg'd; I can endure   150
    Much, till I meet an injury to her,
    Then I am not my self. Farewell, sweet brother,
    How   much   w'are   bound   to   heaven   to   depart
                lovingly![9]   *Exit.*
TOMAZO. Why, here is loves tame madness, thus a man
    Quickly steals into his vexation.   *Exit.* 155

                [ACTUS SECUNDUS. SCENA SECUNDA.]

            Enter DIAPHANTA *and* ALSEMERO.
DIAPHANTA. The place is my charge, you have kept your
                hour,
    And the reward of a just meeting bless you.
    I hear my Lady coming; compleat Gentleman,
    I dare not be too busie with my praises,
    Th'are dangerous[(1)] things to deal with.   *Exit.*
ALSEMERO.   This   goes   5
                well;
    These women are the Ladies Cabinets,
    Things of most pretious trust are lock['d][(1)] into
                'em.
            Enter BEATRICE.

---

[8] *and :* if.
[9] *How much . . . lovingly :*   How much we owe heaven
                                                for preventing a quarrel!

BEATRICE. I have within mine eye all my desires;
　Requests that holy prayers ascend heaven for,
　And brings 'em down to furnish our defects,[1]   10
　Come not more sweet to our necessities,
　Then thou unto my wishes.
ALSEMERO.   W'are so like
　In our expressions, Lady, that unless I borrow
　The same words, I shall never find their equals.
                              [*They embrace and kiss.*]
BEATRICE. How happy were this meeting, this embrace,   15
　If it were free from envy! This poor kiss,
　It has an enemy, a hatefull one,[2]
　That wishes poyson to't[(2)] : how well were I now
　If there were none such name known as Piracquo!
　Nor no such tye as the command of Parents,   20
　I should be but too much blessed.
ALSEMERO.   One good service
　Would strike off[(3)] both your fears, and I'le go neer
                    it too,
　Since you are so distrest; remove the cause,[(4)]
　The command ceases, so there's two fears blown out
　With one and the same blast.
BEATRICE.   Pray let me find you,   25
          sir.
　What might that service be so strangely happy?
ALSEMERO. The honorablest peece 'bout man, Valour.
　I'le send a challenge to Piracquo instantly.
BEATRICE. How? Call you that extinguishing of fear
　When 'tis the onely way to keep it flaming?   30
　Are not you ventured in the action,
　That's all my joyes and comforts? Pray, no more, sir.
　Say you prevaild, [you're][(2)] danger's and not mine
                    then;
　The law[(5)] would claim you from me, or obscurity
　Be made the grave to bury you alive.   35
　I'me glad these thoughts come forth, O keep not one

ACT II. SCENE II.
[1] *furnish our defects:* supply   [2] *a hatefull one :* Alonzo.
what we lack.

Of this condition, sir; here was a course
Found to bring sorrow on her way to death :
The tears would ne'er[3] 'a dried, till dust had
                choak'd 'em.
Blood-guiltiness becomes a fouler visage,—   40
[*Aside.*] And now I think on one,—I was to blame,
I ha' mar'd so good a market with my scorn;[3]
'T had been done questionless; the ugliest creature
 Creation fram'd for some use, yet to see
I could not mark so much where it should be!   45
ALSEMERO. Lady.
BEATRICE. [*Aside.*] Why, men of Art make much of
                poyson,
Keep one to expell another, where was my Art?
ALSEMERO. Lady, you hear not me.
BEATRICE.   I do especially, sir;
The present times are not so sure of our side
As those hereafter may be; we must use 'em then   50
As thrifty folks their wealth, sparingly now,
Till the time opens.
ALSEMERO.   You teach wisdom, Lady.
BEATRICE. Within there, Diaphanta!
                Enter DIAPHANTA.
DIAPHANTA.   Do you call, Madam?
BEATRICE. Perfect[(6)] your service, and conduct this
                Gentleman
The privat way you brought him.
DIAPHANTA.   I shall, Madam.   55
ALSEMERO. My love's as firm as love e'er built upon.
                Exeunt DIAPHANTA *and* ALSEMERO.
                Enter DEFLORES.
DEFLORES. [*Aside.*] I have watcht this meeting, and doe
                wonder much
What shall become of t'other; I'me sure both
Cannot be serv'd unless she transgress; happily
Then I'le put in for one : for if a woman   60

―――――――――

[3] *mar'd so . . . scorn:* spoiled
   the good use of Deflores.

Fly from one point, from him she makes a husband,
She spreads and mounts then like Arithmetick,
One, ten, a hundred, a thousand, ten thousand,[4]
Proves in time Sutler[4] to an Army Royall.
Now do I look to be most richly raild at,   65
Yet I must see her.

BEATRICE. [*Aside.*]   Why, put case I loath'd him
As much as youth and beauty hates a Sepulcher,
Must I needs shew it? Cannot I keep that secret,
And serve my turn upon him?—See, he's here.
Deflores.

DEFLORES. [*Aside.*] Ha, I shall run mad with joy!   70
She call'd me fairly by my name Deflores,
And neither Rogue nor Rascall.

BEATRICE.   What ha' you done
To your face a-late? Y'ave met with some good
                    Physitian,
Y'have prun'd your self me thinks, you were not wont
To look so amorously.

DEFLORES.   Not I,—   75
[*Aside.*] Tis the same Phisnomy to a hair and pimple,
Which she call'd scurvy scarce an hour agoe :
How is this?

BEATRICE.   Come hither, neerer, man.

DEFLORES. [*Aside.*] I'me up to the chin in heaven!

BEATRICE.   Turn,
                    let me see.
[Faugh,][5] tis but the heat of the liver, I perceiv't.   80
I thought it had been worse.

DEFLORES. [*Aside.*]   Her fingers touch't me!
She smels all Amber.

BEATRICE. I'le make a water for you shall cleanse this
Within a fortnight.

DEFLORES.   With your own hands, Lady?

BEATRICE. Yes, mine own sir, in a work of cure   85
I'le trust no other.

---

[4] *Sutler :* Commercial
provisioner.

DEFLORES. [*Aside.*]   'Tis half an act of pleasure
To hear her talk thus to me.
BEATRICE.   When w'are us'd
To a hard face, 'tis not so unpleasing;
It mends still in opinion, hourly mends,
I see it by experience.[7]
DEFLORES. [*Aside.*]   I was blest   90
To light upon this minute; I'le make use on't.
BEATRICE. Hardness becomes the visage of a man well;
It argues service, resolution, manhood,
If cause were of imployment.
DEFLORES.   'Twould be soon seen,
If e'er your Ladiship had cause to use it.   95
I would but wish the honor of a service
So happy as that mounts to.
BEATRICE.   We shall try you—
Oh my Deflores!
DEFLORES. [*Aside.*] How's that?
She calls me hers already, my Deflores!
You were about to sigh out somwhat, Madam.   100
BEATRICE. No, was I? I forgot—Oh!
DEFLORES.   There 'tis agen—
The very fellow on't.
BEATRICE.   You are too quick, sir.
DEFLORES. There's no excuse for't now,[6] I heard it
                          twice, Madam;
That sigh would fain have utterance, take pitty on't,
And lend it a free word; 'las how it labours   105
For liberty. I hear the murmure yet
Beat at your bosome.
BEATRICE.   Would Creation—
DEFLORES. I, well said, that's it.
BEATRICE.   Had form'd me man.
DEFLORES. Nay, that's not it.
BEATRICE.   Oh, 'tis the soul of freedom!
I should not then be forc'd to marry one   110
I hate beyond all depths, I should have power
Then to oppose my loathings, nay remove 'em
For ever from my sight.

DEFLORES.   Oh blest occasion!
Without change to your Sex, you have your wishes.
Claim so much man in me.
BEATRICE.   In thee, Deflores?   115
There's small cause for that.
DEFLORES.   Put it not from me,
It's a service that I kneel for to you.   [*He kneels.*]
BEATRICE. You are too violent to mean faithfully;
There's horror in my service, blood and danger.
Can those be things to sue for?
DEFLORES.   If you knew   120
How sweet it were to me to be imployed
In any act of yours, you would say then
I faild, and us'd not reverence enough
When I receive the charge on't.
BEATRICE. [*Aside.*]   This is much, methinks;
Belike his wants are greedy, and to such   125
Gold tastes like Angels food.[8] [*To* DEFLORES.] Rise.
DEFLORES. I'le have the work first.
BEATRICE. [*Aside.*]   Possible his need
Is strong upon him; [*gives him money*] there's to in-
                    courage thee.
As thou art forward and thy service dangerous,
Thy reward shall be pretious.
DEFLORES.   That I have thought on;   130
I have assur'd my self of that before hand,
And know it will be pretious, the thought ravishes!
BEATRICE. Then take him to thy fury.
DEFLORES.   I thirst for him.
BEATRICE. Alonzo de Piracquo.
DEFLORES.   His end's upon him,
He shal be seen no more.
BEATRICE.   How lovely now   135
Dost thou appear to me! Never was man
Dearlier rewarded.
DEFLORES.   I do think of that.
BEATRICE. Be wondrous carefull in the execution.
DEFLORES. Why, are not both our lives upon the cast?[5]

---

[5] *upon the cast* : of the dice.

BEATRICE. Then I throw all my fears upon thy service.   140
DEFLORES. They ne'er shal rise to hurt you.
BEATRICE.   When the
                deed's done,
  I'le furnish thee with all things for thy flight;
  Thou mayst live bravely in another countrey.
DEFLORES. I, I, wee'l talk of that hereafter.
BEATRICE. [Aside.]   I shall rid
           my self
  Of two inveterate loathings at one time,   145
  Piracquo and his Dog-face.[6]   Exit.
DEFLORES.   Oh my blood![7]
  Methinks I feel her in mine arms already.
  Her wanton fingers combing out this beard,
  And being pleased, praising this bad face :
  Hunger and pleasure—they'l commend sometimes   150
  Slovenly dishes, and feed heartily on 'em,
  Nay, which is stranger, refuse daintier for 'em.
  Some women are odd feeders.—I'me too loud.
  Here comes the man goes supperless to bed,
  Yet shall not rise to-morrow to his dinner.   155
           Enter ALONZO.
ALONZO. Deflores.
DEFLORES.   My kind, honorable Lord.
ALONZO. I am glad I ha' met with thee.
DEFLORES.   Sir.
ALONZO.   Thou canst
        shew me
  The full strength of the Castle.
DEFLORES.   That I can, sir.
ALONZO. I much desire it.
DEFLORES.   And if the ways and straits[8]
  Of some of the passages be not too tedious for you,   160
  I will assure you, worth your time and sight, my Lord.
ALONZO. Puh,[7] that shall be no hinderance.
DEFLORES.   I'me your
      servant then :

---

[6] *Dog-face* : a title for Deflores.   [8] *straits* : narrow places.
[7] *blood* : passion.

'Tis now neer dinner time; 'gainst[9] your Lordships
             rising
I'le have the keys about me.
ALONZO.   Thanks, kind Deflores.
DEFLORES. [*Aside.*] He's safely thrust upon me beyond   165
        hopes.   *Exeunt.*

ACTUS TERTIUS. [SCENA PRIMA.][(1)]

Enter ALONZO *and* DEFLORES.
(*In the Act-time*[1] DEFLORES *hides a naked Rapier.*)
DEFLORES. Yes, here are all the keys; I was afraid, my
            Lord,
  I'de wanted for the postern,[2] this is it.
  I've all, I've all, my Lord : this for the Sconce.[3]
ALONZO. 'Tis a most spacious and impregnable Fort.
DEFLORES. You'l tell me more, my Lord : this discent   5
  Is somwhat narrow, we shall never pass
  Well with our weapons, they'l but trouble us.
ALONZO. Thou sayst true.
DEFLORES.   Pray let me help your Lordship.
ALONZO. 'Tis done. Thanks, kind Deflores.
DEFLORES.   Here are hooks,
      my Lord,
  To hang such things on purpose.
               [*He hangs up the swords.*]
ALONZO.   Lead, I'le follow   10
       thee.
    Exeunt at one door and enter at the other.

9 *'gainst :* before.
  ACT III. SCENE I.
1 *In the Act-time :* In the in-
  terval between the acts.

2 *I'de wanted . . . postern :*
  was lacking the rear-door key.
3 *Sconce :* special fortress.

[ACTUS TERTIUS. SCENA SECUNDA.]

DEFLORES. All this is nothing, you shall see anon
  A place you little dream on.
ALONZO.   I am glad
  I have this leasure : all your masters house
  Imagine I ha' taken a *Gondela*.
DEFLORES. All but my self, sir, [*aside*] which makes up   5
                 my safety;
  [*To* ALONZO.] My Lord, I'le place you at a Casement
                here,
  Will shew you the full strength of all the Castle.
  Look, spend your eye a while upon that object.
ALONZO. Here's rich variety, Deflores.
DEFLORES.   Yes, sir.
ALONZO. Goodly munition.
DEFLORES.   I, there's Ordnance, sir,   10
  No bastard metall, will ring you a peal like Bells
  At greet mens Funerals; keep your eye streight, my
                Lord,
  Take speciall notice of that Sconce before you,
  There you may dwell a-while.
              [*He takes the hidden rapier.*]
ALONZO.   I am upon't.
DEFLORES. And so am I.   [*Stabs him.*]
ALONZO.   Deflores! Oh Deflores,   15
  Whose malice hast thou put on?
DEFLORES.   Doe you question
  A work of secresie? I must silence you.   [*Stabs him.*]
ALONZO. Oh, oh, oh.
DEFLORES.   I must silence you.   [*Stabs him.*]
  So, here's an undertaking wel accomplish'd.
  This vault serves to good use now.—Ha! what's that   20
  Threw sparkles in my eye?—Oh 'tis a Diamond
  He wears upon his finger : it was well found,
  This will approve the work. What, so fast on?
  Not part in death? I'le take a speedy course then,

Finger and all shall off. [*Cuts off the finger.*][1] So,
          now I'le clear   25
The passages from all suspect or fear.

Exit with Body.

[Actus tertius. Scena tertia.]

Enter ISABELLA *and* LOLLIO.

ISABELLA. Why, sirrah?[1] Whence have you commission
  To fetter the doors against me? If you
  Keep me in a Cage, pray whistle to me,
  Let me be doing somthing.

LOLLIO. You shall be doing, if it please you; I'le whistle   5
  to you if you'l pipe after.[2, (1)]

ISABELLA. Is it your Masters pleasure, or your own,
  To keep me in this Pinfold?

LOLLIO. 'Tis for my masters pleasure, lest being taken in
  another mans Corn, you might be pounded in another   10
  place.

ISABELLA. 'Tis very well, and he'l prove very wise.

LOLLIO. He says you have company enough in the house,
  if you please to be sociable, of all sorts of people.

ISABELLA. Of all sorts? Why here's none but fools and
                    mad-men.

LOLLIO. Very well : and where will you find any other,   15
  if you should goe abroad? There's my master and I to
  boot too.

ISABELLA. Of either sort one, a mad-man and a fool.

LOLLIO. I would ev'n participate of both then if I were as
  you; I know y'are half mad already; be half foolish
  too.

ISABELLA. Y'are a brave sawcy Rascall! Come on, sir,   20
  Afford me then the pleasure of your Bedlam;[3]
  You were commending once to day to me,

ACT III. SCENE III.   obey.
[1] *sirrah* : form used to inferiors   [3] *Bedlam* : Madhouse; from
[2] *pipe after* : follow my lead;   Bethlehem Hospital.

Your last come lunatique, what a proper [2]
Body there was without brains to guide it,
And what a pittifull delight appear'd   25
In that defect, as if your wisdom had found
A mirth in madness : pray, sir, let me partake
If there be such a pleasure.

LOLLIO. If I doe not shew you the handsomest, discreet-
est mad-man, one that I may call, the understand-   30
ing [3] mad-man; then say I am a fool.

ISABELLA. Well, a match, I will say so.

LOLLIO. When you have a tast of the mad-man, you shal
(if you please) see Fools Colledge, o'th' side; [4] I seldome lock there, 'tis but shooting a bolt [4] or two,   35
and you are amongst 'em.

                    Exit [and] Enter presently.
Come on, sir, let me see how handsomly you'l behave
your self now.

                    Enter FRANCISCUS. [1]

FRANCISCUS. How sweetly she looks! Oh but there's a
wrinkle in her brow as deep as Philosophy; *Anacreon,*
drink to my Mistress health, I'le pledge it : Stay, stay,
there's a Spider [5] in the cup : No, 'tis but a Grape-   40
stone, swallow it, fear nothing, Poet; so, so, lift
higher.

ISABELLA. Alack, alack, tis too full of pitty
To be laught at; how fell he mad? Canst thou tell?

LOLLIO. For love, Mistress; he was a pretty Poet too,
and that set him forwards first; the Muses then for-   45
sook him, he ran mad for a Chambermaid, yet she
was but a dwarf neither.

FRANCISCUS. Hail, bright *Titania!* [6]
Why standst thou idle on these flowry banks?
Oberon is dancing with his *Dryades;*
I'le gather dazies, primrose, violets,   50
And bind them in a verse of Poesie.

LOLLIO. Not too neer; you see your danger.
                                    [*Shows a whip.*]

---

[4] *o'th' side* : from another angle.

FRANCISCUS. Oh hold thy hand great *Diomed,*⁽⁷⁾
    Thou feedst thy horses well, they shall obey thee;
    Get up, *Bucephalus*⁽⁸⁾ kneels.   *[He kneels.]*   55
LOLLIO. You see how I aw my flock, a Shephard has not
    his dog at more obedience.
ISABELLA. His conscience is unquiet, sure that was
    The cause of this. A proper Gentleman.
FRANCISCUS. Come hither, *Esculapius;*⁽⁹⁾ hide the   60
            poison.
LOLLIO. Well, tis hid.   *[Lowers the whip.]*
FRANCISCUS. Didst thou never hear of one *Tiresias,*⁽¹⁰⁾
    A famous Poet?
LOLLIO. Yes, that kept tame wild-geese.
FRANCISCUS. That's he; I am the man.   65
LOLLIO. No.
FRANCISCUS. Yes, but make no words on't, I was a man
    Seven years agoe.
LOLLIO. A stripling I think you might.
FRANCISCUS. Now I'me a woman, all feminine.   70
LOLLIO. I would I might see that.
FRANCISCUS. *Juno* struck me blind.
LOLLIO. I'le ne'er beleeve that; for a woman, they say,
    has an eye more then a man.
FRANCISCUS. I say she struck me blind.   75
LOLLIO. And *Luna* made you mad; you have two trades
    to beg with.
FRANCISCUS. *Luna* is now big-bellied,⁽¹¹⁾ and there's
            room
    For both of us to ride with *Hecate;*
    I'le drag thee up into her silver sphear,
    And there we'l kick the Dog, and beat the bush   80
    That barks against the Witches of the night,
    The swift *Licanthropi*⁽¹²⁾ that walks the round,
    We'l tear their wolvish skins, and save the sheep.
                [He moves to seize LOLLIO.]
LOLLIO. Is't come to this? Nay, then my poison comes
    forth agen, mad slave; indeed, abuse your Keeper!   85
                  [Shows the whip.]

ISABELLA. I prithee hence with him, now he grows dangerous.

FRANCISCUS. *Sings*.[2] *Sweet love, pitie me,*
Give me leave to lye with thee.

LOLLIO. No, I'le see you wiser first: To your own
kennell.

FRANCISCUS. No noyse, she sleeps, draw all the Curtains   90
round,

Let no soft sound molest the pretty soul,

But love, and love creeps in at a mouse-hole.

LOLLIO. I wo'd you wo'd get into your hole.

Exit FRANCISCUS.

Now, Mistress, I wil bring you another sort, you shal
be fool'd another while; Tony, come hither Tony,   95
look who's yonder, Tony.

Enter ANTONIO.

ANTONIO. Cousin, is it not my Aunt?[5, [3]

LOLLIO. Yes, 'tis one of 'um, Tony.

ANTONIO. He, he, how do you, Uncle?

LOLLIO. Fear him not, Mistress, 'tis a gentle nigget; you
may play with him, as safely with him as with his   100
bawble.

ISABELLA. How long hast thou been a fool?

ANTONIO. Ever since I came hither, Cousin.

ISABELLA. Cousin? I'me none of thy Cousins, fool.

LOLLIO. Oh mistress, fools have always so much wit as
to claim their kindred.   105

Mad-man within. Bounce, bounce, he falls, he falls.

ISABELLA. Heark you, your scholars in the upper room
Are out of order.

LOLLIO. Must I come amongst you there? Keep you the
fool, mistress; I'le go up, and play left-handed *Or-*   110
lando[13] amongst the madmen.   *Exit.*

ISABELLA. Well, sir.

ANTONIO. 'Tis opportuneful now, sweet Lady! Nay,

Cast no amazing eye upon this change.

ISABELLA. Ha!   115

---

5 *Aunt :* Prostitute.

ANTONIO. This shape of Folly shrowds your dearest
                          Love,
   The truest servant to your powerful beauties,
   Whose magick had this force thus to transform me.
ISABELLA. You are a fine Fool indeed.
ANTONIO.   Oh 'tis not strange :
   Love has an intellect that runs through all   120
   The scrutinous Sciences, and like
   A cunning Poet, catches a quantity
   Of every Knowledge, yet brings all home
   Into one mysterie, into one secret
   That he proceeds in.
ISABELLA.   Y'are a parlous[14] Fool.   125
ANTONIO. No danger in me : I bring nought but Love,
   And his soft wounding shafts to strike you with :
   Try but one arrow; if it hurt you,
   I'le stand you twenty back in recompence.
                                   [*He kisses her.*]
ISABELLA. A forward Fool too!
ANTONIO.   This was Love's teaching :   130
   A thousand wayes she[4] fashion'd out my way,
   And this I found the safest and neerest[5]
   To tread the *Gallaxia*6 to my Star.
ISABELLA. Profound, withall : certain you dream'd of
                          this;
   Love never taught it waking.
ANTONIO.   Take no acquaintance   135
   Of these outward Follies; there is within
   A Gentleman that loves you.
ISABELLA.   When I see him,
   I'le speak with him; so in the mean time keep
   Your habit, it becomes you well enough.
   As you are a Gentleman, I'le not discover you;   140
   That's all the favor that you must expect :
   When you are weary, you may leave the school,
   For all this while you have but plaid the Fool.
                   Enter LOLLIO.

6 *Gallaxia :* The Milky-Way.

ANTONIO. And must agen;—He, he, I thank you, Cozen,
    I'le be your Valentine to-morrow morning.   145
LOLLIO. How do you like the Fool, Mistress?
ISABELLA. Passing well, Sir.
LOLLIO. Is he not witty, pretty well for a Fool?
ISABELLA. If he hold on as he begins, he is like
    To come to something.   150
LOLLIO. I, thank a good Tutor : You may put him to't;
    he begins to answer pretty hard questions. Tony, how
    many is five times six?
ANTONIO. Five times six, is six times five.
LOLLIO. What Arithmetician could have answered bet-   155
    ter? How many is one hundred and seven?
ANTONIO. One hundred and seven, is seven hundred and
    one, Cozen.
LOLLIO. This is no wit to speak on; will you be rid of the
    Fool now?   160
ISABELLA. By no means, let him stay a little.
Mad-man within. Catch there, catch the last couple
    in hell! [15]
LOLLIO. Agen, must I come amongst you? Would my
    Master were come home! I am not able to govern
    both these Wards together.   *Exit*
ANTONIO. Why should a minute of Loves hour be lost?   165
ISABELLA. Fie, out agen! I had rather you kept
    Your other posture : you become not your tongue,
    When you speak from your clothes.
ANTONIO.   How can he freeze,
    Lives neer so sweet a warmth? Shall I alone
    Walk through the orchard of the *Hesperides,*   170
    And cowardly not dare to pull an apple?
    This with the red cheeks I must venter for.
                 [He tries to kiss her.]
         Enter LOLLIO *above.*
ISABELLA. Take heed, there's Gyants keep 'em.
LOLLIO. [*Aside.*] How now, fool, are you good at that?
    Have you read *Lipsius?* [16] He's past *Ars Amandi;* [16]   175
    I believe I must put harder questions to him, I per-
    ceive that—

ISABELLA. You are bold without fear too.

ANTONIO.   What should I
     fear,
  Having all joyes about me? Do you[17] smile,
  And Love shall play the wanton on your lip,
  Meet and retire, retire and meet agen :   180
  Look you but cheerfully, and in your eyes
  I shall behold mine own deformity,
  And dresse my self up fairer; I know this shape
  Becomes me not, but in those bright mirrors
  I shall array me handsomly.   185

LOLLIO. Cuckow, Cuckow![7]   *Exit.*

    [Enter] Mad-men above, some as birds, others
               as beasts.

ANTONIO. What are these?

ISABELLA.   Of fear enough[18] to part us;
  Yet are they but our schools of Lunatiques,
  That act their fantasies in any shapes
  Suiting their present thoughts; if sad, they cry;   190
  If mirth be their conceit, they laugh agen.
  Sometimes they imitate the beasts and birds,
  Singing, or howling, braying, barking; all
  As their wilde fansies prompt 'um.

               Enter LOLLIO.

ANTONIO.   These are no fears.

ISABELLA. But here's a large one, my man.   195

ANTONIO. Ha, he, that's fine sport indeed, cousin.

LOLLIO. I would my master were come home, 'tis too
  much for one shepheard to govern two of these flocks;
  nor can I beleeve that one Churchman can instruct
  two benefices at once; there wil be some incurable   200
  mad of the one side, and very fools on the other.
  Come, Tony.

ANTONIO. Prithee, cousin, let me stay here stil.

LOLLIO. No, you must to your Book now you have plaid
  sufficiently.

---

[7] *Cuckow, Cuckow :* Sounding   cuckoldry.
  the alarm for impending

ISABELLA. Your fool is grown wondrous witty.   205
LOLLIO. Well, I'le say nothing; but I do not think but
    he will put you down one of these dayes.
                        Exeunt LOLLIO *and* ANTONIO.
ISABELLA. Here the restrained current might make
                       breach,
    Spite of the watchfull bankers; would a woman stray,
    She need not gad abroad to seek her sin,   210
    It would be brought home one wayes or other :
    The Needles poynt will to the fixed North,
    Such drawing Articks womens beauties are.
               Enter LOLLIO.
LOLLIO. How dost thou, sweet rogue?
ISABELLA. How now?   215
LOLLIO. Come, there are degrees, one fool may be better
    then another.
ISABELLA. What's the matter?
LOLLIO. Nay, if thou giv'st thy mind to Fools-flesh, have
    at thee.   [*He tries to kiss her.*]   220
ISABELLA. You bold slave, you!
LOLLIO. I could follow now as t'other fool did,
    "What should I fear,
    Having all joys about me? Do you but smile,
    And love shall play the wanton on your lip,   225
    Meet and retire, retire and meet agen :
    Look you but cheerfully, and in your eyes,
    I shall behold my own deformity,
    And dress my self up fairer; I know this shape
    Becomes me not—"   230
    And so as it follows, but is not this the more foolish
                  way?
    Come, sweet rogue, kiss me, my little *Lacedemo-*
    nian.[19] Let me feel how thy pulses beat; thou hast
    a thing about thee would doe a man pleasure, I'le lay
    my hand on't.
ISABELLA. Sirrah, no more! I see you have discovered   235
    This loves Knight-arrant, who hath made adventure
    For purchase of my love; be silent, mute,
    Mute as a statue, or his injunction

For me enjoying, shall be to cut thy throat;
I'le do it, though for no other purpose,   240
And be sure hee'l not refuse it.[20]

LOLLIO. My share, that's all; I'le have my fools part with
you.

ISABELLA. No more! Your master.

Enter ALIBIUS.

ALIBIUS.   Sweet, how dost thou?

ISABELLA. Your bounden servant, sir.

ALIBIUS.   Fie, fie, sweet heart,
No more of that.

ISABELLA.   You were best lock me up.   245

ALIBIUS. In my arms and bosome, my sweet Isabella,
I'le lock thee up most neerly. Lollio,
We have imployment, we have task in hand;
At noble Vermanderos, our Castle Captain,
There is a nuptiall to be solemniz'd,—   250
Beatrice-Joanna, his fair daughter, Bride,—
For which the Gentleman hath bespoke our pains,
A mixture of our madmen and our fools,
To finish (as it were) and make the fagg[8]
Of all the Revels, the third night from the first; 255
Onely an unexpected passage over,[9]
To make a frightfull pleasure, that is all,
But not the all I aim at; could we so act it,
To teach it in a wild distracted measure,[10]
Though out of form and figure, breaking times head, 260
It were no matter, 'twould be heald again
In one age or other, if not in this;
This, this, Lollio; there's a good reward begun,
And will beget a bounty, be it known.

LOLLIO. This is easie, sir, I'le warrant you : you have   265
about you Fools and Madmen that can dance very
well; and 'tis no wonder, your best Dancers are not
the wisest men; the reason is, with often jumping they
joult their brains down into their feet, that their wits
lie more in their heels then in their heads.   270

---

[8] *fagg* : end, climax.   [10] *measure* : dance.
[9] *over* : over the stage or floor.

ALIBIUS. Honest Lollio, thou giv'st me a good reason,
  And a comfort in it.
ISABELLA.   Y'ave a fine trade on't,
  Mad-men and Fools are a staple commodity.
ALIBIUS. Oh wife, we must eat, weare clothes, and live;
  Just at the Lawyers Haven[21] we arrive,   275
  By madmen and by fools we both do thrive. *Exeunt.*

[ACTUS TERTIUS. SCENA QUARTA.]

Enter VERMANDERO, ALSEMERO, JASPERINO,
            and BEATRICE.

VERMANDERO. *Valentia* speaks so nobly of you, sir,
  I wish I had a daughter now for you.
ALSEMERO. The fellow of this creature were a partner
  For a Kings love.
VERMANDERO.   I had her fellow once, sir,
  But heaven has married her to joyes eternall;   5
  'Twere sin to wish her in this vale agen.
  Come, sir, your friend and you shall see the pleasures
  Which my health chiefly joyes in.
ALSEMERO. I hear the beauty of this seat largely.[1]
VERMANDERO. It falls much short of that.
                        Exeunt. Manet BEATRICE.
BEATRICE.   So, here's one   10
            step
  Into my fathers favour; time will fix him;
  I have got him now the liberty of the House,
  So wisdome by degrees works out her freedom;
  And if that eye[1] be darkned that offends me,—
  I wait but that Eclipse,—this Gentleman   15
  Shall soon shine glorious in my Fathers liking,
  Through the refulgent[2] vertue of my love.
                Enter DEFLORES.
DEFLORES. [*Aside.*] My thoughts are at a banquet for
                the deed;

ACT III. SCENE IV.
[1] *largely* : praised or boasted of.

I feel no weight in't, 'tis but light and cheap
For the sweet recompence that I set down for't.   20
BEATRICE. Deflores.
DEFLORES.   Lady.
BEATRICE.   Thy looks promise cheerfully.
DEFLORES. All things are answerable,—time, circum-
                                stance,
Your wishes and my service.
BEATRICE.   Is it done then?
DEFLORES. Piracquo is no more.
BEATRICE. My joyes start at mine eyes; our sweet'st   25
                          delights
Are evermore born weeping.
DEFLORES.   I've a token for you.
BEATRICE. For me?
DEFLORES.   But it was sent somwhat unwillingly,
I could not get the Ring without the Finger.
                              [*He shows her the finger.*]
BEATRICE. Bless me! What hast thou done?
DEFLORES.   Why, is that
                        more
Then killing the whole man? I cut his heart-strings.   30
A greedy hand thrust in a dish at Court,
In a mistake, hath had as much as this.
BEATRICE. 'Tis the first token my father made me send
                          him.
DEFLORES. And I made him send it back agen
For his last token; I was loath to leave it,   35
And I'me sure dead men have no use of Jewels;
He was as loath to part with't, for it stuck,
As if the flesh and it were both one substance.
BEATRICE. At the Stags fall the Keeper has his fees :
'Tis soon apply'd, all dead mens fees are yours, Sir;[2]   40
I pray, bury the finger, but the stone

2 *'Tis soon . . . Sir :* Thus the
old saying is applied to this
case.

You may make use on shortly; the true value,
Tak't of my truth, is neer three hundred Duckets.
DEFLORES. 'Twil hardly buy a capcase[3] for ones con-
                          science, tho,
To keep it from the worm, as fine as 'tis.   45
Well, being my fees I'le take it;
Great men have taught me that, or else my merit
Would scorn the way on't.
BEATRICE.   It might justly, sir:
Why thou mistak'st, Deflores, 'tis not given
In state of recompence.
DEFLORES.   No, I hope so, Lady,   50
You should soon witness my contempt too't then.
BEATRICE. Prithee, thou lookst as if thou wer't offended.
DEFLORES. That were strange, Lady, tis not possible
My service should draw such a cause from you.
Offended? Could you think so? That were much   55
For one of my performance, and so warm
Yet in my service.
BEATRICE. 'Twere misery in me to give you cause, sir.
DEFLORES. I know so much, it were so,—misery
In her most sharp condition.
BEATRICE.   'Tis resolv'd then;   60
Look you, sir, here's 3000 golden Florens.[4]
I have not meanly thought upon thy merit.
DEFLORES. What, sallery? Now you move me.
BEATRICE.   How, Deflores?
DEFLORES. Do you place me in the rank of verminous
                          fellows,
To destroy things for wages? Offer gold?   65
The life blood of man! Is any thing
Valued too pretious for my recompence?
BEATRICE. I understand thee not.
DEFLORES.   I could ha' hir'd
A journey-man in murder at this rate,
And mine own conscience might have [kept un-   70
                          sold,][1]
And have had the work brought home.

BEATRICE. [*Aside.*]   I'me in a laby-
        rinth;
What will content him? I would fain be rid of him.
[*To* DEFLORES.] I'le double the sum, sir.
DEFLORES.   You take a
      course
To double my vexation, that's the good you doe.
BEATRICE. [*Aside.*] Bless me! I am now in worse plight   75
      then I was;
I know not what will please him : [*to* DEFLORES]
      for my fears sake
I prithee make away with all speed possible.
And if thou be'st so modest not to name
The sum that will content thee, paper blushes not;
Send thy demand in writing, it shall follow thee,   80
But prithee take thy flight.
DEFLORES.   You must flie too then.
BEATRICE. I?
DEFLORES.   I'le not stir a foot else.
BEATRICE.   What's your meaning?
DEFLORES. Why are not you as guilty, in—I'me sure—
As deep as I? And we should stick together.
Come, your fears counsell you but ill, my absence   85
Would draw suspect upon you instantly;
That were no rescue for you.
BEATRICE. [*Aside.*]   He speaks home.
DEFLORES. Nor is it fit we two, ingag'd so joyntly, .
Should part and live asunder.   [*He tries to kiss her.*]
BEATRICE.   How now, sir?
This shews not well.
DEFLORES.   What makes your lip so strange?   90
This must not be betwixt us.
BEATRICE. [*Aside.*]   The man talks wildly.
DEFLORES. Come, kiss me with a zeal now.
BEATRICE.   Heaven!   I
      doubt[3] him.
DEFLORES. I will not stand so long to beg 'em shortly.

----

[3] *doubt :* fear.

BEATRICE. Take heed, Deflores, of forgetfulness,
  'Twill soon betray us.
DEFLORES.   Take you heed first;   95
  Faith, y'are grown much forgetfull, y'are too blame
                in't.
BEATRICE. [*Aside.*] He's bold, and I am blam'd for't!
DEFLORES.   I have
          eas'd you
  Of your trouble,—think on't,—I'me in pain,
  And must be eas'd of you; 'tis a charity,
  Justice invites your blood to understand me.   100
BEATRICE. I dare not.
DEFLORES.   Quickly!
BEATRICE.   Oh I never shall!
  Speak it yet further off[2] that I may lose
  What has been spoken, and no sound remain on't.
  I would not hear so much offence again
  For such another deed.
DEFLORES.   Soft, Lady, soft;   105
  The last is not yet paid for. Oh, this act
  Has put me into spirit; I was as greedy on't
  As the parcht earth of moisture, when the clouds
                weep.
  Did you not mark, I wrought my self into't,—
  Nay, sued and kneel'd for't : why was all that pains 110
              took?
  You see I have thrown contempt upon your gold,
  Not that I want[4] it [not],[3] for I doe piteously;
  In order I will come unto't, and make use on't,
  But 'twas not held so pretious to begin with;
  For I place wealth after the heels of pleasure,   115
  And were I not resolv'd in my belief
  That thy virginity were perfect in thee,
  I should but take my recompence with grudging,
  As if I had but halfe my hopes I agreed for.
BEATRICE. Why, 'tis impossible thou canst be so wicked, 120
  Or shelter such a cunning cruelty,

---

[4] *want :* need.

To make his death the murderer of my honor.
Thy language is so bold and vitious,
I cannot see which way I can forgive it
With any modesty.
DEFLORES.   Push, you forget your selfe!   125
A woman dipt in blood, and talk of modesty?
BEATRICE. O misery of sin! Would I had been bound
Perpetually unto my living hate
In that Piracquo, then to hear these words.
Think but upon the distance that Creation   130
Set 'twixt thy blood and mine, and keep thee there.
DEFLORES. Look but into your conscience, read me there,
'Tis a true Book, you'l find me there your equall :
Push, flye not to your birth, but settle you
In what the act has made you; y'are no more now,   135
You must forget your parentage to⁵ me,
Y'are the deeds creature, by that name
You lost your first condition; and I challenge you,
As peace and innocency has turn'd you out,
And made you one with me.
BEATRICE.   With thee, foul villain? 140
DEFLORES. Yes, my fair murdress; do you urge me?
Though thou writ'st maid, thou whore in thy affec-
                              tion;
'Twas chang'd from thy first love, and that's a kind
Of whoredome in thy heart, and he's chang'd now,
To bring thy second on, thy Alsemero,   145
Whom (by all sweets that ever darkness tasted)
If I enjoy thee not, thou ne'er enjoyst;
I'le blast the hopes and joyes of marriage,
I'le confess all, my life I rate at nothing.⁽⁵⁾
BEATRICE. Deflores!   150
DEFLORES. I shall rest from all lovers plagues then,
I live in pain now : that shooting eye
Will burn my heart to cinders.
BEATRICE.   O sir, hear me.

⁵ *to :* because of your relation
  to.

DEFLORES. She that in life and love refuses me,
In death and shame my partner she shall be.   155
BEATRICE. [*Kneeling.*] Stay, hear me once for all; I make
thee master
Of all the wealth I have in gold and jewels;
Let me go poor unto my bed with honor,
And I am rich in all things.
DEFLORES.   Let this silence thee,—
The wealth of all *Valentia* shall not buy   160
My pleasure from me;
Can you weep Fate from its determin'd purpose?
So soon may [you][4] weep me.
BEATRICE.   Vengeance begins;
Murder I see is followed by more sins.
Was my creation in the womb so curst,   165
It must ingender with a Viper first?
DEFLORES. Come, rise, and shrowd your blushes in my
bosome;   [*He raises her.*]
Silence is one of pleasures best receipts :
Thy peace is wrought for ever in this yeelding.
'Lasse, how the Turtle[6] pants! Thou'lt love anon   170
What thou so fear'st, and faintst to venture on.
Exeunt.

ACTUS QUARTUS. [SCENA PRIMA.]

[*Dumb Show.*]
Enter Gentlemen, VERMANDERO *meeting them with
action of wonderment at the flight of* PIRACQUO. *Enter*
ALSEMERO, *with* JASPERINO, *and Gallants;* VERMAN-
DERO *poynts to him, the Gentlemen seeming to ap-
plaud the choyce;* [*Exeunt* VERMANDERO,] ALSEMERO,
JASPERINO, *and Gentlemen;* BEATRICE *the Bride fol-
lowing in great state, accompanied with* DIAPHANTA,
ISABELLA, *and other Gentlewomen :* DEFLORES *after
all, smiling at the accident;*[1] ALONZO's *Ghost ap-*

6 *Turtle :* Turtle dove.

pears to DEFLORES *in the midst of his smile, startles him, shewing him the hand whose finger he had cut off. They passe over in great solemnity.*

Enter BEATRICE.

BEATRICE. This fellow has undone me endlessly,
Never was Bride so fearfully distrest;
The more I think upon th'ensuing night,
And whom I am to cope with in embraces,
One [who's][1] ennobled both in blood and mind,   5
So clear in understanding,—that's my plague now,—
Before whose judgement will my fault appear
Like malefactors crimes before Tribunals;
There is no hiding on't, the more I dive
Into my own distress; how a wise man   10
Stands for¹ a great calamity! There's no venturing
Into his bed, what course soe'er I light upon,
Without my shame, which may grow up to danger;
He cannot but in justice strangle me
As I lie by him,[2]—as a cheater use me;   15
'Tis a pretious craft to play with a false Dye
Before a cunning Gamester. Here's his closet,
The key left in't, and he abroad i'th Park;
Sure 'twas forgot, I'le be so bold as look in't.
Bless me! A right Physicians closet 'tis,   20
Set round with vials,[3] every one her mark too.
Sure he does practice Physick for his own use,
Which may be safely calld your great mans Wisdom.
What manuscript lies here? "The Book of Experiment,
Call'd Secrets in Nature"(2): so 'tis, 'tis so;   25
"How to know whether a woman be with child or no."
I hope I am not yet; if he should try tho!
Let me see—folio 45. Here 'tis;
The leaf tuckt down[4] upon't, the place suspitious.
"If you would know whether a woman be with child,   30

ACT IV. SCENE I.
¹ *Stands for :* Symbolizes.

or not, give her two spoonfuls of the white water in
                    Glass C."
Wher's that Glass C : O yonder I see't now,—
"And if she be with child, she sleeps full twelve hours
                 after, if not, not."
None of that water comes into my belly.   35
I'le know you from a hundred; I could break you now
Or turn you into milk, and so beguile
The master of the mystery, but I'le look to you.
Ha! that which is next is ten times worse.
"How to know whether a woman be a maid[2] or not";   40
If that should be apply'd, what would become of me?
Belike he has a strong faith of my purity,
That never yet made proof; but this he calls
"A merry sleight[5] but true experiment, the Author
Antonius Mizaldus. Give the party you suspect the   45
quantity of a spoonful of the water in the glass M,
which upon her that is a maid makes three severall
effects; 'twill make her incontinently[3] gape, then fall
into a sudden sneezing, last into a violent laughing;
else dull, heavy and lumpish."
Where had I been?   50
I fear it, yet 'tis seven hours to bed time.
                Enter DIAPHANTA.
DIAPHANTA. Cuds,[4] Madam, are you here?
BEATRICE. [*Aside.*]   Seeing   that
              wench now,
A trick comes in my mind; 'tis a nice piece[5]
Gold cannot purchase; [*to* DIAPHANTA] I come hither,
              wench,
To look my Lord.   55
DIAPHANTA. [*Aside.*] Would I had such a cause to look
              him too.
[*To* BEATRICE.] Why he's ith' Park, Madam.
BEATRICE. There let him be.

---

[2] *maid :* virgin.   me."
[3] *incontinently :* immediately.   [5] *nice piece :* specially
[4] *Cuds :* Short for "God save   principled girl.

DIAPHANTA.   I, madam, let him compass
  Whole Parks and Forrests, as great Rangers doe;
  At roosting time a little lodge can hold 'em.   60
  Earth-conquering *Alexander,* that thought the world
  Too narrow for him, in the end had but his pit-hole.
BEATRICE. I fear thou art not modest, Diaphanta.
DIAPHANTA. Your thoughts are so unwilling to be known,
               Madam;
  'Tis ever the Brides fashion towards bed-time,   65
  To set light by her joyes, as if she ow'd[6] 'em not.
BEATRICE. Her joys? Her fears, thou wouldst say.
DIAPHANTA.   Fear
          of what?
BEATRICE. Art thou a maid, and talkst so to a maid?
  You leave a blushing bisiness behind,
  Beshrew your heart for't!
DIAPHANTA.   Do you mean good sooth,   70
         madam?
BEATRICE. Well, if I'de thought upon the fear at first,
  Man should have been unknown.
DIAPHANTA.   Is't possible?
BEATRICE. I will give a thousand Duckets to that woman
  Would try what my fear were, and tell me true
  To-morrow, when she gets from't : as she likes   75
  I might perhaps be drawn too't.[7]
DIAPHANTA.   Are you in earnest?
BEATRICE. Do you get the woman, then challenge me,
  And see if I'le flie from't; but I must tell you
  This by the way,—she must be a true maid,
  Else there's no tryall, my fears are not hers else.   80
DIAPHANTA. Nay, she that I would put into your hands,
            madam,
  Shall be a maid.
BEATRICE.   You know I should be sham'd else,
  Because she lies for me.
DIAPHANTA.   Tis a strange humour :

[6] *ow'd :* possessed.   joys it I might perhaps be per-
[7] *as she . . . too't :* as she en-   suaded to do it.

But are you serious still? Would you resigne
Your first nights pleasure, and give money too?   85
BEATRICE. As willingly as live; [*aside*] alas, the gold
    Is but a by-bet to wedge in[8] the honor.
DIAPHANTA. I doe not know how the world goes abroad
    For faith or honesty, there's both requir'd in this.
    Madam, what say you to me, and stray no further?   90
    I've a good mind in troth to earn your money.
BEATRICE. Y'are too quick, I fear, to be a maid.
DIAPHANTA. How? Not a maid? Nay, then you urge me,
                madam;
    Your honorable self is not a truer
    With all your fears upon you,—
BEATRICE. [*Aside.*]   Bad enough then.   95
DIAPHANTA. Then I with all my lightsome joyes about
                me.
BEATRICE. I'me glad to hear't then; you dare put your
                honesty
Upon an easie tryall.
DIAPHANTA.   Easie?—Any thing.
BEATRICE. I'le come to you streight.
DIAPHANTA. [*She goes to the closet.*] She will not search
                me, will she?
Like the fore-woman of a female Jury.[(3)]   100
BEATRICE. [*Bringing a vial.*] Glass M. I, this is it; look,
                Diaphanta,
You take no worse then I do.   [*She drinks.*]
DIAPHANTA.   And in so doing
    I will not question what 'tis, but take it. [*She drinks.*]
BEATRICE. [*Aside.*] Now if the experiment be true, 'twill
                praise it selfe,
And give me noble ease :—Begins already;   105
                [DIAPHANTA *gapes.*]
There's the first symptome; and what hast it makes
To fall into the second, there by this time!
               [DIAPHANTA *sneezes.*]

[8] *a by-bet . . . in :* a side-bet to
  protect.

Most admirable secret! On the contrary
It stirs not me a whit, which most concerns it.
DIAPHANTA. Ha, ha, ha.
BEATRICE. [*Aside.*]   Just in all things and in order,   110
As if 'twere circumscrib'd, one accident
Gives way unto another.
DIAPHANTA.   Ha, ha, ha.
BEATRICE.   How now, wench?
DIAPHANTA. Ha, ha, ha, I am so—so light at heart, ha,
            ha, ha, so pleasurable.
But one swig more, sweet Madam.
BEATRICE.   I, to-morrow,
We shall have time to sit by't.
DIAPHANTA.   Now I'me sad agen.   115
BEATRICE. [*Aside.*] It layes it self so gently too!
                    [*To* DIAPHANTA] Come, wench,
Most honest Diaphanta I dare call thee now.
DIAPHANTA. Pray tell me, madam, what trick call you
                    this?
BEATRICE. I'le tell thee all hereafter; we must study
The carriage of this business.
DIAPHANTA.   I shall carry't well,   120
Because I love the burthen.
BEATRICE.   About midnight
You must not fail to steal forth gently,
That I may use the place.
DIAPHANTA.   Oh fear not, Madam,
I shall be cool by that time : the brides place!
And with a thousand Duckets! I'me for a Justice now,   125
I bring a portion [4] with me; I scorn small fools.
                                            Exeunt.

[ACTUS QUARTUS. SCENA SECUNDA.]

Enter VERMANDERO *and Servant.*
VERMANDERO. I tell thee, knave, mine Honor is in ques-
                    tion,
A thing till now free from suspition,
Nor ever was there cause; who of my Gentlemen
Are absent? Tell me and truly, how many and who.

SERVANT. Antonio, Sir, and Franciscus.   5
VERMANDERO. When did they leave the Castle?
SERVANT. Some ten days since, sir, the one intending to
    Briamata,[1] th'other for *Valentia*.
VERMANDERO. The time accuses 'um, a charge of murder
    Is brought within my Castle gate, Piracquo's murder; 10
    I dare not answer faithfully their absence :
    A strict command of apprehension
    Shall pursue 'um suddenly, and either wipe
    The stain off clear, or openly discover it.
    Provide me winged warrants for the purpose.   15
    See, I am set on agen.   *Exit Servant.*
              Enter TOMAZO.
TOMAZO. I claim a brother of you.
VERMANDERO.   Y'are too hot,
    Seek him not here.
TOMAZO.   Yes, 'mongst your dearest bloods,
    If my peace find no fairer satisfaction;
    This is the place must yeeld account for him,   20
    For here I left him, and the hasty tie
    Of this snatcht marriage, gives strong testimony
    Of his most certain ruine.
VERMANDERO.   Certain falshood!
    This is the place indeed; his breach of faith
    Has too much mar'd both my abused love,   25
    The honorable love I reserv'd for him,
    And mock't my daughters joy; the prepar'd morning
    Blusht at his infidelity; he left
    Contempt and scorn to throw upon those friends
    Whose belief hurt 'em : oh 'twas most ignoble   30
    To take his flight so unexpectedly,[1]
    And throw such publick wrongs on those that lov'd
           him.
TOMAZO. Then this is all your answer.
VERMANDERO.   'Tis too fair
    For one of his alliance[1]; and I warn you

Act IV. Scene ii.
[1] *of his alliance :* of his family
  relationship.

That this place no more see you.   *Exit.*
Enter DEFLORES.

TOMAZO.   The best is,   35
There is more ground to meet a mans revenge on.
Honest Deflores.

DEFLORES.   That's my name indeed.
Saw you the Bride? Good sweet sir, which way took
            she?

TOMAZO. I have blest mine eyes from seeing such a false
            one.

DEFLORES. [*Aside.*] I'de fain get off, this man's not for
            my company,   40
I smell his brothers blood when I come neer him.

TOMAZO. Come hither, kind and true one; I remember
My brother lov'd thee well.

DEFLORES.   O purely, dear sir,
[*Aside.*] Me thinks I am now agen a-killing on him.
He brings it so fresh to me.

TOMAZO.   Thou canst guesse, sirrah,   45
[An][2] honest friend has an instinct of jealousie[2]
At some foul guilty person.

DEFLORES. 'Lasse, sir, I am so charitable, I think none
Worse then my self.—You did not see the Bride then?

TOMAZO. I prithee name her not. Is she not wicked?   50

DEFLORES. No, no, a pretty, easie, round-packt sinner,
As your most Ladies are, else you might think
I flatter'd her; but, sir, at no hand wicked,
Till th'are so old their sins and vices[2] meet,
And they salute Witches; I am call'd, I think, sir: 55
[*Aside.*] His company ev'n o'er-lays[3] my conscience.
                               Exit.

TOMAZO. That Deflores has a wondrous honest heart.
He'l bring it out in time, I'me assur'd on't.
O here's the glorious master of the dayes joy.
I will not be long till he and I do reckon.   60
Enter ALSEMERO.
Sir.

---

[2] *jealousie :* suspicion.   [3] *o'er-lays :* oppresses.

ALSEMERO. You are most welcome.

TOMAZO.   You may call that
  word back,
  I do not think I am, nor wish to be.

ALSEMERO. 'Tis strange you found the way to this
  house then.

TOMAZO. Would I'de ne'er known the cause! I'm none of
  those, sir,
  That come to give you joy, and swill your wine;   65
  'Tis a more pretious liquor that must lay
  The fiery thirst I bring.

ALSEMERO.   Your words and you
  Appear to me great strangers.

TOMAZO.   Time and our swords
  May make us more acquainted; this the businesse,—
  I should have a brother in your Place;   70
  How treachery and malice have dispos'd of him,
  I'me bound to enquire of him which holds his right:
  Which never could come fairly.

ALSEMERO.   You must look
  To answer for that word, sir.

TOMAZO.   Fear you not,
  I'le have it ready drawn at our next meeting.   75
  Keep your day solemn. Farewell, I disturb it not,
  I'le bear the smart with patience for a time.

                                            Exit.

ALSEMERO. 'Tis somwhat ominous—this, a quarrell
                    entred
  Upon this day; my innocence relieves me,
                    Enter JASPERINO.
  I should be wondrous sad else.—Jasperino,   80
  I have newes to tell thee, strange news.

JASPERINO.   I ha' some too,
  I think as strange as yours; would I might keep
  Mine, so my faith and friendship might be kept in't!
  Faith, sir, dispense a little with my zeal,
  And let it cool in this.

ALSEMERO.   This puts me on,[3]   85
  And blames thee for thy slowness.

JASPERINO.   All may prove
                nothing,
Onely a friendly fear that leapt from me, sir.
ALSEMERO. No question it may prove nothing; let's
                partake it tho.[3]
JASPERINO. 'Twas Diaphanta's chance,—for to that
                wench
   I pretend[4] honest love, and she deserves it,—   90
   To leave me in a back part of the house,
   A place we chose for privat conference;
   She was no sooner gone, but instantly
   I heard your brides voyce in the next room to me;
   And lending more attention, found Deflores   95
   Lowder then she.[(4)]
ALSEMERO.   Deflores? Thou art out now.
JASPERINO. You'l tell me more anon.
ALSEMERO.   Still I'le prevent[5]
                thee,
   The very sight of him is poyson to her.
JASPERINO. That made me stagger too, but Diaphanta
   At her return confirm'd it.
ALSEMERO.   Diaphanta!   100
JASPERINO. Then fell we both to listen, and words past
   Like those that chalenge interest in a woman.
ALSEMERO. Peace, quench thy zeal, tis dangerous to thy
                bosom!
JASPERINO. Then truth is full of perill.
ALSEMERO.   Such truths are.
   —O were she the sole glory of the earth,   105
   Had eys that could shoot fire into Kings breasts,
   And toucht, she sleeps not here! Yet I have time
   Though night be neer, to be resolv'd hereof,
   And prithee do not weigh me by my passions.
JASPERINO. I never weigh'd friend so.
ALSEMERO.   Done charitably.   110
   That key will lead thee to a pretty secret,
   By a Chaldean taught me, and I've

---

[4] *pretend* : intend, offer.   [5] *prevent* : forestall.

My study upon some; bring from my closet
A glass inscrib'd there with the letter M,
And question not my purpose.
JASPERINO.   It shall be done, sir.   115
                                                        Exit.
ALSEMERO. How can this hang together? Not an hour
                        since,
Her woman came pleading her Lady's fears,
Deliver'd her for the most timerous virgin
That ever shrunk at mans name, and so modest,
She charg'd her weep out her request to me,   120
That she might come obscurely(5) to my bosome.
                Enter BEATRICE.
BEATRICE. [*Aside.*] All things go well, my womans pre-
                        paring yonder
For her sweet voyage, which grieves me to lose;
Necessity compels it; I lose all else.
ALSEMERO. [*Aside.*] Push, Modesties shrine is set in
                        yonder forehead.   125
I cannot be too sure tho. [*to her*] My Joanna.
BEATRICE. Sir, I was bold to weep a message to you,
Pardon my modest fears.
ALSEMERO. [*Aside.*]   The Dove's not meeker.
She's abus'd, questionless.
                Enter JASPERINO [*with a glass.*]
                        —Oh are you come, sir?
BEATRICE. [*Aside.*] The glass—upon my life! I see the   130
                        letter
JASPERINO. Sir, this is M.
ALSEMERO.   'Tis it.
BEATRICE. [*Aside.*]   I am suspected.
ALSEMERO. How fitly our Bride comes to partake with
                        us!
BEATRICE. What is't, my Lord?
ALSEMERO.   No hurt.
BEATRICE.   Sir, pardon me,
I seldom tast of any composition.
ALSEMERO. But this upon my warrant you shall venture   135
                        on.

BEATRICE. I fear 'twill make me ill.

ALSEMERO.   Heaven forbid that.

BEATRICE. [*Aside*.] I'me put now to my cunning;
             th'effects I know,
   If I can now but feign 'em handsomly.

ALSEMERO. [*Aside to* JASPERINO.] It has that secret
             vertue it ne'er mist, sir,
   Upon a virgin.

JASPERINO. Treble qualitied?   140

                   [BEATRICE *gapes and sneezes*.]

ALSEMERO. By all that's vertuous, it takes there,
                   proceeds!

JASPERINO. This is the strangest trick to know a maid by!

BEATRICE. Ha, ha, ha!
   You have given me joy of heart to drink, my Lord.

ALSEMERO. No, thou hast given me such joy of heart,   145
   That never can be blasted.

BEATRICE.   What's the matter, sir?

ALSEMERO. [*Aside to* JASPERINO.] See, now 'tis setled in
                   a melancholy,
   Keep[s][4] both the time and method. [*to her*]
                   My Joanna!
   Chast as the breath of heaven, or mornings womb,
   That brings the day forth; thus my love incloses thee. 150

                   [*He embraces her*.] *Exeunt*.

             [ACTUS QUARTUS. SCENA TERTIA.]

             Enter ISABELLA *and* LOLLIO.

ISABELLA. Oh heaven! Is this the [weighting][1], (1)
                   moon?
   Does love turn fool, run mad, and all at once?
   Sirrah, here's a mad-man, a-kin to the fool too,
   A lunatick lover.

LOLLIO. No, no, not he I brought the Letter from?   5

ISABELLA. Compare his inside with his out, and tell me.

LOLLIO. The out's mad, I'me sure of that, I had a taste
                   on't.

[*Reads.*] "To the bright *Andromeda*, chiefe Chambermaid to the Knight of the Sun,[2] at the sign of
Scorpio, in the middle Region, sent by the Bellows-
mender of *Aeolus*. Pay the Post." This is stark madness.

ISABELLA. Now mark the inside.

[*She takes the letter and reads.*] "Sweet Lady, having
now cast off this Counterfeit Cover of a mad-man, I
appeare to your best Judgement a true and faithfull
Lover of your beauty."

LOLLIO. He is mad still.

ISABELLA. "If any fault you finde, chide those perfections
in you, which have made[2] me imperfect; 'tis the
same Sun that causeth to grow, and inforceth to
wither,—

LOLLIO. Oh Rogue!

ISABELLA. "Shapes and transhapes, destroys and builds
again; I come in winter to you dismantled of my
proper ornaments; by the sweet splendor of your
cheerful smiles, I spring and live a lover."

LOLLIO. Mad Rascall stil!

ISABELLA. "Tread him not under foot, that shal appear
an honour to your bounties. I remain—mad till I
speak with you, from whom I expect my cure. Yours
all, or one beside himselfe, Franciscus."

LOLLIO. You are like to have a fine time on't; my Master
and I may give over our professions, I do not think
but you can cure fools and madmen faster then we,
with little pains too.

ISABELLA. Very likely.

LOLLIO. One thing I must tell you, Mistris : you perceive, that I am privy to your skill; if I finde you
minister once and set up the trade, I put in for my
thirds; I shall be mad or fool else.

ISABELLA. The first place is thine, beleëve it, Lollio;
If I do fall—

LOLLIO. I fall upon you.

ISABELLA. So.

LOLLIO. Well, I stand to my venture.

ISABELLA. But thy councel now, how shall I deal with
'um?

LOLLIO. [Why,][3] do you mean to deal with 'um?

ISABELLA. Nay, the fair understanding![1] How to use   45
'um.

LOLLIO. Abuse 'um! That's the way to mad the fool, and
make a fool of the madman, and then you use 'um
kindly.[2]

ISABELLA. 'Tis easie, I'll practise; do thou observe it.
The key to thy Wardrobe.

LOLLIO. There—fit your self for 'um, and I'll fit 'um both   50
for you.   [*He gives her the key.*]

ISABELLA. Take thou no further notice then the outside.
Exit.

LOLLIO. Not an inch; I'll put you to the inside.
Enter ALIBIUS.

ALIBIUS. Lollio, art there? Will all be perfect, think'st
thou?

To-morrow night, as if to close up the solemnity :   55
Vermandero expects us.

LOLLIO. I mistrust the madmen most, the fools will do
well enough : I have taken pains with them.

ALIBIUS. Tush, they cannot miss; the more absurdity,
The more commends it, so no rough behaviours   60
Affright the Ladies; they are nice[3] things, thou
know'st.

LOLLIO. You need not fear, Sir, so long as we are there
with our commanding peesles,[3] they'll be as tame
as the ladies themselves.

ALIBIUS. I will see them once more rehearse before they   65
go.

LOLLIO. I was about it, Sir; looke you to the madmens
Morris, and let me alone with the other; there is
one or two that I mistrust their fooling; I'll instruct

ACT IV. SCENE III.   [2] *kindly* : according to their
[1] *Nay . . . understanding* :   natures.
Understand me in the best   [3] *nice* : sensitive.
sense.

them, and then they shall rehearse the whole measure.

ALIBIUS. Do so, I'll see the musick prepar'd : but, Lollio,   70
By the way, how does my wife brook her restraint?
Does she not grudge at it?

LOLLIO. So, so,—she takes some pleasure in the house,
she would abroad else; you must allow her a little
more length, she's kept too short.   75

ALIBIUS. She shall along to Vermandero's with us,
That will serve her for a moneths liberty.

LOLLIO. What's that on your face, Sir?

ALIBIUS. Where, Lollio? I see nothing.

LOLLIO. Cry you mercy, Sir, tis your nose; it shew'd like   80
the trunck(4) of a young Elephant.

ALIBIUS. Away, Rascal! I'll prepare the musick, Lollio.
                                        Exit ALIBIUS.

LOLLIO. Do, Sir, and I'll dance the whilst; Tony, where
art thou, Tony?

                        Enter ANTONIO.

ANTONIO. Here, Cozen, where art thou?   85

LOLLIO. Come, Tony, the footmanship I taught you.

ANTONIO. I had rather ride, Cozen.

LOLLIO. I, a whip take you; but I'll keep you out. Vault
in; look you, Tony,—Fa, la, la, la, la!   [*He dances.*]

ANTONIO. Fa, la, la, la, la.   [*He dances.*]   90

LOLLIO. There, an honour.

ANTONIO. Is this an honour, Cuz?   [*He bows.*]

LOLLIO. Yes, and it please your worship.

ANTONIO. Does honour bend in the hams, Cuz?

LOLLIO. Marry⁴ does it, as low as worship, squireship,   95
nay, yeomandry it self sometimes, from whence it
first stiffened. There, rise a caper.

ANTONIO. Caper after an honour, Cuz?

LOLLIO. Very proper, for honour is but a caper, rise[s][4]
as fast and high, has a knee or two, and falls to th'   100
ground agen. You can remember your figure, Tony?
                                        Exit.

⁴ *Marry :* By Mary.

ANTONIO. Yes, Cozen, when I see thy figure, I can remember mine.

Enter ISABELLA [*dressed like a madwoman.*]

ISABELLA. Hey, how [he][5] treads the air! Shough,
Shough, t'other way! He burns his wings else; here's   105
wax(5) enough below, *Icarus,* more then will be
cancelled5 these eighteen moons; he's down, he's
down! What a terrible fall he had!
Stand up, thou son of *Cretan Dedalus,*
And let us tread the lower Labyrinth;
I'll bring thee to the Clue.(6)   110

ANTONIO. Prethee, Cuz, let me alone.

ISABELLA. Art thou not drown'd?
About thy head I saw a heap of Clouds
Wrapt like a Turkish Turbant; on thy back
A crookt Camelion-colour'd rainbow hung,   115
Like a *Tyara* down unto thy hams.
Let me suck out those Billows in thy belly;
Heark how they rore and rumble in the streets.6, [6]
Bless thee from the Pyrats!

ANTONIO. Pox upon you! Let me alone.   120

ISABELLA. Why shouldst thou mount so high as
                                        Mercury,
Unlesse thou hadst reversion7 of his place?
Stay in the Moon with me, *Endymion,*(7)
And we will rule these wild rebellious waves,
That would have drownd my love.   125

ANTONIO. I'le kick thee if again thou touch me,
Thou wild unshapen Antick; I am no fool,
You Bedlam.

ISABELLA. But you are, as sure as I am, mad.
Have I put on this habit of a frantick,
With love as full of fury to beguile   130
The nimble eye of watchfull jealousie,
And am I thus rewarded?   [*She reveals herself.*]

---

5 *cancelled :* in the form of
 seals.
6 *streets :* a pun on "straits,"

meaning "narrow seas."
7 *reversion :* legal inheritance or
 succession.

ANTONIO. Ha! Dearest beauty!

ISABELLA.   No, I have no beauty now,
   Nor never had, but what was in my garments.
   You a quick-sighted lover? Come not neere me!   135
   Keep your Caparisons, y'are aptly clad;
   I came a feigner to return stark mad.   *Exit.*

Enter LOLLIO.

ANTONIO. Stay, or I shall change condition,
   And become as you are.

LOLLIO. Why, Tony, whither now? Why, fool?   140

ANTONIO. Whose fool, usher of Idiotts? You Coxcomb!
   I have foold too much.

LOLLIO. You were best be mad another while then.

ANTONIO. So I am, stark mad! I have cause enough,
   And I could throw[7] the full effects on thee,   145
   And beat thee like a Fury!

LOLLIO. Doe not, doe not; I shall not forbear the
   Gentleman under the foole, if you doe; alas, I saw
   through your Fox-skin[8] before now : come, I can
   give you comfort; my Mistress loves you, and there is   150
   as arrant a mad-man i' th' house, as you are a foole,
   your Rivall, whom she loves not; if after the mask
   we can rid her of him, you earn her love, she sayes,
   and the fool shall ride her.

ANTONIO. May I beleeve thee?

LOLLIO. Yes, or you may chuse whether you will or no.   155

ANTONIO. She's eas'd of him; I have a good quarrell on't.

LOLLIO. Well, keep your old station yet, and be quiet.

ANTONIO. Tell her I will deserve her love.

LOLLIO. And you are like to have your desire.

[*Exit* ANTONIO.]

Enter FRANCISCUS.

FRANCISCUS. [*Singing.*] "Down, down, down a-down   160
   a-down,—and then with a horse-trick,
   To kick *Latona's*[9] forehead, and break her bow-
      string."

LOLLIO. This is t'other counterfeit, I'l put him out of his
   humor. [*He takes out a letter and reads.*] "Sweet

Lady, having now cast[8] this counterfeit cover of a
mad-man, I appear to your best judgement a true and   165
faithfull lover of your beauty." This is pretty well for
a mad-man.

FRANCISCUS. Ha! What's that?

LOLLIO. "Chide those perfections in you which made
me imperfect."

FRANCISCUS. I am discover'd to the fool.   170

LOLLIO. I hope to discover the fool in you, e'er I have
done with you. "Yours all, or one beside himself,
Franciscus." This mad-man will mend sure.

FRANCISCUS. What do[8] you read, sirrah?

LOLLIO. Your destiny, sir; you'l be hang'd for this trick,   175
and another that I know.

FRANCISCUS. Art thou of counsell with thy mistress?

LOLLIO. Next her Apron strings.

FRANCISCUS. Give me thy hand.

LOLLIO. Stay, let me put your in my pocket first : [*He*   180
puts away the letter.] your hand is true, is it not?[9]
It will not pick? I partly fear it, because I think it
does lye.

FRANCISCUS. Not in a sillable.

LOLLIO. So, if you love my mistress so well as you have
handled the matter here, you are like to be cur'd of   185
your madness.

FRANCISCUS. And none but she can cure it.

LOLLIO. Well, I'le give you over then, and she shall cast
your water next.[10]

FRANCISCUS. Take for thy pains. [*He gives him money.*]   190

LOLLIO. I shal deserve more, sir, I hope; my mistress
loves you, but must have some proof of your love to
her.

FRANCISCUS. There I meet my wishes.

LOLLIO. That will not serve,—you must meet her enemy
and yours.   195

---

8 *cast :* thrown off.   10 Physicians used urine
9 Punning on "hand" and   analysis.
  "handwriting."

FRANCISCUS. He's dead already.

LOLLIO. Will you tell me that, and I parted but now with him?

FRANCISCUS. Shew me the man.

LOLLIO. I, that's a right course now, see him before you kill him in any case, and yet it needs not go so far   200
neither; 'tis but a fool that haunts the house, and my mistris, in the shape of an ideot; bang but his fools coat well-favouredly, and 'tis well.

FRANCISCUS. Soundly, soundly!

LOLLIO. Onely reserve him till the masque be past; and   205
if you find him not now in the dance your self, I'le shew you. In! In! My master.

FRANCISCUS. He handles him like a feather. Hey!

[*Exit dancing.*]

Enter ALIBIUS.

ALIBIUS. Well said;[11] in a readiness, Lollio?

LOLLIO. Yes, sir.   210

ALIBIUS. Away then, and guide them in, Lollio;
Intreat your Mistress to see this sight.
Hark, is there not one incurable fool
That might be beg'd?[12] I have friends.

LOLLIO. I have him for you, one that shall deserve   215
it[(10)] too.   [*Exit* LOLLIO.]

ALIBIUS. Good boy, Lollio.

[*Enter* LOLLIO *with Mad-men and Fools.*]
The Mad-men and Fools dance.

ALIBIUS. 'Tis perfect; well, fit but once these strains,
We shall have coin and credit for our pains. *Exeunt.*

---

[11] *well said :* commonly for "well done" rather than "well spoken."

[12] *is there . . . beg'd :* a way of getting legal control of his estate.

ACTUS QUINTUS. [SCENA PRIMA.]

Enter BEATRICE. *A Clock strikes one.*
BEATRICE. One struck, and yet she lies by't—Oh my
      fears!
  This strumpet serves her own ends, 'tis apparent now,
  Devours the pleasure with a greedy appetite,
  And never minds my honor or my peace,
  Makes havock of my right; but she payes dearly   5
      for't,—
  No trusting of her life with such a secret,
  That cannot rule her blood, to keep her promise.
  Beside, I have some suspition of her faith to me,
  Because I was suspected of my Lord,
  And it must come from her.—Heark, by my horrors!   10
  Another clock strikes two.   *Strike two.*
         Enter DEFLORES.
DEFLORES.   Pist, where are you?
BEATRICE. Deflores?
DEFLORES.   I—is she not come from him yet?
BEATRICE. As I am a living soul, not.
DEFLORES.   Sure the Devill
  Hath sow'd his itch within her; who'd trust
  A waiting-woman?
BEATRICE.   I must trust some body.   15
DEFLORES. Push, they are *Tarmagants.*
  Especially when they fall upon their Masters
  And have their Ladies first fruits;[1] th'are mad
      whelps,
  You cannot stave 'em off from game Royall; then
  You are so harsh and hardy, ask no counsell,   20
  And I could have helpt you to a[n][1] Apothecaries
      daughter
  Would have faln off before eleven, and thank[2] you
      too.
BEATRICE. O me, not yet? This whore forgets her self.
DEFLORES. The Rascal fares so well; look, y'are undone,

    The Day-star, by this hand! See [*Phosphorus*][3]   25
               plain yonder.
BEATRICE. Advise me now to fall upon some ruine,[1]
    There is no counsell safe else.
DEFLORES.   Peace, I ha't now,
    For we must force a rising,[2] there's no remedy.
BEATRICE. How? Take heed of that.
DEFLORES.   Tush, be you quiet,
    Or else give over all.
BEATRICE.   Prithee, I ha' done then.   30
DEFLORES. This is my reach; I'le set some part a-fire
    Of Diaphanta's chamber.
BEATRICE.   How? Fire, sir?
    That may endanger the whole house.
DEFLORES. You talk of danger when your fame's on fire.
BEATRICE. That's true,—do what thou wilt now.
DEFLORES.   Push, I   35
              aim
    At a most rich success, strikes all dead sure;
    The chimney being a-fire, and some light parcels
    Of the least danger in her chamber only,
    If Diaphanta should be met by chance then,
    Far from her lodging, which is now suspitious,   40
    It would be thought her fears and affrights then,
    Drove her to seek for succour; if not seen
    Or met at all, as that's the likeliest,
    For her own shame she'l hasten towards her lodging;
    I will be ready with a piece high-charg'd,[3]   45
    As 'twere to cleanse the chimney : there 'tis proper
               now,
    But she shall be the mark.
BEATRICE.   I'me forc'd to love thee now,
    'Cause thou provid'st so carefully for my honor.

Act V. Scene i.
[1] *fall . . . ruine :* devise something violent.
[2] *force a rising :* disturb the whole house.
[3] *piece high-charg'd :* loaded hunting gun.

DEFLORES. 'Slid, it concerns the safety of us both,
Our pleasure and continuance.
BEATRICE.   One word now, prithee,—   50
How for the servants?
DEFLORES.   I'le dispatch them,
Some one way, some another in the hurry,
For Buckets, Hooks, Ladders; fear not you;
The deed shall find its time, and I've thought since
Upon a safe conveyance for the body too.   55
How this fire purifies wit! Watch you your minute.
BEATRICE. Fear keeps my soul upon't, I cannot stray
                          from't.
               Enter ALONZO'S GHOST.
DEFLORES. Ha! What art thou that tak'st away the light
'Twixt that starr and me? I dread thee not,
'Twas but a mist of conscience.—All's clear agen.   60
                                              Exit.
BEATRICE. Who's that, Deflores? Bless me! It slides by,
                              [*Exit* GHOST.]
Some ill thing haunts the house; 't has left behind it
A shivering sweat upon me; I'me afraid now,
This night hath been so tedious; oh this strumpet!
Had she a thousand lives, he should not leave her   65
Till he had destroyd the last.—List, oh my terrors!
Three struck by St. Sebastians.   *Struck 3 a-clock.*
[VOICES] WITHIN. Fire, fire, fire!
BEATRICE. Already! How rare is that mans speed!
How heartily he serves me! His face loathes one,   70
But look upon his care, who would not love him?
The East is not more beauteous then his service.
[VOICES] WITHIN. Fire, fire, fire!
Enter DEFLORES [*and*] *servants : passe over, ring a Bell.*
DEFLORES. Away, dispatch! Hooks, buckets, ladders;
                    thats well said,—
The fire-bell rings, the chimney works,—my charge;   75
The piece is ready.   *Exit.*
BEATRICE.   Here's a man worth loving!
               Enter DIAPHANTA.
Oh y'are a jewel!

DIAPHANTA.   Pardon frailty,[2] Madam,
In troth I was so well, I ev'n forgot my self.
BEATRICE. Y'have made trim work.
DIAPHANTA.   What?
BEATRICE.   Hie quickly
                    to your chamber,
Your reward follows you.
DIAPHANTA.   I never made   80
So sweet a bargain.   *Exit.*
                Enter ALSEMERO.
ALSEMERO.   Oh my dear Joanna,
Alas, art thou risen too? I was coming,
My absolute treasure.
BEATRICE.   When I mist you,
I could not chuse but follow.
ALSEMERO.   Th'art all sweetness!
The fire is not so dangerous.
BEATRICE.   Think you so, sir?   85
ALSEMERO. I prithee tremble not : believe me, 'tis not.
                Enter VERMANDERO, JASPERINO.
VERMANDERO. Oh bless my house and me!
ALSEMERO.   My Lord your
                    father.
                Enter DEFLORES *with a Piece.*
VERMANDERO. Knave, whither goes that piece?
DEFLORES.   To scour
                    the chimney.   *Exit.*
VERMANDERO. Oh well said, well said![3]
That fellow's good on all occasions.   90
BEATRICE. A wondrous necessary man, my Lord.
VERMANDERO. He hath a ready wit, he's worth 'em all,
                    sir;
Dog at a house a-fire,[4] I ha' seen him sindg'd ere
                now :   *The piece goes off.*
Ha, there he goes.
BEATRICE.   'Tis done.
ALSEMERO.   Come, sweet, to bed now;
Alas, thou wilt get cold.

BEATRICE.   Alas, the fear keeps that   95
 out;
 My heart will find no quiet till I heare
 How Diaphanta, my poor woman, fares;
 It is her chamber, sir, her lodging chamber.
VERMANDERO. How should the fire come there?
BEATRICE. As good a soul as ever Lady countenanc'd,   100
 But in her chamber negligent and heavy;
 She scap't a Mine[4] twice.[4]
VERMANDERO.   Twice?
BEATRICE.   Strangely twice,
 sir.
VERMANDERO. Those sleepy sluts are dangerous in a
 house,
 And they be ne'er so good.
    Enter DEFLORES.
DEFLORES.   Oh poor virginity!
 Thou hast paid dearly for't.
VERMANDERO.   Bless us! What's that?[5]   105
DEFLORES. A thing you all knew once,—Diaphanta's
 burnt.
BEATRICE. My woman, oh my woman!
DEFLORES.   Now the flames
 Are greedy of her,—burnt, burnt, burnt to death, sir.
BEATRICE. Oh my presaging soul!
ALSEMERO.   Not a tear more,
 I charge you by the last embrace I gave you   110
 In bed before this rais'd us.
BEATRICE.   Now you tie me;
 Were it my sister, now she gets no more.
    Enter Servant.
VERMANDERO. How now?
SERVANT. All danger's past, you may now take your
 rests, my Lords; the fire is throughly quencht; ah   115
 poore Gentlewoman, how soon was she stifled!
BEATRICE. Deflores, what is left of her interre,

[4] *scap't . . . twice*: had two
close calls.

And we as mourners all will follow her :
I will intreat that honour to my servant,
Ev'n of my Lord himself.
ALSEMERO.   Command it, sweetness.   120
BEATRICE. Which of you spied the fire first?
DEFLORES.   'Twas I,
          Madam.
BEATRICE. And took such pains in't too? A double good-
                              ness!
'Twere well he were rewarded.
VERMANDERO.   He shall be,
Deflores, call upon me.
ALSEMERO.   And upon me, sir.
                    Exeunt [all but DEFLORES.]
DEFLORES. Rewarded? Pretious, here's a trick beyond 125
                    me!
I see in all bouts, both of sport and wit,
Always a woman strives for the last hit.   *Exit.*

                [Actus quintus. Scena secunda.]

                    Enter TOMAZO.
TOMAZO. I cannot taste the benefits of life
With the same relish I was wont to do.
Man I grow weary of, and hold his fellowship
A treacherous bloody friendship; and because
I am ignorant in whom my wrath should settle,   5
I must think all men villains, and the next
I meet, whoe'er he be, the murderer
Of my most worthy brother.—Ha! What's he?
          Enter DEFLORES, *passes over the Stage.*
Oh, the fellow that some call honest Deflores;
But me thinks honesty was hard bested[1]   10
To come there for a lodging, as if a Queen
Should make her Palace of a Pest-house;[1]

Act V. Scene ii.
[1] *Pest-house :* Hospital for
plague victims.

I find a contrariety in nature
Betwixt that face and me,—the least occasion
Would give me game upon him;[2] yet he's so foul   15
One would scarce touch [him][1] with a sword he
                    loved
And made account of, so most deadly venemous,
He would go neer to poyson any weapon
That should draw blood on him; one must resolve
Never to use that sword again in fight,   20
In way of honest manhood, that strikes him;
Some river must devour't, 'twere not fit
That any man should find it.—What agen?
                 Enter DEFLORES.
He walks a' purpose by, sure, to choke me up,
To infect my blood.
DEFLORES.   My worthy noble Lord.   25
TOMAZO. Dost offer to come neer and breath upon me?
                              [*He strikes him.*]
DEFLORES. A blow!   [*He draws his sword.*]
TOMAZO.   Yea, are you so prepar'd?
I'le rather like a souldier die by th' sword
Then like a Polititian by thy poyson.   [*He draws.*]
DEFLORES. Hold, my Lord, as you are honorable!   30
TOMAZO. All slaves that kill by poyson are still[3] cowards.
DEFLORES. [*Aside.*] I cannot strike, I see his brothers
                    wounds
Fresh bleeding in his eye, as in a Crystall.
[*To him.*] I will not question this, I know y'are noble.
I take my injury with thanks given, Sir,   35
Like a wise Lawyer; and as a favour
Will wear it for the worthy hand that gave it.
[*Aside.*] Why this from him, that yesterday appeard
So strangely loving to me?
Oh but instinct is of a subtler strain,   40
Guilt must not walk so neer his lodge agen;
He came neer[2] me now.   *Exit.*

[2] *Would give . . . him:* Make   [3] *still:* always.
fighting him a pleasure.

TOMAZO. All league with mankind I renounce for ever,
  Till I find this murderer; not so much
  As common curtesie, but I'le lock up :   45
  For in the state of ignorance I live in,
  A brother may salute his brothers murderer,
  And wish good speed to th' villain in a greeting.
     Enter VERMANDERO, ALIBIUS, *and* ISABELLA.
VERMANDERO. Noble Piracquo.
TOMAZO.   Pray keep on your way,
               sir.
  I've nothing to say to you.
VERMANDERO.   Comforts bless you sir.   50
TOMAZO. I have forsworn complement, in troth I have,
               sir;
  As you are meerly man, I have not left
  A good wish for you, nor any here.
VERMANDERO. Unless you be so far in love with grief,
  You will not part from't upon any tearms,   55
  We bring that news will make a welcome for us.
TOMAZO. What newes can that be?
VERMANDERO.   Throw no scornfull
          smile
  Upon the zeal I bring you, tis worth more, sir;
  Two of the chiefest men I kept about me
  I hide not from the law, or your just vengeance.   60
TOMAZO. Ha!
VERMANDERO. To give your peace more ample satisfac-
          tion,
  Thank these discoverers.
TOMAZO.   If you bring that calm,
  Name but the manner I shall ask forgiveness in
  For that contemptuous smile upon you :   65
  I'le perfect it with reverence that belongs
  Unto a sacred altar.   [*He kneels.*]
VERMANDERO.   Good sir, rise;
  Why now you over-doe as much a' this hand,
  As you fell short a' tother. Speak, Alibius.
ALIBIUS. 'Twas my wifes[3] fortune,—as she is most   70
         lucky

At a discovery,—to find out lately
Within our Hospital of Fools and mad-men,
Two counterfeits slipt into these disguises;
Their names Franciscus and Antonio.

VERMANDERO. Both mine, sir, and I ask no favour for   75
                              'em.

ALIBIUS. Now that which draws suspition to their habits,
The time of their disguisings agrees justly
With the day of the murder!

TOMAZO.   O blest revelation!

VERMANDERO. Nay more, nay more, sir,—Ile not spare
                              mine own
In way of justice,—they both faign'd a journey   80
To *Br[i]amata,* and so wrought out their leaves;
My love was so abus'd in't.

TOMAZO.   Time's too pretious
To run in waste now; you have brought a peace
The riches of five kingdoms could not purchase;
Be my most happy conduct, I thirst for 'em;   85
Like subtile lightning will I wind about 'em,
And melt their marrow in 'em.   *Exeunt.*

[ACTUS QUINTUS. SCENA TERTIA.]

Enter ALSEMERO *and* JASPERINO.

JASPERINO. Your confidence, I'me sure, is now of proof.
The prospect from the Garden has shew'd
Enough for deep suspition.

ALSEMERO.   The black masque[1]
That so continually was worn upon't,
Condemnes the face for ugly ere't be seen,—   5
Her despite to him, and so seeming bottomless.

JASPERINO. Touch it home then, 'tis not a shallow probe
Can search this ulcer soundly; I fear you'l find it

ACT V. SCENE III.
[1] *The . . . masque :* Deflores'
ugliness.

    Full of corruption; 'tis fit I leave you,
    She meets you opportunely from that walk,   10
    She took the back door at his parting with her.
                              Exit JASPERINO.
ALSEMERO. Did my fate wait for this unhappy stroke
    At my first sight of woman?—She's here.
                 Enter BEATRICE.
BEATRICE. Alsemero!
ALSEMERO.   How do you?
BEATRICE.   How do I?
    Alas! How do you? You look not wel.   15
ALSEMERO. You read me well enough, I am not well.
BEATRICE. Not well, sir? Is't in my power to better you?
ALSEMERO. Yes.
BEATRICE.   Nay, then y'are cur'd again.
ALSEMERO. Pray resolve me one question, Lady.
BEATRICE.   If I can.
ALSEMERO. None can so sure. Are you honest?   20
BEATRICE. Ha, ha, ha,—that's a broad question, my Lord.
ALSEMERO. But that's not a modest answer, my Lady:
    Do you laugh? My doubts are strong upon me.
BEATRICE. 'Tis innocence that smiles, and no rough brow
    Can take away the dimple in her cheek.   25
    Say I should strain a tear to fill the vault,[2]
    Which would you give the better faith to?
ALSEMERO. 'Twere but hypocrisie of a sadder colour,
    But the same stuff; neither your smiles nor tears
    Shall move or flatter me from my belief,   30
    You are a Whore.
BEATRICE.   What a horrid sound it hath!
    It blasts a beauty to deformity;
    Upon what face soever that breath falls,
    It strikes it ugly : oh you have ruin'd
    What you can ne'er repair agen.
ALSEMERO.   I'le all   35
    Demolish and seek out truth within you,
    If there be any left, let your sweet tongue

[2] *vault* : vault of the heavens.

Prevent[3] your hearts rifling; there I'le ransack
And tear out my suspition.
BEATRICE.   You may, sir,
  'Tis an easie passage; yet, if you please,   40
  Shew me the ground whereon you lost your love;
  My spotlesse vertue may but tread on that
  Before I perish.
ALSEMERO.   Unanswerable!
  A ground you cannot stand on; you fall down
  Beneath all grace and goodness, when you set   45
  Your ticklish heel on't; there was a vizor[4]
  O'er that cunning face, and that became you,
  Now Impudence in triumph rides upon't;
  How comes this tender reconcilement else
  'Twixt you and your despight, your rankerous loath-   50
      ing,
  Deflores? He that your eye was sore at sight of,
  He's now become your arms supporter, your
  Lips Saint.
BEATRICE.   Is there the cause?
ALSEMERO.   Worse,—your lusts Devill,
  Your adultery!
BEATRICE.   Would any but your self say that,
  'Twould turn him to a villain.
ALSEMERO.   'Twas witnest   55
  By the counsell of your bosome, Diaphanta.
BEATRICE. Is your witness dead then?
ALSEMERO.   'Tis to be fear'd,
  It was the wages of her knowledge; poor soule,
  She liv'd not long after the discovery.
BEATRICE. Then hear a story of not much less horror   60
  Then this your false suspition is beguild with;
  To your beds scandal, I stand up innocence,
  Which even the guilt of one black other deed
  Will stand for proof of,—your love has made me
  A cruell murdress,—
ALSEMERO.   Ha!

---

[3] *Prevent :* Forestall.   [4] *vizor :* mask.

BEATRICE.   A bloody one.   65
  I have kist poyson for't, stroakt a serpent;
  That thing of hate, worthy in my esteem
  Of no better imployment, and him most worthy
  To be so imployd, I caus'd to murder
  That innocent Piracquo, having no   70
  Better means then that worst, to assure
  Your self to me.
ALSEMERO.   Oh the place it self e'er since
  Has crying been for vengeance, the Temple
  Where blood and beauty first unlawfully
  Fir'd their devotion, and quencht the right one;   75
  'Twas in my fears at first, 'twill have it now;
  Oh thou art all deform'd!
BEATRICE.   Forget not, sir,
  It for your sake[1] was done; shall greater dangers
  Make the less welcome?
ALSEMERO.   Oh thou shouldst have gone
  A thousand leagues about to have avoided   80
  This dangerous bridge of blood,—here we are lost!
BEATRICE. Remember I am true unto your bed.
ALSEMERO. The bed it selfe's a Charnell, the sheets
                  shrowds
  For murdered Karkasses; it must ask pawse
  What I must do in this, meantime you shall   85
  Be my prisoner onely,—enter my Closet.
                    Exit BEATRICE.
  Ile be your Keeper yet. Oh in what part
  Of this sad story shall I first begin?—
          Enter DEFLORES.
                Ha!
  This same fellow has put me in.[5] Deflores!
DEFLORES. Noble Alsemero!
ALSEMERO.   I can tell you   90
  Newes, sir; my wife has her commended to you.
DEFLORES. That's news indeed, my Lord; I think she
             would

[5] *put me in* : given me my cue.

Commend me to the gallows if she could,
She ever lov'd me so well,—I thank her.
ALSEMERO. What's this blood upon your band, Deflores?   95
DEFLORES. Blood? No, sure, 'twas washt since.
ALSEMERO.   Since when, man?
DEFLORES. Since t'other day I got a knock
In a Sword and Dagger School; I think 'tis out.
ALSEMERO. Yes, 'tis almost out, but 'tis perceiv'd tho.
I had forgot my message; this it is,   100
What price goes murder?
DEFLORES.   How, sir?
ALSEMERO.   I ask you, sir;
My wife's behind hand with you, she tells me,
For a brave bloody blow you gave for her sake
Upon Piracquo.
DEFLORES.   Upon? 'Twas quite through him sure;
Has she confest it?
ALSEMERO.   As sure as death to both of you,   105
As much more then that.
DEFLORES.   It   could   not   be   much
                                        more;
'Twas but one thing, and that—she's a Whore.
ALSEMERO. I[t][2] could not chuse but follow; oh cun-
                        ning Divels!
How   should   blind   men   know   you   from   fair   fac'd
                        saints?
BEATRICE *within*. He lies. the villain does be-lye me!   110
DEFLORES. Let me go to her, sir.
ALSEMERO.   Nay, you shal to her.
Peace, crying Crocodile, your sounds are heard!
Take your prey to you. Get you into her, sir.
                                        Exit DEFLORES.
I'le be your pander[3] now; rehearse agen
Your Scene of lust, that you may be perfect   115
When you shall come to act it to the black audience
Where howls and gnashings shall be musick to you.
Clip your adultress freely, 'tis the pilot
Will guide you to the *Mare mortuum*,[6]

_____

[6] *Mare mortuum* : Dead Sea.

Where you shall sink to fadoms bottomless.   120
  Enter VERMANDERO, ALIBIUS, ISABELLA, TOMAZO,
            FRANCISCUS, *and* ANTONIO.
VERMANDERO. Oh, Alsemero, I have a wonder for you.
ALSEMERO. No, sir, 'tis I, I have a wonder for you.
VERMANDERO. I have suspition neer as proof it self
  For Piracquo's murder.
ALSEMERO.   Sir, I have proof
  Beyond suspition, for Piracquo's murder.   125
VERMANDERO. Beseech you hear me, these two have
                  been disguis'd
  E'er since the deed was done.
ALSEMERO.   I have two other
  That were more close disguis'd then your two could
                  be,
  E'er since the deed was done.
VERMANDERO. You'l hear me,—these mine own serv-
                  ants,—   130
ALSEMERO. Hear me,—those nearer then your servants
  That shall acquit them, and prove them guiltless.
FRANCISCUS. That may be done with easie truth, sir.
TOMAZO. How is my cause bandied through your de-
                  laies!
  'Tis urgent in blood, and calls for hast;   135
  Give me a brother alive or dead;
  Alive, a wife with him, if dead, for both
  A recompence for murder and adultery.[1]
BEATRICE *within.* Oh, oh, oh!
ALSEMERO.   Heark, 'tis comming to you.
DEFLORES *within.* Nay, I'le along for company.
BEATRICE *within.*   Oh, oh! 140
VERMANDERO. What horrid sounds are these?
ALSEMERO. Come forth, you twins of mischief.
  Enter DEFLORES *bringing in* BEATRICE [*wounded.*]
DEFLORES. Here we are; if you have any more
  To say to us, speak quickly, I shall not
  Give you the hearing else; I am so stout yet,   145
  And so, I think, that broken rib[2] of mankind.
VERMANDERO. An Host of enemies entred my Citadell,
  Could not amaze like this. Joanna, Beatrice-Joanna!

BEATRICE. O come not neer me, sir, I shall defile you;
 I am that of your blood was taken from you   150
 For your better health; look no more upon't,
 But cast it to the ground regardlessly;
 Let the common sewer[4] take it from distinction
 Beneath the starres; upon yon Meteor[3]
 Ever hang[5] my fate, 'mongst things corruptible; 155
 I ne'er could pluck it from him, my loathing
 Was Prophet to the rest, but ne'er beleev'd;
 Mine honour fell with him, and now my life.
 Alsemero, I am a stranger to your bed,
 Your bed was coz'ned[7] on the nuptiall night, 160
 For which your false bride died.
ALSEMERO.   Diaphanta!
DEFLORES. Yes, and the while I coupled with your mate
 At barly-break;[4] now we are left in hell.
VERMANDERO. We are all there, it circumscribes[5] here.
DEFLORES. I lov'd this woman in spight of her heart, 165
 Her love I earn'd out of Piracquos murder.
TOMAZO. Ha, my brothers murtherer!
DEFLORES.   Yes, and her honors
      prize
 Was my reward; I thank life for nothing
 But that pleasure, it was so sweet to me
 That I have drunk up all, left none behinde 170
 For any man to pledge me.
VERMANDERO.   Horrid Villain!
 Keep life in him for further tortures.
DEFLORES.   No!
 I can prevent you, here's my penknife still;
 It is but one thread more, [*stabs himself*]—and now
      'tis cut.
 Make haste, Joanna, by that token[6] to thee,— 175
 Canst not forget,[8] so lately put in mind,
 I would not goe to leave thee far behind. *Dyes.*

---

[7] *coz'ned :* cheated, deceived. [8] *Canst . . . forget :* You cannot
            forget.

BEATRICE. Forgive me, Alsemero, all forgive,
   'Tis time to die, when 'tis a shame to live.   *Dyes.*
VERMANDERO. Oh my name is entred now in that record, 180
   Where till this fatall hour 'twas never read.
ALSEMERO. Let it be blotted out, let your heart lose it,
   And it can never look you in the face,
   Nor tell a tale behind the back of life
   To your dishonor; justice hath so right   185
   The guilty hit, that innocence is quit
   By proclamation, and may joy agen.
   Sir, your are sensible of what truth hath done,
   'Tis the best comfort that your grief can find.
TOMAZO. Sir, I am satisfied, my injuries   190
   Lie dead before me; I can exact no more,
   Unless my soul were loose, and could o'er-take
   Those black fugitives, that are fled from thence,[6], (7)
   To take a second vengeance; but there are wraths
   Deeper then mine ('tis to be fear'd) about 'em. 195
ALSEMERO. What an opacous body had that moon
   That last chang'd on us? Here's beauty chang'd
   To ugly whoredom : here servant obedience
   To a master-sin, imperious murder :
   I, a suppos'd husband, chang'd embraces   200
   With wantonness, but that was paid before;
   Your(8) change is come too, from an ignorant wrath
   To knowing friendship. Are there any more on's?
ANTONIO. Yes, sir, I was chang'd too, from a little Asse as
   I was, to a great Fool as I am; and had like to ha' 205
   been chang'd to the gallows, but that you know my
   Innocence[9] always excuses me.
FRANCISCUS. I was chang'd from a little wit to be stark
                 mad,
   Almost for the same purpose.
ISABELLA.   Your change is still behind,[10]
   But best deserve your transformation.
   You are a jealous Coxcomb,[11] keep Schools of Folly, 210

[9] *Innocence :* Pun on "idiocy."   She addresses Alibius.
[10] *still behind :* still to come.   [11] *Coxcomb :* Fool.

And teach your Scholars how to break your own
   head.
ALIBIUS. I see all apparent, wife, and will change now
 Into a better husband, and never keep Scholars
 That shall be wiser then my self.
ALSEMERO. Sir, you have yet a sons duty living,   215
 Please you accept it; let that your sorrow
 As it goes from your eye, goe from your heart,
 Man and his sorrow at the grave must part.

EPILOGUE.

ALSEMERO. All we can doe, to Comfort one another,
 To stay a Brothers sorrow for a Brother,
 To Dry a Child from the kinde Fathers eyes—
 Is to no purpose, it rather multiplies :
 Your only smiles have power to cause re-live
 The Dead agen, or in their Rooms to give
 Brother a new Brother, Father a Child;
 If these appear, All griefs are reconcil'd.

           Exeunt omnes.

FINIS.

THE REVENGER'S TRAGEDY

BY

CYRIL TOURNEUR

THE
REVENGERS
TRAGÆDIE.

As it hath beene sundry times Acted,
by the Kings Maiesties
Seruants.

AT LONDON
Printed by G. E ı d, and are to be sold at his
house in Fleete-lane at the signe of the
Printers-Presse.
1 6 0 8.

[DRAMATIS PERSONAE.

The DUKE.
LUSSURIOSO,[1] *the Duke's Son.*
SPURIO, *a Bastard.*
AMBITIOSO, *the Duchess' Eldest Son.*
SUPERVACUO,[2] *the Duchess' Second Son.*
The YOUNGEST SON *of the Duchess.*
VINDICE, *the Revenger, called* PIATO *in disguise,*⎫ *Brothers*
HIPPOLITO, *also called* CARLO, ⎬ *of* CASTIZA.
ANTONIO, ⎫
PIERO, ⎬ *Nobles.*
DONDOLO.[3]

Nobles, Judges, Gentlemen, Officers,
Keeper, Servants.

The DUCHESS.
CASTIZA.
GRATIANA,[4] *Mother of* CASTIZA.]

[SCENE.
A CITY IN ITALY.]

Act I. [Scene i.]

Enter VINDICE [, *carrying a skull*]; *the* DUKE, DUCHESS,
LUSSURIOSO *her sonne*, SPURIO *the bastard,*
with a traine passe over the Stage with
Torch-light.

VINDICE. Duke, royall letcher! goe, gray-hayrde adultery,
  And thou his sonne as impious steept as hee :
  And thou his bastard, true-begott in evill :
  And thou his Dutchesse, that will doe[1] with Divill,
  Foure exlent Characters.—O that marrow-lesse age   5
  Would stuffe the hollow Bones with dambd desires,
  And 'stead of heate kindle infernall fires
  Within the spend-thrift veynes of a drye Duke,
  A parcht and juicelesse luxur.[2, (1)] O God! one
  That has scarce bloud inough to live upon;   10
  And hee to ryot it like a sonne and heyre!
  O the thought of that
  Turnes my abused heart-strings into fret.[3]
                [*He looks at the skull.*]
  Thou sallow picture of my poysoned love,
  My studies ornament, thou shell of Death,   15
  Once the bright face of my betrothed Lady,
  When life and beauty naturally fild out
  These ragged imperfections;
  When two heaven-pointed Diamonds were set
  Into those unsightly Rings;—then 'twas a face   20
  So farre beyond the artificiall shine
  Of any womans bought complexion,
  That the uprightest man, (if such there be,
  That sinne but seaven times a day), broke custome
  And made up eight with looking after her.   25
  Oh she was able to ha' made a Usurers sonne
  Melt all his patrimony in a kisse,
  And what his father fiftie yeares told,[4]

Act I. Scene i.
[1] *doe;* do the sexual act.   [3] *fret :* discontented music.
[2] *luxur :* lecher.   [4] *told :* counted up.

To have consumde, and yet his sute beene cold :
But oh accursed Pallace!   30
Thee, when thou wert appareld in thy flesh,
The old Duke poyson'd,
Because thy purer part would not consent
Unto his palsey-lust, for old men lust-full
Do show like young men angry, eager, violent,   35
Out-bid, like their limited performances.
O ware an old man hot and vicious!
"Age, as in gold, in lust is covetous."
Vengence, thou murders Quit-rent,[2] and whereby
Thou showst[1] thy selfe Tennant to Tragedy,   40
Oh keepe thy day, houre, minute, I beseech,
For those thou hast determind. Hum, who e'er[2]
                    knew
Murder unpayd? Faith, give Revenge her due,
Sh'as kept touch hetherto.—Be merry, merry,
Advance thee, O thou terror to fat folkes,   45
To have their costly three-pilde[3] flesh worne off
As bare as this; for banquets, ease, and laughter
Can make great men, as greatnesse goes by clay,
But wise men little are more great then they.
            Enter [his][3] brother HIPPOLITO.
HIPPOLITO. Still sighing o'er deaths vizard?
VINDICE.   Brother,   50
            welcome,
What comfort bringst thou? How go things at Court?
HIPPOLITO. In silke and silver, brother : never braver.
VINDICE.   Puh,
Thou playst upon my meaning. Pree-thee, say,
Has that bald Madam, Opportunity,
Yet thought upon's? Speake, are we happy yet?   55
Thy wrongs and mine are for one scabberd fit.
HIPPOLITO. It may prove happinesse.
VINDICE.   What ist may prove?
Give me to tast.
HIPPOLITO.   Give me your hearing then.
You know my place at Court.

VINDICE.   I, the Dukes Chamber,
But tis a marvaile thourt not turnd out yet!   60
HIPPOLITO. Faith, I have beene shoovd at, but twas still
                    my hap
To hold by th' Dutchesse skirt,[4]—you gesse at that,—
Whome such a Coate keepes up can ne'er fall flat.
But to the purpose—
Last evening, predecessor unto this,   65
The Dukes sonne warily enquird for me,
Whose pleasure I attended : he began
By policy to open and unhuske me
About the time and common rumour :
But I had so much wit to keepe my thoughts   70
Up in their built houses, yet afforded him
An idle satisfaction without danger;
But the whole ayme and scope of his intent
Ended in this, conjuring me in private
To seeke some strange digested fellow forth,   75
Of ill-contented nature, either disgracst
In former times, or by new groomes displacst
Since his Step-mothers nuptialls,—such a bloud,
A man that were for evill onely good;
To give you the true word, some base-coynd Pander.   80
VINDICE. I reach you, for I know his heate is such,
Were there as many Concubines as Ladies
He would not be contaynd, he must flie out :
I wonder how ill featurde, vilde proportiond,
That one should be, if she were made for woman,   85
Whom, at the Insurrection of his lust,
He would refuse for once. Heart, I thinke none.
Next to a skull, tho more unsound then one,
Each face he meetes he strongly doates upon.
HIPPOLITO. Brother, y'ave truly spoke him!   90
He knowes not you, but Ile sweare you know him.
VINDICE. And therefore Ile put on[5] that knave for once,
And be a right man then, a man a' th' Time;
For to be honest is not to be i' th' world.

[5] *put on :* pretend to be.

Brother, Ile be that strange composed fellow.   95
HIPPOLITO. And Ile prefer[6] you, brother.
VINDICE.   Go to,[4] then,
  The smallst advantage fattens wronged men.
  It may point out occasion;(5) if I meete her,
  Ile hold her by the fore-top fast ynough;[7]
  Or like the French Moale,[8, (6)] heave up hayre and   100
                      all.
  I have a habit[9] that wil fit it quaintly.
             [*Enter* GRATIANA *and* CASTIZA.]
  Here comes our Mother.
HIPPOLITO.   And sister.
VINDICE.   We must quoyne.[10]
  Women are apt, you know, to take false money,
  But I dare stake my soule for these two creatures,
  Onely excuse excepted, that they'le swallow   105
  Because their sex is easy in beleefe.(7)
GRATIANA.[5] What newes from Cour[t],[6] sonne
                      Carlo?
HIPPOLITO.   Faith, Mother,
  Tis whisperd there the Duchesse yongest sonne
  Has playd a Rape on Lord Antonios wife.
GRATIANA. On that relligious Lady!   110
CASTIZA. Royall bloud monster! he deserves to die,
  If Italy had no more hopes but he.
VINDICE. Sister, y'ave sentenc'd most direct and true,
  The Lawes a woman, and would she were you.
  Mother, I must take leave of you.   115
GRATIANA. Leave for what?
VINDICE.   I intend speedy travaile.
HIPPOLITO. That he do's, Madam.
GRATIANA.   Speedy indeed!
VINDICE. For since my worthy fathers funerall,
  My life's unnaturally to me, e'en compeld,
  As if I liv'd now, when I should be dead.   120

---

[6] *prefer :* recommend.   [8] *French Moale :* Head tumor.
[7] *Ile hold . . . ynough :* The [9] *habit :* costume.
  mythical Occasion had a fore-   [10] *quoyne :* coin; feign.
  lock for grasping.

GRATIANA. Indeed, he was a worthy Gentleman,
　Had his estate beene fellow to his mind.
VINDICE. The Duke did much deject him.
GRATIANA.　　　　　　　　　　　　　Much!
VINDICE.　　　　　　　　　　　　　　　　　Too much;
　And through disgrace oft smotherd in his spirit,
　When it would mount; surely I thinke hee dyed　　　125
　Of discontent, the Noblemans consumption.
GRATIANA. Most sure he did.
VINDICE.　　　　　　　　　Did he? 'lack,—you know all,
　You were his mid-night secretary.
GRATIANA.　　　　　　　　　　　No,
　He was too wise to trust me with his thoughts.
VINDICE. [*Aside.*] Yfaith, then, father, thou wast wise in-　130
　　　　　　deed,
　"Wives are but made to go to bed and feede."—
　Come, mother, sister : youle bring me onward,
　　　　　　brother?
HIPPOLITO. I will.
VINDICE. [*Aside.*] Ile quickly turne into another.
　　　　　　　　　　　　　　　　　　　　Exeunt.

[Act I. Scene ii.]

Enter the old DUKE, LUSSURIOSO *his sonne, the* DUCHESS,
　　[SPURIO] *the Bastard, the* DUCHESS' *two sonnes*
　　AMBITIOSO *and* SUPERVACUO; *the third, her*
　　　yongest, brought out with Officers for the
　　　　　　Rape. Two Judges.
DUKE. Duchesse, it is your yongest sonne, we're sory
　His violent Act has e'en drawne bloud of honor
　And staind our honors,
　Throwne inck upon the for-head[1] of our state,
　Which envious[1] spirits will dip their pens into　　　5
　After our death, and blot us in our Toombes;

ACT I. SCENE II.
[1] *envious :* malicious.

For that which would seeme treason in our lives
Is laughter when we're dead. Who dares now whisper
That dares not then speake out, and e'en proclaime
With lowd words and broad pens our closest shame.   10
I. JUDGE. Your grace hath spoke like to your silver
                    yeares,
Full of confirmed gravity; for what is it to have
A flattering false insculption on a Toombe :
And in mens hearts reproch? The boweld[2] Corps
May be seard in,[2] but with free tongue I speake,   15
"The faults of great men through their seare[1]
                    clothes breake."
DUKE. They do, we're sory for't; it is our fate
To live in feare and die to live in hate.
I leave him to your sentance; dome him, Lords,—
The fact[3] is great,—whilst I sit by and sigh.   20
DUCHESS. [Kneeling.] My gracious Lord, I pray be
                    mercifull;
Although his trespasse far exceed his yeares,
Thinke him to be your owne, as I am yours.
Call him not sonne-in-law[3] : the law I feare
Wil fal too soone upon his name and him :   25
Temper his fault with pitty!
LUSSURIOSO.   Good my Lord,
Then twill not tast so bitter and unpleasant
Upon the Judges pallat, for offences
. Gilt o'er with mercy show like fayrest women,
Good onely for their[2] beauties, which washt off,[2]   30
No sin is ouglier.
AMBITIOSO.   I beseech your grace,
Be soft and mild; let not Relentlesse Law
Looke with an iron for-head on our brother.
SPURIO. [Aside.] He yeelds small comfort yet,—hope he
                    shall die;
And if a bastards wish might stand in force   35
Would all the court were turnde into a coarse.[4]

---

[2] *seard in :* wrapped in waxed   [3] *fact :* deed (of crime).
   sheets.   [4] *coarse :* corpse.

DUCHESS. No pitty yet? Must I rise fruitlesse then?

                                        [*She rises.*]

    A wonder in a woman! Are my knees
    Of such lowe mettall that without Respect—
I. JUDGE. Let the offender stand forth;   40
    Tis the Dukes pleasure that Impartiall Doome
    Shall take first hold of his uncleane attempt,
    A Rape! Why, tis the very core of lust,
    Double Adultery.
YOUNGEST SON.[3] So, Sir.
II. JUDGE.   And which was worse,
    Committed on the Lord Antonioes wife,   45
    That Generall honest Lady. Confesse, my Lord,
    What mov'd you too't.
YOUNGEST SON.   Why flesh and blood, my Lord.
    What should move men unto a woman else.
LUSSURIOSO. O do not jest thy doome! Trust not an axe
    Or sword too far; the Law is a wise serpent   50
    And quickly can beguile thee of thy life.
    Tho marriage onely has mad thee my brother,
    I love thee so far; play not with thy Death.
YOUNGEST SON. I thanke you, troth,—good admonitions,
                faith,
    If Ide the grace now to make use of them.   55
I. JUDGE. That Ladyes name has spred such a faire wing
    Over all Italy, that if our Tongs
    Were sparing toward the Fact, Judgment it selfe
    Would be condemned and suffer in mens thoughts.
YOUNGEST SON. Well then, tis done, and it would please   60
                me well
    Were it to doe agen : sure shees a Goddesse,
    For Ide no power to see her, and to live.
    It falls out true in this, for I must die;
    Her beauty was ordaynd to be my scaffold.
    And yet, me[4] thinks, I might be easier ceast,[4], (4)   65
    My fault being sport, let me but die in jest.
I. JUDGE. This be the sentence.—
DUCHESS. O keept upon your Tongue, let it not slip;
    Death too soone steales out of a Lawyers lip.

Be not so cruell-wise!
I. JUDGE.   Your Grace must pardon us,   70
'Tis but the Justice of the Lawe.
DUCHESS.   The Lawe
Is growne more subtill then a woman(5) should be.
SPURIO. [*Aside.*] Now, now he dyes; rid 'em away.
DUCHESS. [*Aside.*] O what it is to have an old-coole
                         Duke,
To bee as slack in tongue as in performance.   75
I. JUDGE. Confirmde, this be the doome irrevocable.
DUCHESS. Oh!
I. JUDGE.   To-morrow early,—
DUCHESS.   Pray, be a-bed, my Lord.
I. JUDGE. Your Grace much wrongs your selfe.
AMBITIOSO.   No, 'tis
                    that tongue;
Your too much right dos do us too much wrong.
I. JUDGE. Let that offender—
DUCHESS.   Live and be in health.   80
I. JUDGE. Be on a Scaffold—
DUKE.   Hold, hold, my Lord.
SPURIO. [*Aside.*]   Pox on't,[5]
What makes my Dad speake now?
DUKE. We will defer the judgement till next sitting;
    In the meane time let him be kept close prisoner :
    Guard, beare him hence.
AMBITIOSO. [*Aside.*]   Brother, this makes for thee;   85
    Feare not, weele have a trick to set thee free.
YOUNGEST SON. [*Aside.*] Brother, I will expect it from
                         you both;
    And in that hope I rest.
SUPERVACUO.   Farewell, be merry.
                    Exit [YOUNGEST SON] *with a garde.*
SPURIO. Delayd, deferd! Nay then, if judgement have
    Cold blood, flattery and bribes will kill it.   90
DUKE. About it, then, my Lords, with your best powers;
    More serious businesse calls upon our houres.
                         Exeunt. Manet DUCHESS.

DUCHESS. Wast ever knowne step-Dutchesse was so
        milde
  And calme as I? Some now would plot his death
  With easie Doctors, those loose living men,   95
  And make his witherd Grace fall to his Grave,
  And keepe Church better.
  Some second wife would do this, and dispatch
  Her double loathd Lord at meate,[6] and sleepe.
  Indeed 'tis true an old mans twice a childe;   100
  Mine cannot speake, one of his single words
  Would quite have freed my yongest deerest sonne
  From death or durance, and have made him walke
  With a bold foote upon the thornie law,
  Whose Prickles should bow under him; but 'tis not,   105
  And therefore wedlock faith shall be forgot,
  Ile kill him in his fore-head; hate there feede,
  That wound is deepest, tho it never bleed[5]:
             [*Enter* SPURIO.]
  And here comes hee whom my heart points unto,
  His bastard sonne, but my loves true-begot;   110
  Many a wealthy letter have I sent him,
  Sweld up with Jewels, and the timorous man
  Is yet but coldly kinde;
  That Jewel's mine that quivers in his eare,
  Mocking his Maisters chilnesse and vaine feare.   115
  H'as spide me now.
SPURIO.   Madame, your Grace so private?
  My duety on your hand.
DUCHESS. Upon my hand, sir! Troth, I thinke youde feare
  To kisse my hand too if my lip stood there.
SPURIO. Witnesse I would not, Madam. [*He kisses her.*]
DUCHESS.   Tis a wonder,   120
  For ceremonie has made many fooles;
  It is as easie way unto a Dutchesse
  As to a Hatted-dame,[6] (if her love answer),
  But that by timorous honors, pale respects,

[5] The horns of the cuckolded
husband.

Idle degrees of feare, men make their wayes   125
   Hard of themselves. What have you thought of me?
SPURIO. Madam, I ever thinke of you in duty,
   Regard, and—
DUCHESS.   Puh! upon my love, I meane.
SPURIO. I would 'twere love, but 'tis[7] a fowler name
   Then lust; you are my fathers wife,—your Grace may   130
                 gesse now
   What I could call it.
DUCHESS.   Why, th'art his sonne but falsly;
   Tis a hard question whether he begot thee.
SPURIO. Ifaith[8] 'tis true too; Ime an uncertaine man,
   Of more uncertaine woman; may be his groome
   A' th' stable begot me,—you know I know not.   135
   Hee could ride a horse well, a shrewd[9] suspition,
              marry!
   Hee was wondrous tall, hee had his length, yfaith,
   For peeping over halfe shut holy-day windowes.[8]
   Men would desire him light.[6] When he was a-foote
   He made a goodly show under a Pent-house,   140
   And when he rid, his Hatt would check the signes,
   And clatter Barbers Basons.[7]
DUCHESS.   Nay, set you a-horse-
            back once,
   Youle ne'er light off.
SPURIO.   Indeed, I am a beggar.[8]
DUCHESS. That's more the signe thou art Great.—
   But to our love.   145
   Let it stand firme both in thought and minde,
   That the Duke was thy Father, as no doubt then
   Hee bid faire fort, thy injurie is the more;
   For had hee cut thee a right Diamond,
   Thou hadst beene next set in the Duke-doomes Ring,   150
   When his worne selfe, like Ages easie slave,
   Had dropt out of the Collet[7] into th' Grave.
   What wrong can equall this? Canst thou be tame

---

[6] *light* : to alight. See note.   [7] *Collet* : where the stone rests
                                   in a ring.

And thinke uppon't?

SPURIO.   No—mad, and thinke upon't.

DUCHESS. Who would not be revengd of such a father,   155
    E'en in the worst way? I would thanke that sinne
    That could most injury him, and bee in league with it.
    Oh what a griefe 'tis, that a man should live
    But once ith world, and then to live a Bastard,
    The curse a' the wombe, the theefe of Nature,̓   160
    Begot against the seaventh commandement,
    Halfe dambd in the conception, by the justice
    Of that unbribed everlasting law.

SPURIO. Oh, Ide a hot-backt Divill to my father!

DUCHESS. Would not this mad e'en patience, make bloud   165
               rough?
    Who but an Eunuch would not sinne?—his bed
    By one false minute disinherited.

SPURIO.[10] I, there's the vengeance that my birth was
               wrapt in!
    Ile be revengd for all. Now, hate, begin;
    Ile call foule Incest but a Veniall sinne.   170

DUCHESS. Cold still: in vaine then must a Dutchesse
               woo?

SPURIO. Madam, I blush to say what I will doo.

DUCHESS. Thence flew sweet comfort,—earnest[8] and
               farewell.   [*She kisses him.*]

SPURIO. Oh, one incestuous kisse picks open hell.

DUCHESS. Faith, now, old Duke, my vengeance shall   175
               reach high,
    Ile arme thy brow with womans Herauldrie.   *Exit.*

SPURIO. Duke, thou didst do me wrong, and by thy Act
    Adultery is my nature;
    Faith, if the truth were knowne, I was begot
    After some gluttonous dinner, some stirring dish   180
    Was my first father, when deepe healths went round
    And Ladies cheekes were painted red with Wine,
    Their tongue as short and nimble as their heeles,

---

[8] *earnest:* pledge of future rewards.

Uttering words sweet and thick; and when they
                     [rose],[11]
Were merrily disposd to fall agen.   185
In such a whispring and with-drawing houre,
When base male-Bawds kept Centinell at staire-head
Was I stolne softly; oh—damnation met
The sinne of feasts, drunken adultery.
I feele it swell me; my revenge is just,   190
I was begot in impudent Wine and Lust :
Step-mother, I consent to thy desires;
I love thy mischiefe well, but I hate thee
And those three Cubs thy sonnes, wishing confusion,
Death, and disgrace may be their Epitaphs.   195
As for my brother, the Dukes onely sonne,
Whose birth is more beholding to report
Then mine, and yet perhaps as falsely sowne.
(Women must not be trusted with their owne).
Ile loose my dayes upon him, hate-all I;   200
Duke, on thy browe Ile drawe my Bastardie.
For indeed a bastard by nature should make
                 Cuckolds,
Because he is the sonne of a Cuckold-maker.   *Exit.*

[Act I. Scene iii.]

Enter vindice *and* hippolito, vindice *in*
disguise to attend L[ord] lussurioso
the Dukes sonne.

vindice. What, brother, am I farre inough from my
        selfe?
hippolito. As if another man had beene sent whole
   Into the world, and none wist how he came.
vindice. It wil confirme me bould : the child a' th'
        Court;
   Let blushes dwell i' th' Country. Impudence!   5
   Thou Goddesse of the pallace, Mistris of Mistresses,
   To whom the costly perfumd people pray,
   Strike thou my fore-head into dauntlesse Marble,

Mine eyes to steady Saphires : turne my visage,
And if I must needes glow, let me blush inward   10
That this immodest season may not spy
That scholler in my cheekes, foole-bashfullnes,
That Maide in the old time, whose flush of Grace
Would never suffer her to get good cloaths;
Our maids are wiser, and are lesse ashamd;   15
Save[1] Grace the bawde,[(1)] I seldome heare Grace
             nam'd!

HIPPOLITO. Nay, brother, you reach out a' th' Verge[(2)]
             now.—

      [*Enter* LUSSURIOSO *with servants.*]

Sfoote, the Dukes sonne; settle your lookes.

VINDICE. Pray, let me not be doubted.

HIPPOLITO. My Lord—

LUSSURIOSO.   Hippolito?—Be absent, leave us.   20
         [*Exit servants.* VINDICE *retires.*]

HIPPOLITO. My Lord, after long search, wary inquiryes,
And politick siftings, I made choise of yon fellow,
Whom I gesse rare for many deepe imployments;
This our age swims within him : and if Time[(3)]
Had so much hayre, I should take him for Time,   25
He is so neere kinne to this present minute.

LUSSURIOSO. Tis ynough,
We thanke thee : yet words are but great-mens
            blanckes,[2, (4)]
Gold, tho it be dum, do's utter the best thankes.
           [*He gives him money.*]

HIPPOLITO. Your plenteous honor.—An exlent fellow, my   30
            Lord.

LUSSURIOSO. So,[[1]] give us leave.—   [*Exit* HIPPOLITO.]
         Welcome, bee not far
    off,
We must bee better acquainted. Push! be bould
With us,—thy hand.

VINDICE.   With all my heart yfaith!

ACT I. SCENE III.   [2] *words are . . . blanckes :*
[1] *Save :* Except for.   paper promises to pay.

How dost, sweete Musk-cat,—when shall we lie to-
          gither?[1]

LUSSURIOSO. [*Aside.*] Wondrous knave!   35
  Gather him into bouldnesse, sfoote, the slave's
  Already as familiar as an Ague,
  And shakes me at his pleasure.—Friend, I can
  Forget my selfe in private, but else where,
  I pray do you remember me.   40

VINDICE. Oh very well, sir.—I conster[3] my selfe sawcy.

LUSSURIOSO. What hast beene?
  Of what profession?

VINDICE.   A bone-setter.

LUSSURIOSO.   A bone-setter?

VINDICE. A bawde, my Lord,
  One that setts bones togither.

LUSSURIOSO. [*Aside.*]   Notable bluntnesse!   45
  Fit, fit for me, e'en traynd up to my hand.—
  Thou hast beene Scrivener[5] to much knavery then.

VINDICE. Foole[2] to abundance, sir; I have beene
          witnesse
  To the surrenders of a thousand virgins,
  And not so little;   50
  I have seene Patrimonyes washt a-peices,
  Fruit-feilds turnd into bastards,
  And in a world of Acres,
  Not so much dust due to the heire 'twas left too
  As would well gravell[4] a petition.   55

LUSSURIOSO. [*Aside.*] Fine villaine! Troth, I like him
          wonderously,
  Hees e'en shapt for my purpose.—Then thou knowst
  Ith world strange lust?

VINDICE.   O Dutch lust! fulsome lust!
  Druncken procreation, which begets so many drunck-
          ards;[6]
  Some father dreads not (gonne to bedde in wine) to
        slide from the mother,   60

---

[3] *conster :* construe.   [4] *gravell :* make sand to dry the
                              ink.

And cling the daughter-in-law;
Some Uncles are adulterous with their Neeces,
Brothers with brothers wives. O howre of Incest!
Any kin now next to the Rim a' th' sister
Is mans meate in these dayes; and in the morning,   65
When they are up and drest, and their maske on,
Who can perceive this, save that eternall eye
That sees through flesh and all? Well, if any thing be
      dambd,
It will be twelve a' clock at night; that twelve
Will never scape;   70
It is the *Judas* of the howers, wherein
Honest salvation is betrayde to sin.

LUSSURIOSO. In troth, it is, too, but let this talke glide.
It is our bloud to erre, tho hell gapte lowde;
Ladies know *Lucifer* fell, yet still are proude.   75
Now, sir, wert thou as secret as thou'rt subtil,
And deepely fadomd into all estates,
I would embrace thee for a neere imployment;
And thou shouldst swell in money, and be able
To make lame beggers crouch to thee.

VINDICE.   My Lord,—   80
Secret! I ne'er had that disease a' th' mother,[5]
I praise my father : why are men made closse
But to keepe thoughts in best? I grant you this,—
Tell but some woman a secret over night,
Your doctor may finde it in the urinall ith morning;   85
But, my Lord,—

LUSSURIOSO.   So, thou'rt confirm:d in mee,
And thus I enter[7] thee.   [*He gives him money.*]

VINDICE.   This Indian divill[6]
Will quickly enter any man but a Usurer;
He prevents that by entring the divill first.

LUSSURIOSO. Attend me.[7] I am past my depth in lust,   90
And I must swim or drowne; all my desires

---

[5] *Secret! I . . . mother :* Since
  women cannot keep secrets.
[6] *Indian divill :* Gold from the
Indies.
[7] *Attend me :* Listen carefully
to me.

Are leveld at a Virgin not far from Court,
To whom I have convayde by Messenger
Many waxt Lines,[8] full of my neatest spirit,[8]
And jewells that were able to ravish her   95
Without the helpe of man; all which and more
Shee—foolish chast—sent back, the messengers
Receiving frownes for answeres.
VINDICE.   Possible?
Tis a rare *Phaenix*[9] who e'er she bee;
If your desires be such, she so repugnant,   100
In troth, my Lord, Ide be revengde and marry her.
LUSSURIOSO. Push! the doury of her bloud and of her
                              fortunes
Are both too meane,—good ynough to be bad withal.
Ime one of that number can defend
Marriage is good : yet rather keepe a friend;[9]   105
Give me my bed by stealth—there's true delight.
What breeds a loathing in't, but night by night?
VINDICE. A very fine relligion!
LUSSURIOSO.   Therefore thus,—
Ile trust thee in the businesse of my heart,
Because I see thee wel experienc'st   110
In this Luxurious day wherein we breath.
Go thou, and with a smooth enchaunting tongue
Bewitch her eares, and Couzen[10] her of all Grace.
Enter upon the portion[11] of her soule,
Her honor, which she calls her chastity,   115
And bring it into expence[12]; for honesty
Is like a stock of money layd to sleepe,
Which, ne'er so little broke, do's never keep.
VINDICE. You have gi'n't the Tang, yfaith, my Lord.
Make knowne the Lady to me, and my braine   120
Shall swell with strange Invention : I will move it
Till I expire with speaking, and drop downe
Without a word to save me;—but Ile worke—

---

[8] *neatest spirit :* inspiration of
wine unmixed with water.
[9] *friend :* paramour.

[10] *Couzen :* Cheat.
[11] *portion :* inherited treasure.
[12] *expence :* use.

LUSSURIOSO. We thanke thee, and will raise thee: re-
    ceive her name.
  It[3] is the only daughter to Madame   125
  Gratiana, the late widdow.
VINDICE. [*Aside.*] Oh, my sister, my sister!
LUSSURIOSO.   Why dost
    walke aside?[3]
VINDICE. My Lord, I was thinking how I might begin,
  As thus, "Oh Ladie!"—or twenty hundred devices;
  Her very bodkin will put a man in.[13]   130
LUSSURIOSO. I, or the wagging of her haire.
VINDICE. No, that shall put you in, my Lord.
LUSSURIOSO. Shal't? Why, content. Dost know the
    daughter then?
VINDICE. O exlent well—by sight.
LUSSURIOSO.   That was her brother
  That did prefer thee to us.
VINDICE.   My Lord, I thinke so,   135
  I knew I had seene him some where.—
LUSSURIOSO. And therefore, pree-thee, let thy heart to
    him
  Be as a Virgin closse.
VINDICE.   Oh [my][4] good Lord!
LUSSURIOSO. We may laugh at that simple age within
    him;—
VINDICE. Ha, ha, ha!   140
LUSSURIOSO. Himselfe being made the subtill instrument
  To winde up[(10)] a good fellow.
VINDICE.   That's I, my Lord.
LUSSURIOSO. That's thou,
  To entice and worke his sister.
VINDICE. A pure novice!
LUSSURIOSO.   'Twas finely manag'd.   145
VINDICE. Gallantly carried;
  A prety-perfumde villaine!
LUSSURIOSO.   I've bethought me.

---

[13] *put . . . in:* give him an
  entry.

If she proove chast still[14] and immoveable,
Venture upon the Mother, and with giftes
As I will furnish thee, begin with her.   150
VINDICE. Oh[5] fie, fie! that's the wrong end, my Lord.
  Tis meere impossible that a mother by any gifts
  Should become a bawde to her owne Daughter!
LUSSURIOSO. Nay, then, I see thou'rt but a puny[15]
  In the subtill Mistery of a woman.[5]   155
  Why, tis held now no dainty dish : the name
  Is so in league with age that now adaies
  It do's Eclipse three quarters of a Mother.
VINDICE. Dost so, my Lord?
  Let me alone then to Eclipse the fourth.   160
LUSSURIOSO. Why, well sayd, come, Ile furnish thee; but
                        first
  Sweare to be true in all.
VINDICE.   True?
LUSSURIOSO.   Nay, but sweare!
VINDICE. Sweare?—I hope your honor little doubts my
                        fayth.
LUSSURIOSO. Yet for my humours sake, cause I love
                        swearing.
VINDICE. Cause you love swearing,—slud,[16] I will.   165
LUSSURIOSO. Why, ynough;
  Ere long looke to be made of better stuff.
VINDICE. That will do well indeed, my Lord.
LUSSURIOSO. Attend me.   [Exit.]
VINDICE. Oh,   170
  Now let me burst, I've eaten Noble poyson!
  We are made strange fellowes, brother, innocent
                        villaines.
  Wilt not be angry when thou hearst on't, thinkst
                        thou?
  Ifayth, thou shalt. Sweare me to foule my sister!
  Sword, I durst make a promise of him to thee;   175
  Thou shalt dis-heire him, it shall be thine honor;

---

[14] *still* : continually.   [16] *slud* : by God's blood.
[15] *puny* : novice.

And yet, now angry froath is downe in me,
It would not prove the meanest policy
In this disguize to try the fayth of both.
Another might have had the selfe-same office,   180
Some slave that would have wrought effectually,
I, and perhaps o'er-wrought em; therefore I,
Being thought travayld,[11] will apply my selfe
Unto the selfe-same forme, forget my nature,
As if no part about me were kin to em,   185
So touch[17] 'em, tho I durst almost for good
Venture my lands in heaven upon their [blood].[6]

Exit.

[ACT I. SCENE IV.]

Enter the discontented Lord ANTONIO, *whose*
wife the Duchesses yongest Sonne ravisht;
he Discovering[1] *the body of her dead to*
certaine Lords: [PIERO] *and* HIPPOLITO.

ANTONIO.[1] Draw neerer, Lords, and be sad witnesses
Of a fayre comely building newly falne,
Being falsely undermined : violent rape
Has playd a glorious act. Behold, my Lords,
A sight that strikes man out of me!   5
PIERO. That vertuous Lady!
ANTONIO.   President[1] for wives!
HIPPOLITO. The blush of many weomen, whose chast
                          presence
Would e'en call shame up to their cheekes, and make
Pale wanton sinners have good colours.—
ANTONIO.   Dead!
Her honor first drunke poyson, and her life,   10
Being fellowes in one house, did pledge her honour.
PIERO. O greefe of many!
ANTONIO.   I markt not this before,—
A prayer-Booke, the pillow to her cheeke;

17 *touch :* test.

ACT I. SCENE IV.
1 *President :* Precedent.

This was her rich confection, and another
Plac'd in her right hand, with a leafe tuckt up,   15
Poynting to these words,
Melius virtute mori, Quam per Dedecus vivere.[2, (2)]
True and effectuall it is indeed.
HIPPOLITO. My Lord, since you envite us to your
                              sorrowes,
Lets truely tast 'em, that with equall comfort,   20
As to our selves we may releive your wrongs;
We have greefe too, that yet walkes without Tong,
Curae leves loquuntur, Majores stupent.[3, (3)]
ANTONIO. You deale with truth, my Lord.
Lend me but your Attentions, and Ile cut   25
Long greefe into short words : last revelling night,
When Torch-light made an artificiall noone
About the Court, some Courtiers in the maske,
Putting on better faces then their owne,
Being full of frawde and flattery : amongst whome,   30
The Ducheses yongest sonne (that moth to honor)
Fild up a Roome, and with long lust to eat
Into my wearing,—amongst all the Ladyes
Singled out that deere forme, who ever liv'd
As cold in Lust as shee is now in death,   35
(Which that step-Duches' Monster knew to well),
And therefore, in the height of all the revells,
When Musick was hard lowdest, Courtiers busiest,
And Ladies great with laughter—O Vitious minute!
Unfit but for relation to be spoke of;   40
Then, with a face more impudent then his vizard,
He harried her amidst a throng of Panders
That live uppon damnation of both kindes,
And fed the ravenous vulture of his lust,
(O death to thinke ont!) She, her honor forcst,   50
Deemd it a nobler dowry for her name
To die with poyson, then to live with shame.

---

[2] *Melius virtute . . . vivere :*
Better to die virtuous than live
dishonorable.

[3] *Curae leves . . . stupent :*
Light cares find tongue,
greater ones do not.

HIPPOLITO. A wondrous Lady, of rare fire compact!
   Sh'as made her name an Empresse by that act.
PIERO. My Lord, what judgement followes the offender?   55
ANTONIO. Faith, none, my Lord, it cooles and is deferd.
PIERO. Delay the doome for rape?
ANTONIO. O you must note who tis should die,
   The Duchesse' sonne; sheele looke to be a saver,[4]
   "Judgment in this age is nere kin to favour."   60
HIPPOLITO. Nay then, step forth, thou Bribelesse officer;
                      [*He draws his sword.*]
   I bind you all in steele to bind you surely.
   Heer let your oths meet, to be kept and payd,
   Which else will sticke like rust, and shame the blade;
   Strengthen my vow that, if at the next sitting   65
   Judgment speake all in gold and spare the bloud
   Of such a serpent, e'en before their seats,
   To let his soule out, which long since was found
   Guilty in heaven.
ALL.   We sweare it and will act it!
ANTONIO. Kind Gentlemen, I thanke you in mine Ire.   70
HIPPOLITO. Twere pitty
   The ruins of so faire a Monument
   Should not be dipt in the defacers bloud.
PIERO. Her funerall shall be wealthy, for her name
   Merits a toombe of pearle. My Lord Antonio,   75
   For this time wipe your Lady from your eyes;
   No doubt our greefe and youres may one day court
                it,
   When we are more familiar with Reveng.
ANTONIO. That is my comfort, Gentlemen, and I joy
   In this one happiness above the rest,   80
   Which will be cald a miracle at last,
   That—being an old man—Ide a wife so chast. *Exeunt.*

Act II. Scene i.

Enter CASTIZA, *the sister.*
CASTIZA. How hardly shall that mayden be beset,
　Whose onely fortunes are her constant thoughts,
　That has no other childes-part but her honor,
　That Keepes her lowe and empty in estate.
　Maydes and their honors are like poore beginners;　5
　Were not sinne rich there would be fewer sinners.
　Why had not vertue a revennewe? Well,
　I know the cause, twold have impoverish'd hell.
　　　　　[*Enter* DONDOLO.]
　How now, Dondolo?
DONDOLO. Madona, there is one, as they say, a thing of　10
　flesh and blood, a man—I take him by his beard—that
　would very desireously mouth to mouth with you.
CASTIZA. What's that?
DONDOLO. Show his teeth in your company.
CASTIZA. I understand thee not.　15
DONDOLO. Why, speake with you, Madona!
CASTIZA. Why,[1] say so, mad-man, and cut off a great
　　　　　deale
　Of durty way; had it not beene better spoke
　In ordinary words that one would speake with me?[1]
DONDOLO. Ha, ha, that's as ordinary as two shillings; I　20
　would strive a litle to show my self in my place; a
　Gentleman-usher scornes to use the Phrase and
　fanzye of a servingman.
CASTIZA. Yours be your own,[2] sir; go direct him
　　　　　hether.
　　　　　[*Exit* DONDOLO.]
　I hope some happy tidings from my brother
　That lately travayld, whome my soule affects.[1]　25
　Here he comes.

Act II. Scene i.
[1] *affects :* feels affection for.

Enter VINDICE, *her brother disguised.*

VINDICE. Lady, the best of wishes to your sexe,—
Faire skins and new gownes.

CASTIZA.   Oh they shall thanke
you, sir.

Whence this?

VINDICE. Oh from a deere and worthy friend,—
Mighty!

CASTIZA. From whome?

VINDICE.   The Dukes sonne!

CASTIZA.   Receive that!   30
[*She gives*] *a boxe a' th' eare to her Brother.*
I swore I'de put anger in my hand,
And passe the Virgin limits[1] of my selfe
To him that next appear'd in that base office,
To be his sinnes Atturney. Beare to him
That figure of my hate upon thy cheeke   35
Whilst tis yet hot, and Ile reward thee fort.
Tell him my honor shall have a rich name,
When severall harlots shall share his with shame.
Farewell, commend me to him in my hate!   *Exit.*

VINDICE. It is the sweetest Boxe that e'er my nose came   40
nye,
The finest drawne-worke cuffe that e'er was worne;
Ile love this blowe for ever, and this cheeke
Shall still hence forward take the wall[2] of this.
Oh Ime above my tong : most constant sister,
In this thou hast right honorable showne;   45
Many are cald by their honour that have none.
Thou art approv'd for ever in my thoughts;
It is not in the power of words to taynt thee;
And yet for the salvation of my oth,
As my resolve in that point, I will lay   50
Hard seige unto my Mother, tho I know
A *Syrens* tongue could not bewitch her so.
[*Enter* GRATIANA.]

---

[2] *take the wall :* have the more
honorable place.

Masse, fitly here she comes! Thankes, my disguize.
Madame, good afternoone.
GRATIANA.   Y'are welcome, sir.
VINDICE. The Next[3] of Italy commends him to you,   55
   Our mighty expectation, the Dukes sonne.
GRATIANA. I thinke my selfe much honord, that he
                        pleases
   To ranck me in his thoughts.
VINDICE.   So may you, Lady:
   One that is like to be our suddaine Duke;
   The Crowne gapes for him every tide, and then   60
   Commander o'er us all. Do but thinke on him;
   How blest were they now that could pleasure him
   E'en with any thing almost.
GRATIANA.   I, save their honor.
VINDICE. Tut, one would let a little of that go too,
   And ne'er be seene in't: ne'er be seene [in't],[3]   65
                        marke you.
   Ide winck and let it go.—
GRATIANA.   Marry, but I would not.
VINDICE. Marry, but I would, I hope; I know you would
                        too,
   If youd that bloud now which you gave your
                        daughter;
   To her indeed tis, this wheele[4] comes about.
   That man that must be all this, perhaps ere morning   70
   (For his white father do's but moulde away)
   Has long desirde your daughter.
GRATIANA.   Desirde?
VINDICE. Nay, but heare me;
   He desirs now, that will command hereafter,
   Therefore be wise,—I speake as more a friend   75
   To you then him; Madam, I know y'are poore,
   And 'lack the day,
   There are too many poore Ladies already.
   Why should you vex[5] the number? Tis despisd;

---

[3] Next: Next in rule.   [5] vex: aggravate by increasing.
[4] wheele: of Fortune.

Live wealthy, rightly understand the world,   80
And chide away that foolish Country girle
Keepes company with your daughter, chastity.
GRATIANA. Oh[4] fie, fie, the riches of the world can-
                not hire
A mother to such a most unnatural taske.[4]
VINDICE. No, but a thousand Angells[2] can;   85
Men have no power, Angells must worke you too't.
The world descends into such base-borne evills
That forty Angells can make fourescore divills;
There will be fooles still, I perceive, still foole[s].[5]
Would I be poore, dejected, scornd of greatnesse,   90
Swept from the Pallace; and see other daughters
Spring with the dewe a' th' Court, having mine owne
So much desir'd and lov'd—by the Dukes sonne?
No, I would raise my state upon her brest
And call her eyes my Tennants; I would count   95
My yearely maintenance upon her cheekes :
Take Coach upon her lip, and all her partes
Should keepe men after men, and I would ride
In pleasure upon pleasure.
You tooke great paines for her, once when it was;   100
Let her requite it now, tho it be but some;
You brought her forth, she may well bring you home.
GRATIANA. O heavens! this over-comes me!
VINDICE. [*Aside.*] Not, I hope, already.
GRATIANA. [*Aside.*] It is too strong for me; men know   105
                that know us,
We are so weake their words can overthrow us.
He toucht me neerely, made my vertues bate,
When his tongue struck upon my poore estate.
VINDICE. [*Aside.*] I e'en quake to proceede, my spirit
                turnes edge!
I feare me she's unmotherd, yet Ile venture;   110
"That woman is all male, whome none can Enter."—[3]
What thinke you now, Lady, speake, are you wiser?
What sayd advancement to you? Thus it sayd,
The daughters fall lifts up the mothers head :
Did it not, Madame? But Ile sweare it does   115

In many places; tut, this age feares no man.

"Tis no shame to be bad, because tis common."

GRATIANA. I, that's the comfort on't.

VINDICE. The comfort on't!

I keepe the best for last; can these perswade you

To forget heaven—and—

GRATIANA. I, these are they,—

VINDICE. Oh! 120

GRATIANA. That enchant our sexe;

These are the means that governe our affections,—that woman

Will not be troubled with the mother(4) long,

That sees the comfortable shine of you;

I blush to thinke what for your sakes Ile do. 125

VINDICE. [Aside.] O suffring heaven,6 with thy invisible finger,

E'en at this Instant turne the pretious side

Of both mine eye-balls inward, not to see my selfe.

GRATIANA. Looke you, sir.

VINDICE. Holla.

GRATIANA. Let this thanke your paines.

VINDICE. O you'r a kind [Madam].[6] 130

GRATIANA. Ile see how I can move.

VINDICE. Your words will sting.

GRATIANA. If she be still chast, Ile ne'er call her mine.

VINDICE. [Aside.] Spoke truer then you ment it.

GRATIANA. Daughter Castiza.

[Enter CASTIZA.]

CASTIZA. Madam.

VINDICE. O shees yonder.

Meet her. [Aside.] Troupes of celestiall Soldiers gard 135 her heart.

Yon dam has devills ynough to take her part.

CASTIZA. Madam, what makes yon evill offic'd man

In presence of you?

6 O . . . heaven : O heaven
that allows such things!

GRATIANA.   Why?
CASTIZA.   He lately brought
  Immodest writing sent from the Dukes sonne,
  To tempt me to dishonorable Act.   140
GRATIANA. Dishonorable Act?—good honorable foole,
  That wouldst be honest, cause thou wouldst be so,
  Producing no one reason but thy will.
  And 't'as a good report, pretely commended,
  But pray by whome?—meane[7] people, ignorant   145
              people.
  The better sort, Ime sure, cannot abide it,
  And by what rule shouldst we square out our lives,
  But by our betters actions? Oh, if thou knew'st
  What 'twere to loose it, thou would never keepe it!
  But there's a cold curse layd upon all Maydes,   150
  Whilst other[s][7] clip[8] the Sunne they clasp the
             shades!
  Virginity is paradice, lockt up;
  You cannot come by your selves without fee,
  And twas decreed that man should keepe the key.
  Deny advancement, treasure, the Dukes sonne!   155
CASTIZA. I cry you mercy, Lady, I mistooke you.
  Pray, did you see my Mother? Which way went you?
  Pray God I have not lost her.
VINDICE. [*Aside.*]   Prittily put by.
GRATIANA. Are you as proud to me, as coye to him?
                   [*She strikes her.*]
  Doe you not know me now?
CASTIZA.   Why, are you shee?   160
  The world's so changd, one shape into another,
  It is a wise childe now that knowes her mother.
VINDICE. [*Aside.*] Most right, ifaith.
GRATIANA. I owe your cheeke my hand
  For that presumption now, but Ile forget it.   165
  Come, you shall leave those childish 'haviours,
  And understand your Time. Fortunes flow to you,—
  What, will you be a Girle?

---

[7] *meane* : socially low.   [8] *clip* : embrace.

If all feard drowning, that spye waves a-shoare,
Gold would grow rich, and all the Marchants poore.   170
CASTIZA. It is a pritty saying of a wicked one,
But, me thinkes now, it dos not show so well
Out of your mouth,—better in his.
VINDICE. [*Aside.*] Faith, bad inough in both,
Were I in earnest, as Ile seeme no lesse.—   175
I wonder, Lady, your owne mothers words
Cannot be taken, not stand in full force.
'Tis honestie you urge; what's honestie?
'Tis but heavens beggar, and what woman is
So foolish to keepe honesty,   180
And be not able to keepe her-selfe? No,
Times are growne wiser and will keepe lesse
                                    charge. (5)
A Maide that Has small portion now entends
To breake up house and live upon her friends.
How blest are you, you have happinesse alone!   185
Others must fall to thousands, you to one
Sufficient in him-selfe to make your fore-head (6)
Dazle the world with Jewels, and petitionary people
Start at your presence.
GRATIANA. Oh, if I were yong, I should be ravisht!   190
CASTIZA. I, to loose your honour.
VINDICE. Slid, how can you loose your honor?
To deale with my Lords Grace;
Heele adde more honour to it by his Title.
Your Mother will tell you how.
GRATIANA.   That I will.   195
VINDICE. O thinke upon the pleasure of the Pallace,
Secured ease and state, the stirring meates
Ready to move out of the dishes,
That e'en now quicken when thei'r eaten!
Banquets abroad by Torch-light, Musicks, sports,   200
Bare-headed vassailes, that had ne'er the fortune
To keepe on their owne Hats, but let hornes were
                                    em! (7)
Nine Coaches waiting—hurry, hurry, hurry.
CASTIZA. I, to the Divill.

VINDICE. [*Aside.*] I, to the Divill.—To th' Duke, by my   205
　　　　　faith.
GRATIANA. I, to the Duke : daughter, youde scorne to
　　　　　thinke
A' th' Divill, and[9] you were there once.
VINDICE. [*Aside.*] True, for most there are as proud
　　As he for his heart, ifaith.—
　　Who'de sit at home in a neglected roome,   210
　　Dealing her short-liv'de beauty to the pictures,
　　That are as use-lesse as old men, when those
　　Poorer in face and fortune then her-selfe
　　Walke with a hundred Acres on their backs,
　　Faire Medowes cut into Greene fore-parts? Oh!   215
　　It was the greatest blessing ever happened to women,
　　When Farmers sonnes agreed and met agen,
　　To wash their hands and come up[10] Gentlemen.
　　The common-wealth has flourisht ever since,—
　　Lands that were meat[11] by the Rod,—that labor's
　　　　　　　　　spar'd,—   220
　　Taylors ride downe, and measure em by the yeard.
　　Faire trees, those comely fore-tops[8] of the Field,
　　Are cut to maintaine head-tires[12]—much untold.[13]
　　All thrives but Chastity, she lyes a-cold.
　　Nay, shall I come neerer to you? Marke but this :   225
　　Why[8] are there so few honest women, but
　　Because 'tis the poorer profession?
　　That's accounted best that's best followed;
　　Least in trade, least in fashion,
　　And that's not honesty, beleeve it; and doe   230
　　But note the loue and dejected price of it :
　　"Loose but a Pearle, we search and cannot brooke
　　　　　　　　it;[9]
But that once gone, who is so mad to looke it?"[8]
GRATIANA. Troth, he sayes true.
CASTIZA.　　　　　　　　False! I defie you both!

---

9 *and* : if.　　　　　　　　11 *meat* : measured.
10 *come up* : come up to　　12 *head-tires* : headdresses.
　London.　　　　　　　　　13 *untold* : uncounted.

I have endur'd you with an eare of fire;   235
Your Tongues have struck hotte yrons on my face.
Mother, come from that poysonous woman there.(10)
GRATIANA. Where?
CASTIZA. Do you not see her? Shee's too inward
        then.(10)
Slave, perish in thy office! You heavens, please   240
Hence-forth to make the Mother a disease,
Which first begins with me; yet I've out-gon you.
                       Exit.
VINDICE. [*Aside.*] O Angels, clap your wings upon the
        skyes,
And give this Virgin Christall plaudities!
GRATIANA. Peevish, coy, foolish!—But returne this an-   245
        swer;
My Lord shall be most welcome, when his pleasure
Conducts him this way. I will sway mine owne,
Women with women can worke best alone.   *Exit.*
VINDICE. Indeed, Ile tell him so.
O more uncivill, more unnaturall,   250
Then those base-titled creatures that looke downe-
        ward!
Why do's not heaven turne black, or with a frowne
Undoo the world? Why do's not earth start up
And strike the sinnes that tread uppon't? Oh,
Wert not for gold and women, there would be no   255
        damnation;
Hell would looke like a Lords Great Kitchin without
        fire in't.
But 'twas decreed before the world began,
That they should be the hookes to catch at man. *Exit.*

[ACT II. SCENE II.]

Enter LUSSURIOSO *with* HIPPOLITO, VINDICE's *brother.*
LUSSURIOSO. I much applaud
Thy judgement. Thou art well read in a fellow;[1]
And 'tis the deepest Arte to studie man.

I know this, which I never learnt in schooles,
The world's divided into knaves and fooles.   5
HIPPOLITO. [*Aside.*] Knave, in your face, my Lord,—be-
        hinde your back,—[1]
LUSSURIOSO. And I much thanke thee, that thou hast
        preferd
A fellow of discourse well mingled,
And whose braine Time hath seasond.
HIPPOLITO. [*Aside.*]   True, my Lord,
We shall finde season once, I hope;—O villaine!   10
To make such an unnaturall slave of me,—but—
       [*Enter* VINDICE *disguised.*]
LUSSURIOSO. Masse, here he comes.
HIPPOLITO. [*Aside.*] And now shall I have free leave to
        depart.
LUSSURIOSO. Your absence. Leave us.
HIPPOLITO. [*Aside.*]   Are not my thoughts
        true?
I must remoove; but, brother, you may stay;   15
Heart, we are both made Bawdes a new-found way.
                     Exit.

LUSSURIOSO. Now we're an even number, a third man's
        dangerous,
Especially her brother; say, be free,
Have I a pleasure toward?
VINDICE.   Oh my Lord!
LUSSURIOSO. Ravish me in thine answer; art thou rare?   20
Hast thou beguilde her of salvation,
And rubd hell o'er with hunny? Is she a woman?
VINDICE. In all but in Desire.
LUSSURIOSO.   Then shee's in nothing.
I bate in courage now.
VINDICE.   The words I brought
Might well have made indifferent honest naught.[1]   25
A right good woman in these dayes is changde
Into white money[2] with lesse labour farre;

ACT II. SCENE II.
[1] *naught :* naughty, evil.   [2] *white money :* silver.

Many a Maide has turn'd to Mahomet
With easier working; I durst undertake
Upon the pawne and forfeit of my life,   30
With halfe those words to flat a Puritanes wife.
But she is closse and good; yet 'tis a doubt
By this time. Oh the mother, the mother!
LUSSURIOSO. I never thought their sex had beene a
                                wonder
Untill this minute; what fruite from the Mother?   35
VINDICE. [*Aside.*] Now must I blister my soule, be for-
                                sworne,
Or shame the woman that receiv'd mee first.
I will be true; thou liv'st not to proclaime;
Spoke to a dying man, shame has no shame.—
My Lord.
LUSSURIOSO. Whose that?
VINDICE.   Here's none but I, my Lord.   40
LUSSURIOSO. What would thy hast utter?
VINDICE.   Comfort.
LUSSURIOSO.   Welcome.
VINDICE. The Maide being dull, having no minde to
                                travell(2)
Into unknowne lands, what did me i' straight
But set spurs to the Mother; golden spurs
Will put her to a false gallop in a trice.   45
LUSSURIOSO. Ist possible that in this
The Mother should be dambd before the daughter?
VINDICE. Oh,[2] that's good manners, my Lord; the
                                Mother for
Her age must goe formost, you know.[2]
LUSSURIOSO. Thou'st spoke that true, but where comes
                                in this comfort?   50
VINDICE. In a fine place, my Lord,—the unnaturall
                                mother
Did with her tong so hard be-set her honor,
That the poore foole was struck to silent wonder;
Yet still the maid, like an unlighted Taper,
Was cold and chast, save that her Mothers breath   55
Did blowe fire on her cheekes. The girle departed,

But the good antient Madam, halfe mad, threwe me
These promissing words, which I tooke deepely note
                              of;
"My Lord shall be most wellcome,—"
LUSSURIOSO.   Faith, I thanke
                              her.
VINDICE. "When his pleasure conducts him this way."   60
LUSSURIOSO. That shall be soone, ifath.
VINDICE.   "I will sway mine
                              owne."
LUSSURIOSO. Shee do's the wiser, I commend her fort.
VINDICE. "Women with women can worke best alone."
LUSSURIOSO. By[3] this light! and so they can; give 'em
    Their due, men are not comparable to 'em.   65
VINDICE. No, that's true, for you shall have one woman
    Knit[3] more in a hower, then any man
    Can Ravell agen in seaven and twenty yeare.[3]
LUSSURIOSO. Now my desires are happy; Ile make 'em
                    free-men now.
    Thou art a pretious fellow, faith, I love thee;   70
    Be wise and make it thy revennew,—beg, leg![3]
    What office couldst thou be Ambitious for?
VINDICE. Office,[4] my Lord!
    Marry, if I might have my wish, I would
    Have one that was never begd yet.   75
LUSSURIOSO. Nay, then thou canst have none.
VINDICE.   Yes, my
                    Lord;
    I could picke out another office yet.
    Nay, and keepe a horse and drab[4] uppont.
LUSSURIOSO. Prethee, good bluntnes, tell me.
VINDICE. Why, I would desire but this, my Lord;   80
    To have all the fees[5] behind the Arras, and all
    The farthingales that fal plumpe about twelve a'
                    clock
    At night upon the Rushes.[4]

[3] *beg, leg* : bow for a favor.

LUSSURIOSO. Thou'rt[5] a mad apprehensive[4] knave;
   Dost thinke to make any great purchase of that?   85
VINDICE. Oh tis an unknowne thing, my Lord; I wonder
   T'as been mist so long![5]
LUSSURIOSO. Well, this night Ile visit her, and tis till then
   A yeare in my desires.—Farewell, attend;
   Trust me with thy preferment.[5]   *Exit.*
VINDICE.   My lov'd Lord.—   90
   Oh, shall I kill him a'th' wrong-side now? No!
   Sword, thou wast never a back-biter yet.
   Ile peirce him to his face; he shall die looking upon
         me;
   Thy veines are sweld with lust, this shall unfill 'em;
   Great men were Gods, if beggers could not kil 'em.   95
   Forgive me, heaven, to call my mother wicked.
   Oh lessen not[6] my daies upon the earth,
   I cannot honor her. By this, I feare me,
   Her tongue has turnd my sister into use.
   I was a villaine not to be forsworne   100
   To this our lecherous hope, the Dukes sonne;
   For Lawiers, Merchants, some divines, and all,
   Count beneficiall perjury[7] a sin small.
   It shall go hard yet, but Ile guard her honor,
   And keepe the portes sure.   105
           Enter HIPPOLITO.
HIPPOLITO. Brother, how goes the world? I would know
         newes
   Of you, but I have newes to tell you.
VINDICE. What, in the name of knavery?
HIPPOLITO.   Knavery, fayth;
   This vicious old Duke's worthily abusde;[6]
   The pen of his bastard writes him Cuckold!   110
VINDICE. His bastard?
HIPPOLITO.   Pray, beleeve it; he and the
        Duchesse,
   By night meete in their linnen; they have been seene

---

[4] *apprehensive* : witty,
  intelligent.
[5] *preferment* : advancement.
[6] *abusde* : deceived.

By staire-foote panders.

VINDICE.   Oh sin foule and deepe!
Great faults are winckt at when the Duke's a-sleepe.
See, see, here comes the Spurio.
                    [*Enter* SPURIO *with two men.*]
HIPPOLITO.   Monstrous Luxur!   115
VINDICE. Unbrac'd[7] : two of his valiant bawdes with
                    him.
O there's a wicked whisper; hell is in his eare.
Stay, let's observe his passage.—   [*They retire.*]
SPURIO. Oh, but are you sure on't?
SERVANT. My Lord, most sure on't, for twas spoke by   120
                    one
That is most inward with the Dukes sonnes lust :
That he intends within this houre to steale
Unto Hippolitoes sister, whose chast life
The mother has corrupted for his use.
SPURIO.   Sweete word, sweete occasion! fayth then,   125
                    brother,
Ile disinherit you in as short time
As I was when I was begot in hast :
Ile dam you at your pleasure : pretious deed!
After your lust, oh twill be fine to bleede.
Come, let our passing out be soft and wary.   130
                                        Exeunt.
VINDICE. Marke, there, there, that step, now to the
                    Duches;
This their second meeting writes the Duke Cuckold
With new additions, his hornes newly revived :
Night! thou that lookst like funerall Heraulds fees[8]
Torne downe betimes ith morning, thou hangst fittly   135
To Grace those sins that have no grace at all.
Now tis full sea a-bed over the world,
There's jugling of all sides; some that were Maides
E'en at Sun set are now perhaps ith Toale-booke.[8]
This woman in immodest thin apparell   140

---

[7] *Unbrac'd :* Without outer gar-   [8] *Toale-booke :* Book of horses
ment (doublet); in his shirt.   for sale at a fair.

Lets in her friend by water; here a Dame
Cunning, naylẹs lether-hindges to a dore,
To avoide proclamation.
Now Cuckolds are a-quoyning,[9] apace, apace, apace,
    apace!
And carefull sisters spinne that thread ith night,   145
That does maintaine them and their bawdes ith daie.
HIPPOLITO. You flow well, brother!
VINDICE.   Puh, I'me shallow
    yet,
Too sparing and too modest; shall I tell thee?
If every trick were told that's dealt by night,
There are few here that would not blush out-right. 150
HIPPOLITO. I am of that beleefe too. Whose this comes?
     [*Enter* LUSSURIOSO.]
VINDICE. The Dukes sonne up so late?—Brother, fall
    back,
And you shall learne some mischeife.
        [HIPPOLITO *retires.*]
         My good Lord.
LUSSURIOSO. Piato, why the man I wisht for! Come,
I do embrace this season for the fittest   155
To tast of that yong Lady.
VINDICE. [*Aside.*]   Heart and' hell.
HIPPOLITO. [*Aside.*] Dambd villaine.
VINDICE. [*Aside.*] I ha' no way now to crosse it, but to
    kill him.
LUSSURIOSO. Come, only thou and I.
VINDICE.   My Lord, my Lord.
LUSSURIOSO. Why dost thou start us?   160
VINDICE. Ide almost forgot—the bastard!
LUSSURIOSO.   What of him?
VINDICE. This night, this houre—this minute, now—
LUSSURIOSO. What? what?
VINDICE.   Shadowes the Duchesse—
LUSSURIOSO.   Horrible
    word!

[9] *a-quoyning :* being coined.

VINDICE. And like strong poyson eates
    Into the Duke your fathers fore-head.
LUSSURIOSO.   Oh!   165
VINDICE. He makes horne royall.
LUSSURIOSO.   Most ignoble slave!
VINDICE. This is the fruite of two beds.
LUSSURIOSO.   I am mad.
VINDICE. That passage he trod warily.
LUSSURIOSO.   He did?
VINDICE. And husht his villaines every step he tooke.
LUSSURIOSO. His villaines? Ile confound them.   170
VINDICE. Take 'em finely, finely now.
LUSSURIOSO. The Duchesse Chamber-doore shall not
           controule mee.
        Exeunt [LUSSURIOSO *and* VINDICE.]   ·
HIPPOLITO. Good, happy, swift! There's gunpowder ith
           Court,
    Wilde fire at mid-night; in this heedlesse fury
    He may show violence to crosse himselfe.   175
    Ile follow the Event.   *Exit.*

[ACT II. SCENE III.][(1)]

[*The* DUKE *and* DUCHESS *are discovered in bed.*]
Enter againe [LUSSURIOSO *and* VINDICE *disguised.*]
LUSSURIOSO. Where is that villaine?
VINDICE. Softly, my Lord, and you may take 'em
           twisted.
LUSSURIOSO. I care not how!
VINDICE.   Oh twill be glorious,
    To kill 'em doubled, when thei'r heapt; be soft, my
           Lord.
LUSSURIOSO. Away, my spleene is not so lazy; thus   5
           and thus
    Ile shake their eye-lids ope, and with my sword
    Shut 'em agen for ever.— [*They approach the bed.*]
           Villain! Strumpet!
DUKE. You upper Guard, defend us!

DUCHESS.   Treason, treason!
DUKE. Oh take mee not in sleepe!
    I have great sins; I must have daies,   10
    Nay, months, deere sonne, with penitential heaves,
    To lift 'em out, and not to die uncleere.
    O thou wilt kill me both in heaven and here.
LUSSURIOSO. I am amazde to death!
DUKE.   Nay, villaine traytor,
    Worse then the fowlest Epithite, now Ile gripe thee   15
    E'en with the Nerves of wrath, and throw thy head
    Amongst the Lawyers! Gard!
        Enter Nobles and sonnes [AMBITIOSO *and* SUPER-
                VACUO, *with* HIPPOLITO.]
I. NOBLE. How comes the quiet of your Grace disturbd?
DUKE. This boye, that should be my selfe after mee,
    Would be my selfe before me, and in heate   20
    Of that ambition bloudily rusht in,
    Intending to depose me in my bed.
II. NOBLE. Duty and naturall-loyalty for-fend.
DUCHESS. He cald his Father villaine, and me strumpet,
    A word that I abhorre to 'file[1] my lips with.   25
AMBITIOSO. That was not so well done, Brother.
LUSSURIOSO. I am abusde.—
    I know ther's no excuse can do me good.
VINDICE. [*Aside to* HIPPOLITO.] Tis now good policie to
                be from sight;
    His vicious purpose to our sisters honour   30
    Is crost beyond our thought.
HIPPOLITO. You little dreamt his Father slept heere.
VINDICE. Oh 'twas farre beyond me.
    But since it fell so;—without fright-full word[s],[1]
    Would he had kild him, 'twould have easde our   35
                swords.
                [VINDICE *and* HIPPOLITO *flee.*][2]
DUKE. Be comforted our Duchesse, he shall dye.

    ACT II. SCENE III.
1 '*file :* defile.

LUSSURIOSO. Where's this slave-pander now? out of mine
                              eye?
   Guiltie of this abuse.
                     Enter SPURIO *with his villaines.*
SPURIO. Y'are villaines, Fablers;
   You have knaves chins and harlots tongues, you lie,   40
   And I will dam you with one meale a day.
I. SERVANT. O good my Lord!
SPURIO.   Sbloud! you shall never
                              sup.
II. SERVANT. O I beseech you, sir.
SPURIO.   To let my sword
   Catch cold so long and misse him.
I. SERVANT.   Troth, my Lord,
   Twas his intent to meete there.
SPURIO.   Heart, hee's yonder!   45
   Ha, what newes here? Is the day out a' th' socket[2]
   That it is Noone at Mid-night?—the Court up?
   How comes the Guard so sawcie with his elbowes?
LUSSURIOSO. The Bastard here?
   Nay, then the truth of my intent shall out.   50
   My Lord and Father, heare me.
DUKE.   Beare him hence.
LUSSURIOSO. I can with loyaltie excuse—
DUKE. Excuse? To prison with the Villaine!
   Death shall not long lag after him.
SPURIO. [*Aside.*] Good, ifaith, then 'tis not much amisse.   55
LUSSURIOSO. Brothers, my best release lies on your
                              tongues;
   I pray, perswade for mee.
AMBITIOSO. It is our duties : make your selfe sure of us.
SUPERVACUO. Weele sweate in pleading.
LUSSURIOSO. And I may live to thanke you.   60
                     Exeunt [LUSSURIOSO *and guards.*]
AMBITIOSO. [*Aside.*] No, thy death shall thanke me
                              better.

[2] *Is . . . socket :* Is the eye of
heaven (sun) out of its place?

SPURIO. [*Aside.*] Hee's gon : Ile after him
And know his trespasse, seeme to beare a part
In all his ills, but with a *Puritane* heart.
                              Exit [SPURIO *with his villains.*]
AMBITIOSO. [*Aside.*] Now, brother, let our hate and love
                              be woven   65
So subtilly together, that in speaking one
Word for his life, we may make three for his death;
The craftiest pleader gets most gold for breath.
SUPERVACUO. Set on, Ile not be farre behinde you,
                              brother.
DUKE. Ist[3] possible a sonne   70
Should bee disobedient as farre as the sword?
It is the highest, he can goe no farther.[3]
AMBITIOSO. My gratious Lord, take pitty.—
DUKE.   Pitty, boyes?
AMBITIOSO. Nay, weed be loth to moove your Grace too
                              much;
Wee know the trespasse is unpardonable,   75
Black, wicked, and unnaturall.
SUPERVACUO. In a Sonne, oh Monstrous!
AMBITIOSO.   Yet, my Lord,
A Dukes soft hand stroakes the rough head of law,
And makes it lye smooth.
DUKE.   But my hand shall ne'er
                              doot.
AMBITIOSO. That, as you please, my Lord.
SUPERVACUO.   We must   80
                    needs confesse,
Some father would have enterd into hate
So deadly pointed, that before his eyes
Hee would ha' seene the execution sound,
Without corrupted favour.
AMBITIOSO.   But, my Lord,
Your Grace may live the wonder of all times,   85
In pardning that offence which never yet
Had face to beg a pardon.
DUKE.   Hunny, how's this?

AMBITIOSO. Forgive him, good my Lord, hee's your
             owne sonne,
  And I must needs say, 'twas the vildlier[3] done.
SUPERVACUO. Hee's the next heire, yet this true reason   90
             gathers,
  None can possesse that dispossesse their fathers :
  Be mercifull.—
DUKE. [*Aside.*] Here's no Step-mothers-wit.
  Ile trie 'em both upon their love and hate.
AMBITIOSO. Be mercifull—altho—
DUKE.   You have prevaild.
  My wrath like flaming waxe hath spent itselfe;   95
  I know 'twas but some peevish Moone[4] in him :
  Goe, let him bee releasd.
SUPERVACUO. [*Aside.*]   Sfoote, how now, Brother?
AMBITIOSO. Your Grace doth please to speake beside
             your spleene;
  I would it were so happy.
DUKE.   Why, goe release him.
SUPERVACUO. O my good Lord, I know the fault's too   100
             weighty
  And full of generall loathing, too inhumaine,
  Rather by all mens voyces worthy death.
DUKE. Tis true too; here then, receive this signet.
  Doome shall passe,
  Direct it to the Judges; he shall dye   105
  Ere many dayes. Make hast.
AMBITIOSO.   All speed that may be
  We could have wisht his burthen not so sore,
  We knew your Grace did but delay before.   *Exeunt.*
DUKE. Here's Envie with a poore thin cover or't,
  Like Scarlet hid in lawne,[5] easily spide through.   110
  This their ambition by the Mothers side
  Is dangerous, and for safetie must be purgd.
  I will prevent their envies; sure, it was
  But some mistaken furie in our sonne,

---

[3] *vildlier :* more vilely.   (lune).
[4] *Moone :* Notion, lunacy   [5] *lawne :* white linen.

Which these aspiring boyes would climbe upon: 115
He shall bee releasde suddainly.
Enter Nobles.
I. NOBLE. Good morning to your Grace.
DUKE.   Welcome, my
                    Lords.   [*They kneel.*]
II. NOBLE. Our knees shall take away the office of
    Our feete for ever,
    Unlesse your Grace bestow a fathers eye   120
    Upon the Clouded fortunes of your sonne,
    And in compassionate vertue grant him that
    Which makes e'en meane men happy—libertie.
DUKE. How seriously their loves and honors woo
    For that which I am about to pray them doo.   125
    —Rise,[4] my Lords, your knees signe his release;
    We freely parden him.
I. NOBLE. We owe your Grace much thankes, and he
                    much   duety.   *Exeunt.*
DUKE. It well becomes that Judge to nod at crimes,
    That dos commit greater himselfe and lives.   130
    I may forgive a disobedient error,
    That expect pardon for adultery,
    And in my old daies am a youth in lust :
    Many a beauty have I turnd to poyson
    In the deniall, covetous of all.   135
    Age hot is like a Monster to be seene :
    My haires are white, and yet my sinnes are Greene.

ACT III. [SCENE I.]

Enter AMBITIOSO *and* SUPERVACUO.
SUPERVACUO. Brother, let my opinion sway you once,—
    I speake it for the best,—to have him die
    Surest and soonest. If the signet come
    Unto the judges hands, why then his doome
    Will be deferd till sittings and Court-daies,   5
    Juries and further; fayths are bought and sold,
    Oths in these daies are but the skin of gold.

AMBITIOSO. In troth, tis true too!

SUPERVACUO.   Then lets set by the
    Judges
And fall to the Officers; tis but mistaking
The Duke our fathers meaning, and where he nam'd   10
"Ere many daies," tis but forgetting that
And have him die i' th' morning.

AMBITIOSO.   Excellent!
Then am I heire—Duke in a minute.

SUPERVACUO. [*Aside.*]   Nay,
And he[1] were once pufft out, here is a pinne
Should quickly prick your bladder.

AMBITIOSO.   Blest[2] occasion!   15
He being packt, weele have some trick and wile
To winde our yonger brother out of prison,
That lies in for the Rape; the Ladies dead
And peoples thoughts will soone be buried.

SUPERVACUO. We may with safty do't, and live and   20
    feede;
The Duchesse-sonnes are too proud to bleed.

AMBITIOSO. We are yfaith, to say true.—Come, let's not
    linger,
Ile to the Officers; go you before
And set an edge upon the Executioner.

SUPERVACUO. Let me alone to grind him.   *Exit.*

AMBITIOSO.   Meete; farewell.   25
I am next now; I rise just in that place
Where thou'rt cut off,[3] upon thy Neck, kind
    brother,
The falling of one head lifts up another.   *Exit.*

[ACT III. SCENE II.]

Enter with the Nobles, LUSSURIOSO *from pryson.*

LUSSURIOSO. My Lords, I am so much indebted to your
    loves,
For this,—O this delivery.

I. NOBLE.   But our dueties, my Lord,

Unto the hopes that growe in you.
LUSSURIOSO. If ere I live to be my selfe, Ile thanke you.
O liberty, thou sweete and heavenly Dame!   5
But hell, for pryson is too milde a name.   *Exeunt.*

[Act III. Scene iii.]

Enter AMBITIOSO *and* SUPERVACUO *with Officers.*
AMBITIOSO. Officers, here's the Dukes signet, your firme
                            warrant,
Brings the command of present death a-long with it
Unto our brother, the Dukes sonne; we are sory
That we are so unnaturally employde
In such an unkinde Office, fitter farre   5
For enemies then brothers.
SUPERVACUO.   But you know,
The Dukes command must be obayde.
I. OFFICER. It must and shal, my Lord—this morning
                            then;
So suddainely?
AMBITIOSO. I, alasse, poore—good soule;
Hee must breake fast betimes,[1] the executioner   10
Stands ready to put forth his cowardly valour.
II. OFFICER. Already?
SUPERVACUO. Already, ifath,—O sir, destruction hies,
And that is least Impudent, soonest dyes.
I. OFFICER. Troth, you say true, my Lord; we take our   15
                            leaves.
Our Office shall be sound; weele not delay
The third part of a minute.
AMBITIOSO.   Therein you showe
Your selves good men and upright officers.
Pray, let him die as privat as he may;
Doe him that favour, for the gaping people   20
Will but trouble him at his prayers,

Act III. Scene ii.
[1] *betimes :* early.

And make him curse and sweare, and so die black.[1]
Will you be so far Kind?

I. OFFICER.   It shall be done, my Lord.

AMBITIOSO. Why, we do thanke you; if we live to be,
    You shall have a better office.

II. OFFICER.   Your good Lord-shippe.   25

SUPERVACUO. Commend us to the scaffold in our teares.

I. OFFICER. Weele weepe and doe your commendations.

Exeunt.

AMBITIOSO. Fine fooles in office!

SUPERVACUO.   Things fall out so fit.

AMBITIOSO. So happily! Come, brother, ere next clock
    His head will be made serve a bigger block.[2] *Exeunt.*   30

[ACT III. SCENE IV.]

Enter in prison[1] [*the* DUCHESS' YOUNGEST SON,
            with his Keeper.]

YOUNGEST SON. Keeper.

KEEPER.   My Lord.

YOUNGEST SON.   No newes lately from
                our brothers?
    Are they unmindfull of us?

KEEPER. My Lord, a messenger came newly in,
    And brought this from 'em.   [*He gives him a letter.*]

YOUNGEST SON. Nothing but paper comforts?   5
    I look'd for my delivery before this,
    Had they beene worth their oths.—Prethee be from
                us.   [*Exit* KEEPER.]
    Now, what say you, forsooth; speake out, I pray.
    [*He reads the*] *Letter.* "Brother, be of good cheere."
    Slud, it begins like a whore, with good cheere.   10
    "Thou shalt not be long a prisoner."
    Not five and thirty yeare, like a banqrout,[1]—I thinke
                so.

                                    ACT III. SCENE IV.
[2] Play on "block" as "hat-size."   [1] *banqrout :* bankrupt.

"We have thought upon a device to get thee out by a
             tricke!"
By a tricke? Pox a' your tricke, and it be so long
             a-playing.
"And so rest comforted, be merry and expect it sud-   15
             daynely."
Be merry? Hang merry, draw and quarter merry!
Ile be mad. Ist[2] not strange that a man
Should lie in a whole month for a woman?
Well, wee shall see how suddaine our brothers
Will bee in their promise; I must expect   20
Still a trick. I shall not bee long a prisoner.
How now, what newes?[2]
            [*Enter* KEEPER.]
KEEPER. Bad newes, my Lord; I am discharg'd of you.
YOUNGEST SON. Slave, calst thou that bad newes? I
            thanke you, brothers.
KEEPER. My Lord, twill prove so; here come the Officers, 25
    Into whose hands I must commit you. [*Exit* KEEPER.]
YOUNGEST SON. Ha, Officers! What, why?
            [*Enter* OFFICERS.]
I. OFFICER. You must pardon us, my Lord,
    Our Office must be sound; here is our warrant,
    The signet from the Duke; you must straight suffer.   30
YOUNGEST SON. Suffer? Ile suffer you to be gon; Ile suffer
            you
To come no more; what would you have me suffer?
II. OFFICER. My Lord, those words were better chang'd
            to praiers;
    The time's but breife with you; prepare to die.
YOUNGEST SON. Sure, tis not so.
III. OFFICER.   It is too true, my Lord.   35
YOUNGEST SON. I tell you, tis not, for the Duke my father
    Deferd me till next sitting, and I looke
    E'en every minute, threescore times an houre,
    For a release, a trick wrought by my brothers.
I. OFFICER. A trick, my Lord? If you expect such   40
            comfort,
    Your hope's as fruitlesse as a barren woman :

Your brothers were the unhappy messengers
That brought this powerfull token for your death.
YOUNGEST BROTHER. My brothers? No, no.
II. OFFICER.   Tis most true,
    my Lord.
YOUNGEST BROTHER. My brothers to bring a warrant for   45
    my death?
How strange this showes!
III. OFFICER.   There's no delaying time.
YOUNGEST BROTHER. Desire 'em hether, call 'em up,—my
    brothers?
They shall deny it to your faces.
I. OFFICER.   My Lord,
They're far ynough by this, at least at Court;
And this most strickt command they left behinde 'em,   50
When griefe swum in their eyes; they show'd like
    brothers,
Brim-full of heavy sorrow, but the Duke
Must have his pleasure.
YOUNGEST SON.   His pleasure?
I. OFFICER. These were their last words which my mem-
    ory beares,
"Commend us to the Scaffold in our teares."   55
YOUNGEST SON. Pox drye their teares! What should I do
    with teares?
I hate em worse then any Cittizens sonne
Can hate salt water; here came a letter now,
New-bleeding from their Pens, scarce stinted yet.
Would Ide beene torne in peeces when I tore it.   60
Looke, you officious whoresons, words of comfort,
"Not long a Prisoner."
I. OFFICER. It sayes true in that, sir, for you must suffer
    presently.
YOUNGEST SON. A villanous Duns[2] upon the letter knav-
    ish exposition.

---

[2] *Duns*: From Duns Scotus, me-   distinctions, hence "dunce."
dieval philosopher of subtle

Looke you then here sir : "Weele get thee out by a   65
         trick,"
Sayes hee.
ii. OFFICER. That may hold too, sir, for you know
  A Trick is commonly foure Cardes,[3] which was meant
  By us foure officers.
YOUNGEST SON.   Worse and worse dealing.
i. OFFICER. The houre beckens us,
  The heads-man waites; lift up your eyes to heaven.   70
YOUNGEST SON. I thanke you, faith,—good, pritty-
        holsome counsell.
I should looke up to heaven, as you sedd,
Whilst he behinde me cozens me of my head.
I, that's the Trick.
iii. OFFICER.   You delay too long, my Lord.
YOUNGEST SON. Stay, good Authorities Bastards; since I   75
        must
Through Brothers perjurie dye, O let me venome
Their soules with curses.
i. OFFICER.   Come, tis no time to curse.
YOUNGEST SON. Must I bleed then, without respect of
        signe?[4, (1)] Well—
My fault was sweet sport, which the world approves;
I dye for that which every woman loves.   *Exeunt.*   80

[Act III. Scene v.]

Enter VINDICE [*disguised*], *with* HIPPOLITO
his brother.

VINDICE. O sweete, delectable, rare, happy, ravishing!
HIPPOLITO. Why what's the matter, brother?
VINDICE.   O tis able
  To make a man spring up, and knock his for-head[(1)]
  Against yon silvar seeling.
HIPPOLITO.   Pre-thee, tell me,

---

[3] *A Trick . . . Cardes*: In the   [4] *signe*: of the Zodiac.
game of Primero.

Why may not I pertake with you? You vowde once   5
To give me share to every tragick thought.

VINDICE. By th' Masse, I thinke I did too;
Then Ile divide it to thee.—The old Duke,
Thinking my outward shape and inward heart
Are cut out of one peice (for he that prates his   10
    secrets,
His heart stands a' th' out-side) hires me by price:
To greete him with a Lady
In some fit place vaylde from the eyes a' th' Court,
Some darkned blushlesse Angle, that is guilty
Of his fore-fathers lusts and great-folkes riots,   15
To which I easily (to[1] maintaine my shape)
Consented, and did wish his impudent grace
To meete her here in this un-sunned lodge,
Where-in tis night at noone, and here the rather
Because, unto the torturing of his soule,   20
The Bastard and the Duchesse have appoynted
Their meeting too in this luxurious circle,
Which most afflicting sight will kill his eyes
Before we kill the rest of him.

HIPPOLITO. Twill yfaith! Most dreadfully digested![1]   25
I see not how you could have mist me, brother.

VINDICE. True, but the violence of my joy forgot it.

HIPPOLITO. I, but where's that Lady now?

VINDICE.   Oh, at that
    word
I'me lost againe! You cannot finde me yet;
I'me in a throng of happy Apprehensions.   30
Hee's suted for a Lady; I have tooke care
For a delitious lip, a sparkling eye,—
You shall be witnesse, brother;
Be ready, stand with your hat off.   *Exit.*

HIPPOLITO. Troth, I wonder what Lady it should be?   35
Yet tis no wonder, now I thinke againe,

ACT III. SCENE v.
1 *digested :* planned.

To have a Lady stoope to a Duke, that stoopes unto
    his men.
Tis common to be common through the world :
And there's more private common shadowing vices
Then those who are knowne both by their names and   40
    prices;
Tis part of my alleagance to stand bare
To the Dukes Concubine,—and here she comes.
    Enter VINDICE, *with the skull of his love drest*
        up in Tires.[2]
VINDICE. Madame, his grace will not be absent long.
    Secret? Ne'er doubt us, Madame; twill be worth
    Three velvet gownes to your Ladyship. Knowne?   45
    Few Ladies respect that disgrace, a poore thin shell!
    Tis the best grace you have to do it well;
    Ile save your hand that labour, Ile unmaske you.
        [He reveals the skull.]
HIPPOLITO. Why brother, brother!
VINDICE. Art thou beguild now? Tut, a Lady can,   50
    At such,—all hid,—beguile a wiser man.
    Have I not fitted the old surfetter
    With a quaint peice of beauty? Age and bare bone
    Are e'er allied in action; here's an eye
    Able to tempt a great man—to serve God,   55
    A prety hanging lip, that has forgot now to dissemble;
    Me thinkes this mouth should make a swearer
        tremble,
    A drunckard claspe his teeth and not undo 'em
    To suffer wet damnation to run through 'em.
    Here's a cheeke keepes her colour, let the winde go   60
        whistle.
    Spout Raine, we feare thee not; be hot or cold,
    All's one with us. And is not he absurd,
    Whose fortunes are upon their faces set,
    That feare no other God but winde and wet?
HIPPOLITO. Brother, y'ave spoke that right;   65
    Is this the forme that living shone so bright?

[2] *Tires :* Headdress.

VINDICE. The very same,
   And now me thinkes I cold e'en chide my selfe
   For doating on her beauty, tho her death
   Shall be revengd after no common action;   70
   Do's the Silke-worme expend her yellow labours
   For thee? For thee dos she undoe herselfe?
   Are Lord-ships sold to maintaine Lady-ships
   For the poore benefit of a bewitching minute?
   Why dos yon fellow falsify hie-waies   75
   And put his life betweene the Judges lippes,
   To refine such a thing, keepes horse and men
   To beate their valours for her?
   Surely wee're all mad people, and they
   Whome we thinke are, are not,—we mistake those;   80
   Tis we are mad in scence, they but in clothes.
HIPPOLITO. Faith, and in clothes too we,—give us our
                     due.
VINDICE. Dos every proud and selfe-affecting Dame
   Camphire[3] her face for this, and grieve her Maker
   In sinfull baths of milke,—when many an infant   85
                     starves
   For her superfluous out-side,—all for this?
   Who now bids twenty pound a night, prepares
   Musick, perfumes, and sweete-meates? All are husht,
   Thou maist lie chast now! It were fine, me thinkes,
   To have thee seene at Revells, forgetfull feasts,   90
   And uncleane Brothells; sure twould fright the sinner
   And make him a good coward, put a Reveller
   Out of his Antick amble,
   And cloye an Epicure with empty dishes?
   Here might a scornefull and ambitious woman   95
   Looke through and through her selfe;—see, Ladies,
                     with false formes
   You deceive men, but cannot deceive wormes.—
   Now to my tragick businesse. Looke you, brother,
   I have not fashiond this onely for show

[3] *Camphire* : white and trans-
   lucent cosmetic.

And uselesse property;[4] no, it shall beare a part   100
E'en in it[s][2] owne Revenge. This very skull,
Whose Mistris the Duke poysoned, with this drug,
The mortall curse of the earth, shall be revengd
In the like straine, and kisse his lippes to death.
As much as the dumbe thing can, he shall feele :   105
What fayles in poyson, weele supply in steele.
HIPPOLITO. Brother, I do applaud thy constant venge-
                    ance,—
The quaintnesse of thy malice,—above thought.
            [VINDICE *poisons the lips of the skull*
                    and re-attires it.]
VINDICE. So—tis layde on : now come and welcome,
                    Duke,
I have her for thee. I protest it, brother,   110
Me thinkes she makes almost as faire a fine
As some old gentlewoman in a Periwig.
Hide thy face now for shame; thou hadst neede have
                    a Maske now.
Tis vaine when beauty flowes; but when it fleetes,
This would become graves better then the streetes.   115
HIPPOLITO. You have my voice in that. [*Noises within.*]
                    Harke, the Duke's
            come.
VINDICE. Peace, let's observe what company he brings,
And how he do's absent 'em, for you knowe
Heele wish all private.—Brother, fall you back a little
With the bony Lady.
HIPPOLITO.   That I will.   [*He retires.*]   120
VINDICE. So, so;—now nine years vengeance crowde into
                    a minute.
            [*Enter the* DUKE *and Gentlemen.*]
DUKE. You shall have leave to leave us, with this charge
Upon your lives; if we be mist by th' Duchesse
Or any of the Nobles, to give out
We're privately rid forth.
VINDICE.   Oh happinesse!   125

---

[4] *property :* theatrical prop.

DUKE. With some few honorable gentlemen, you may
        say;
  You may name those that are away from Court.
GENTLEMAN. Your will and pleasure shall be done, my
        Lord.   [*Exeunt gentlemen.*]
VINDICE. "Privatly rid forth!"
  He strives to make sure worke on't. [*He advances.*]
                    Your good grace!   130
DUKE. Piato, well done. Hast brought her? What Lady
        ist?
VINDICE. Faith,[3] my Lord,
  A Country Lady, a little bashfull at first,
  As most of them are; but after the first kisse,
  My Lord, the worst is past with them; your grace   135
  Knowes now what you have to doo;
  Sh'as some-what a grave looke with her—but—[3]
DUKE. I love that best; conduct her.
VINDICE. [*Aside.*]   Have at all.[5]
DUKE. In gravest lookes the greatest faultes seeme lesse;
  Give me that sin that's rob'd in Holines.   140
VINDICE. [*Aside.*] Back with the Torch; brother, raise
        the perfumes.
DUKE. How sweete can a Duke breath? Age has no fault.
  Pleasure should meete in a perfumed mist.
  Lady, sweetely encountred; I came from Court,
  I must bee bould with you.   [*He kisses the skull.*]
                Oh, what's this? Oh!   145
VINDICE. Royall villaine! White divill![2]
DUKE.   Oh!
VINDICE. Brother, place the Torch here, that his af-
        frighted eye-balls
  May start into those hollowes. Duke, dost knowe
  Yon dreadfull vizard?[6] View it well; tis the skull
  Of Gloriana, whom thou poysonedst last.   150
DUKE. Oh, 'tas poysoned me!
VINDICE. Didst not know that till now?

---

[5] *Have . . . all :* Venture every-   [6] *vizard :* visage.
  thing; shoot the works.

DUKE.   What are you two?

VINDICE. Villaines—all three! The very ragged bone
   Has beene sufficiently revengd.

DUKE. Oh Hippolito, call treason!   [*He falls.*]   155

HIPPOLITO. Yes, my good Lord,—treason! treason! trea-
                     son!   *Stamping on him.*

DUKE. Then I'me betrayde.

VINDICE. Alasse, poore Lecher! in the hands of knaves,
   A slavish Duke is baser then his slaves.

DUKE. My teeth are eaten out.

VINDICE.   Hadst any left?   160

HIPPOLITO. I thinke but few.

VINDICE. Then those that did eate are eaten.

DUKE.   O my tongue!

VINDICE. Your tongue? Twill teach you to kisse closer,
   Not like a [S]lobbering[4] *Dutchman.* You have
                  eyes still :
   Looke, monster, what a Lady hast thou made me   165
                  [*He discovers himself.*]
   My once betrothed wife.

DUKE. Is it thou, villaine? nay then—

VINDICE. 'Tis I, 'tis Vindice, tis I!

HIPPOLITO. And let this comfort thee : our Lord and
                  Father
   Fell sick upon the infection of thy frownes,   170
   And dyed in sadnesse; be that thy hope of life.

DUKE.   Oh!

VINDICE. He had his toung, yet greefe made him die
                  speechlesse.
   Puh, tis but early yet; now Ile begin
   To stick thy soule with Ulcers. I will make
   Thy spirit grievous sore; it shall not rest,   175
   But like some pestilent man, tosse in thy brest.
   Marke me, duke,
   Thou'rt a renowned, high, and mighty Cuckold.

DUKE.   Oh!

VINDICE. Thy Bastard, thy bastard rides a-hunting in
                  thy browe.

DUKE. Millions of deaths!

VINDICE.   Nay, to afflict thee more,   180
  Here in this lodge they meete for damned clips;
  Those eyes shall see the incest of their lips.

DUKE. Is there a hell besides this, villaines?

VINDICE.   Villaine?
  Nay, heaven is just, scornes are the hires[7] of scornes;
  I ne'er knew yet Adulterer without hornes.   185

HIPPOLITO. Once ere they dye 'tis quitted.

                                    [*Noises within.*]

VINDICE.   Harke, the musicke;
  Their banquet is preparde, they're comming.—

DUKE. Oh, kill me not with that sight.

VINDICE. Thou shalt not loose that sight for all thy
                      Duke-doome.

DUKE. Traytors, murderers!   190

VINDICE. What! is not thy tongue eaten out yet?
  Then weele invent a silence. Brother, stifle the Torch.

DUKE. Treason, murther!

VINDICE. Nay, faith, weele have you husht now with
                      thy dagger.
  Naile downe his tongue, and mine shall keepe posses-   195
                      sion
  About his heart; if hee but gaspe hee dyes,
  Wee dread not death to quittance[8] injuries. Brother,
  If he but winck,[9] not brooking the foule object,
  Let our two other hands teare up his lids,
  And make his eyes like Comets shine through blood;   200
  When the bad bleedes, then is the Tragedie good.

HIPPOLITO. Whist,[10] brother, musick's at our eare; they
                      come.

        Enter the Bastard meeting the Dutchesse.

SPURIO. Had not that kisse a taste of sinne, 'twere
                      sweete.

DUCHESS. Why, there's no pleasure, sweet, but it is sin-
                      full.

---

[7] *hires :* rewards.   [9] *winck :* close his eyes.
[8] *quittance :* pay back.   [10] *Whist :* Be quiet.

SPURIO. True, such a bitter sweetnesse fate hath given,   205
    Best side to us, is the worst side to heaven.
DUCHESS. Push, come : 'tis the old Duke, thy doubtfull
                    Father,
    The thought of him rubs heaven in thy way;
    But I protest by yonder waxen fire,
    Forget him, or Ile poyson him.   210
SPURIO. Madam, you urge a thought which ne'er had
                life.
    So deadly doe I loath him for my birth,
    That if hee tooke mee haspt within his bed,
    I would adde murther to adultery,
    And with my sword give up his yeares to death.   215
DUCHESS. Why, now thou'rt sociable; let's in and feast.
    Lowdst Musick sound : pleasure is Banquets[5]
              guest.   *Exeunt.*
DUKE. I cannot brooke—   [*He dies.*]
VINDICE.   The Brooke[3] is turnd to bloud.
HIPPOLITO. Thanks to lowd Musick.
VINDICE.   Twas our friend indeed.
    'Tis state in Musicke for a Duke to bleed :   220
    The Duke-dome wants a head, tho yet unknowne;
    As fast as they peepe up, lets cut 'em downe. *Exeunt.*

[ACT III. SCENE VI.]

Enter the Duchess' two sonnes, AMBITIOSO *and*
SUPERVACUO.

AMBITIOSO. Was not his execution rarely plotted?
    We are the Dukes sonnes now.
SUPERVACUO. I, you may thanke my policie for that.
AMBITIOSO. Your policie for what?
SUPERVACUO. Why, wast not my invention, brother,   5
    To slip the Judges? And in lesser compasse,
    Did not I draw the modell[1] of his death,
    Advizing you to suddaine officers
    And e'en extemporall execution.
AMBITIOSO. Heart, twas a thing I thought on too.   10

SUPERVACUO. You thought ont too? Sfoote, slander not
                  your thoughts
With glorious untruth; I know twas from you.[1]
AMBITIOSO. Sir, I say twas in my head.
SUPERVACUO.   I, like your braines
            then,
Ne'er to come out as long as you liv'd.
AMBITIOSO. You'd have the honor on't, forsooth, that   15
                  your wit
Lead him to the scaffold.
SUPERVACUO.   Since it is my due,
Ile publish't, but Ile ha't in spite of you.
AMBITIOSO. Me thinkes, y'are much too bould; you
                  should a little
Remember us, brother, next to be honest Duke.
SUPERVACUO. [*Aside.*] I, it shall be as easie for you to be   20
                  Duke,
As to be honest, and that's never ifaith.
AMBITIOSO. Well, cold he is by this time, and because
Wee're both ambitious, be it our amity
And let the glory be sharde equally.
SUPERVACUO.   I am content to
            that.
AMBITIOSO. This night our yonger brother shall out of   25
                  prison;
I have a trick.
SUPERVACUO. A trick! pre-thee, what ist?
AMBITIOSO. Weele get him out by a wile.
SUPERVACUO.   Pre-thee, what
            wile?
AMBITIOSO. No, sir, you shall not know it, till't be done;
For then you'd sweare twere yours.
        [*Enter an Officer, with a head.*]
SUPERVACUO. How now, what's he?
AMBITIOSO.   One of the officers.   30
SUPERVACUO. Desired newes.

ACT III. SCENE VI.
[1] *from you* : not on your mind.

AMBITIOSO. How now, my friend?

OFFICER. My Lords, under your pardon, I am allotted
  To that desertlesse office, to present you
  With the yet bleeding head.

SUPERVACUO. [*Aside.*] Ha, ha, excellent.

AMBITIOSO. [*Aside.*] All's sure our owne : Brother,
  canst weepe, thinkst thou?   35
  Twould grace our Flattery much; thinke of some
  Dame,
  Twill teach thee to dissemble.

SUPERVACUO. [*Aside.*] I have thought;—now for your
  selfe.

AMBITIOSO. Our sorrowes are so fluent,
  Our eyes o'er-flow our toungs; words spoake in teares   40
  Are like the murmures of the waters,—the sound
  Is lowdly heard, but cannot be distinguisht.

SUPERVACUO. How dyed he, pray?

OFFICER. O full of rage and
  spleene.

SUPERVACUO. He dyed most valiantly then; we're glad
  to heare it.

OFFICER. We could not woo[1] him once to pray.   45

AMBITIOSO. He showd himselfe a Gentleman in that :
  Give him his due.

OFFICER. But in the steed of prayer,
  He drew forth oaths.

SUPERVACUO. Then did hee pray, deere heart,
  Although you understood him not.

OFFICER. My Lords,
  E'en at his last, with pardon bee it spoake,   50
  Hee curst you both.

SUPERVACUO. Hee curst us? 'Lasse, good soule.

AMBITIOSO. It was not in our powers, but the Dukes
  pleasure.
  [*Aside.*] Finely dissembled a' both sides, sweete fate,—
  O happy opportunitie!

Enter LUSSURIOSO.

LUSSURIOSO. Now, my Lords.

BOTH. Oh!—   55

LUSSURIOSO. Why doe you shunne mee, Brothers?
  You may come neerer now;
  The savor of the prison has for-sooke mee.
  I thanke such kinde Lords as your selves, I'me free.
AMBITIOSO. Alive!
SUPERVACUO.   In health!
AMBITIOSO.   Releasd!
  We were both e'en amazd with joy to see it.   60
LUSSURIOSO. I am much to thanke you.
SUPERVACUO. Faith, we spar'd no toung unto my Lord
                the Duke.
AMBITIOSO. I know your delivery, brother,
  Had not beene halfe so sudden but for us.
SUPERVACUO. O how we pleaded!
LUSSURIOSO.   Most deserving   65
                brothers,
  In my best studies I will thinke of it. *Exit* LUSSURIOSO.
AMBITIOSO. O death and vengeance!
SUPERVACUO.   Hell and torments!
AMBITIOSO. Slave, camst thou to delude us?
OFFICER.   Delude you,
                my Lords?
SUPERVACUO. I, villaine, where's this head now?
OFFICER.   Why heere,
                my Lord;
  Just after his delivery, you both came   70
  With warrant from the Duke to be-head your
                brother.
AMBITIOSO. I, our brother, the Dukes sonne.
OFFICER. The Dukes sonne, my Lord, had his release
                before you came.
AMBITIOSO. Whose head's that; then?
OFFICER. His whom you left command for, your owne   75
                brothers.
AMBITIOSO. Our brothers? O furies!
SUPERVACUO. Plagues!
AMBITIOSO.   Confusions!
SUPERVACUO. Darkenesse!
AMBITIOSO.   Divils!

SUPERVACUO. Fell it out so accursedly?
AMBITIOSO.   So damnedly?
SUPERVACUO. Villaine, Ile braine thee with it.
OFFICER.   O my good   80
            Lord!
SUPERVACUO. The Divill over-take thee.
AMBITIOSO.   O fatall!
SUPERVACUO. O prodigious to our blouds!
AMBITIOSO.   Did we dissemble?
SUPERVACUO. Did we make our teares woemen for thee?
AMBITIOSO. Laugh and rejoyce for thee?
SUPERVACUO. Bring warrant for thy death?
AMBITIOSO.   Mock off thy   85
            head?
SUPERVACUO. You had a trick, you had a wile, forsooth.
AMBITIOSO. A murren[2] meete 'em!
    There's none of these wiles that ever come to good :
    I see now, there is nothing sure in mortalitie but mor-
            talitie.
    Well, no more words,—shalt be revengd ifaith.   90
    Come, throw off clouds now, brother; thinke of
            vengeance
    And deeper setled hate;
                    sirrah,[2] sit fast,
    Weele pull downe all, but thou shalt downe at last.
                                       Exeunt.

                    Act IV. Scene i.

            Enter LUSSURIOSO *with* HIPPOLITO.
LUSSURIOSO. Hippolito.
HIPPOLITO.   My Lord :
    Has your good Lordship ought to command me in?
LUSSURIOSO. I pre-thee, leave us.
HIPPOLITO. How's this?—come and leave us?
LUSSURIOSO.   Hippolito.   5

2 *murren :* plague.

HIPPOLITO. Your honor, I stand ready for any dutious
                emploiment.   5
LUSSURIOSO. Heart, what makst thou here?
HIPPOLITO. [*Aside.*] A pritty Lordly humor:
   He bids me to bee present, to depart;
   Some-thing has stung his honor.
LUSSURIOSO. Bee neerer, draw neerer: 10
   Ye are not so good, me thinkes, Ime angry with you.
HIPPOLITO. With me, my Lord? Ime angry with my
                selfe fort.
LUSSURIOSO. You did preferre a goodly fellow to me,
   Twas wittily elected, twas; I thought
   Had beene a villaine, and he prooves a Knave—   15
   To mee a Knave.
HIPPOLITO. I chose him for the best, my Lord;
   Tis much my sorrow, if neglect in him
   Breed discontent in you.
LUSSURIOSO. Neglect?—twas will: Judge of it,   20
   Firmely to tell of an incredible Act,
   Not to be thought, lesse to be spoken of,
   Twixt my Step-mother and the Bastard,—oh!
   Incestuous sweetes betweene 'em.
HIPPOLITO. Fye! my Lord.   25
LUSSURIOSO. I, in kinde loyaltie to my fathers fore-head,
   Made this a desperate arme, and in that furie
   Committed treason on the lawfull bed,
   And with my sword e'en rac'd[1] my fathers bosome,
   For which I was within a stroake of death.   30
HIPPOLITO. Alack! Ime sorry. [*Aside.*] Sfoote! just upon
                the stroake
   Jars in my brother; twill be villanous Musick.
           Enter VINDICE [*disguised*].
VINDICE. My honored Lord.
LUSSURIOSO. Away! pre-thee forsake us; heereafter
                weele not know thee.

   ACT IV. SCENE I.
[1] *rac'd :* razed.

VINDICE. Not know me, my Lord! Your Lordship cannot   35
           choose.—
LUSSURIOSO. Begon, I say; thou art a false knave.
VINDICE. Why, the easier to be knowne, my Lord.
LUSSURIOSO. Push, I shall proove too bitter with a word,
    Make thee a perpetuall prisoner,
    And laye this yron-age[1] upon thee.   40
VINDICE. [*Aside.*] Mum,
    For there's a doome would make a woman dum.
    Missing the bastard next him, the winde's come
           about;
    Now tis my brothers turne to stay, mine to goe out.
                         Exit VINDICE.
LUSSURIOSO. Has greatly moov'd me.
HIPPOLITO.   Much to blame ˌifaith.   45
LUSSURIOSO. But Ile recover, to his ruine.—Twas told me
           lately,—
    I know not whether falslie,—that you'd a brother.
HIPPOLITO. Who, I? Yes, my good Lord, I have a
           brother.
LUSSURIOSO. How chance the Court ne'ere saw him? of
           what nature?
    How does he apply his houres?
HIPPOLITO.   Faith, to curse Fates,   50
    Who, as he thinkes, ordaind him to be poore,—
    Keepes at home, full of want and discontent.
LUSSURIOSO. [*Aside.*] There's hope in him, for discontent
           and want
    Is the best clay to mould a villaine off.—
    Hippolito, wish him repaire to us;   55
    If there be ought in him to please our bloud,
    For thy sake weele advance him and build faire
    His meanest fortunes : for it is in us
    To reare up Towers from cottages.
HIPPOLITO. It is so, my Lord; he will attend your honour,   60
    But hee's a man in whom much melancholy dwels.
LUSSURIOSO. Why, the better : bring him to Court.
HIPPOLITO. With willingnesse and speed.

[*Aside.*] Whom he cast off e'en now, must now
    succeed;
Brother, disguise must off,   65
In thine owne shape now Ile prefer thee to him :
How strangely does himselfe worke to undo him.
                                Exit.

LUSSURIOSO. This fellow will come fitly; he shall kill
    That other slave that did abuse my spleene
    And made it swell to Treason. I have put   70
    Much of my heart into him, hee must dye.
    He that knowes great mens secrets and proves slight,[2]
    That man ne'er lives to see his Beard turne white.
    I, he shall speede him : Ile employ the[1] brother;
    Slaves are but Nayles to drive out one another.   75
    Hee being of black condition,[3] sutable
    To want and ill content, hope of preferment
    Will grinde him to an Edge.
              The Nobles enter.[2]
I. NOBLE. Good dayes unto your honour.
LUSSURIOSO. My kinde Lords, I do returne the like.   80
II. NOBLE. Sawe you my Lord the Duke?
LUSSURIOSO. My Lord and Father,—is he from Court?
I. NOBLE. Hee's sure from Court,
    But where, which way his pleasure tooke, we know
           not;
    Nor can we heare ont.   85
          [*More Nobles enter.*]
LUSSURIOSO. Here come those should tell.
    Sawe you my Lord and Father?
III. NOBLE. Not since two houres before noone, my Lord,
    And then he privately ridde forth.
LUSSURIOSO. Oh hee's [rid][3] forth.   90
I. NOBLE. Twas wondrous privately.
II. NOBLE. There's none ith Court had any knowledge
        ont.
LUSSURIOSO. His Grace is old and sudden; tis no treason

[2] *slight :* untrustworthy.

[3] *black condition :* melancholy
nature.

To say, the Duke my Father has a humor,
Or such a Toye about him; what in us   95
Would appeare light, in him seemes vertuous.
iii. noble. Tis Oracle, my Lord.   *Exeunt.*

[Act IV. Scene ii.]

Enter vindice *and* hippolito, vindice *out of his*
disguise.

hippolito. So so, all's as it should be, y'are your selfe.
vindice. How that great villaine puts me to my shifts!
hippolito. Hee that did lately in disguize reject thee
  Shall, now thou art thy selfe, as much respect thee.
vindice. Twill be the quainter fallacie; but brother,   5
  Sfoote, what use will hee put me to now, thinkst
                      thou?
hippolito. Nay, you must pardon me in that, I know
                      not :
  H'as some employment for you, but what tis
  Hee and his Secretary[(1)]—the Divell—knowes best.
vindice. Well, I must suite my toung to his desires,   10
  What colour so e'er they be, hoping at last
  To pile up all my wishes on his brest.
hippolito. Faith, Brother, he himselfe showes the way.
vindice. Now the Duke is dead, the realme is clad in
                      claye :
  His death being not yet knowne, under his name   15
  The people still are governd. Well, thou his sonne
  Art not long-liv'd; thou shalt not joy his death.
  To kill thee then I should most honour thee;
  For twould stand firme in every mans beliefe,
  Thou'st a kinde[1] child, and onely dyedst with griefe. 20
hippolito. You fetch about well, but let's talke in
                      present;
  How will you appeare in fashion different

Act IV. Scene ii.
[1] *kinde :* natural.

As well as in apparrell, to make all things possible :
If you be but once tript, wee fall for ever.
It is not the least pollicie to bee doubtfull;[2]   25
You must change tongue[(2)]—familiar was your first.
VINDICE. Why, Ile beare me in some straine of melan-
                    cholie,
And string my selfe with heavy-sounding Wyre,
Like such an Instrument that speakes merry things
                    sadly.
HIPPOLITO. Then tis as I meant;   30
I gave you out at first in discontent.
VINDICE. Ile turne my selfe, and then—
           [*Enter* LUSSURIOSO.]
HIPPOLITO. Sfoote, here he comes : hast thought
                  uppont?
VINDICE. Salute him, feare not me.
LUSSURIOSO.   Hippolito.
HIPPOLITO. Your Lordship.
LUSSURIOSO.   What's he yonder?   35
HIPPOLITO. Tis Vindice, my discontented Brother,
Whom, 'cording to your will I'ave brought to Court.
LUSSURIOSO. Is that thy brother? Beshrew me, a good
                  presence;
I wonder h'as beene from the Court so long.
Come neerer.   40
HIPPOLITO. Brother, Lord Lussurioso the Duke['s][1]
                  sonne.
LUSSURIOSO. Be more neere to us,—welcome,—neerer
                  yet.
VINDICE. How don you? God you god den.[3]
    Snatches of[f] his hat and makes legs to him.
LUSSURIOSO. We thanke thee.
How strangly such a course-homely salute   45
Showes in the Pallace, where we greete in fire,—
Nimble and desperate tongues. Should we name

[3] *God . . . den :* God give you
[2] *doubtfull :* hesitant.   good day.

God in a salutation, 'twould ne'ere be stood on't—
                      heaven!
Tell me, what has made thee so melancholy.

VINDICE. Why, going to Law.   50

LUSSURIOSO. Why, will that make a man mellancholy?

VINDICE. Yes, to looke long upon inck and black
buckrom. I went mee to law in *Anno Quadragesimo
secundo*,[3] and I waded out of it in *Anno sextagesimo tertio*.[4]

LUSSURIOSO. What, three and twenty years in law?   55

VINDICE. I have knowne those that have beene five and
fifty, and all about Pullin[4] and Pigges.

LUSSURIOSO. May it bee possible such men should
                      breath,
To vex the Tearmes[5] so much.

VINDICE. Tis foode to some, my Lord. There are olde   60
men at the present, that are so poysoned with the af-
fectation of law-words, (having had many suites
canvast) that their common talke is nothing but
Barbery Lattin[6] : they cannot so much as pray but in
law, that their sinnes may be remov'd with a writ of   65
Error, and their soules fetcht up to heaven with a
sasarara.[7]

[LUSSURIOSO.][2] It seemes most strange to me;
Yet all the world meetes round in the same bent :
Where the heart's set, there goes the tongues consent.
How dost apply thy studies, fellow?

VINDICE. Study?—why, to thinke how a great rich man   70
lies a-dying, and a poore Cobler toales the bell for
him. How he cannot depart the world, and see the
great chest stand before him; when hee lies speech-
lesse, how hee will point you readily to all the boxes,
and when hee is past all memory,—as the gosseps   75
gesse,—then thinkes hee of forffetures and obliga-
tions; nay, when to all mens hearings he whurles and

---

4 *Pullin* : Poultry.
5 *Tearmes* : Legal sessions.

6 *Barbery Lattin* : Barbarous
  Latin.
7 *sasarara* : writ of *certiorari.*

rotles in the throate, hee's bussie threatning his poore
Tennants. And this would last me now some seaven
yeares thinking or there abouts. But I have a Conceit[8] a-comming in picture upon this; I drawe it my   80
selfe, which ifaith, la, Ile present to your honor; you
shall not chose but like it, for your Lordship shall
give me nothing for it.

LUSSURIOSO. Nay, you misstake me then,
    For I am publisht bountifull inough.
    Let's tast of your conceit.   85

VINDICE. In picture, my Lord?

LUSSURIOSO.   I, in picture.

VINDICE. Marry, this it is—"A usuring Father to be
    boyling in hell, and his sonne and Heire with a
    Whore dancing over him."

HIPPOLITO. [*Aside.*] H'as par'd him to the quicke.

LUSSURIOSO. The conceit's pritty, ifaith,   90
    But tak't upon my life, twill ne'er be likt.

VINDICE. No?—why Ime sure the whore will be likt well
    enough.

HIPPOLITO. [*Aside.*] I, if she were out a' th' picture,
    heede like her then himselfe.

VINDICE. And as for the sonne and heire, he shall be an   95
    eyesore to no young Revellers, for hee shall bee
    drawne in cloth of gold breeches.

LUSSURIOSO. And thou hast put my meaning in the
                    pockets,
    And canst not draw that out; my thought was this,
    To see the picture of a usuring father   100
    Boyling in hell, our richmen would ne'er like it.

VINDICE. O true, I cry you heartly mercy! I know the
    reason, for some of 'em had rather be dambd indeed
    then dambd in colours.[9]

LUSSURIOSO. [*Aside.*] A parlous melancholy!—has wit   105
                    enough
    To murder any man, and Ile give him meanes.—

---

[8] *Conceit* : Imaginative con-   [9] *in colours* : by a trick.
ception.

I thinke thou art ill monied.

VINDICE.   Money, ho, ho!

'T'as beene my want so long, tis now my scoffe.

Ive e'en forgot what colour silver's off.

LUSSURIOSO. [*Aside.*] It hits as I could wish.

VINDICE.   I get good   110

                    cloths

Of those that dread my humour, and for table-roome

I feed on those that cannot be rid of me.

LUSSURIOSO. Somewhat to set thee up withall.

                    [*He gives him money.*]

VINDICE. O mine eyes!

LUSSURIOSO.   How now, man?

VINDICE.   Almost strucke

                    blind;

This bright unusuall shine, to me seemes proud;   115

I dare not looke till the sunne be in a cloud.

LUSSURIOSO. I thinke I shall afecte[10] his melancholy.

How are they now.

VINDICE.   The better for your asking.

LUSSURIOSO. You shall be better yet if you but fasten

Truly on my intent; now yare both present   120

I will unbrace such a close private villayne

Unto your vengfull swords, the like ne'er heard of,

Who hath disgrac'd you much and injur'd us.

HIPPOLITO. Disgraced us, my Lord?

LUSSURIOSO.   I, Hippolito.

I kept it here till now that both your angers   125

Might meete him at once.

VINDICE.   Ime covetuous

To know the villayne.

LUSSURIOSO.   You know him, that slave Pandar

Piato, whome we threatened last

With irons in perpetuall prisonment.

VINDICE. [*Aside.*] All this is I.

HIPPOLITO.   Ist he, my Lord?   130

LUSSURIOSO. Ile tell you,—you first preferd him to me.

10 *afecte :* get to like.

VINDICE. Did you, brother?

HIPPOLITO.   I did indeed.

LUSSURIOSO. And the ingreatfull villayne,
　To quit that kindnes, strongly wrought with me,
　Being—as you see—a likely man for pleasure,   135
　With jewels to corrupt your virgin sister.

HIPPOLITO. Oh villaine!

VINDICE.   He shall surely die that did it.

LUSSURIOSO. I, far from thinking any Virgin harme,
　Especially knowing her to be as chast
　As that part which scarce suffers to be toucht,—   140
　Th' eye,—would not endure him.

VINDICE. Would you not, my Lord?
　Twas wondrous honorably donne.

LUSSURIOSO. But with some [fine][3] frownes kept him
　　　　　　　　　out.

VINDICE. Out, slave!   145

LUSSURIOSO. What did me he? but in revenge of that,
　Went of his owne free will to make infirme
　Your sisters honor, whome I honor with my soule
　For chast respect, and not prevayling there,
　(As twas but desperate folly to attempt it,)   150
　In meere spleene, by the way, way-laies your mother,
　Who'se honor being coward—as it seemes—
　Yeelded by little force.

VINDICE.   Coward indeed!

LUSSURIOSO. He, proud of their advantage, (as he
　　　　　　　　　thought),
　Brought me these newes for happy; but I,—heaven
　　　　　　　　　forgive mee for't!   155

VINDICE. What did your honour?

LUSSURIOSO.   In rage pusht him from
　　　　　　　　　mee,
　Trampled beneath his throate, spurnd him, and
　　　　　　　　　bruizd :
　Indeed, I was too cruell, to say troth.

HIPPOLITO. Most Nobly managde!

VINDICE. [*Aside.*] Has not heaven an eare? Is all the
　　　　　　　　　lightning wasted?   160

LUSSURIOSO. If I now were so impatient in a modest
                         cause,
  What should you be?
VINDICE.   Full mad; he shall not live
  To see the Moone change.
LUSSURIOSO.   He's about the Pallace;
  Hippolito, intice him this way, that thy brother
  May take full marke of him.   165
HIPPOLITO. Heart!—that shall not neede, my Lord;
  I can direct him so far.
LUSSURIOSO.   Yet, for my hates sake,
  Go, winde(5) him this way; Ile see him bleede my
                         selfe.
HIPPOLITO. [*Aside.*] What now, brother?
VINDICE. [*Aside.*] Nay, e'en what you will; y'are put
                         to't, brother.   170
HIPPOLITO. [*Aside.*] An impossible taske, Ile sweare,
  To bring him hither that's already here.
                                   Exit HIPPOLITO.
LUSSURIOSO. Thy name? I have forgot it.
VINDICE.   Vindice, my
                 Lord.
LUSSURIOSO. Tis a good name, that.
VINDICE.   I, a Revenger.
LUSSURIOSO. It dos betoken courage; thou shouldst be   175
                 valiant,
  And kill thine enemies.
VINDICE.   That's my hope, my Lord.
LUSSURIOSO. This slave is one.
VINDICE.   Ile doome him.
LUSSURIOSO. Then Ile praise thee.
  Do thou observe[11] me best, and Ile best raise thee.
                      Enter HIPPOLITO.
VINDICE. Indeed, I thanke you.   180
LUSSURIOSO. Now, Hippolito, where's the slave Pandar?
HIPPOLITO. Your good Lordship

[11] *observe* : obey, follow.

Would have a loathsome sight of him, much offen-
sive.
Hee's not in case now to be seene, my Lord.
The worst[6] of all the deadly sinnes is in him :   185
That beggerly damnation, drunkennesse.
LUSSURIOSO. Then he's a double-slave.
VINDICE. [*Aside.*] Twas well convaide, upon a suddaine
wit.
LUSSURIOSO. What, are you both
Firmely resolvd? Ile see him dead my selfe.   190
VINDICE. Or else, let not us live.
LUSSURIOSO. You may direct your brother to take note
of him.
HIPPOLITO. I shall.
LUSSURIOSO. Rise but in this, and you shall never fall.
VINDICE. Your honours Vassayles.   195
LUSSURIOSO. [*Aside.*] This was wisely carried.
Deepe policie in us makes fooles of such :
Then must a slave die, when he knowes too much.
                                        Exit LUSSURIOSO.
VINDICE. O thou almighty patience! tis my wonder
That such a fellow, impudent and wicked,   200
Should not be cloven as he stood :
Or with a secret winde burst open!
Is there no thunder left, or ist kept up
In stock for heavier vengeance? [*Thunder.*] There it
goes!
HIPPOLITO. Brother, we loose our selves.
VINDICE.   But I have found   205
it,
Twill hold, tis sure; thankes, thankes to any spirit
That mingled it mongst my inventions.
HIPPOLITO. What ist?
VINDICE.   Tis sound and good, thou shalt per-
take it.
I'me hir'd to kill my selfe.
HIPPOLITO.   True.
VINDICE.   Pree-thee, marke it.
And the old Duke being dead, but not convaide,   210

For he's already mist too, and you know :
Murder will peepe out of the closest huske.
HIPPOLITO.   Most   true.
VINDICE. What say you then to this device;
  If we drest up the body of the Duke.—
HIPPOLITO. In that disguise of yours.
VINDICE.   Y'are quick, y'ave   215
              reacht it.
HIPPOLITO. I like it wonderously.
VINDICE. And being in drinck, as you have publisht him,
  To leane him on his elbowe, as if sleepe had caught
              him :
  Which claimes most interest in such sluggy men.
HIPPOLITO. Good yet, but here's a doubt.   220
  [We],[4] thought by th' Dukes sonne to kill that
              pandar,
  Shall, when he is knowne, be thought to kill the
              Duke.
VINDICE. Neither,[5] O thankes! It is substantiall;[7]
  For that disguize being on him, which I wore,
  It wil be thought I, which he calls the Pandar,   225
  Did kil the Duke, and fled away in his
  Apparell, leaving him so disguiz'd,
  To avoide swift pursuite.
HIPPOLITO.   Firmer and firmer.
VINDICE. Nay, doubt not; tis in graine, I warrant it
  Hold collour.[5]
HIPPOLITO. Let's about it.
VINDICE. But by the way too, now I thinke on't,   230
              brother;
  Let's conjure that base divill out of our Mother.
                                          Exeunt.

[ACT IV. SCENE III.]

Enter the DUCHESS *arme in arme with the Bastard :*
he seemeth lasciviously to her; after them,
enter SUPERVACUO, *running with a rapier; his*
Brother [AMBITIOSO] *stops him.*

SPURIO. Madam, unlock your selfe; should it be seene,
    Your arme would be suspected.
DUCHESS. Who ist that dares suspect or this or these?[1]
    May not we deale our favours where we please?
SPURIO. I'me confident you may.   *Exeunt.*   5
AMBITIOSO. Sfoot! brother, hold.
SUPERVACUO.   Woult let the Bastard
          shame us?
AMBITIOSO. Hold, hold, brother! there's fitter time then
          now.
SUPERVACUO. Now, when I see it.
AMBITIOSO.   Tis too much seene
          already.
SUPERVACUO. Seene and knowne.
    The Nobler she's, the baser is shee growne.   10
AMBITIOSO. If she were bent lasciviously, the fault
    Of mighty women that sleepe soft,—O death,
    Must she needes chuse such an unequall sinner—
    To make all worse?
SUPERVACUO. A Bastard, the Dukes Bastard! Shame
          heapt on shame!   15
AMBITIOSO. O our disgrace!
    Most women have small waste the world through-
          out;
    But their[1] desires are thousand miles about.
SUPERVACUO. Come, stay not here, let's after and
          prevent,
    Or els thei'le sinne faster then weele repent. *Exeunt.*   20

[ACT IV. SCENE IV.]

Enter VINDICE *and* HIPPOLITO, *bringing out there*
Mother, one by one shoulder, and the other by
the other, with daggers in their hands.

VINDICE. O thou, for whom no name is bad ynough!

GRATIANA. What meanes my sonnes? What, will you
                                murder me?

VINDICE. Wicked, unnaturall Parent![1]

HIPPOLITO.   Feend of women!

GRATIANA. Oh, are sonnes turnd monsters? Helpe!

VINDICE. In vaine.   5

GRATIANA. Are you so barbarous to set Iron nipples
    Upon the brest that gave you suck?

VINDICE.   That brest
    Is turnd to Quarled[(1)] poyson.

GRATIANA. Cut not[(2)] your daies for't; am not I your
                                mother?

VINDICE. Thou dost usurpe that title now by fraud,   10
    For in that shell of mother breeds a bawde.

GRATIANA. A bawde? O name far loathsomer then hell!

HIPPOLITO. It should be so, knewst thou thy Office well.

GRATIANA. I hate it.

VINDICE. Ah, ist possible? *Thou onely*—you powers on   15
                                hie,
    That women should dissemble when they die.

GRATIANA. Dissemble?

VINDICE.   Did not the Dukes sonne direct
    A fellow of the worlds condition hither,
    That did corrupt all that was good in thee?
    Made thee uncivilly forget thy selfe   20
    And worke our sister to his lust?

GRATIANA.   Who—I?
    That had beene monstrous! I defie that man
    For any such intent; none lives so pure
    But shall be soild with slander.
    Good sonne, beleive it not.

VINDICE.   Oh, I'me in doubt   25
  Whether I'me my selfe or no!
  Stay, let me looke agen upon this face.
  Who shall be sav'd when mothers have no grace?
HIPPOLITO. Twould make one halfe dispaire.
VINDICE.   I was the man.
  Defie me now! Let's see,—do't modestly.   30
GRATIANA. O hell unto my soule!
VINDICE. In that disguize, I, sent from the Dukes sonne,
  Tryed you, and found you base mettell,
  As any villaine might have donne.
GRATIANA. O no, no tongue but yours could have   35
              bewitcht me so.
VINDICE. O nimble in damnation, quick in tune!
  There is no divill could strike fire so soone :
  I am confuted in a word.
GRATIANA. Oh sonnes, forgive me! To my selfe Ile prove
              more true.
  You that should honor me, I kneele to you.   40
              [*She kneels and weeps.*]
VINDICE. A mother to give ayme to her owne daughter!
HIPPOLITO. True, brother,—how far beyond nature to't,
  Tho many Mothers do't!
VINDICE. Nay, and you draw teares once, go you to bed;
  Wee will make you blush and change to red.   45
  Brother, it raines; twill spoile your dagger, house it.
HIPPOLITO. Tis done.
VINDICE. Yfaith, tis a sweete shower, it dos much good;
  The fruitfull grounds and meadowes of her soule
  Has beene long dry : powre downe, thou blessed   50
              dew!
  Rise, Mother; troth, this shower has made you higher.
GRATIANA. O you heavens, take this infectious spot out
              of my soule!
  Ile rence it in seaven waters of mine eyes.
  Make my teares salt ynough to tast of grace.
  To weepe is to our sexe naturally given,   55
  But to weepe truely, that's a gift from heaven.
VINDICE. Nay, Ile kisse you now. Kisse her, brother.

Let's marry her to our soules, wherein's no lust,
And honorably love her.
HIPPOLITO.   Let it be.
VINDICE. For honest women are so seld[2] and rare,   60
Tis good to cherish those poore few that are.
Oh you of easie waxe! do but imagine,
Now the disease has left you, how leprously
That Office would have cling'd unto your forehead.
All mothers that had any gracefull hue   65
Would have worne maskes to hide their face at you.
It would have growne to this,—at your foule name,
Greene-collour'd maides would have turnd red with
                    shame.
HIPPOLITO. And then, our sister full of hire and
                    bassenesse!
VINDICE. There had beene boyling lead agen.   70
[The] Dukes[3] sonnes great Concubine!
A drab of State, a cloath a' silver slut,
To have her traine borne up, and her soule traile i'
                    th' durt.
HIPPOLITO. Great, too miserably great!—rich to be
                    eternally wretched.
VINDICE. O common madnesse!   75
Aske but the thrivingst harlot in cold bloud,
Sheed give the world to make her honour good.
Perhaps youle say,—but onely to th' Dukes sonne
In private. Why, shee first begins with one,
Who afterward to thousand prooves a whore :   80
"Breake Ice in one place, it will crack in more."
GRATIANA. Most certainly applyed.
HIPPOLITO. Oh Brother, you forget our businesse.
VINDICE. And well remembred; joye's a subtill elfe,
I thinke man's happiest when he forgets himselfe.   85
Farewell, once dryed, now holy-watred Meade;
Our hearts weare Feathers that before wore Lead.
GRATIANA. Ile give you this,—that one I never knew,
Plead better for and gainst the Divill, then you.
VINDICE. You make me proud ont.   90
HIPPOLITO. Commend us in all vertue to our Sister.

VINDICE. I, for the love of heaven, to that true maide.
GRATIANA. With my best words.
VINDICE.   Why that was motherly
                    sayd.   *Exeunt.*
GRATIANA. I wonder now what fury did transport me.
    I feele good thoughts begin to settle in me.   95
    Oh with what fore-head [3] can I looke on her,
    Whose honor I've so impiouslie beset.
    And here shee comes.
                    [*Enter* CASTIZA.]
CASTIZA. Now, mother, you have wrought with me so
                    strongly,
    That what for my advancement, as to calme   100
    The trouble of your tongue, I am content.
GRATIANA. Content to what?
CASTIZA.   To do as you have wisht me,
    To prostitute my brest to the Dukes sonne,
    And put my selfe to common Usury.
GRATIANA. I hope you will not so.
CASTIZA.   Hope you I will not?   105
    That's not the hope you looke to be saved in.
GRATIANA. Truth, but it is.
CASTIZA.   Do not deceive your selfe.
    I am, as you, e'en out of Marble wrought.
    What would you now? Are yee not pleasde yet with
                    me?
    You shall not wish me to be more lascivious   110
    Then I intend to be.
GRATIANA.   Strike not me cold.
CASTIZA. How often have you chargd me on your
                    blessing
    To be a cursed woman? When you knew
    Your blessing had no force to make me lewd,
    You laide your cursse upon me. That did more;   115
    The mothers curse is heavy,—where that fights,
    Sonnes set in storme and daughters loose their lights.
GRATIANA. Good childe, deare maide, if there be any
                    sparke
    Of heavenly intellectuall fire within thee,

Oh let my breath revive it to a flame!   120
Put not all out with womans wilfull follyes.
I am recoverd of that foule disease
That haunts too many mothers; kinde, forgive me.
Make me not sick in health. If then
My words prevailde when they were wickednesse,   125
How much more now, when they are just and good!
CASTIZA. I wonder what you meane. Are not you she
For whose infect perswasions I could scarce
Kneele out my prayers, and had much adoo
In three houres reading, to untwist so much   130
Of the black serpent as you wound about me.
GRATIANA. Tis unfruitfull, [child],[4] tedious to re-
                    peate what's past;
Ime now your present Mother.
CASTIZA.   Push, now 'tis too late.
GRATIANA. Bethinke agen, thou knowst not what thou
                    sayst.
CASTIZA. No?—deny advancement, treasure, the Dukes   135
                    sonne?
GRATIANA. O see,. I spoke those words, and now they
                    poyson me.
What will the deed do then?
Advancement?—true, as high as shame can pitch.
For Treasure—who e'er knew a harlot rich?
Or could build by the purchase of her sinne   140
An hospitall to keepe their bastards in.
The Dukes sonne—oh when woemen are yong
                    Courtiers,
They are sure to be old beggars.
To know the miseries most harlots taste,
Thoudst wish thy selfe unborne, when thou art un-   145
                    chast.
CASTIZA. O mother, let me twine about your necke,
And kisse you till my soule melt on your lips.
I did but this to trie you.
GRATIANA.   O, speake truth.
CASTIZA. Indeed, I did not;[4] for no tong has force
To alter me from honest.   150

If maydens would, mens words could have no power;
A vergin honor is a christall Tower,
Which—being weake—is guarded with good spirits;
Untill she basely yeelds, no ill inherits.[1]

GRATIANA. O happy child! faith and thy birth hath   155
   saved me.
Mongst thousand daughters, happiest of all others,
[Be][5] thou a glasse for maides, and I for mothers.
           Exeunt.

[ACT V. SCENE I.]

Enter VINDICE *and* HIPPOLITO,
[*with the Duke's corpse.*]

VINDICE. So, so, he leanes well; take heede you wake
 him not, brother.
HIPPOLITO. I warrant you my life for yours.
VINDICE. That's a good lay, for I must kill my selfe.
 Brother, that's I : that sits for me : do you marke it.   5
 And I must stand ready here to make away my selfe
 yonder. I must sit to bee kild, and stand to kill my
 selfe. I could varry it not so little as thrice over agen;
 'tas some eight returnes,[1] like Michelmas Tearme.
HIPPOLITO. That's enow, a' conscience.   10
VINDICE. But, sirrah, dos the Dukes sonne come single?
HIPPOLITO. No, there's the hell on't. His faith's too
 feeble to go alone; hee brings flesh-flies after him,
 that will buzze against supper time, and hum for his
 comming out.
VINDICE. Ah, the fly-flop of vengeance beate 'em to   15
 peeces! Here was the sweetest occasion, the fittest
 houre, to have made my reveng familiar with him,—
 show him the body of the Duke his father, and how
 quaintly he died, like a Polititian, in hugger-mugger,[1]
 made no man acquainted with it,—and in Catas-

ACT IV. SCENE IV.   ACT V. SCENE I.
[1] *inherits :* can possess her. [1] *hugger-mugger :* secrecy.

trophe[2] [slay][11] him over his fathers brest! And   20
oh, I'me mad to loose such a sweete opportunity!

HIPPOLITO. Nay, push, pree-thee be content! There's no
remedy present. May not hereafter times open in as
faire faces as this?

VINDICE. They may, if they can paint so well.

HIPPOLITO. Come, now to avoide al suspition, let's for-   25
sake this roome, and be going to meete the Dukes
sonne.

VINDICE. Content,—I'me for any wether. Heart, step
closse; here hee comes.

                    Enter LUSSURIOSO.

HIPPOLITO. My honor'd Lord.

LUSSURIOSO.   Oh me! you both present?

VINDICE. E'en newly, my Lord, just as your Lordship   30
enterd now. About this place we had notice given hee
should bee, but in some loathsome plight or other.

HIPPOLITO. Came your honour private?

LUSSURIOSO. Private inough for this : onely a few
Attend my comming out.

HIPPOLITO. [*Aside.*] Death rotte those few.   35

LUSSURIOSO. Stay, yonder's the slave.

VINDICE. Masse, there's the slave indeed, my Lord.
[*Aside.*] Tis a good child; he calls his Father slave.

LUSSURIOSO. I, that's the villaine, the dambd villaine :
                    softly.
Tread easie.

VINDICE. Push, I warrant you, my Lord,   40
Weele stiflle in our breaths.

LUSSURIOSO.   That will do well.
Base roague, thou sleepest thy last. [*Aside.*] Tis
                    policie
To have him killd in's sleepe, for if he wakt
Hee would betray all to them.

VINDICE. But, my Lord—

LUSSURIOSO.   Ha,—what sayst?   45

2 *Catastrophe* : Conclusion.

VINDICE. Shall we kill him now hee's drunke?

LUSSURIOSO.   I,—best of all.

VINDICE. Why, then hee will ne'er live to be sober.

LUSSURIOSO. No matter, let him reele to hell.

VINDICE. But being so full of liquor, I feare hee will put
    out all the fire.   50

LUSSURIOSO. Thou art a mad beast.

VINDICE. And leave none to warme your Lordships Gols³
    withall; for he that dyes drunke⁽²⁾ falls into hell fire
    like a Bucket a' water, qush, qush.

LUSSURIOSO. Come, be ready; nake[2] your swords;
               thinke of your wrongs.   55
    This slave has injur'd you.

VINDICE. Troth, so he has, and he has paide well fort.

LUSSURIOSO. Meete with him now.

VINDICE.   Youle beare us out,
    my Lord?

LUSSURIOSO. Puh, am I a Lord for nothing, thinke you?
    Quickly now.

VINDICE.   Sa, sa, sa! [*He stabs the Duke's corpse.*]
                    Thumpe, there he lyes.   60

LUSSURIOSO. Nimbly done. Ha! Oh, villaines, murderers!
    Tis the old Duke my father.

VINDICE.   That's a jest.

LUSSURIOSO. What—stiffe and colde already?
    O pardon me to call you from your names :
    Tis none of your deed. That villaine Piato,   65
    Whom you thought now to kill, has murderd him
    And left him thus disguizd.

HIPPOLITO.   And not unlikely.

VINDICE. O rascall, was he not ashamde
    To put the Duke into a greasie doublet?

LUSSURIOSO. He has beene cold and stiff—who knowes   70
               how long?

VINDICE. [*Aside.*] Marry, that do I.

³ *Gols :* Hands (cant word of
unknown origin).

LUSSURIOSO. No words, I pray, off any thing entended.
VINDICE. Oh my Lord.
HIPPOLITO. I would faine have your Lordship thinke
                that we
Have small reason to prate.   75
LUSSURIOSO. Faith, thou sayst true. Ile forth-with send
                to Court
For all the Nobles, Bastard, Duchesse—all—[3]
How here by miracle wee found him dead,
And in his rayment that foule villaine fled.
VINDICE. That will be the best way, my Lord, to cleere   80
Us all : let's cast about to be cleere.
LUSSURIOSO. Ho, Nencio, Sordido, and the rest!
         Enter all [his attendants].
I. [SERVANT]. My Lord.
II. [SERVANT].   My Lord.
LUSSURIOSO. Be wittnesses of a strange spectacle.
Choosing for private conference that sad roome,   85
We found the Duke my father gealde in bloud.
I. [SERVANT]. My Lord the Duke!—Run, hie thee,
                Nencio.
Startle the Court by signifying so much.
                    [*Exit* NENCIO.]
VINDICE. [*Aside.*] Thus much by wit a deepe Revenger
                can,—
When murder's knowne,—to be the cleerest man.   90
We're fordest off, and with as bould an eye
Survay his body, as the standers by.
LUSSURIOSO. My royall father, too basely let bloud
By a malevolent slave!
HIPPOLITO. [*Aside.*] Harke, he calls thee slave agen.
VINDICE. [*Aside.*]   H'as
                lost, he may.   95
LUSSURIOSO. Oh sight! Looke hether, see, his lips are
                gnawn
With poyson.
VINDICE. How?—his lips? By th' masse, they bee.
O villaine! O roague! O slave! O rascall!

HIPPOLITO. [*Aside.*] O good deceite, he quits[4] him with
        like tearmes.
I. [VOICE *within*]. Where?
II. [VOICE *within*].   Which way?   100
    [*Enter* AMBITIOSO *and* SUPERVACUO, *with Nobles*
        and Gentlemen.]
AMBITIOSO. Over what roofe hangs this prodigious
        Comet,
  In deadly fire.
LUSSURIOSO.   Behold, behold, my Lords!
  The Duke my father's murderd by a vassaile
  That owes[5] this habit[6] and here left disguisde.
      [*Enter the* DUCHESS *with* SPURIO.]
DUCHESS. My Lord and husband.
[I. NOBLE].   Reverend Majesty.   105
[II. NOBLE]. I have seene these cloths often attending on
        him.
VINDICE. [*Aside.*] That Nobleman has bin ith Country,
        for he dos not lie.
SUPERVACUO. [*Aside.*] Learne of our mother, let's dis-
        semble to.
  I am glad hee's vanisht; so, I hope, are you.   110
AMBITIOSO. [*Aside.*] I, you may take my word fort.
SPURIO. Old Dad dead?
  I, one of his cast sinnes, will send the Fates
  Most hearty commendations by his owne sonne;
  Ile tug in the new streame till strength be done.   115
LUSSURIOSO. Where be those two, that did affirme to us
  My Lord the Duke was privately rid forth?
I. [GENTLEMAN]. O pardon us, my Lords, hee gave that
        charge
  Upon our lives, if he were mist at Court,
  To answer so; hee rode not any where.   120
  We left him private with that fellow here.
VINDICE. [*Aside.*] Confirmde.
LUSSURIOSO. O heavens, that false charge was his death!

---

[4] *quits* : repays.   [6] *habit* : clothing.
[5] *owes* : owns.

Impudent Beggars! durst you to our face
Maintaine such a false answer? Beare him straight   125
To execution.
1. [GENTLEMAN]. My Lord!
LUSSURIOSO.   Urge me no more.
In this the excuse may be cal'd halfe the murther.
VINDICE. [*Aside.*] You've sentencde well.
LUSSURIOSO.   Away, see it
                    be done.
               [*Exit* GENTLEMAN *under guard.*]
VINDICE. [*Aside.*] Could you not stick? See what con-
                    fession doth.
Who would not lie when men are hangd for truth?   130
HIPPOLITO. [*Aside.*] Brother, how happy is our venge-
                    ance!
VINDICE. [*Aside.*] Why, it hits
Past the apprehension of indifferent wits.
LUSSURIOSO. My Lord, let post-horse be sent
Into all places to intrap the villaine.   135
VINDICE. [*Aside.*] Post-horse! ha, ha.
[1.] NOBLE. My Lord, we're som-thing bould to know
                    our duety.
Your father's accidentally departed;
The titles that were due to him meete you.
LUSSURIOSO. Meete me? I'me not at leisure, my good   140
                    Lord.
I've many greefes to dispatch out a' th' way.
[*Aside.*] Welcome, sweete titles.—Talke to me, my
                    Lords,
Of sepulchers, and mighty Emperors bones;
That's thought for me.
VINDICE. [*Aside.*] So, one may see by this   145
How forraine markets7 goe :
Courtiers have feete a' th' nines, and tongues a' th'
                    twelves;8
They flatter Dukes and Dukes flatter them-selves.

                              8 Tongues three sizes larger than
7 Alienated or abandoned titles.   feet.

[II.] NOBLE. My Lord, it is your shine must comfort us.

LUSSURIOSO. Alas, I shine in teares, like the Sunne in   150
           Aprill.

[I.] NOBLE. You'r now my Lords grace.

LUSSURIOSO. My Lords grace! I perceive youle have it
           so.

[II.] NOBLE. Tis but your owne.

LUSSURIOSO. Then, heavens give me grace to be so!

VINDICE. [*Aside.*] He praies wel for him-selfe.   155

[I.] NOBLE. [*to the* DUCHESS.] Madame, all sorrowes
     Must runne their circles into joyes; no doubt
     But time wil make the murderer bring forth him-selfe.

VINDICE. [*Aside.*] He were an Asse then, yfaith.

[I.] NOBLE. In the meane season,   160
     Let us bethinke the latest funerall honors
     Due to the Dukes cold bodie;—and withall
     Calling to memory our new happinesse
     Spreade in his royall sonne, Lords, Gentlemen,
     Prepare for Revells.

VINDICE. [*Aside.*] Revells!   165

[I.] NOBLE. Time hath severall falls;
     Greefes lift up joyes, feastes put downe funeralls.

LUSSURIOSO. Come then, my Lords, my favours to you
           all.
     [*Aside.*] The Duchesse is suspected fowly bent;
     Ile beginne Dukedome with her banishment.   170
         Exeunt [LUSSURIOSO], *Nobles and* DUCHESS.

HIPPOLITO. [*Aside.*] Revells!

VINDICE. [*Aside.*]   I, that's the word, we are
           firme yet;
     Strike one straine more, and then we crowne our wit.
                     Exeunt Brothers.

SPURIO. Well, have [at] the[4] fayrest marke,—
     So sayd the Duke when he begot me;
     And if I misse his heart or neere about,   175
     Then have at any;—a Bastard scornes to be out.
                      [*Exit.*]

SUPERVACUO. Not'st thou that Spurio, brother?

AMBITIOSO. Yes, I note him to our shame.

supervacuo. He[5] shall not live; his haire shall not
           grow much longer.
In this time of Revells, tricks may be set a-foote.   180
Seest thou yon new Moone? It shall out-live
The new Duke by much; this hand shall dispossesse
Him, then we're mighty.[5]
A maske is treasons licence, that build upon;
Tis murders best face when a vizard's[9] on.[3]   185
                  Exit supervacuo.
ambitioso. Ist so? Tis very good.
And do you thinke to be Duke then, kinde brother?
Ile see faire play; drop one, and there lies tother.
                  Exit ambitioso.

[Act V. Scene ii.]

Enter vindice *and* hippolito, *with* piero *and*
other Lords.

vindice. My Lords, be all of Musick! Strike old griefes
            into other countries
That flow in too much milke, and have faint livers,
Not daring to stab home their discontents :
Let our hid flames breake out, as fire, as lightning,
To blast this villanous Dukedome, vext with sinne;   5
Winde up[1] your soules to their full height agen!
piero. How?
i. [lord].   Which way?
[ii. lord].   Any way : our wrongs are such,
We cannot justly be revengde too much.
vindice. You shall have all enough :—Revels are toward,   10
And those few Nobles that have long suppressd you
Are busied to the furnishing of a Maske,
And do affect[1] to make a pleasant taile ont.
The Masking suites are fashioning; now comes in
That which must glad us all—wee too take patterne   15

                     Act V. Scene ii.
[9] *vizard :* mask.   [1] *affect :* desire.

Of all those suites, the colour, trimming, fashion,
E'en to an undistinguisht hayre almost :
Then entring first, observing the true forme,
Within a straine or two we shall finde leasure
To steale our swords out handsomly;   20
And when they thinke their pleasure sweete and
                              good,
In midst of all their joyes, they shall sigh bloud.
PIERO. Weightily, effectually!
III. [LORD]   Before the tother Maskers
                    come—
VINDICE. We're gone, all done and past.
PIERO. But how for the Dukes guard?
VINDICE.   Let that alone;   25
By one and one their strengths shall be drunke
                    downe. (2)
HIPPOLITO. There are five hundred Gentlemen in the
                    action,
That will apply them-selves, and not stand idle.
PIERO. Oh, let us hug our bosomes!2
VINDICE.   Come, my Lords,
Prepare for deeds; let other times have words.   30
                              Exeunt.

[ACT V. SCENE III.]

In a dum shew, the possessing¹ of the young Duke,
with all his Nobles : then sounding Musick.
A furnisht Table is brought forth : then
enters the Duke and his Nobles to the
banquet. A blasing-star
appeareth.

[I.] NOBLE. Many harmonious houres, and choisest
                    pleasures
Fill up the royall numbers of your yeares.

2 *let us . . . bosomes :* be secret   ACT V. SCENE III.
  and resolute.   1 *possessing :* coronation.

LUSSURIOSO. My Lords, we're pleasd to thanke you,—
tho we know
Tis but your duety now to wish it so.
[II.] NOBLE. That shine makes us all happy.
III. NOBLE.   His   Grace   5
                        frounes.
II. NOBLE. Yet we must say he smiles.
I. NOBLE.   I thinke we must.
LUSSURIOSO. [*Aside*.] That foule-Incontinent Duchesse
we have banisht;
The Bastard shall not live : after these Revells
Ile begin strange ones; hee and the stepsonnes
Shall pay their lives for the first subsidies.   10
We must not frowne so soone, else t'ad beene now.
I. NOBLE. My gratious Lord, please you prepare for
pleasure;
The maske is not far off.
LUSSURIOSO.   We are for pleasure.
Beshrew thee! what art thou—madst me start?
Thou hast committed treason.—A blazing star! (1)   15
I. NOBLE. A blazing star! O where, my Lord?
LUSSURIOSO.   Spy out.
II. NOBLE. See, see, my Lords, a wondrous-dreadful one!
LUSSURIOSO. I am not pleasd at that ill-knotted fire,
That bushing-flaring star,—am not I Duke?
It should not quake me now : had it appeard   20
Before it,² I might then have justly feard.
But yet, they say, whom art and learning Weds :
When stars wear[1] locks, they threaten great-mens
heads.
Is it so? You are read, my Lords.
I. NOBLE. May it please your Grace,   25
It showes great anger.
LUSSURIOSO.   That dos not please our Grace.
II. NOBLE. Yet here's the comfort, my Lord; many times,

2 Before the fact of becoming
Duke.

When it seemes most [near],[2] it threatnes fardest
    off.

LUSSURIOSO. Faith, and I thinke so too.

I. NOBLE.   Beside, my Lord,
    You'r gracefully establisht with the loves   30
    Of all your subjects : and for naturall death,
    I hope it will be threescore years a-comming.

LUSSURIOSO. True,—no more but threescore years?

I. NOBLE. Fourescore, I hope, my Lord.

II. NOBLE.   And fivescore, I.

III. NOBLE. But tis my hope, my Lord, you shall ne'er   35
    die.

LUSSURIOSO. Give me thy hand, these others I rebuke;
    He that hopes so, is fittest for a Duke :
    Thou shalt sit next me. Take your places, Lords,
    We're ready now for sports, let 'em set on.
    You thing! we shall forget you quite anon.   40

III. NOBLE. I heare 'em comming, my Lord.

    Enter the Maske of Revengers, the two Brothers
    [VINDICE *and* HIPPOLITO], *and two Lords more.*

LUSSURIOSO. Ah, tis well.

    [*Aside.*] Brothers, and Bastard, you dance next in
        hell.

    The Revengers daunce. At the end, steale out
    their swords, and these foure kill the foure
    at the Table, in their Chaires.
    It thunders.

VINDICE. Marke, Thunder!
    Dost know thy kue, thou big-voyc'st cryer?   45
    Dukes groanes are thunders watch-words.

HIPPOLITO. So, my Lords, you have ynough.

VINDICE. Come, let's away,—no lingring.

HIPPOLITO.   Follow,—goe!

           Exeunt [*all but* VINDICE.]

VINDICE. No power is angry when the lust-ful die;
    When thunder claps, heaven likes the tragedy.   50

                    Exit VINDICE.

LUSSURIOSO. Oh, oh.

Enter the other Maske of entended murderers, Step-
*sons [*AMBITIOSO, SUPERVACUO*]; Bastard [*SPURIO*];*
and a fourth man, comming in dauncing; the
*Duke [*LUSSURIOSO*] recovers a little in*
voyce, and groanes,—calls "a guard,
treason." At which they all start
out of their measure,[3] and
turning towards the
Table, they finde
them all to be
murdered.

SPURIO. Whose groane was that?
LUSSURIOSO.   Treason!—a guard!
AMBITIOSO. How now?—all murderd!
SUPERVACUO.   Murderd!
IV. [LORD]. And those his Nobles?
AMBITIOSO.   Here's a labour sav'd;
    I thought to have sped him. Sbloud! how came this?   55
[SUPERVACUO].[3] Then I proclaime my selfe! Now I
        am Duke.
AMBITIOSO. Thou Duke! Brother, thou liest.
                [*He slays* SUPERVACUO.]
SPURIO. Slave, so dost thou!   [*He slays* AMBITIOSO.]
IV. [LORD]. Base villayne, hast thou slaine my Lord
        and Maister?   [*He slays* SPURIO.]
   Enter the first men [, VINDICE, HIPPOLITO, *and*
       the two Lords].
VINDICE. Pistolls! treason! murder! Helpe, guard my
        Lord the Duke!   60
    [*Enter* ANTONIO *and the Guard.*]
HIPPOLITO. Lay hold upon this Traytor!
               [*They seize* IV. LORD.]
LUSSURIOSO.   Oh.
VINDICE. Alasse, the Duke is murderd!
HIPPOLITO.   And the Nobles.
VINDICE. Surgeons, Surgeons!—[*Aside.*] Heart, dos he
        breath so long?

[3] *measure :* dance.

ANTONIO. A piteous tragedy! able to [make][4]
    An old-mans eyes bloud-shot.
LUSSURIOSO.   Oh.   65
VINDICE. Looke to my Lord the Duke. [*Aside.*] A venge-
    ance throttle him.—
    Confesse, thou murdrous and unhollowed man,
    Didst thou kill all these?
IV. [LORD].   None but the Bastard, I.
VINDICE. How came the Duke slaine then?
IV. [LORD]. We found him so.
LUSSURIOSO.   O villaine!   70
VINDICE. Harke!
LUSSURIOSO.   Those in the maske did murder us.
VINDICE. Law! you now, sir.
    O marble impudence! will you confesse now?
IV. [LORD]. Sbloud![5] tis all false.
ANTONIO. Away with that foule monster,   75
    Dipt in a Princes bloud.
IV. [LORD].   Heart, tis a lye!
ANTONIO. Let him have bitter execution.
              [*Exit* IV. LORD *under guard.*]
VINDICE. [*Aside.*] New marrow!—No, I cannot be
          exprest.—
    How faires my Lord the Duke?
LUSSURIOSO.   Farewel to al,
    He that climes highest has the greatest fall;   80
    My tong is out of office.
VINDICE. Ayre, Gentlemen, ayre!
    [*He whispers to* LUSSURIOSO.] Now thoult not
    prate ont; twas Vindice murdred thee.
LUSSURIOSO. Oh.
VINDICE. [*Whispers.*]   Murdred thy Father.
LUSSURIOSO. Oh.
VINDICE. [*Whispers.*] And I am he—tell no-body.[(2)]   85
                  [LUSSURIOSO *dies.*]
    So, so, the Duke's departed.
ANTONIO. It was a deadly hand that wounded him;
    The rest, ambitious who should rule and sway

After his death, were so made all away.

VINDICE. My Lord was unlikely.[4]

HIPPOLITO.   Now the hope   90
Of Italy lyes in your reverend yeares.

VINDICE. Your hayre will make the silver age agen,
When there was fewer but more honest men.

ANTONIO. The burden's weighty and will presse age
downe.

May I so rule that heaven may keepe the crowne.   95

VINDICE. The rape of your good Lady has beene quited
With death on death.

ANTONIO.   Just is the Lawe above.
But of al things it puts me most to wonder
How the old Duke came murdred.

VINDICE.   Oh, my Lord.

ANTONIO. It was the strangeliest carried; I not heard of
the like.   100

HIPPOLITO. Twas all doune for the best, my Lord.

VINDICE. All for your graces good. We may be bould to
speake it now.
Twas some-what witty carried, tho we say it;
Twas we two murdred him.

ANTONIO.   You two?

VINDICE. None else ifaith, my Lord—nay, twas well   105
managde.

ANTONIO. Lay hands upon those villaines.

VINDICE.   How!—on us?

ANTONIO. Beare 'em [to][6] speedy execution.

VINDICE. Heart, wast not for your good, my Lord?

ANTONIO. My good?—away with 'em—such an ould man
as he!
You that would murder him would murder me.   110

VINDICE. Ist come about?

HIPPOLITO.   Sfoote, brother, you begun.

VINDICE. May not we set as well as the Dukes sonne?
Thou hast no conscience,—are we not revengde?

---

[4] *unlikely :* unpromising.

Is there one enemy left alive amongst those?
Tis time to die, when we are our selves our foes.   115
When murd[r]ers[7] shut deeds closse, this curse does
              seale 'em;
If none disclose 'em, they them selves reveale 'em!
This murder might have slept in tonglesse brasse,—
But for our selves,—and the world dyed an asse.
Now I remember too, here was Piato   120
Brought forth a knavish sentance once;
No doubt (said he) but time
Will make the murderer bring forth himselfe.
Tis well he died, he was a witch.[5]
And now, my Lord, since we are in for ever :   125
This worke was ours, which else might have beene
              slipt,
And if we list, we could have Nobles clipt,
And go for lesse then beggers; but we hate
To bleed so cowardly. We have ynough,
Yfaith, we're well, our Mother turnd, our Sister true;   130
We die after a nest of Dukes,—adue.
       Exeunt [VINDICE *and* HIPPOLITO *under guard.*]
ANTONIO. How subtilly was that murder closde.[6] Beare
        up
Those tragick bodies; tis a heavy season :
Pray heaven their bloud may wash away all treason.
               [*Exeunt omnes.*]

             FINIS.

---

[5] Because he could prophesy.   [6] *closde :* disclosed.

THE BROKEN HEART

BY

JOHN FORD

THE
BROKEN
HEART.

A Tragedy.

ACTED
By the K I N G's Majesties Seruants
at the priuate Houſe in the
B L A C K-F R I E R S.

Fide Honor.

LONDON:
Printed by *I. B.* for H V G H B E E S T O N, and are to
be ſold at his Shop, neere the *Caſtle* in
Corne-bill ℈ 6 3 3.

TO THE MOST WORTHY DESERVER
OF THE NOBLEST TITLES IN HONOUR,
William, Lord Craven, [1] *Baron of Hamsteed-Marshall.*

MY LORD :

The glory of a *great name*, acquired by a greater glory of *Action*, hath in all ages liv'd the truest chronicle to his owne Memory. In the practise of which Argument, *your grouth* to perfection (even in youth) hath appear'd so sincere, so un-flattering a *Penne-man;* that   5
Posterity cannot with more delight read the merit of *Noble endeavours,* then *noble endeavours* merit thankes from Posterity to be read with delight. Many Nations, many eyes, have beene witnesses of your *Deserts,* and lov'd Them : Be pleas'd then, with the freedome of your own Nature, to admit ONE   10
amongst All, particularly into the list of such as honour a faire Example of Nobilitie. There is a kinde of humble *Ambition,* not un-commendable, when the silence of study breakes forth into Discourse, coveting rather encouragement then Applause; yet herein *Censure* commonly is too severe an Auditor,   15
without the moderation of an able *Patronage.* I have ever beene slow in courtship of greatnesse, not ignorant of such defects as are frequent to *Opinion :* but the Justice of your Inclination to *Industry,* emboldens my weaknesse, of confidence, to rellish an   20
experience of *your Mercy,* as many brave Dangers have tasted of *your Courage.* Your Lordship strove to be knowne to the world (when the world knew you least) by voluntary but excellent *Attempts :* Like Allowance I plead of being knowne to your Lordship (in this low presumption) by tendring to a favourable   25
entertainment, [1] a *Devotion* offred from a heart, that can be as truely sensible of any least respect, as ever professe[d] [2] the owner in my best, my readiest services,

A Lover of your naturall Love to Vertue,
John Ford.

THE SCEANE,
SPARTA. [1]

THE SPEAKERS NAMES, FITTED TO THEIR QUALITIES.

AMYCLAS,	*Common to the Kings of Laconia.*
ITHOCLES, *Honour of lovelinesse,*	*A favourite.*
ORGILUS, *Angry,*	*Sonne to* CROTOLON.
BASSANES, *Vexation,*	*A jealous Nobleman.*
ARMOSTES, *An appeasor,*	*A Counsellor of State.*
CROTOLON, *Noyse,*	*Another Counsellor.*
PROPHILUS, *Deare,*	*Friend to* ITHOCLES.
NEARCHUS, *Young Prince,*	*Prince of Argos.*
TECNICUS, *Artist,*	*A Philosopher.*
HEMOPHIL, [1] *Glutton,* ⎱	
GRONEAS, *Tavernhaunter,* ⎰	*Two Courtiers.*
AMELUS, *Trusty,*	*Friend to* NEARCHUS.
PHULAS, *Watchfull,*	*Servant to* BASSANES.

[*Lords, Courtiers, Officers, Attendants, etc.*]

CALANTHA, *Flower of beauty,*	*The Kings daughter.*
PENTHEA, *Complaint,*	*Sister to* ITHOCLES [*and wife of* BASSANES].
EUPHRANEA, *Joy,*	*A Maid of Honor* [*and daughter of* CROTOLON].
CHRISTALLA, *Christall,* ⎱	
PHILEMA, *A kisse,* ⎰	*Maids of Honour.*
GRAUSIS, *Old Beldam,*	*Overseer of* PENTHEA.

PERSONS INCLUDED.

THRASUS, *Fiercenesse,*	*Father of* ITHOCLES.
APLOTES, *Simplicity,*	ORGILUS *so disguis'd.*

The Prologue.

Our Scaene is *Sparta*. HE whose best of *Art*
Hath drawne *this Peece,* cals it the *Broken Heart.*
The Title lends no expectation here
Of apish laughter, or of some lame Jeere
At place or persons; no pretended clause[1]   5
Of jests fit for a brothell Courts applause
From vulgar admiration : such low songs,
Tun'd to unchast eares, suit not modest tongues.
The Virgine Sisters[2] then deserv'd fresh bayes
When *Innocence* and *Sweetnesse* crown'd their layes :   10
Then vices gasp'd for breath, whose whole Commerce
Was whip'd to Exile by unblushing verse.
This law we keepe in our Presentment now,
Not to take freedome more then we allow;
What may be here thought a *fiction,* when Times   15
               youth
Wanted some riper yeares, was knowne *A Truth*[(1)] :
In which, if words have cloath'd the subject right,
You may pertake a Pitty with Delight.

Actus primus. [Scaena prima.]

Enter CROTOLON *and* ORGILUS.
CROTOLON. Dally not further; I will know the reason
  That speeds thee to this journey.
ORGILUS.   Reason! Good Sir,
  I can yeeld many.
CROTOLON.   Give me one, a good one;
  Such I expect, and ere we part must have :
  Athens? Pray, why to *Athens?* You intend not   5
  To kicke against the world, turne Cynicke, Stoicke,
  Or read the Logicke Lecture, or become

---

[1] *pretended :* offered conclusion.　　[2] *Virgine Sisters :* Muses.

An *Areopagite*,[1] and Judge in causes
Touching the Common-wealth? For, as I take it,
The budding of your chin cannot prognosticate   10
So grave an honour.

ORGILUS.   All this I acknowledge.

CROTOLON. You doe : then, Son, if books and love of
                knowledge
Enflame you to this travell, here in Sparta
 You may as freely study.

ORGILUS.   'Tis not that, Sir.

CROTOLON. Not that, Sir! As a father I command thee   15
To acquaint me with the truth.

ORGILUS.   Thus I obey 'ee :
After so many quarrels, as dissention,
Fury, and Rage had brauch't[1] in blood, and some-
                times
With death to such confederates as sided
With now dead *Thrasus* and your selfe, my Lord,   20
Our present King, Amyclas, reconcil'd
Your eager swords, and Seal'd a gentle peace :
Friends you profest your selves, which to confirme,
A resolution for a lasting league
Betwixt your Families was entertain'd,   25
By joyning in a *Hymenean*[2] bond
Me and the faire Penthea, onely daughter
To *Thrasus*.

CROTOLON.   What of this?

ORGILUS.   Much, much, deere sir.
A freedome of converse, an enterchange
Of holy and chast love so fixt our soules   30
In a firme grouth of holy union,[1] that no Time
Can eat into the pledge; we had enjoy'd
The sweets our vowes expected, had not cruelty
Prevented all those triumphs we prepar'd for,
By *Thrasus* his untimely death.

ACT I. SCENE I.
[1] *Areopagite :* member of the
Athenian court.

CROTOLON.   Most certaine.   35
ORGILUS. From this time sprouted up that poysonous
        stalke
 Of *Aconite*,(3) whose ripened fruit hath ravisht
 All health, all comfort of a happy life :
 For Ithocles, her brother, proud of youth,
 And prouder in his power, nourisht closely²   40
 The memory of former discontents.
 To glory in revenge, by cunning partly,
 Partly by threats, 'a³ wooes at once, and forces
 His virtuous sister to admit a marriage
 With Bassanes, a Noble-man, in honour   45
 And riches, I confesse, beyond my fortunes.
CROTOLON. All this is no sound reason to importune
 My leave for thy departure.
ORGILUS.   Now it followes.
 Beauteous Penthea, wedded to this torture
 By an insulting⁴ brother, being secretly   50
 Compeld to yeeld her virgine freedome up
 To him who never can usurpe her heart
 Before contracted mine, is now so yoak'd
 To a most barbarous thraldome, misery,
 Affliction, that he savors not humanity   55
 Whose sorrow melts not into more then pitty
 In hearing but her name.
CROTOLON.   As how, pray?
ORGILUS.   Bassanes,
 The man that calls her wife, considers truly
 What Heaven of perfections he is Lord of,
 By thinking faire Penthea his : this thought   60
 Begets a kinde of Monster-Love, which Love
 Is nurse unto a feare so strong and servile,
 As brands all dotage with a Jealousie.
 All eyes who gaze upon that shrine of beauty,
 He doth resolve,⁵ doe homage to the miracle;   65
 Some one, he is assur'd, may now or then

---

² *closely* : secretly.   ⁴ *insulting* : overbearing.
³ *'a* : he.   ⁵ *resolve* : is certain.

(If opportunity but sort⁶) prevaile :
So much out of a selfe-unworthinesse
His feares transport him, not that he findes cause
In her obedience, but his owne distrust.   70
CROTOLON. You spin out your discourse.
ORGILUS.   My griefs are
    violent.
For, knowing how the Maid was heretofore
Courted by me, his jealousies grow wild
That I should steale againe into her favours,
And undermine her vertues : which the gods   75
Know I nor dare nor dreame of : hence, from hence
I undertake a voluntary exile.
First, by my absence to take off the cares
Of Jealous Bassanes, but chiefly, Sir,
To free Penthea from a hell on earth :   80
Lastly, to lose the memory of something
Her presence makes to live in me afresh.
CROTOLON. Enough, my Orgilus, enough! To *Athens,*
I give a full consent :—Alas, good Lady!—
Wee shall heare from thee often?
ORGILUS.   Often.
CROTOLON.   See,   85
Thy Sister comes to give a farewell.
        Enter EUPHRANEA.
EUPHRANEA.   Brother.
ORGILUS. Euphranea, thus upon thy cheekes I print
A brothers kisse, more carefull of thine honour,
Thy health, and thy well-doing then my life.
Before we part, in presence of our father,   90
I must preferre a suit to 'ee.
EUPHRANEA.   You may stile it,
My brother, a command.
ORGILUS.   That you will promise
To passe never to any man, how ever worthy,
Your faith, till with our Fathers leave
I give a free consent.

⁶ *sort :* arrange it.

CROTOLON.   An easie motion![7]   95
  I'le promise for her, Orgilus.
ORGILUS.   Your pardon;
  Euphranea's oath must yeeld me satisfaction.
EUPHRANEA. By *Vesta's* sacred fires[(4)] I sweare.
CROTOLON.   And I
  By great Apollo's beames joyne in the vow;
  Not without thy allowance, to bestow her   100
  On any living.
ORGILUS.   Deere Euphranea,
  Mistake me not; farre, farre 'tis from my thought,
  As farre from any wish of mine, to hinder
  Preferment to an honourable bed,
  Or fitting Fortune : thou art young and handsome;   105
  And 'twere injustice—more, a tyrannie—
  Not to advance thy merit. Trust me, Sister,
  It shall be my first care to see thee match'd
  As may become thy choyce, and our contents :
  I have your oath.
EUPHRANEA.   You have : but meane you, brother,   110
  To leave us as you say?
CROTOLON.   I, I, Euphranea :
  He has just grounds direct him : I will prove
  A father and a brother to thee.
EUPHRANEA.   Heaven
  Does looke into the secrets of all hearts :
  Gods, you have mercy with 'ee, else—
CROTOLON.   Doubt[8] nothing.   115
  Thy brother will returne in safety to us.
ORGILUS. Soules sunke in sorrowes never are without
                 'em;
  They change fresh ayres, but beare their griefes about
             'em.   *Exeunt omnes.*

---

[7] *motion :* proposal.   [8] *Doubt :* Fear.

[ACTUS PRIMUS. SCAENA SECUNDA.]

Flourish. Enter AMYCLAS *the King,* ARMOSTES,
        PROPHILUS, *and attendants.*

AMYCLAS. The Spartane gods are gracious; our humility
   Shall bend before their Altars, and perfume
   Their Temples with abundant sacrifice.
   See, Lords, Amyclas your old King, is entring
   Into his youth againe. I shall shake off   5
   This silver badge of age, and change this snow
   For haires as gay as are *Apollo's* lockes;
   Our heart leaps in new vigour!
ARMOSTES.   May old time
   Run backe to double your long life, great Sir!
AMYCLAS. It will, it must, Armostes; thy bold Nephew,   10
   Death-braving Ithocles, brings to our gates
   Triumphs and peace upon his conquering sword.
   Laconia is a monarchy at length;
   Hath in this latter warre trod underfoot
   Messenes pride; *Messene*(1) bowes her necke   15
   To Lacedemons royalty : O 'twas
   A glorious victory, and doth deserve
   More then a Chronicle—a Temple, Lords,
   A Temple to the name of Ithocles!—
   Where didst thou leave him, Prophilus?
PROPHILUS.   At *Pephon,*(2)   20
   Most gracious Soveraigne; twenty of the noblest
   Of the *Messenians* there attend your pleasure
   For such conditions as you shall propose,
   In setling peace and liberty of life.
AMYCLAS. When comes your friend the General?
PROPHILUS.   He promis'd   25
   To follow with all speed convenient.
Enter CROTOLON, CALANTHA, CHRISTALLA, PHILEMA
        [*with a garland*] *and* EUPHRANEA.
AMYCLAS. Our daughter!—Deere Calantha, the happy
                        newes,

The conquest of *Messene*, hath already
Enrich'd thy knowledge.
CALANTHA.   With the circumstance
And manner of the fight related faithfully   30
By Prophilus himselfe; but pray, Sir, tell me,
How doth the youthfull Generall demeane
His actions in these fortunes?
PROPHILUS.   Excellent Princesse,
Your owne faire eyes may soone report a truth
Unto your judgement, with what moderation,   35
Calmenesse of nature, measure, bounds and limits
Of thankefulnesse and joy, 'a doth digest
Such amplitude of his successe, as would
In others, moulded of a spirit lesse cleare,
Advance 'em to comparison with heaven.   40
But Ithocles—
CALANTHA.   Your friend.
PROPHILUS.   He is so, Madam,
In which the period of my Fate consists :
He, in this Firmament of honour, stands
Like a Starre fixt, not mov'd with any thunder
Of popular applause, or sudden lightning   45
Of selfe-opinion : he hath serv'd his Country
And thinks 'twas but his duty.
CROTOLON.   You describe
A miracle of man.
AMYCLAS.   Such, Crotolon,
On forfeit of a Kings word, thou wilt finde him.
                                              Flourish.
Harke, warning of his comming! All attend him.   50
    Enter ITHOCLES, HEMOPHIL, *and* GRONEAS : *the*
        rest of the Lords ushering him in.
Returne into these armes, thy home, thy sanctuary,
Delight of Sparta, treasure of my bosome,
Mine owne, owne Ithocles.
ITHOCLES.   Your humblest subject.
ARMOSTES. Proud of the blood I claime an Interest in,
As brother to thy mother, I embrace thee,   55
Right noble Nephew.

ITHOCLES.   Sir, your love's too partiall.
CROTOLON. Our Country speakes by me, who by thy
                              valour,
Wisdome and service shares in this great action,
Returning thee, in part of thy due merits,
A generall welcom.
ITHOCLES.   You exceed in bounty.   60
CALANTHA.   Christalla,   Philema,   the   Chaplet.(3)—
                              Ithocles,
Upon the wings of Fame, the singular
And chosen fortune of an high attempt
Is borne so past the view of common sight,
That I my selfe, with mine owne hands, have wrought   65
To crowne thy Temples, this provinciall garland.(4)
Accept, weare, and enjoy it, as our gift
Deserv'd, not purchas'd.
ITHOCLES.   Y'are a royall mayd.
AMYCLAS. Shee is in all our daughter.
ITHOCLES.   Let me blush,
Acknowledging how poorely I have serv'd,   70
What nothings I have done, compar'd with th'
                              honours
Heap'd on the issue of a willing minde;
In that lay mine ability, that onely.
For who is he so sluggish from his birth,
So little worthy of a name or country,   75
That owes not out of gratitude for life,
A debt of Service, in what kinde soever
Safety or Counsaile of the Common-wealth
Requires for paiment?
CALANTHA.   'A speaks truth.
ITHOCLES.   Whom heaven
Is pleas'd to stile victorious, there, to such,   80
Applause runs madding, like the drunken priests
In *Bacchus* sacrifices, without Reason,
Voycing the Leader-on a Demi-god :
When as, indeed, each common souldiers blood
Drops downe as current coyne in that hard purchase,   85
As his whose much more delicate condition

Hath suckt the milke of ease. Judgement commands,
But Resolution executes : I use not
Before this royall presence, these fit sleights,[1]
As in contempt of such as can direct :   90
My speech hath other end, not to attribute
All praise to one mans fortune, which is strengthed
By many hands.—For instance, here is Prophilus,
A Gentleman (I cannot flatter truth)
Of much desert; and, though in other ranke,   95
Both Hemophil and Groneas were not missing
To wish their Countries peace; for, in a word,
All there did strive their best, and 'twas our duty.

AMYCLAS. Courtiers turne souldiers?—We vouchsafe our
                              hand,—

                    [*They all kiss his hand.*]

Observe your great example.

HEMOPHIL.   With all diligence.   100

GRONEAS. Obsequiously and hourely.

AMYCLAS.   Some repose
After these toyles are needfull; we must thinke on
Conditions for the Conquered; they expect 'em.
On.—Come, my Ithocles.

                    [PROPHILUS *offers his arm to* EUPHRANEA.]

EUPHRANEA.   Sir, with your favour,
I need not a supporter.

PROPHILUS.   Fate instructs me.   105

     Exeunt. Manent HEMOPHIL, GRONEAS, CHRISTALLA
          et PHILEMA. HEMOPHIL *stayes* CHRISTALLA,
                    GRONEAS, PHILEMA.

CHRISTALLA. With me?

PHILEMA.   Indeed, I dare not stay.

HEMOPHIL.   Sweet Lady,
Souldiers are blunt,—your lip.

CHRISTALLA.   Fye, this is rudenesse;
You went not hence such creatures.

Act I. Scene ii.
[1] *fit sleights :* proper remarks of
self depreciation.

GRONEAS.   Spirit of valour
  Is of a mounting nature.
PHILEMA.   It appeares so :
  Pray, in earnest, how many men apeece   110
  Have you two beene the death of?
GRONEAS.   Faith, not many;
  We were compos'd of mercy.
HEMOPHIL.   For our daring
  You heard the Generals approbation
  Before the King.
CHRISTALLA.   You "wish'd your Countries peace" :
  That shew'd your charity. Where are your spoyles,   115
  Such as the Souldier fights for?
PHILEMA.   They are comming.
CHRISTALLA. By the next Carrier, are they not?
GRONEAS.   Sweet Philema,
  When I was in the thickest of mine enemies,
  Slashing off one mans head, anothers nose,
  Anothers armes and legs,—
PHILEMA.   And   altogether.[1]   120
GRONEAS. Then would I with a sigh remember thee;
  And cry, "Deare Philema, 'tis for thy sake
  I doe these deeds of wonder!"—dost not love me
  With all thy heart now?
PHILEMA.   Now as heretofore.
  I have not put my love to use,[2] the principall   125
  Will hardly yeeld an Interest.
GRONEAS.   By *Mars,*
  I'le marry thee.
PHILEMA.   By *Vulcan,*[(5)] y'are forsworne,
  Except my mind doe alter strangely.
GRONEAS.   One word.
CHRISTALLA. You lye beyond all modesty,—forbeare me.
HEMOPHIL. I'le make thee mistresse of a City, 'tis   130
  Mine owne by conquest.
CHRISTALLA.   By petition; sue for't

---

[2] *use :* usury.

In *Forma pauperis*[3] :—City? Kennell.[6] Gallants,
Off with your F[e]athers,[2] put on aprons, Gallants;
Learne to reele,[4] thrum,[5] or trim a Ladies dog,[7]
And be good quiet soules of peace, Hobgoblins.   135

HEMOPHIL. Christalla!

CHRISTALLA.   Practise to drill hogs, in hope
To share in the Acorns. Souldiers? Corn-cutters;[8]
But not so valiant : they oft-times draw blood,
Which you durst never doe. When you have practis'd
More wit, or more civility, wee'll ranke 'ee   140
I' th' list of men : till then, brave things at armes,
Dare not to speake to us,—most potent Groneas.

PHILEMA. And Hemophil the hardy,—at your services.

                    Exeunt CHRISTALLA *et* PHILEMA.

GRONEAS. They scorne us as they did before we went.

HEMOPHIL. Hang 'em! Let us scorne them and be re-   145
                    veng'd.

GRONEAS. Shall we?

HEMOPHIL.   We will; and when we sleight them
                    thus,
Instead of following them, they'll follow us.
It is a womans nature.

GRONEAS.   'Tis a scurvy one. *Exeunt.*[3]

                [ACTUS PRIMUS. SCAENA TERTIA.]

        Enter TECNICUS, *a Philosopher, and* ORGILUS
            disguised like a Scholler of his.

TECNICUS. Tempt not the Stars, young man; thou canst
                    not play
With the severity of Fate : this change
Of habit[1] and disguise in outward view
Hides not the secrets of thy soule within thee

---

[3] *Forma pauperis :* as a pauper,   [5] *thrum :* make tufts in cloth.
    free of charges in court.   ACT I. SCENE III.
[4] *reele :* wind thread.   [1] *habit :* clothing.

From their quicke-piercing eyes, which dive at all   5
    times
Downe to thy thoughts : in thy aspect I note
A consequence of danger.
ORGILUS.   Give me leave,
  Grave Tecnicus, without fore-dooming[1] destiny,
  Under thy roofe to ease my silent griefes,
  By applying to my hidden wounds the balme   10
  Of thy Oraculous Lectures : if my fortune
  Run such a crooked by-way as to wrest
  My steps to ruine, yet thy learned precepts
  Shall call me backe, and set my footings streight :
  I will not court the world.
TECNICUS.   Ah, Orgilus,   15
  Neglects in young men of delights and life
  Run often to extremities; they care not
  For harmes to others, who contemne their owne.
ORGILUS. But I, most learned Artist, am not so much
  At ods with Nature, that I grutch the thrift[2]   20
  Of any true deserver : nor doth malice
  Of present hopes so checke them with despaire,
  As that I yeeld to thought of more affliction
  Then what is incident to frailty[3] : wherefore
  Impute not this retired course of living   25
  Some little time, to any other cause
  Then what I justly render : the information
  Of an unsetled minde, as the effect
  Must clearely witnesse.
TECNICUS.   Spirit of truth inspire thee!
  On these conditions I conceale thy change,   30
  And willingly admit thee for an Auditor.
  I'le to my study.
ORGILUS.   I to contemplations,
  In these delightfull walkes.—   [*Exit* TECNICUS.]
                    Thus metamorphiz'd,
  I may without suspition hearken after

2 *thrift :* reward.

3 *frailty :* common human
nature.

Pentheas usage and Euphraneas faith :   35
Love, thou art full of mystery! The Deities
Themselves are not secure in searching out
The secrets of those flames, which hidden wast
A breast made tributary to the Lawes
Of beauty; Physicke yet hath never found   40
A remedy to cure a Lovers wound.
Ha! who are those that crosse yon private walke
Into the shadowing grove, in amorous foldings?
    PROPHILUS *passeth over, supporting* EUPHRANEA,
              and whispering.
My Sister, O my Sister! 'Tis Euphranea
With Prophilus, supported too; I would   45
It were an Apparition; Prophilus
Is Ithocles his friend : it strangely puzles[1] me.
Againe? Helpe me, my booke; this Schollers habit
Must stand my privilege : my mind is busie,
Mine eyes and eares are open.
                  Walke by, reading.
    Enter againe PROPHILUS *and* EUPHRANEA.
PROPHILUS.   Doe not wast   50
The span of this stolne time (lent by the gods
For precious use) in nicenesse!4 Bright Euphranea,
Should I repeat old vowes or study new
For purchase of beleefe to my desires,—
ORGILUS. [*Aside.*] Desires!
PROPHILUS.   My service, my integrity,—   55
ORGILUS. [*Aside.*] That's better.
PROPHILUS.   I should but repeat a
        lesson
Oft conn'd without a prompter but thine eyes.
My Love is honourable,—
ORGILUS. [*Aside.*]   So was mine
To my Penthea : chastly honourable.
PROPHILUS. Nor wants there more addition to my wish   60
Of happinesse then having thee a wife,
Already sure of Ithocles, a friend

---

4 *nicenesse :* scrupulous shyness.

Firme and un-alterable.

ORGILUS. [*Aside.*]   But a brother
More cruell then the grave.

EUPHRANEA.   What can you looke for
In answer to your noble protestations,   65
From an unskilfull[5] mayd, but language suited
To a divided minde?

ORGILUS. [*Aside.*] Hold out, Euphranea!

EUPHRANEA. Know, Prophilus, I never under-valued
(From the first time you mentioned worthy love)
Your merit, meanes, or person : it had beene   70
A fault of judgement in me, and a dulnesse
In my affections, not to weigh and thanke
My better Starres, that offered me the grace
Of so much blisfulnesse. For to speake truth,
The law of my desires kept equall pace   75
With yours, nor have I left that resolution;
But onely, in a word, what-ever choyce
Lives nearest in my heart, must first procure
Consent both from my father and my brother,
Ere he can owne me his.

ORGILUS. [*Aside.*]   She is forsworne else.   80

PROPHILUS. Leave me that taske.

EUPHRANEA.   My brother, ere he parted
To *Athens,* had my oath.

ORGILUS. [*Aside.*]   Yes, yes, 'a had sure.

PROPHILUS. I doubt not, with the meanes the Court
                                    supplies,
But to prevaile at pleasure.

ORGILUS. [*Aside.*]   Very likely.

PROPHILUS. Meane time, best, dearest, I may build my   85
                                    hopes
On the foundation of thy constant suffrance
In any opposition.[6]

EUPHRANEA.   Death shall sooner
Divorce life and the joyes I have in living,

---

[5] *unskilfull :* innocent.

[6] *constant . . . opposition :*

faithfulness under opposing
forces.

Then my chast vowes from truth.

PROPHILUS.   On thy faire hand
I seale the like.

ORGILUS. [*Aside.*] There is no faith in woman.—   90
Passion! O be contained! My very heart strings
Are on the Tenters.[7]

EUPHRANEA.   Sir, we are over-heard;
Cupid protect us : 'twas a stirring, Sir,
Of some one neere.

PROPHILUS.   Your feares are needlesse, Lady;
None have accesse into these private pleasures,   95
Except some neere in Court or bosome Student
From Tecnicus his Oratory,[2] granted
By speciall favour lately from the King
Unto the grave Philosopher.

EUPHRANEA.   Me thinkes
I heare one talking to himselfe : I see him.   100

PROPHILUS. 'Tis a poore Scholler, as I told you, Lady.

ORGILUS. [*Aside.*] I am discovered.—Say it : is it possible,
With a smooth tongue, a leering countenance,
Flattery, or force of reason (—I come t'ee, Sir)
To turne, or to appease the raging Sea?   105
Answer to that.—Your Art? What Art to catch
And hold fast in a net the Sunnes small Atomes?
No, no; they'll out, they'll out; ye may as easily
Out-run a Cloud driven by a Northerne blast
As fiddle-faddle so. Peace, or speake sense.[3]   110

EUPHRANEA. Call you this thing a Scholler? 'Las, hee's
                                    lunaticke.

PROPHILUS. Observe him, sweet, 'tis but his recreation.

ORGILUS. But will you heare a little! You are so teatchy,
You keepe no rule in argument; Philosophy
Workes not upon impossibilities,   115
But naturall conclusions.—Mew!—absurd;[4]
The metaphisicks are but speculations[5]
Of the celestiall bodies, or such accidents[6]
As not mixt perfectly, in the Ayre ingendred,

---

[7] *Tenters :* Stretching hooks.

Appeare to us unnaturall; that's all.   120
Prove it;—yet, with a reverence to your gravity,
I'le baulke illiterate sawcinesse, submitting
My sole opinion to the touch[8] of writers.
PROPHILUS. Now let us fall in with him.

                                        [*They approach.*]
ORGILUS.   Ha, ha, ha!
These   Apish   boyes,   when   they   but   tast   the   125
                Grammates[9]
And principals of Theory, imagine
They can oppose their teachers. Confidence
Leads many into errors.
PROPHILUS.   By your leave, Sir.
EUPHRANEA. Are you a Scholler, friend?
ORGILUS.   I am, gay creature,
With pardon of your Deities, a mushrome   130
On whom the dew of heaven drops now and then:
The Sunne shines on me too, I thanke his beames;
Sometime I feele their warmth, and eat and sleepe.
PROPHILUS. Does Tecnicus read to thee?[10]
ORGILUS.   Yes, forsooth,
He is my master surely; yonder dore   135
Opens upon his Study.
PROPHILUS.   Happy creatures;
Such people toyle not, sweet, in heats of State,
Nor sinke in thawes of greatnesse: their affections
Keepe order with the limits of their modesty:
Their love is love of vertue.—What's thy name?   140
ORGILUS. Aplotes, sumptuous master, a poore wretch.
EUPHRANEA. Dost thou want any thing?
ORGILUS.   Books, *Venus,*
                books.
PROPHILUS. Lady, a new conceit[11] comes in my thought,
And most availeable for both our comforts.
EUPHRANEA. My Lord.—

[8] *touch* : touchstone, test by   [10] *read to thee* : teach you by
  authorities.   lecturing.
[9] *Grammates* : Fundamentals.   [11] *conceit* : idea.

PROPHILUS.   Whiles I endevour to deserve   145
   Your fathers blessing to our loves, this Scholler
   May daily at some certaine houres attend
   What notice I can write of my successe,
   Here in this grove, and give it to your hands :
   The like from you to me; so can we never,   150
   Barr'd of our mutuall speech, want sure intelligence;
   And thus our hearts may talke when our tongues
             cannot.
EUPHRANEA. Occasion is most favourable; use it.
PROPHILUS. Aplotes, wilt thou wait us twice a day,
   At nine i' th' morning, and at foure at night,   155
   Here in this Bower, to convey such letters
   As each shall send to other? Doe it willingly,
   Safely, and secretly, and I will furnish
   Thy Study, or what else thou canst desire.
ORGILUS. *Jove,* make me thankfull, thankfull, I beseech   160
            thee,
   Propitious *Jove!* I will prove sure and trusty.
   You will not faile me bookes?
PROPHILUS.   Nor ought besides
   Thy heart can wish. This Ladies name's Euphranea,
   Mine Prophilus.
ORGILUS.   I have a pretty memory;
   It must prove my best friend.—I will not misse   165
   One minute of the houres appointed.
PROPHILUS.   Write
   The bookes thou wouldst have bought thee in a note,
   Or take thy selfe some money.
ORGILUS.   No, no money :
   Money to Schollers is a spirit invisible,
   We dare not finger it; or bookes, or nothing.   170
PROPHILUS. Bookes of what sort thou wilt : doe not
            forget
   Our names.
ORGILUS.   I warrant 'ee, I warrant 'ee.
PROPHILUS. Smile, *Hymen,* on the grouth of our desires,
   Wee'll feed thy torches with eternall fires.
     Exeunt [PROPHILUS *and* EUPHRANEA]. *Manet* ORGILUS.

ORGILUS. Put out thy Torches, *Hymen*, or their light   175
    Shall meet a darkenesse of eternall night.
    Inspire me, *Mercury*, with swift deceits;
    Ingenious Fate has lept into mine armes
    Beyond the compasse of my braine!—Mortality
    Creeps on the dung of earth and cannot reach   180
    The riddles which are purpos'd by the gods.
    Great Arts best write themselves in their owne stories;
    They dye too basely who out-live their glories.   *Exit.*

ACTUS SECUNDUS. SCAENA PRIMA.

Enter BASSANES *and* PHULAS.

BASSANES. I'le have that window next the street dam'd
                  up;
    It gives too full a prospect to temptation,
    And courts a Gazers glances : there's a lust
    Committed by the eye, that sweats and travels,[1]
    Plots, wakes, contrives, till the deformed bear-whelpe   5
    Adultery be lick'd[(1)] into the act,
    The very act; that light shall be dam'd up;
    D'ee heare, Sir?
PHULAS.   I doe heare, my Lord; a Mason
    Shall be provided suddenly.[2]
BASSANES.   Some Rogue,
    Some Rogue of your confederacy, factor[3]   10
    For slaves and strumpets, to convey close packets[4]
    From this spruce springall[(2)] and the tother
                  youngster,
    That gawdy Eare-wrig,[5, (3)] or my Lord, your
                   Patron,
    Whose pensioner you are.—I'le tear thy throat out,
    Sonne of a Cat, ill-looking Hounds-head—rip up   15

ACT II. SCENE I.   [3] *factor :* agent.
[1] *travels :* labors.   [4] *close packets :* secret letters.
[2] *suddenly :* immediately.   [5] *Eare-wrig :* Insinuator.

Thy ulcerous maw, if I but scent a paper,
A scroll, but halfe as big as what can cover
A wart upon thy nose, a spot, a pimple,
Directed to my Lady : it may prove
A mystical preparative to lewdnesse.   20
PHULAS. Care shall be had.—I will turne every thread
    About me to an eye.—[*Aside.*] Here's a sweet life.
BASSANES. The City houswives, cunning in the traffique
    Of Chamber-merchandise, set all at price
    By whole-sale, yet they wipe their mouthes and   25
            simper,
    Cull,⁶ kisse, and cry "Sweet-hart," and stroake the
            head
    Which they have branch'd,⁷ and all is well againe :
    Dull clods of dirt, who dare not feele the rubs
    Stucke on [their][¹] fore-heads!
PHULAS.   'Tis a villanous world;
    One cannot hold his owne in't.
BASSANES.   Dames at Court,   30
    Who flaunt in riots, runne another byas⁸ :
    Their pleasure heaves the patient Asse that suffers
    Upon the stilts of Office, titles, Incomes;
    Promotion justifies the shame and sues for't :
    Poore Honour! thou art stab'd, and bleed'st to death   35
    By such unlawfull hire. The Country mistresse
    Is yet more wary, and in blushes hides
    What ever trespasse drawes her troth to guilt;
    But all are false. On this truth I am bold.
    No woman but can fall, and doth, or would.—   40
    Now for the newest newes about the Citie;
    What blab the voyces, sirrah?[²]
PHULAS.   O my Lord,
    The rarest, quaintest, strangest, tickling newes
    That ever—
BASSANES.   Hey da! up and ride⁽⁴⁾ me, Rascall!
    What is't?

---

⁶ *Cull :* Embrace.   ⁸ *byas :* course.
⁷ *branch'd :* with horns.

PHULAS. Forsooth, they say the King has mew'd[9]   45
   All his gray beard, in stead of which is budded
   Another of a pure Carnation colour,
   Speckled with Greene and Russet.
BASSANES.   Ignorant blocke!
PHULAS. Yes truly, and 'tis talkt about the streets,
   That since Lord Ithocles came home, the Lyons   50
   Never left roaring, at which noyse the Beares
   Have danc'd their very hearts out.
BASSANES.   Dance out thine too.
PHULAS. Besides, Lord Orgilus is fled to *Athens*
   Upon a fiery Dragon, and 'tis thought
   'A never can returne.
BASSANES.   Grant it, *Apollo*.   55
PHULAS. Moreover, please your Lordship, 'tis reported
   For certaine, that who ever is found jealous
   Without apparant proofe that's wife is wanton,
   Shall be divorc'd : but this is but she-newes,—
   I had it from a midwife. I have more yet.   60
BASSANES. Anticke,[10] no more! Ideots and stupid
                        fooles
   Grate my calamities. Why to be faire
   Should yeeld presumption of a faulty soule!—
   Looke to the doores.
PHULAS. [*Aside.*]   The horne[5] of plenty crest him.
                                        Exit PHULAS.
BASSANES. Swormes of confusion huddle in my thoughts   65
   In rare distemper. Beauty! O it is
   An unmatcht blessing or a horrid curse.
        Enter PENTHEA *and* GRAUSIS,[3] *an old Lady.*
   Shee comes, she comes! So shoots the morning forth,
   Spangled with pearles of transparent dew;
   The way to poverty is to be rich,   70
   As I in her am wealthy, but for her
   In all contents a Bankrupt.—Lov'd Penthea,
   How fares my hearts best joy?

9 *mew'd :* lost (like a falcon its   10 *Anticke :* Fool.
feathers).

GRAUSIS.   In sooth not well,
   She is so over-sad.
BASSANES.   Leave chattering, Mag-pye.—
   Thy brother is return'd, sweet, safe and honour'd   75
   With a Triumphant victory : thou shalt visit him;
   We will to Court, where, if it be thy pleasure,
   Thou shalt appeare in such a ravishing lustre
   Of Jewels above value, that the Dames
   Who brave it there,[11] in rage to be out-shin'd,   80
   Shall hide them in their Closets and unseene
   Fret in their teares; whiles every wondring eye
   Shall crave none other brightnesse but thy presence.
   Choose thine owne recreations; be a Queene
   Of what delights thou fanciest best, what company,   85
   What place, what times; doe any thing, doe all things
   Youth can command, so thou wilt chase these clouds
   From the pure firmament of thy faire lookes.
GRAUSIS. Now 'tis well said, my Lord! What, Lady,
                 laugh!
   Be merry, time is precious.
BASSANES.   Furies whip thee.   90
PENTHEA. Alas, my Lord, this language to your Hand-
                 maid
   Sounds as would musicke to the deafe : I need
   No braveries nor cost of Art to draw
   The whitenesse of my name into offence;
   Let such (if any such there are) who covet   95
   A curiosity of admiration
   By laying out their plenty to full view,
   Appeare in gawdy out-sides; my attires
   Shall suit the inward fashion of my minde;
   From which, if your opinion nobly plac'd   100
   Change not the Livory your words bestow,
   My Fortunes with my hopes are at the highest.
BASSANES. This house, me thinkes, stands somewhat too
              much inward;

[11] *Who brave it there* : Who
   glorify themselves.

It is too melancholy; wee'll remove
Nearer the Court; or what thinks my Penthea   105
Of the delightfull Island we command?
Rule me as thou canst wish.

PENTHEA.   I am no Mistresse;
Whither you please, I must attend; all wayes
Are alike pleasant to me.

GRAUSIS.   Island? Prison!
A prison is as gaysome : wee'll no Islands :   110
Marry, out upon 'em! Whom shall we see there?
Sea-guls, and Porpises,[4] and water-rats,
And Crabs, and Mewes,[12] and Dogfish! Goodly
                    geere
For a young Ladies dealing, or an old ones!
On no termes Islands; I'le be stew'd first.   115

BASSANES.   Grausis,
You are a Jugling Bawd.—This sadnesse, sweetest,
Becomes not youthfull blood.—[*Aside to* GRAUSIS.] I'le
                    have you pounded.—
For my sake put on a more chearefull mirth;
Thou't marre thy cheekes and make me old in
                    griefes.—
[*Aside to* GRAUSIS.] Damnable Bitch-foxe!

GRAUSIS.   I am thicke 120
                    of hearing
Still[13] when the wind blowes Southerly. What
                    think 'ee,
If your fresh Lady breed young bones, my Lord?
Wood not a chopping[6] boy d'ee good at heart?
But as you said,—

BASSANES.   I'le spit thee on a stake,
Or chop thee into collops.[7]

GRAUSIS.   Pray, speake louder. 125
Sure, sure, the wind blowes South still.

PENTHEA.   Thou prat'st
                    madly.

---

[12] *Mewes* : another term for sea-   [13] *Still* : Always.
gull.

BASSANES. 'Tis very hot; I sweat extreamely.—
                    Enter PHULAS.
                                                    Now?
PHULAS. A heard of Lords, Sir.
BASSANES.   Ha?
PHULAS.   A flock of Ladies.
BASSANES. Where?
PHULAS.   Shoalds of horses.
BASSANES.   Peasant, how?
PHULAS.   Caroches[14]
    In drifts,—th' one enter, th' other stand without, sir.   130
    And now I vanish.   *Exit* PHULAS.
            Enter PROPHILUS, HEMOPHIL, GRONEAS,
                  CHRISTALLA, *and* PHILEMA.
PROPHILUS.   Noble Bassanes.
BASSANES. Most welcome, Prophilus, Ladies,' Gentlemen;
    To all my heart is open, you all honour me.
    [*Aside.*] A tympany[(8)] swels in my head already.—
    Honour me bountifully.—[*Aside.*] How they flutter,   135
    Wagtailes and Jayes together!
PHOPHILUS.   From your brother,
    By virtue of your love to him, I require
    Your instant presence, fairest.
PENTHEA.   He is well, Sir?
PROPHILUS. The gods preserve him ever! Yet, deare
                            beauty,
    I finde some alteration in him lately,   140
    Since his returne to Sparta. My good Lord,
    I pray use no delay.
BASSANES.   We had not needed
    An invitation, if his sisters health
    Had not fallen into question.—Hast, Penthea,
    Slacke not a minute : Lead the way, good Prophilus,   145
    I'le follow step by step.
PROPHILUS.   Your arme, faire Madam.
            Exeunt omnes sed[15] BASSANES *and* GRAUSIS.

---

[14] *Caroches :* Coaches.   [15] *omnes sed :* all but.

BASSANES. One word with your old Bawdship : th' hadst
                                bin better
Raild   at   the   sinnes[5]   thou   worshipst,   then   have
                                thwarted
My will. I'le use thee cursedly.
GRAUSIS.   You dote,
You are beside your selfe. A Politician   150
In jealousie? No, y'are too grosse, too vulgar.
Pish! teach not me my trade, I know my cue :
My crossing you sinks me into her trust,
By which I shall know all : my trade's a sure one.
BASSANES. Forgive me, Grausis; 'twas consideration   155
I rellisht not,[16] but have a care now.
GRAUSIS.   Feare not,
I am no new-come-too't.
BASSANES.   Thy life's upon it,
And so is mine. My Agonies are infinite.
                                        Exeunt omnes.

[ACTUS SECUNDUS. SCAENA SECUNDUS.]

Enter ITHOCLES *alone.*
ITHOCLES. Ambition! 'tis of vipers[1] breed, it knawes
A passage through the wombe that gave it motion.
Ambition! like a seeled Dove,[1] mounts upward,
Higher and higher still, to pearch on clouds,
But tumbles headlong downe with heavier ruine.   5
So squibs and crackers flye into the ayre,
Then onely breaking with a noyse, they vanish
In stench and smoke : Morality appli'd
To timely practice, keeps the soule in tune,
At whose sweet musicke all our actions dance;   10
But this is forme of books and schoole-tradition,[2, (2)]
It physicks not the sicknesse of a minde

---

[16] *I rellisht not :* a fine point I   sewn shut.
did not appreciate.   [2] *schoole-tradition :* scholastic
ACT II. SCENE II.   teaching.
[1] *seeled Dove :* with eyelids

Broken with griefes : strong Feavers are not eas'd
With counsell, but with best receipts and meanes :
Meanes, speedy meanes, and certaine! that's the cure.   15
         Enter ARMOSTES *and* CROTOLON.
ARMOSTES. You sticke, Lord Crotolon, upon a point
  Too nice,[3] and too unnecessary. Prophilus
  Is every way desertfull. I am confident
  Your wisdome is too ripe to need instruction
  From your sonnes tutillage.
CROTOLON.   Yet not so ripe,   20
  My Lord Armostes, that it dares to dote
  Upon the painted meat of smooth perswasion,
  Which tempts me to a breach of faith.
ITHOCLES.   Not yet
  Resolv'd, my Lord? Why, if your sonnes consent
  Be so availeable, wee'll write to *Athens*   25
  For his repaire to Sparta. The Kings hand
  Will joyne with our desires; he has beene mov'd too't.
ARMOSTES. Yes, and the King himselfe importun'd
              Crotolon
  For a dispatch.
CROTOLON.   Kings may command, their wils
  Are Lawes not to be questioned.
ITHOCLES.   By this marriage   30
  You knit a union so devout, so hearty,
  Betweene your loves to me, and mine to yours,
  As if mine owne blood had an interest in it;
  For Prophilus is mine, and I am his.
CROTOLON. My Lord, my Lord!
ITHOCLES.   What, good Sir? Speak   35
          your thoght.
CROTOLON. Had this sincerity beene reall once,
  My Orgilus had not beene now un-wiv'd,
  Nor your lost Sister buried in a Bride-bed.
  Your Unckle here, Armostes, knowes this truth,
  For had your father Thrasus liv'd,—but peace   40
  Dwell in his grave : I have done.

[3] *nice :* finicky.

ARMOSTES.   Y'are bold and bitter.

ITHOCLES. [*Aside.*] 'A presses home the injury, it
        smarts.—
No reprehensions, Uncle, I deserve 'em.
Yet, gentle Sir, consider what the heat
Of an unsteady youth, a giddy braine,   45
Greene indiscretion, flattery of greatnesse,
Rawnesse of judgement, wilfulnesse in folly,
Thoughts vagrant as the wind, and as uncertaine,
Might lead a boy in yeeres too; 'twas a fault,
A Capitall fault, for then I could not dive   50
Into the secrets of commanding Love :
Since when, experience by the extremities (in others)
Hath forc'd me to collect.[4] And trust me, Crotolon,
I will redeeme those wrongs with any service
Your satisfaction can require for currant.[5]   55

ARMOSTES. Thy acknowledgement is satisfaction.
What would you more?

CROTOLON.   I'me conquered : if Euphranea
Her selfe admit the motion, let it be so.
I doubt not my sonnes liking.

ITHOCLES.   Use my fortunes,
Life, power, sword, and heart, all are your owne.   60

    Enter BASSANES, PROPHILUS, CALANTHA, PENTHEA,
      EUPHRANEA, CHRISTALLA, PHILEMA, *and* GRAUSIS.

ARMOSTES. The Princesse with your sister.

CALANTHA.   I present 'ee
A stranger here in Court, my Lord, for did not
Desire of seeing you draw her abroad,
We had not beene made happy in her company.

ITHOCLES. You are a gracious Princesse.—Sister, wed-   65
     locke
Holds too severe a passion in your nature,
Which can engrosse all duty to your husband,
Without attendance on so deare a mistresse.
'Tis not my brothers pleasure, I presume,
T' immure her in a chamber.

---

[4] *collect :* realize, infer.   [5] *currant :* present value.

BASSANES.   'Tis her will,   70
  Shee governes her owne houres; noble Ithocles,
  We thanke the gods for your successe and welfare.
  Our Lady has of late beene indispos'd,
  Else we had waited on you with the first.
ITHOCLES. How does Penthea now?
PENTHEA.   You best know, brother,   75
  From whom my health and comforts are deriv'd.
BASSANES. [*Aside.*] I like the answer well; 'tis sad[6] and
                      modest;
  There may be tricks yet, tricks.—Have an eye,
                      Grausis.
CALANTHA. Now, Crotolon, the suit we joyn'd in must
                      not
  Fall by too long demurre.
CROTOLON.   'Tis granted, Princesse,   80
  For my part.
ARMOSTES.   With condition that his sonne
  Favour the Contract.
CALANTHA.   Such delay is easie.
  The joyes of marriage make thee, Prophilus,
  A proud deserver of Euphranea's love,
  And her of thy desert.
PROPHILUS.   Most sweetly gracious.   85
BASSANES. The joyes of marriage are the heaven on
                  earth,
  Life's paradise, great Princesse, the soules quiet,
  Sinewes of concord, earthly immortality,
  Eternity of pleasures; no restorative's
  Like to a constant woman.—[*Aside.*] (But where is   90
                  she?
  'Twould puzzle all the gods but to create
  Such a new monster.)—I can speake by proofe,
  For I rest in *Elizium*, 'tis my happinesse.
CROTOLON. Euphranea, how are you resolv'd, speak
                freely,
  In your affections to this Gentleman?   95

[6] *sad :* serious.

EUPHRANEA. Nor more, nor less, then as his love assures
                              me,
  Which (if your liking with my brothers warrants)
  I cannot but approve in all points worthy.
CROTOLON. So, so. [*to* PROPHILUS.] I know your answer.
ITHOCLES.   'T had
                           bin pitty
  To sunder hearts so equally consented.   100
                  Enter HEMOPHIL.
HEMOPHIL. The King, Lord Ithocles, commands your
                           presence;
  And, fairest Princesse, yours.
CALANTHA.   We will attend him.
                  Enter GRONEAS.
GRONEAS. Where are the Lords? All must unto the King
  Without delay : the Prince of *Argos*—
CALANTHA.   Well, Sir?
GRONEAS. Is comming to the Court, sweet Lady.
CALANTHA.   How!   105
  The Prince of *Argos*?
GRONEAS.   'Twas my fortune, Madam,
  T' enjoy the honour of these happy tidings.
ITHOCLES. Penthea!
PENTHEA.   Brother?
ITHOCLES.   'Let me an howre hence
  Meet you alone, within the Palace grove;
  I have some secret with you.—Prethee,[1] friend,   110
  Conduct her hither, and have speciall care
  The walks be clear'd of any to disturbe us.
PROPHILUS. I shall.
BASSANES. [*Aside.*] How's that?
ITHOCLES.   Alone, pray be alone.—
  I am your creature, princesse.—On, my Lords.
                     Exeunt [all but] BASSANES.
BASSANES. Alone, alone! What meanes that word   115
                        "alone"?
  Why might not I be there?—Hum!—hee's her brother;
  Brothers and sisters are but flesh and blood,
  And this same whorson Court-ease is temptation

To a rebellion in the veins : —besides,
His fine friend Prophilus must be her guardian.   120
Why may not he dispatch a businesse nimbly
Before the other come?—or—pandring, pandring,
For one another? Bee't to sister, mother,
Wife, couzen, any thing, 'mongst youths of mettall,
Is in request : it is so—stubborne Fate!   125
But if I be a Cuckold, and can know it,
I will be fell,[7] and fell.

Enter GRONEAS.

GRONEAS.   My Lord, y'are call'd for.
BASSANES. Most hartily I thanke ye. Where's my wife,
                                         pray?
GRONEAS. Retir'd amongst the Ladies.
BASSANES.   Still I thanke 'ee :
There's an old waiter[8] with her; saw you her too?   130
GRONEAS. She sits i' th' presence Lobby fast asleepe, Sir.
BASSANES. Asleepe? 'sleepe, Sir!
GRONEAS.   Is your Lordship troubled?
You will not to the King?
BASSANES.   Your humblest Vassaile.
GRONEAS. Your servant, my good Lord.
BASSANES.   I wait your footsteps.
Exeunt.

[ACTUS SECUNDUS. SCAENA TERTIA.]

[*Enter*] PROPHILUS [*and*] PENTHEA.
PROPHILUS. In this walke, Lady, will your brother find
                     you :
And with your favour, give me leave a little
To worke a preparation. In his fashion
I have observ'd of late, some kind of slacknesse
To such alacrity as Nature[1]   5
And custome tooke delight in : Sadnesse growes
Upon his recreations, which he hoards

---

[7] *fell :* cruel.   [8] *waiter :* servant.

In such a willing silence, that to question
The grounds will argue [little] skill[2] in friendship,
And lesse good manners.
PENTHEA.   Sir, I'me not inquisitive   10
Of secrecies without an invitation.
PROPHILUS. With pardon, Lady, not a sillable
Of mine implyes so rude a sense; the drift—
         Enter ORGILUS [*disguised as* APLOTES].
[*To* ORGILUS.] Doe thy best
To make this Lady merry for an houre.   *Exit.*   15
ORGILUS. Your will shall be law, Sir.
PENTHEA.   Prethee,[3] leave me;
I have some private thoughts I would account with:
Use thou thine owne.
ORGILUS.   Speake on, faire nimph; our
                         soules
Can dance as well to musicke of the Spheares
As any's who have feasted with the gods.   20
PENTHEA. Your Schoole[1] terms are too troublesome.
ORGILUS.   What heaven
Refines mortality from drosse of earth,
But such as uncompounded beauty hallowes
With glorified perfection?
PENTHEA.   Set thy wits
In a lesse wild proportion.
ORGILUS.   Time can never   25
On the white table of unguilty faith
Write counterfeit dishonour; turne those eyes
(The arrowes of pure love) upon that fire
Which once rose to a flame, perfum'd with vowes
As sweetly scented as the Incense smoking   30
[On *Vesta's* Altars, Virgin teares (like[4]
The holiest odours)] sprinkled dewes to feed 'em,[5]
And to increase their fervour.
PENTHEA.   Be not franticke.
ORGILUS. All pleasures are but meere imagination,
Feeding the hungry appetite with steame   35
And sight of banquet, whilst the body pines,
Not relishing the reall[2] tast of food;

Such is the leannesse of a heart divided
From entercourse of troth-contracted loves;
No horror should deface that precious figure   40
Seal'd with the lively stampe of equall[3] soules.

PENTHEA. Away! some fury hath bewitch'd thy tongue :
The breath of ignorance that flyes from thence,
Ripens a knowledge in me of afflictions
Above all suffrance.—Thing of talke, be gone.   45
Be gone without reply.

ORGILUS.   Be just, Penthea,
In thy commands : when thou send'st forth a doome
Of banishment, know first on whom it lights;
Thus I take off the shrowd, in which my cares
Are folded up from view of common eyes.   50
                    [*He throws off his hood.*]
What is thy sentence next?

PENTHEA.   Rash man, thou layest
A blemish on mine honour with the hazard
Of thy too desperate life : yet I professe,
By all the Lawes of ceremonious wedlocke,
I have not given admittance to one thought   55
Of female change, since cruelty enforc'd
Divorce betwixt my body and my heart :
Why would you fall from goodnesse thus?

ORGILUS.   O rather
Examine me how I could live to say
I have bin much, much wrong'd; 'tis for thy sake   60
I put on this Imposture; deare Penthea,
If thy soft bosome be not turn'd to marble,
Thou't pitty our calamities; my Interest
Confirmes me thou art mine still.

PENTHEA.   Lend your hand;
With both of mine I claspe it thus, thus kisse it,   65
Thus kneele before ye.

ORGILUS.   You instruct my duty.
                    [*They kneel, with clasped hands.*]

PENTHEA. We may stand up.—Have you ought else to
                              urge
Of new demand? As for the old, forget it;

'Tis buried in an everlasting silence,
And shall be, shall be ever. What more would ye?   70
ORGILUS. I would possesse my wife, the equity
    Of very reason bids me.
PENTHEA.   Is that all?
ORGILUS. Why, 'tis the all of me my selfe.
PENTHEA.   Remove
    Your steps some distance from me.

                                        [*He retires.*]
                        At this space
A few words I dare change; but first put on   75
Your borrowed shape.

                        [*He puts on his hood.*]
ORGILUS.   You are obey'd, 'tis done.
PENTHEA. How, Orgilus, by promise I was thine,
    The heavens doe witnesse; they can witnesse too
    A rape done on my truth : how I doe love thee
    Yet, Orgilus, and yet, must best appeare   80
    In tendering thy freedome; for I find
    The constant preservation of thy merit,
    By thy not daring to attempt my fame
    With injury of any loose conceit,
    Which might give deeper wounds to discontents :   85
    Continue this faire race,[1] then though I cannot
    Adde to thy comfort, yet I shall more often
    Remember from what fortune I am fallen,
    And pitty mine owne ruine.—Live, live happy,.
    Happy in thy next choyce, that thou maist people   90
    This barren age with vertues in thy issue :
    And O, when thou art married, thinke on me
    With mercy, not contempt : I hope thy wife,
    Hearing my story, will not scorne my fall :
    Now let us part.
ORGILUS.   Part! Yet advise thee better :   95
    Penthea is the wife to Orgilus,
    And ever shall be.

    ACT II. SCENE III.
[1] *race :* course of action.

PENTHEA.   Never shall nor will.

ORGILUS. How!

PENTHEA.   Heare me, in a word I'le tell thee why :
    The Virgin dowry which my birth bestow'd
    Is ravish'd by another : my true love   100
    Abhorres to thinke that Orgilus deserved
    No better favours then a second bed.

ORGILUS. I must not take this reason.

PENTHEA.   To confirme it,
    Should I outlive my bondage, let me meet
    Another worse then this, and lesse desir'd,   105
    If of all the men alive thou shouldst but touch
    My lip or hand againe.

ORGILUS.   Penthea, now
    I tell 'ee, you grow wanton in my sufferance.[2]
    Come, sweet, th' art mine.

PENTHEA.   Uncivill Sir, forbeare,
    Or I can turne affection into vengeance;   110
    Your reputation (if you value any)
    Lyes bleeding at my feet. Unworthy man,
    If ever henceforth thou appeare in language,
    Message, or letter, to betray my frailty,
    I'le call thy former protestations lust,   115
    And curse my Starres for forfeit of my judgement.
    Goe thou, fit onely for disguise and walkes,
    To hide thy shame : this once I spare thy life;
    I laugh at mine owne confidence; my sorrowes
    By thee are made inferiour to my fortunes.   120
    If ever thou didst harbour worthy love,
    Dare not to answer. My good Genius[(4)] guide me,
    That I may never see thee more.—Goe from me.

ORGILUS. I'[l]e[6] teare my vaile of politicke French off,
    And stand up like a man resolv'd to doe.   125
    Action, not words, shall shew me.—O Penthea!
                           Exit ORGILUS.

PENTHEA. 'A sigh'd my name sure as he parted from me.

---

2 *wanton . . . sufferance :* reck-   obey.
  less in making me suffer and

I feare I 'was too rough : alas, poore Gentleman,
'A look'd not like the ruines of his youth
But like the ruines of those ruines. Honour,   130
How much we fight with weaknesse to preserve thee.
          Enter BASSANES *and* GRAUSIS.
BASSANES. Fye on thee! Damb thee, rotten magot, damb
                              thee!
Sleepe? Sleepe at Court? And now? Aches,(5)
                              convulsions,
Impostumes,³ rhe[u]mes,[7] gouts, palsies clog thy
                              bones
A dozen yeeres more yet.
GRAUSIS.   Now y'are in humors.   135
BASSANES. Shee's by her selfe, there's hope of that; shee's
                              sad too,
Shee's in strong contemplation : yes, and fixt;
The signes are wholesome.
GRAUSIS.   Very wholsome, truly.
BASSANES. Hold your chops, night mare.—Lady, come;
                              your brother
Is carried to his closet; you must thither.   140
PENTHEA. Not well, my Lord?
BASSANES.   A sudden fit, 'twill off;
Some surfeit or disorder.—How doest, deerest?
PENTHEA. Your newes is none o' th' best.
          Enter PROPHILUS.
PROPHILUS.   The chiefe of men,
The excellentest(6) Ithocles, desires
Your presence, Madam.
BASSANES.   We are hasting to him.   145
PENTHEA. In vaine we labour in this course of life
To piece our journey out at length, or crave
Respite of breath; our home is in the grave.
BASSANES. Perfect Philosophy : then[8] let us care
To live so that our reckonings may fall even   150
When w'are to make account.[8]
PROPHILUS.   He cannot feare

³ *Impostumes :* Ulcers.

Who builds on noble grounds : sicknesse or paine
Is the deservers exercise, and such
Your vertuous brother to the world is knowne.
Speake comfort to him, Lady, be all gentle;   155
Starres fall but in the grossenesse of our sight;
A good man dying, th' Earth doth lose a light.

Exeunt omnes.

Actus tertius. Scaena prima.

Enter TECNICUS, *and* ORGILUS *in his owne shape.*
TECNICUS. Be well advis'd; let not a resolution
    Of giddy rashnesse choake the breath of reason.
ORGILUS. It shall not, most sage Master.
TECNICUS.   I am jealous[1] :
    For if the borrowed shape so late put on
    Inferr'd a consequence, we must conclude   5
    Some violent designe of sudden nature
    Hath shooke that shadow off, to flye upon
    A new-hatch'd execution : Orgilus,
    Take heed thou hast not (under our integrity)
    Shrowded unlawfull plots : our mortall eyes   10
    Pierce not the secrets of your [heart],[1] the gods
    Are onely privie to them.
ORGILUS.   Learned Tecnicus,
    Such doubts are causelesse, and to cleere the truth
    From misconceit,[2] the present State commands me.
    The Prince of *Argos* comes himselfe in person   15
    In quest of great Calantha for his Bride,
    Our kingdomes heire; besides, mine onely sister,
    Euphranea, is dispos'd[3] to Prophilus.
    Lastly, the King is sending letters for me
    To *Athens,* for my quicke repaire to Court.   20
    Please to accept these Reasons.
TECNICUS.   Just ones, Orgilus,

ACT III. SCENE II.   [2] *misconceit :* misconception.
[1] *jealous :* suspicious.   [3] *dispos'd :* betrothed.

Not to be contradicted : yet beware
Of an unsure foundation; no faire colours
Can fortifie a building faintly joynted.
I have observ'd a growth in thy aspect   25
Of dangerous extent, sudden, and (looke too't)
I might adde—certaine—

ORGILUS.   My aspect? Could Art
Runne through mine inmost thoughts, it should not
                                          sift
An inclination there more then what suited
With justice of mine honour.

TECNICUS.   I beleeve it.   30
But know then, Orgilus, what honour is :
Honour consists not in a bare opinion
By doing any act that feeds content,
Brave in appearance, 'cause we thinke it brave :
Such honour comes by accident, not nature,   35
Proceeding from the vices of our passion,
Which makes our reason drunke. But reall(1) Honour
Is the reward of vertue, and acquir'd
By Justice or by valour, which for Bases
Hath Justice to uphold it. He then failes   40
In honour, who for lucre [or][2] Revenge
Commits thefts, murthers, Treasons and Adulteries,
With such like, by intrenching on just Lawes,
Whose sov'raignty is best preserv'd by Justice.
Thus, as you see how honour must be grounded   45
On knowledge, not opinion—for opinion
Relyes on probability and Accident,
But knowledge on Necessity and Truth—
I leave thee to the fit consideration
Of what becomes the grace of reall Honour,   50
Wishing successe to all thy vertuous meanings.

ORGILUS. The gods increase thy wisdome, reverend
                                          Oracle,
And in thy precepts make me ever thrifty.⁴

⁴ *thrifty* : careful in observance.

TECNICUS. I thanke thy wish.—   *Exit* ORGILUS.
                              Much mystery of Fate
  Lyes hid in that mans fortunes; Curiosity⁵   55
  May lead his actions into rare attempts;
  But let the gods be moderators⁽²⁾ still,
  No humane power can prevent their will.
         Enter ARMOSTES [*with a box*].
  From whence come 'ee?
ARMOSTES.   From King Amyclas; (pardon
  My interuption of your Studies).—Here   60
  In this seal'd box he sends a treasure deare
  To him as his Crowne; 'a prayes your gravity
  You would examine, ponder, sift and bolt
  The pith and circumstance of every tittle
  The scroll within containes.
TECNICUS.   What is't, Armostes?   65
ARMOSTES. It is the health of Sparta, the Kings life,
  Sinewes and safety of the Common-wealth,
  The summe of what the Oracle deliver'd,
  When last he visited the propheticke Temple
  At *Delphos;*⁽³⁾ what his reasons are, for which   70
  After so long a silence he requires
  You[r]⁽³⁾ counsaile now, grave man, his majesty
  Will soone himselfe acquaint you with.
TECNICUS. [*Taking the box.*]   *Apollo*
  Inspire my Intellect.—The Prince of *Argos*
  Is entertain'd?
ARMOSTES.   He is, and has demanded   75
  Our Princesse for his wife; which I conceive
  One speciall cause the King importunes you
  For resolution of the Oracle.
TECNICUS. My duty to the King, good peace to Sparta,
  And faire day to Armostes!
ARMOSTES.   Like to Tecnicus!   80
             Exeunt [*severally.*]

⁵ *Curiosity :* Strange personal
  traits.

[ACTUS TERTIUS. SCAENA SECUNDA.]

Soft Musicke. A Song.
Can you paint a thought? or number
Every fancy in a slumber?
Can you count soft minutes roving
From a dyals point by moving?
Can you graspe a sigh? or lastly,   5
Rob a Virgins honour chastly?
   No, O no; yet you may
     Sooner doe both that and this,
     This and that, and never misse,
   Then by any praise display   10
     Beauties beauty, such a glory
     As beyond all Fate, all Story,
      All armes, all arts,
      All loves, all hearts,
     Greater then those, or they,   15
     Doe, shall, and must obey.
During which time, enters PROPHILUS, BASSANES,
   PENTHEA, GRAUSIS, *passing over the Stage;*
    BASSANES *and* GRAUSIS *enter againe*
    softly, stealing to severall stands,[1]
      and listen.

BASSANES. All   silent,   calme,   secure.—Grausis,   no
       creaking?
 No noyse? Dost heare nothing?
GRAUSIS.   Not a mouse,
 Or whisper of the winde.
BASSANES.   The floore is matted,
 The bed posts sure are steele or marble.—Souldiers   20
 Should not affect (me thinkes) straines so effeminate;
 Sounds of such delicacy are but fawnings
 Upon the sloth of Luxury[1] : they heighten

ACT III. SCENE II.
[1] *Luxury :* Lechery.

Cinders of covert lust up to a flame.
GRAUSIS. What doe you meane, my Lord? Speak low;   25
            that gabling
Of yours will but undoe us.
BASSANES.   Chamber-combats
  Are felt, not h[e]ard.[1]
PROPHILUS. [*Within.*]   'A wakes.
BASSANES.   What's that?
ITHOCLES. [*Within.*]   Who's there?
  Sister? All quit the roome else.
BASSANES.   'Tis consented.
                Enter PROPHILUS.
PROPHILUS. Lord Bassanes, your brother would be
                private,
  We must forbeare; his sleepe hath newly left him.   30
  Please 'ee withdraw?
BASSANES.   By any meanes, 'tis fit.
PROPHILUS. Pray, Gentlewoman, walke too.
GRAUSIS.   Yes, I will, Sir.
                            Exeunt omnes.
  ITHOCLES *discovered*(2) *in a Chayre, and* PENTHEA.
ITHOCLES. Sit nearer, sister, to me, nearer yet;
  We had one Father, in one wombe tooke life,
  Were brought up twins together, yet have liv'd   35
  At distance like two strangers. I could wish
  That the first pillow whereon I was cradell'd
  Had prov'd to me a grave.
PENTHEA.   You had beene happy :
  Then had you never knowne that sinne of life
  Which blots all following glories with a vengeance,   40
  For forfeiting the last will of the dead,
  From whom you had your being.
ITHOCLES.   Sad Penthea,
  Thou canst not be too cruell; my rash spleene
  Hath with a violent hand pluck'd from thy bosome
  A lover-blest heart, to grind it into dust,   45
  For which mine's now a-breaking.
PENTHEA.   Not yet, heaven,
  I doe beseech thee : first let some wild fires

Scorch, not consume it; may the heat be cherisht
With desires infinite, but hopes impossible.

ITHOCLES. Wrong'd soule, thy prayers are heard.

PENTHEA.   Here, lo,
              I breathe,   50
A miserable creature led to ruine
By an unnaturall brother.

ITHOCLES.   I consume
In languishing affections[2] for that trespasse,
Yet cannot dye.

PENTHEA.   The handmaid to the wages
[Of   Country   toyle   drinkes   the   untroubled   55
              streames][2]
With leaping kids, and with the bleating lambes;
And so allayes her thirst secure, whiles I
Quench my hot sighes with fleetings of my teares.

ITHOCLES. The labourer doth eat his coursest bread,
Earn'd with his sweat, and lyes him downe to sleepe,   60
Which[3] every bit I touch turnes in disgestion
To gall, as bitter as Penthea's curse.
Put me to any pennance for my tyranny,
And I will call thee mercifull.

PENTHEA.   Pray kill me,
Rid me from living with a jealous husband,   65
Then we will joyne in friendship, be againe
Brother and sister.—Kill me, pray : nay, will 'ee?

ITHOCLES. How does thy Lord esteeme thee?

PENTHEA.   Such an one
As onely you have made me, a faith-breaker,
A spotted whore; forgive me, I am one   70
In art,[3] not in desires; the gods must witnesse.

ITHOCLES. Thou dost belye thy friend.[3]

PENTHEA.   I doe not, Ithocles;
For she that's wife to Orgilus, and lives
In knowne Adultery with Bassanes,
Is at the best a whore. Wilt kill me now?   75
The ashes of our parents will assume

---

[2] *affections* : passions.   [3] *friend* : lover.

Some dreadfull figure, and appeare to charge
Thy bloody gilt, that hast betray'd their name
To infamy, in this reproachfull match.

ITHOCLES. After my victories abroad, at home   80
I meet despaire; ingratitude of nature
Hath made my actions monstrous : thou shalt stand
A Deity, my sister, and be worship'd
For thy resolved martyrdome : wrong'd maids
And married wives shall to thy hallowed shrine   85
Offer their orisons, and sacrifice
Pure Turtles[4] crown'd with mirtle, if thy pitty
Unto a yeelding brothers pressure lend
One finger but to ease it.

PENTHEA.   O no more!

ITHOCLES. Death waits to waft me to the Stygian bankes,   90
And free men from this Chaos of my bondage,
And till thou wilt forgive, I must indure.

PENTHEA. Who is the Saint you serve?

ITHOCLES.   Friendship, or [tie][4]
Of birth to any but my sister, durst not
Have mov'd that question; as a secret, Sister,   95
I dare not murmure to my selfe.

PENTHEA.   Let me,—
By your new protestations I conjure 'ee,—
Partake her name.

ITHOCLES.   Her name,—'tis,—'tis,—I dare not.

PENTHEA. All your respects are forg'd.[5]

ITHOCLES.   They are not.—
                          Peace!
Calantha is—the Princesse, the Kings daughter,   100
Sole heire of Sparta.—Me most miserable,
Doe I now love thee? For my injuries
Revenge thy selfe with bravery,[6] and gossip
My treasons to the Kings eares. Doe; Calantha
Knowes it not yet, nor Prophilus, my nearest.   105

---

4 *Turtles :* Turtle doves.   ing on false pretenses.
5 *All . . . forg'd :* You are refus-   6 *bravery :* sarcastic insult.

PENTHEA. Suppose you were contracted to her, would
                              it not
  Split even your very soule to see her father
  Snatch her out of your armes against her will,
  And force her on the Prince of *Argos?*
ITHOCLES.   Trouble not
  The fountaines of mine eyes with thine owne story,   110
  I sweat in blood for 't.
PENTHEA.   We are reconcil'd :
  Alas, Sir, being children, but two branches
  Of one stocke, 'tis not fit we should divide :
  Have comfort, you may find it.
ITHOCLES.   Yes, in thee :
  Onely in thee, Penthea mine.
PENTHEA.   If sorrowes   115
  Have not too much dull'd my infected braine,
  I'le cheere invention for an active straine.[7]
ITHOCLES. Mad man! why have I wrong'd a maid so
                              excellent?
   Enter BASSANES *with a ponyard;*[8] PROPHILUS,
     GRONEAS, HEMOPHIL *and* GRAUSIS.
BASSANES. I can forbeare no longer : more I will not :
  Keepe off your hands, or fall upon my point :   120
  Patience is tyr'd, for like a slow-pac'd Asse
  Ye ride my easie nature, and proclaime
  My sloth to vengeance a reproach and property.[9]
ITHOCLES. The meaning of this rudenesse?
PROPHILUS.   Hee's distracted.
PENTHEA. O˙my griev'd Lord!
GRAUSIS.   Sweet Lady, come not 125
                              neere him;
  He holds his perilous weapon in his hand
  To pricke 'a cares not whom, nor where,—see, see, see.
BASSANES. My birth is noble; though the popular blast
  Of vanity, as giddy as thy youth,

---

[7] *cheere . . . straine :* try to
  think of something to do.
[8] *ponyard :* dagger.

[9] *property :* personal trait of
  character.

Hath rear'd thy name up to bestride a cloud,   130
Or progresse in the Chariot of the Sunne,
I am no clod of trade, to lackey pride,
Nor like your slave of expectation[10] wait
The baudy hinges of your dores, or whistle
For mysticall conveyance to your bed-sports.   135
GRAUSIS. Fine humors! They become him.
HEMOPHIL.   How 'a stares,
Struts, puffes, and sweats : most admirable[11] lunacy!
ITHOCLES. But that I may conceive the spirit of wine
Has took possession of your soberer custome,
I'de say you were unmannerly.
PENTHEA.   Deare brother,—   140
BASSANES. Unmannerly!—Mew, Kitling,[12]—smooth for-
                              mality
Is usher to the ranknesse of the blood,
But Impudence beares up the traine : indeed, sir,
Your fiery mettall, or your springall blaze
Of huge renowne, is no sufficient Royalty   145
To print upon my forehead the scorne "Cuckold."
ITHOCLES. His Jealousie has rob'd him of his wits,
'A talkes 'a knowes not what.
BASSANES.   Yes, and 'a knowes
To whom 'a talkes; to one that franks[13] his lust
In Swine-security of bestiall incest.   150
ITHOCLES. Hah, devill!
BASSANES.   I will hallo't, though I blush more
To name the filthinesse than thou to act it.
ITHOCLES. Monster!
PROPHILUS.   Sir, by our friendship—
PENTHEA.   By our bloods,—
Will you quite both undoe us, Brother?
GRAUSIS.   Out on him!
These are his megrims,[14] firks,[15] and melancholies.   155
HEMOPHIL. Well said, old Touch-hole. (4)

10 *slave of expectation :* servant   13 *franks :* feeds like an animal.
  for reward.   14 *megrims :* fantasies.
11 *admirable :* incredible.   15 *firks :* whims.
12 *Kitling :* Kitten.

GRONEAS.   Kick him out
  at dores.
PENTHEA. With favour, let me speake.—My Lord, what
                    slacknesse
  In my obedience hath deserv'd this rage?
  Except humility and silent[5] duty
  Have drawne on your unquiet, my simplicity   160
  Ne'er studied your vexation.
BASSANES.   Light of beauty!
  Deale not ungently with a desperate wound!
  No breach of reason dares make warre with her
  Whose lookes are soveraignty, whose breath is balme.
  O that I could preserve thee in fruition   165
  As in devotion!
PENTHEA.   Sir, may every evill
  Lock'd in *Pandora's* box(5) showre (in your
                    presence)
  On my unhappy head, if since you made me
  A partner in your bed, I have been faulty
  In one unseemely thought against your honour.   170
ITHOCLES. Purge not his griefes, Penthea.
BASSANES.   Yes, say on,
  Excellent creature.—Good,[16] be not a hinderance
  To peace and praise of vertue.—O my senses
  Are charm'd with sounds caelestiall.—On, deare, on;
  I never gave you one ill word; say, did I?   175
  Indeed I did not.
PENTHEA.   Nor, by *Juno's* forehead,
  Was I e'er guilty of a wanton error.
BASSANES. A goddesse! Let me kneele.
GRAUSIS.   Alas, kind Animall!
ITHOCLES. No,—but for pennance.
BASSANES.   Noble sir, what is it?
  With gladnesse I embrace it; yet, pray let not   180
  My rashnesse teach you to be too unmercifull.
ITHOCLES. When you shall shew good proofe that manly
                    wisdome

[16] *Good :* Good sir.

Not over-sway'd by passion or opinion,
Knowes how to lead judgement, then this Lady,
Your wife, my sister, shall returne in safety   185
Home, to be guided by you; but till first
I can, out of cleare evidence, approve[17] it,
Shee shall be my care.
BASSANES.   Rip my bosome up!
I'le stand the execution with a constancy:
This torture is unsufferable.
ITHOCLES.   Well, Sir,   190
I dare not trust her to your fury.
BASSANES.   But
Penthea sayes not so.
PENTHEA.   She needs no tongue
To plead excuse, who never purpos'd wrong.
HEMOPHIL. [to GRAUSIS.] Virgin of reverence and an-
                              tiquity,
Stay you behind.
GRONEAS.   The Court wants not your diligence. 195
          Exeunt omnes sed[18] BASSANES *and* GRAUSIS.
GRAUSIS. What will you doe, my Lord? My Lady's gone;
I am deny'd to follow.
BASSANES.   I may see her,
Or speake to her once more.
GRAUSIS.   And feele her too, man;
Be of good cheare; she's your owne flesh and bone.
BASSANES. Diseases desperate must find cures alike: 200
She swore she has beene true.
GRAUSIS.   True, on my modesty.
BASSANES. Let him want truth who credits not her
                              vowes.
Much wrong I did her, but to her brother infinite;
Rumor will voyce me the contempt of manhood,
Should I run on thus. Some way I must try   205
To out-doe Art,[6] and cry 'a[19] Jealousie.[6]
                              Exeunt omnes.

17 *approve*: certify.   19 *cry 'a*: exclaim against.
18 *omnes sed*: all but.

.

[Actus tertius. Scaena tertia.]

Flourish. Enter AMYCLAS, NEARCHUS *leading* CALANTHA,
ARMOSTES, CROTOLON, EUPHRANEA, CHRISTALLA,
PHILEMA *and* AMELUS.

AMYCLAS. Cozen of *Argos*, what the heavens have
        pleas'd
  In their unchanging Counsels to conclude
  For both our Kingdomes weale, we must submit to :
  Nor can we be unthankfull to their bounties,
  Who, when we were even creeping to our [grave],[1]   5
  Sent us a daughter, in whose birth our hope
  Continues of succession : as you are
  In title next, being grandchilde to our Aunt,
  So we in heart desire you may sit nearest
  Calantha's love; since we have ever vow'd   10
  Not to inforce affection by our will,
  But by her owne choyce to confirme it gladly.
NEARCHUS. You speake the nature of a right just father :
  I come not hither roughly to demand
  My Cozens thraldome, but to free mine owne :   15
  Report of great Calantha's beauty, vertue,
  Sweetnesse, and singular perfections, courted
  All eares to credit what I finde was publish'd
  By constant truth : from which, if any service
  Of my desert can purchase faire construction,   20
  This Lady must command it.
CALANTHA.   Princely Sir,
  So well you know how to professe observance,[1]
  That you instruct your hearers to become
  Practitioners in duty, of which number
  I'le study to be chiefe.
NEARCHUS.   Chiefe, glorious Virgine,   25
  In my devotions, as in all mens wonder.

  ACT III. SCENE III.
[1] *observance :* courtly service.

AMYCLAS. Excellent Cozen, we deny no libertie;
   Use thine owne opportunities.—Armostes,
   We must consult with the Philosophers;
   The businesse is of weight.
ARMOSTES.   Sir, at your pleasure.   30
AMYCLAS. You told me, Crotolon, your sonne's return'd
   From *Athens.* Wherefore comes 'a not to Court,
   As we commanded?
CROTOLON.   He shall soone attend
   Your royall will, great Sir.
AMYCLAS.   The marriage
   Betweene young Prophilus and Euphranea   35
   Tasts of too much delay.
CROTOLON.   My Lord,—
AMYCLAS.   Some pleasures
   At celebration of it would give life
   To th' entertainment of the Prince our kinsman :
   Our Court weares gravity more then we rellish.
ARMOSTES. Yet the heavens smile on all your high at-   40
                        tempts,
   Without a Cloud.
CROTOLON.   So may the gods protect us.
CALANTHA. A Prince a subject?
NEARCHUS.   Yes, to beauties scepter :
   As all hearts kneele, so mine.
CALANTHA.   You are too Courtly.
   [*Enter*] *to them* ITHOCLES, ORGILUS, [*and*] PROPHILUS.
ITHOCLES. Your safe returne to Sparta is most welcome;
   I joy to meet you here, and as occasion   45
   Shall grant us privacy, will yeeld you reasons
   Why I should covet to deserve the title
   Of your respected friend : for—without Complement—
   Beleeve it, Orgilus, 'tis my ambition.
ORGILUS. Your Lordship may command me, your poore   50
                        servant.
ITHOCLES. [*Aside.*] So amorously close!—close so soone?
                        —my heart!
PROPHILUS. What sudden change is next?
ITHOCLES.   Life to the King!

To whom I here present this Noble gentleman,
New come from *Athens;* Royall Sir, vouchsafe
Your gracious hand in favour of his merit.   55
CROTOLON. [*Aside.*] My sonne preferr'd[2] by Ithocles!
AMYCLAS.   Our bounties
Shall open to thee, Orgilus; for instance,—
Harke in thine eare,—if out of those inventions
Which flow in *Athens*, tho hast there ingrost[3]
Some rarity of wit to grace the Nuptials   60
Of thy faire sister, and renowne our Court
In th' eyes of this young Prince, we shall be debtor
To thy conceit; thinke on't.
ORGILUS.   Your Highnesse honors me.
NEARCHUS. My tongue and heart are twins.
CALANTHA.   A noble birth,
Becomming such a father.—Worthy Orgilus,   65
You are a guest most wish'd for.
ORGILUS.   May my duty
Still rise in your opinion, sacred Princesse.
ITHOCLES. Euphranea's brother, sir, a Gentleman
Well worthy of your knowledge.
NEARCHUS.   We embrace him,
Proud of so deare acquaintance.
AMYCLAS.   All prepare   70
For Revels and disport : the joyes of *Hymen,*
Like *Phoebus* is his lustre, puts to flight
All mists of dulnesse; crowne the houres with glad-
                          nesse :
No sounds but musicke, no discourse but mirth!
CALANTHA. Thine arme, I prethee,[2] Ithocles.—Nay,   75
                          good
My Lord, keepe on your way, I am provided.
NEARCHUS. I dare not disobey.
ITHOCLES.   Most heavenly Lady!
                                        Exeunt.

---

[2] *preferr'd :* presented for   [3] *ingrost :* acquired.
promotion.

[ACTUS TERTIUS. SCAENA QUARTA.]

    Enter CROTOLON [*and*] ORGILUS.
CROTOLON. The King hath spoke his mind.
ORGILUS.   His will he
    hath :
 But were it lawfull to hold plea against
 The power of greatnesse, not the reason, haply
 Such under-shrubs as subjects sometimes might
 Borrow of Nature[1] Justice, to informe   5
 That licence soveraignty holds without checke
 Over a meeke obedience,—
CROTOLON.   How resolve you
 Touching your sisters marriage? Prophilus
 Is a deserving and a hopefull youth.
ORGILUS. I envy not his merit, but applaud it :   10
 Could [wish][1] him thrift[1] in all his best desires,
 And with a willingnesse inleague our blood
 With his, for purchase of full growth in friendship.
 He never touch'd on any wrong that malic'd
 The honour of our house, nor stirr'd our peace; 15
 Yet, with your favour, let me not forget
 Under whose wing he gathers warmth and comfort,
 Whose creature he is bound, made, and must live so.
CROTOLON. Sonne, sonne, I find in thee a harsh condi-
    tion,
 No curtesie can winne it; 'tis too ranckorous.   20
ORGILUS. Good Sir, be not severe in your construction;
 I am no stranger to such easie calmes
 As sit in tender bosomes : Lordly Ithocles
 Hath grac'd my entertainment in abundance,—
 Too humbly hath descended from that height   25
 Of arrogance and spleene which wrought the rape
 On griev'd Penthea's purity; his scorne

ACT III. SCENE IV.
[1] *thrift :* success.

Of my untoward fortunes is reclaim'd
Unto a Courtship, almost to a fawning :
I'le kisse his foot, since you will have it so.   30
CROTOLON. Since I will have it so?—Friend, I will have it
                                       so,
Without our ruine by your politike plots,
Or Wolfe of hatred snarling in your breast;
You have a spirit, Sir, have ye? A familiar[2]
That poasts i' th' ayre for your intelligence?   35
Some such *Hobgoblin* hurried you from *Athens,*
For yet you come unsent for.
ORGILUS.   If unwelcome,
I might have found a grave there.
CROTOLON.   Sure your businesse
Was soone dispatch'd, or your mind alter'd quickly.
ORGILUS. 'Twas care, Sir, of my health, cut short my   40
                                  journey;
For there a generall infection
Threatens a desolation.
CROTOLON.   And I feare
Thou hast brought backe a worse infection with thee,
Infection of thy mind, which, as thou sayst,
Threatens the desolation of our family.   45
ORGILUS. Forbid it, our deare Genius![3] I will rather
Be made a Sacrifice on *Thrasus'* monument,
Or kneele to Ithocles, his sonne, in dust,
Then wooe a fathers curse! My sisters marriage
With Prophilus is from my heart confirm'd :   50
May I live hated, may I dye despis'd,
If I omit to further it in all
That can concerne me!
CROTOLON.   I have beene too rough,
My duty to my King made me so earnest;
Excuse it Orgilus.
ORGILUS.   Deare Sir,—
    Enter to them PROPHILUS, EUPHRANEA, ITHOCLES,
              GRONEAS, [*and*] HEMOPHIL.

---

[2] *familiar :* demon.   [3] *Genius :* Generative spirit.

CROTOLON.   Here comes   55
   Euphranea, with Prophilus and Ithocles.
ORGILUS. Most honored!—ever famous!
ITHOCLES.   Your true friend,
   On earth not any truer.—With smooth eyes
   Looke on this worthy couple; your consent
   Can onely make them one.
ORGILUS.   They have it.—Sister,   60
   Thou pawn'dst to me an oath, of which ingagement
   I never will release thee, if thou aym'st
   At any other choyce then this.
EUPHRANEA.   Deare brother,
   At him or none.
CROTOLON.   To which my blessing's added.
ORGILUS. Which, till a greater ceremony perfect,—   65
   Euphranea, lend thy hand,—here, take her, Prophilus.
   Live long a happy man and wife; and further,
   That these in presence may conclude an omen,
   Thus for a Bridall song I close my wishes :
     Comforts lasting, Loves increasing,   70
     Like soft houres never ceasing;
     Plenties pleasure, *peace* complying,
     Without jarres, or tongues envying;[4]
     Hearts by holy Union wedded
     More then theirs by custome bedded;   75
     Fruitfull *issues; life* so graced,
     Not by age to be defaced;
     Budding, as the yeare ensu'th,
     Every spring another *youth :*
     All what thought can adde beside,   80
     Crowne this *Bridegroome* and this *Bride.*
PROPHILUS. You have seal'd joy close to my soule :
              Euphranea,
   Now I may call thee mine.
ITHOCLES.   I but exchange
   One good friend for another.

  4 *tongues envying :* ill will,
   malice.

ORGILUS.   If these Gallants
Will please to grace a poore invention,   85
By joyning with me in some slight devise,
I'le venture on a straine my younger dayes
Have studied for delight.
HEMOPHIL.   With thankfull willingnesse
I offer my attendance.
GRONEAS.   No endevour
Of mine shall faile to shew it selfe.
ITHOCLES.   We will   90
All joyne to wait on thy directions, Orgilus.
ORGILUS. O my good Lord, your favours flow towards
A too unworthy worme; but, as you please,—
I am what you will shape me.
ITHOCLES.   A fast friend.
CROTOLON. I thanke thee, sonne, for this acknowledge-   95
                                    ment;
It is a sight of gladnesse.
ORGILUS.   But my duty.
                                    Exeunt omnes.

[ACTUS TERTIUS. SCAENA QUINTA.]

Enter CALANTHA, PENTHEA, CHRISTALLA, [*and*]
                          PHILEMA.
CALANTHA. Whoe'er would speake with us, deny his en-
                                    trance;
Be carefull of our charge.
CHRISTALLA.   We shall, madam.
CALANTHA. Except the King himselfe, give none admit-
                                    tance,
Not any.
PHILEMA. Madam, it shall be our care.
                          Exeunt [CHRISTALLA *and* PHILEMA].
CALANTHA. Being alone, Penthea, you have granted[1]   5
The oportunity you sought, and might
At all times have commanded.
PENTHEA.   'Tis a benefit

Which I shall owe your goodnesse even in death for :
My glasse of life, sweet Princesse, hath few minutes
Remaining to runne downe; the sands are spent,   10
For by an inward messenger I feele
The summons of departure short and certaine.
CALANTHA. You feed too much your melancholly.
PENTHEA.   Glories
Of humane greatnesse are but pleasing dreames,
And shadowes soone decaying : on the stage   15
Of my mortality, my youth hath acted
Some scenes of vanity, drawne out at length
By varied pleasures, sweetned in the mixture,
But Tragicall in issue; Beauty, pompe,
With every sensuality our giddinesse   20
Doth frame an Idoll, are unconstant friends
When any troubled passion makes assault
On the unguarded Castle of the mind.
CALANTHA. Contemne not your condition for the proofe
Of bare opinion onely : to what end   25
Reach all these Morall texts?
PENTHEA.   To place before 'ee
A perfect mirror, wherein you may see
How weary I am of a lingring life,
Who count the best a misery.
CALANTHA.   Indeed
You have no little cause; yet none so great   30
As to distrust a remedy.
PENTHEA.   That remedy
Must be a winding sheet, a fold of lead,
And some untrod-on corner in the earth.
Not to detaine your expectation, Princesse,
I have an humble suit.
CALANTHA.   Speake, I enjoy it.   35
[PENTHEA.][2] Vouchsafe then to be my Executrix,
And take that trouble on 'ee, to dispose
Such Legacies as I bequeath impartially :
I have not much to give, the paines are easie;
Heaven will reward your piety, and thanke it   40
When I am dead; for sure I must not live,—

I hope I cannot.

CALANTHA.   Now beshrew thy sadnesse;
Thou turn'st me too much woman.   [*She weeps.*]

PENTHEA. [*Aside.*]   Her faire eyes
Melt into passion; then I have assurance
Encouraging my boldnesse.—In this paper   45
My Will was Character'd; which you, with pardon,
Shall now know from mine owne mouth.

CALANTHA.   Talke on, prethee,[3]
It is a pretty earnest.[1]

PENTHEA.   I have left me
But three poore Jewels to bequeath; the first is
My youth, for though I am much old in griefes,   50
In yeares I am a child.

CALANTHA.   To whom that?[4]

PENTHEA. To Virgin wives, such as abuse not wedlocke
By freedome of desires, but covet chiefly
The pledges of chast beds for tyes of love,
Rather than ranging of their blood : and next   55
To married maids, such as preferre the number
Of honorable issue in their vertues,
Before the flattery of delights by marriage,—
May those be ever young!

CALANTHA.   A second Jewell
You meane to part with.

PENTHEA.   'Tis my Fame, I trust,   60
By scandall yet untouch'd; this I bequeath
To Memory, and Times old daughter, Truth :
If ever my unhappy name find mention
When I am falne to dust, may it deserve
Beseeming charity without dishonour.   65

CALANTHA. How handsomely thou playst with harm-
                        lesse sport
Of meere[2] imagination; speak the last,
I strangely like thy will.

PENTHEA.   This Jewell, Madam,

ACT III. SCENE v.
[1] *earnest :* legacy.   [2] *meere :* pure.

Is dearely precious to me; you must use
The best of your discretion to imploy   70
This gift as I entend it.
CALANTHA.   Doe not doubt me.
PENTHEA. 'Tis long agone since first I lost my heart;
Long I have liv'd without it, else for certaine
I should have given that too; but in stead
Of it, to great Calantha, Sparta's heire,   75
By service bound, and by affection vow'd,
I doe bequeath in holiest rites of love
Mine onely brother Ithocles.
CALANTHA.   What saydst thou?
PENTHEA. Impute not, heaven-blest Lady, to ambition,
A faith as humbly perfect as the prayers   80
Of a devoted supplicant can indow it :
Looke on him, Princesse, with an eye of pitty;
How like the ghost of what he late appear'd
'A moves before you.
CALANTHA. [Aside.]   Shall I answer here,
Or lend my eare too grossely?
PENTHEA.   First, his heart   85
Shall fall in Cynders, scorch'd by your disdaine,
Ere he will dare, poore man, to ope an eye
On these divine lookes, but with low-bent thoughts
Accusing such presumption; as for words,
'A dares not utter any but of service :   90
Yet this lost creature loves 'ee.—Be a Princesse
In sweetnesse as in blood; give him his doome,
Or raise him up to comfort.
CALANTHA.   What new change
Appeares in my behaviour that thou dar'st
Tempt my displeasure?
PENTHEA.   I must leave the world   95
To revell [in] Elizium,[5] and 'tis just
To wish my brother some advantage here :
Yet by my best hopes, Ithocles is ignorant
Of this pursuit. But if you please to kill him,
Lend him one angry looke, or one harsh word,   100
And you shall soone conclude how strong a power

Your absolute authority holds over
His life and end.

CALANTHA.   You have forgot, Penthea,
How still I have a father.

PENTHEA.   But remember
I am a sister, though to me this brother   105
Hath beene, you know, unkinde : O most unkinde!

CALANTHA. Christalla, Philema, where are 'ee?—Lady,
Your checke lyes in my silence.

                Enter CHRISTALLA *and* PHILEMA.

BOTH.   Madam, here.

CALANTHA. I thinke 'ee sleepe, 'ee drones; wait on
                            Penthea
Unto her lodging.—[*Aside.*] Ithocles? Wrong'd Lady!   110

PENTHEA. My reckonings are made even; Death or Fate
Can now nor strike too soone, nor force too late.

                                                Exeunt.

                ACTUS QUARTUS. SCAENA PRIMA.

                Enter ITHOCLES *and* ARMOSTES.

ITHOCLES. Forbeare your Inquisition; curiosity
Is of too subtill and too searching nature :
In feares of love too quicke, too slow of credit :
I am not what you doubt me.[1]

ARMOSTES.   Nephew, be then
As I would wish;—all is not right.—Good heaven   5
Confirme your Resolutions for dependance
On worthy ends which may advance your quiet.

ITHOCLES. I did the Noble Orgilus much injury,
But griev'd Penthea more : I now repent it,—
Now, Uncle, now; this "Now" is now too late :   10
So provident is folly in sad issue,
That after-wit, like Bankrupts debts, stand[s][1]
                            tallyed

    ACT IV. SCENE I.
    [1] *doubt me :* fear me to be.

Without all possibilities of payment :
Sure he's an honest, very honest Gentleman,
A man of single[2] meaning.
ARMOSTES.   I beleeve it :   15
Yet, Nephew, 'tis the tongue informes our eares;
Our eyes can never pierce into the thoughts,
For they are lodg'd too inward :—but I question
No truth in Orgilus.—The Princesse, Sir.
ITHOCLES. The Princesse? Ha!
ARMOSTES.   With her the Prince of   20
                    Argos.
        Enter NEARCHUS *leading* CALANTHA, AMELUS,
                CHRISTALLA, [*and*] PHILEMA.
NEARCHUS. Great faire one, grace my hopes with any
                instance
Of Livery,[3] from the allowance of your favour;
This little sparke—   [*He tries to take a ring.*]
CALANTHA.   A Toy.
NEARCHUS.   Love feasts on Toyes,
For *Cupid* is a child;—vouchsafe this bounty :
It cannot be [de]ny'd.[2]
CALANTHA.   You shall not value,   25
Sweet Cozen, at a price, what I count cheape,
So cheape, that let him take it who dares stoope for't,
And give it at next meeting to a Mistresse;
Shee'le thanke him for't, perhaps.
                    Casts it to ITHOCLES.
AMELUS.   The Ring, Sir, is
The Princesses,—I could have tooke it up.   30
ITHOCLES. Learne manners, prethee.[3]—To the blessed
                owner,
Upon my knees.
            [*He kneels and offers it to* CALANTHA.]
NEARCHUS.   Y'are sawcy.
CALANTHA.   This is pretty!
I am, belike, a Mistresse.—Wondrous pretty!

2 *single :* direct and sincere.   wear as a sign of favor.
3 *Livery :* Personal article to

 Let the man keepe his fortune, since he found it;
He's worthy on't.—On, Cozen.
ITHOCLES.   Follow, Spaniell, 35
 I'le force 'ee to a fawning else.
AMELUS.   You dare not.
    Exeunt. Manent ITHOCLES *and* ARMOSTES.
ARMOSTES. My Lord, you were too forward.
ITHOCLES.   Looke 'ee,
     Uncle :
Some such there are whose liberall contents
Swarme without care in every sort of plenty;
Who, after full repasts, can lay them downe 40
To sleepe; and they sleepe, Uncle : in which silence
Their very dreames present 'em choyce of pleasures :
Pleasures (observe me, Uncle) of rare object :
Here heaps of gold, there Increments of honors;
Now change of garments, then the votes of people; 45
Anon varieties of beauties, courting
In flatteries of the night, exchange of dalliance,—
Yet these are still but dreames : give me felicity
Of which my senses waking are partakers,—
A reall, visible, materiall happinesse : 50
And then too, when I stagger in expectance
Of the least comfort that can cherish life.—
I saw it, Sir, I saw it! for it came
From her owne hand.
ARMOSTES.   The Princesse threw it t'ee.—
ITHOCLES. True, and she said—well I remember what. 55
 Her Cozen Prince would beg it.
ARMOSTES.   Yes, and parted
 In anger at your taking on't.
ITHOCLES.   Penthea!
 Oh thou hast pleaded with a powerfull language!
I want a fee to gratifie thy merit.[4] [4]
 But I will doe—
ARMOSTES. What is't you say?

---

[4] *I want . . . merit :* I lack   deserve.
 means to reward you as you

ITHOCLES.   In anger!   60
   In anger let him part; for could his breath,
   Like whirlewinds, tosse such servile slaves as licke
   The dust his footsteps print into a vapour,
   It durst not stirre a haire of mine; it should not,
   I'de rend it up by th' roots first. To be any thing   65
   Calantha smiles on, is to be a blessing
   More sacred than a petty-Prince of *Argos*
   Can wish to equall, or in worth or Title.
ARMOSTES. Containe your selfe, my Lord; *Ixion,*[(1)]
                    ayming
   To embrace *Juno*, bosom'd but a cloud,   70
   And begat *Centaures :* 'tis an usefull morall;
   Ambition hatch'd in clouds of meere opinion
   Proves but in birth a prodigie.[5]
ITHOCLES.   I thanke 'ee;
   Yet, with your Licence, I should seeme uncharitable
   To gentler Fate, if, rellishing the dainties   75
   Of a soules setled peace, I were so feeble
   Not to digest it.
ARMOSTES.   He deserves small trust
   Who is not privy Counsellor to himselfe.
     Enter NEARCHUS, ORGILUS, *and* AMELUS.
NEARCHUS. Brave me?
ORGILUS.   Your Excellence mistakes his
                temper,
   For Ithocles in fashion of his mind   80
   Is beautifull, soft, gentle, the cleare mirror
   Of absolute perfection.
AMELUS.   Was't your modesty
   Term'd any of the Prince his servants "Spaniell"?
   Your Nurse sure taught you other language.
ITHOCLES.   Language!
NEARCHUS. A gallant Man at armes is here : a Doctor   85
   In feats of Chivalry,—blunt, and rough spoken,
   Vouchsafing not the fustian of civility,
   Which [less] rash[5] spirits stile good manners.

[5] *prodigie :* monster.

ITHOCLES. Manners?

ORGILUS. No more, Illustrious Sir; 'tis matchlesse Ithocles.

NEARCHUS. You might have understood who I am.

ITHOCLES. Yes,   90
  I did—else—but the presence calm'd[6] th' affront;
  Y'are Cozen to the Princesse.

NEARCHUS. To the King too;
  A certaine Instrument that lent supportance
  To your Collossicke greatnesse :—to that King too,
  You might have added.

ITHOCLES. There is more divinity   95
  In beauty[(2)] then in Majesty.

ARMOSTES. O fie, fie!

NEARCHUS. This odde youths pride turnes hereticke in
          loyalty.
  Sirrah! low Mushroms never rivall Cedars.

                Exeunt NEARCHUS *and* AMELUS.

ITHOCLES. Come backe! What pittifull dull thing am I
  So to be tamely scoulded at? Come backe!   100
  Let him come backe and eccho once againe
  That scornefull sound of "Mushrome"; painted colts,
  Like Heralds coats guilt o'er with Crownes and
             Scepters,
  May bait a muzled[6] Lion.

ARMOSTES. Cozen, Cozen,
  Thy tongue is not thy friend.

ORGILUS. In point of honour   105
  Discretion knowes no bounds. Amelus told me
  'Twas all about a little Ring.

ITHOCLES. A Ring
  The Princesse threw away, and I tooke up :
  Admit she threw't to me,—what arme of brasse
  Can snatch it hence? No, could 'a grind the hoope   110
  To powder, 'a might sooner reach my heart
  Then steale and weare one dust on't.—Orgilus,
  I am extreamely wrong'd.

[6] *calm'd :* the royal presence
  prevented violence.

ORGILUS.   A Ladies favour
  Is not to be so slighted.
ITHOCLES.   Slighted!
ARMOSTES.   Quiet
  These vaine unruly passions, which will render ye   115
  Into a madnesse.
ORGILUS.   Griefes will have their vent.
        Enter TECNICUS [*with a scroll*].
ARMOSTES. Welcome; thou com'st in season, reverend
               man,
  To powre the balsome of a supplying patience
  Into the festering wound of ill-spent fury.
ORGILUS. [*Aside.*] What makes He here?
TECNICUS.   The hurts are
        yet but mortall,[7, (3)]   120
  Which shortly will prove deadly. To the King,
  Armostes, see in safety thou deliver
  This seal'd up counsaile; bid him with a constancy
  Peruse the secrets of the gods :—O Sparta,
  O Lacedemon! double nam'd, but one   125
  In fate : when Kingdomes reele (marke well my
        Saw[8])
  Their heads must needs be giddy : tell the King
  That henceforth he no more must enquire after
  My aged head : *Apollo* wils it so;
  I am for *Delphos*.
ARMOSTES.   Not without some conference   130
  With our great master?
TECNICUS.   Never more to see him,—
  A greater Prince commands me.—Ithocles,
    When youth is ripe, and Age from time doth
        part,
    The livelesse trunke shall wed the Broken
        Heart.
ITHOCLES. What's this, if understood?

[7] *but mortall :* only threatening   [8] *Saw :* Proverbial saying.
  death.

TECNICUS.   List, Orgilus,   135
   Remember what I told thee long before;
   These teares shall be my witnesse.
ARMOSTES.   'Las, good man!
TECNICUS. Let craft with curtesie a while conferre,
   Revenge proves its owne Executioner.
ORGILUS. Darke sentences are for Apollo's Priests :   140
   I am not *Oedipus*.⁹
TECNICUS.   My howre is come;
   Cheare up the King : farewell to all.—O Sparta!
   O Lacedemon!   *Exit* TECNICUS.
ARMOSTES. If propheticke fire
   Have warm'd this old mans bosome, we might construe
   His words to fatall sense.
ITHOCLES.   Leave to the powers   145
   Above us the effects of their decrees;
   My burthen lyes within me. Servile feares
   Prevent no great effects.—Divine Calantha!
ARMOSTES. The gods be still propitious.
                        Exeunt. Manet ORGILUS.
ORGILUS.   Something oddly
   The booke-man prated; yet 'a talk'd it weeping :   150
    "Let craft with curtesie a while conferre,
    Revenge proves its owne executioner."
   Conne it againe; for what? It shall not puzzle me;
   'Tis dotage of a withered braine.—Penthea
   Forbad me not her presence; I may see her   155
   And gaze my fill : why, see her then I may,
   When, if I faint to speake, I must be silent.
                        Exit ORGILUS.

---

⁹ *Oedipus* : He solved the riddle
  of the Sphinx.

[Actus quartus.   Scaena secunda.]

Enter BASSANES, GRAUSIS, *and* PHULAS.

BASSANES. Pray, use your Recreations, all the service
   I will expect is quietnesse amongst 'ee :
   Take liberty at home, abroad, at all times,
   And in your charities appease the gods,
   Whom I with my distractions have offended.   5
GRAUSIS. Faire blessings on thy heart!
PHULAS. [*Aside.*]   Here's a rare change!
   My Lord, to cure the itch, is surely gelded.
   The Cuckold in conceit[1] hath cast his hornes!
BASSANES. Betake 'ee to your severall occasions,
   And wherein I have heretofore beene faulty,   10
   Let your constructions mildly passe it over;
   Henceforth I'le study reformation,—more
   I have not for employment.
GRAUSIS.   O sweet man!
   Thou art the very hony-combe of honesty.
PHULAS. The garland of good-will.[(1)]—Old Lady, hold up   15
   Thy reverend snout and trot behind me softly,
   As it becomes a Moile[2] of ancient carriage.
                  Exeunt. Manet BASSANES.
BASSANES. Beasts onely capable of sense[3] enjoy
   The benefit of food and ease with thankfulnesse :
   Such silly creatures, with a grudging, kicke not   20
   Against the portion Nature hath bestow'd :
   But men endow'd with reason, and the use
   Of reason, to distinguish from the chaffe
   Of abject scarcity the Quintescence,[(2)]
   Soule, and Elixar of the Earths abundance,   25
   The treasures of the Sea, the Ayre, nay heaven,
   Repining at these glories of creation,
   Are verier beasts than beasts; and of those beasts

Act IV. Scene ii.   [2] *Moile :* Mule.
[1] *in conceit :* in imagination.   [3] *sense :* sensuality.

The worst am I,—I, who was made a Monarch
Of what a heart could wish for, a chast wife,   30
Endevour'd what in me lay, to pull downe
That Temple built for adoration onely,
And level't in the dust of causelesse scandall :
But to redeeme a sacrilege so impious,
Humility shall powre before the deities   35
I have incenst a largenesse[1] of more patience
Then their displeased Altars can require :
No tempests of commotion shall disquiet
The calmes of my composure.

                Enter ORGILUS.

ORGILUS.   I have found thee,
Thou patron of more horrors then the bulke   40
Of manhood, hoop'd about with ribs of Iron,
Can cramb within thy brest : Penthea, Bassanes,
Curst by thy Jealousies,—more, by thy dotage,—
Is left a prey to words.

BASSANES.   Exercise
Your trials for addition to my pennance;   45
I am resolv'd.

ORGILUS.   Play not with misery
Past cure : some angry Minister of Fate hath
Depos'd the Empresse of her soule, her reason,
From its most proper Throne; but what's the miracle
More new, I, I have seene it, and yet live.   50

BASSANES. You may delude my senses, not my judge-
           ment :
'Tis anchor'd into a firme resolution;
Dalliance of Mirth or Wit can ne'er unfixe it.
Practice yet further.

ORGILUS.   May thy death of love to her
Damne all thy comforts to a lasting fast   55
From every joy of life! Thou barren rocke,
By thee we have bee[n][2] split in ken of harbour.

Enter ITHOCLES, PENTHEA *her haire about her eares,*
      [ARMOSTES,] PHILEMA, [*and*] CHRISTALLA.

ITHOCLES. Sister, looke up; your Ithocles, your brother

Speakes t'ee : why doe you weepe? Deere, turne not
    from me.
Here is a killing sight : lo, Bassanes,   60
A lamentable object.
ORGILUS.   Man, dost see't?
Sports are more gamesome; am I yet in merriment?
Why dost not laugh?
BASSANES.   Divine and best of Ladies,
Please to forget my out-rage! Mercy ever
Cannot but lodge under a [roof][3] so excellent : 65
I have cast off that cruelty of frenzy
Which once appear'd Impostors,[4] and then jugled
To cheat my sleeps of rest.
ORGILUS.   Was I in earnest?
PENTHEA. Sure, if we were all Sirens, we should sing
    pittifully;
And 'twere a comely musicke, when in parts   70
One sung anothers knell : the Turtle[4] sighes
When he hath lost his mate; and yet some say
'A must be dead first : 'tis a fine deceit
To passe away in a dreame : indeed, I've slept
With mine eyes open a great while. No falshood 75
Equals a broken faith; there's not a haire
Sticks on my head but like a leaden Plummet
It sinkes me to the grave : I must creepe thither.
The journy is not long.
ITHOCLES.   But thou, Penthea,
Hast many yeeres, I hope, to number yet,   80
Ere thou canst travell that way.
BASSANES.   Let the [Sun][5] first
Be wrap'd up in an everlasting darknesse,
Before the light of nature, chiefly form'd
For the whole worlds delight, feele an Ecclipse
So universall.
ORGILUS. Wisdome, looke 'ee,   85
Begins to rave :—art thou mad too, antiquity?
PENTHEA. Since I was first a wife, I might have beene

4 *Turtle :* Dove.

Mother to many pretty pratling Babes :
They would have smil'd when I smil'd, and for
           certaine
I should have cry'd when they cry'd;—truly, brother,   90
My father would have pick'd me out a husband,
And then my little ones had beene no bastards :
But 'tis too late for me to marry now,
I am past child-bearing; 'tis not my fault.

BASSANES. Fall on me, if there be a burning *Etna*,   95
And bury me in flames! Sweats hot as sulphure
Boyle through my pores! Affliction hath in store
No torture like to this.

ORGILUS.   Behold a patience!
Lay by thy whyning gray dissimulation;
Doe something worth a Chronicle. Shew Justice   100
Upon the Author of this mischiefe; dig out
The Jealousies that hatch'd this thraldome first
With thine owne ponyard[5] : every anticke rapture
Can roare as thine does.

ITHOCLES.   Orgilus, forbeare.

BASSANES. Disturbe him not; it is a talking motion[6]   105
Provided for my torment : what a foole am I
To bawdy[6] passion? Ere I'le speake a word
I will looke on and burst.

PENTHEA. [*to* ORGILUS.]   I lov'd you once.

ORGILUS. Thou didst, wrong'd creature, in despite of
           malice;
For it I love thee ever.

PENTHEA.   Spare your hand;   110
Beleeve me, I'le not hurt it.

ORGILUS.   Paine my heart too.[7]

[PENTHEA.][8] Complaine not though I wring it hard :
           I'le kisse it;
O 'tis a fine soft palme : harke, in thine eare,—
Like whome doe I looke, prethee?[9]—nay, no
           whispering.

---

[5] *ponyard :* dagger.   [6] *talking motion :* puppet.

Goodnesse! we had beene happy : too much hap-   115
            pinesse
Will make folke proud, they say,—but that is he,—
                        Points at ITHOCLES.
And yet he paid for't home; alas, his heart
Is crept into the cabinet of the Princesse;
We shall have points[7] and bridelaces.[8] Remember
When we last gather'd Roses in the garden   120
I found my wits, but truly you lost yours :
That's He, and still 'tis He.[3]
ITHOCLES.   Poore soule, how idely
  Her fancies guide her tongue.
BASSANES.   Keepe in, vexation,
  And breake not into clamour.
ORGILUS.   She has tutor'd me :
  Some powerfull inspiration checks my lazinesse :   125
  Now let me kisse your hand, griev'd beauty.
PENTHEA.   Kisse it.
  Alacke, alacke, his lips be wondrous cold;
  Deare soule, h'as lost his colour : have 'ee seene
  A straying heart? All crannies! Every drop
  Of blood is turn'd to an Amethist,[4]   130
  Which married Bachelours hang in their eares.
ORGILUS. Peace usher her into *Elizium* :
  If this be madnesse, madnesse is an Oracle.
                        Exit ORGILUS.
ITHOCLES. Christalla, Philema, when slept my sister?
  Her ravings are so wild.
CHRISTALLA.   Sir, not these ten dayes.   135
PHILEMA. We watch by her continually; besides,
  We cannot any way pray her to eat.
BASSANES. Oh—misery of miseries!
PENTHEA.   Take comfort,
  You may live well, and dye a good old man :
  By yea and nay, an oath not to be broken,   140
  If you had joyn'd our hands once in the Temple,—

                [8] *bridelaces :* ties for sprigs of
[7] *points :* tagged laces.   rosemary ("remembrance").

'Twas since my father dy'd, for had he liv'd
He would have don't :—I must have call'd you father.
Oh my wrack'd honour, ruin'd by those Tyrants,
A cruell brother, and a desperate dotage!   145
There is no peace left for a ravish'd wife
Widdow'd by lawlesse marriage; to all memory,
Penthea's, poore Penthea's name is strumpeted :
But since her blood was season'd by the forfeit
Of noble shame with mixtures of pollution,   150
Her blood ('tis just) be henceforth never heightned
With tast of sustenance. Starve; let that fulnesse
Whose plurisie⁹ hath fever'd faith and modesty,—
Forgive me : O I faint!

ARMOSTES.   Be not so wilfull,
Sweet Neece, to worke thine owne destruction.   155

ITHOCLES.   Nature
Will call her daughter monster;—what! not eat?
Refuse the onely ordinary meanes
Which are ordain'd for life? Be not, my sister,
A murthresse to thy selfe.—Hear'st thou this, Bas-
    sanes?

BASSANES. Fo! I am busie; for I have not thoughts   160
Enow to thinke all shall be well anon;
'Tis tumbling in my head : there is a mastery
In Art to fatten and keepe smooth the outside;
Yes, and to comfort up the vitall spirits
Without the helpe of food,—fumes or perfumes,   165
Perfumes or fumes : let her alone, I'le search out
The tricke on't.

PENTHEA.   Lead me gently; heavens reward ye :
Griefes are sure friends; they leave, without controule,
Nor cure nor comforts for a leprous soule.

                    Exeunt the maids supporting PENTHEA.

BASSANES. I grant t'ee; and will put in practice instantly   170
What you shall still admire : 'tis wonderfull,
'Tis super singular, not to be match'd :

⁹ *plurisie :* excess.

Yet when I've don't, I've don't; ye shall thanke mee.
Exit BASSANES.

ARMOSTES. The sight is full of terror.

ITHOCLES.   On my soule
  Lyes such an infinite clogge of massie dulnesse,   175
  As that I have not sense enough to feele it.
  See, Uncle, th' augury[10] thing returnes againe,
  Shall's welcome him with Thunder? We are haunted,
  And must use exorcisme to conjure downe
  This spirit of malevolence.

ARMOSTES.   Mildly, Nephew.   180
Enter NEARCHUS *and* AMELUS.

NEARCHUS. I come not, Sir, to chide your late disorder,
  Admitting that th' inurement to a roughnesse
  In Souldiers of your yeares and fortunes, chiefly
  So lately prosperous, hath not yet shooke off
  The custome of the warre in houres of leisure :   185
  Nor shall you need excuse, since y'are to render
  Account to that faire Excellence, the Princesse,
  Who in her private Gallery expects it
  From your owne mouth alone : I am a messenger
  But to her pleasure.

ITHOCLES.   Excellent Nearchus,   190
  Be Prince still of my services, and conquer
  Without the combat of dispute; I honour 'ee.

NEARCHUS. The King is on a sudden indispos'd,
  Physicians are call'd for; 'twere fit, Armostes,
  You should be neere him.

ARMOSTES.   Sir, I kisse your hands.   195
Exeunt. Manent NEARCHUS *and* AMELUS.

NEARCHUS. Amelus, I perceive Calantha's bosome
  Is warm'd with other fires then such as can
  Take strength from any fuell of the love
  I might addresse to her : young Ithocles,
  Or ever I mistake, is Lord ascendant[5]   200
  Of her devotions; one, to speake him truly,
  In every disposition nobly fashioned.

AMELUS. But can your Highnesse brooke to be so rival'd,
  Considering th' inequality of the persons?

NEARCHUS. I can, Amelus; for affections injur'd   205
    By tyrannie, or rigour of compulsion,
    Like Tempest-threatned Trees unfirmely rooted,
    Ne'er spring to timely growth : observe, for instance,
    Life-spent Penthea and unhappy Orgilus.
AMELUS. How does your grace determine?
NEARCHUS.   To be jealous 210
    In publike of what privately I'le further;
    And though they shall not know, yet they shall finde
               it.

[ACTUS QUARTUS. SCAENA TERTIA.]

Enter HEMOPHIL *and* GRONEAS *leading* AMYCLAS,
and placing him in a Chayre, followed by
ARMOSTES [*with a box*], CROTOLON,
and PROPHILUS.

AMYCLAS. Our daughter is not neere?
ARMOSTES.   She is retired, Sir,
    Into her gallery.
AMYCLAS.   Where's the Prince our Cozen?
PROPHILUS. New walk'd into the Grove, my Lord.
AMYCLAS.   All
          leave us
    Except Armostes, and you, Crotolon;
    We would be private.
PROPHILUS.   Health unto your Majesty.   5
        Exeunt PROPHILUS, HEMOPHIL, *and* GRONEAS.
AMYCLAS. What, Tecnicus is gone?
ARMOSTES.   He is—to *Delphos;*
    And to your Royall hands presents this box.
AMYCLAS. Unseale it, good Armostes, therein lyes
    The secrets of the Oracle; out with it.
           [ARMOSTES *takes out the scroll.*]
    Apollo live our patron : read, Armostes.   10
ARMOSTES. "The plot in which the Vine takes root
    Begins to dry from head to foot,
    The stocke soone withering, want of sap

Doth cause to quaile the budding grape :
But from the neighboring Elme, a dew   15
Shall drop and feed the Plot anew."

AMYCLAS. That is the Oracle; what exposition
Makes the Philosopher?

ARMOSTES.   This briefe one onely :
"The plot is Sparta, the dry'd Vine the King;
The quailing grape his daughter; but the thing   20
Of most importance, not to be reveal'd,
Is a neere Prince, the Elme; the rest conceal'd.
                                          Tecnicus."

AMYCLAS. Enough; although the opening[1] of this Riddle
Be but it selfe a Riddle, yet we construe   25
How neere our lab'ring age drawes to a rest :
But must Calantha quaile too—that young grape
Untimely budded? I could mourne for her;
Her tendernesse hath yet deserv'd no rigor
So to be crost by Fate.

AMYCLAS.   You misapply, Sir,—   30
With favour let me speake it—what *Apollo*
Hath clouded in hid sense : I here conjecture
Her marriage with some neighb'ring Prince, the dew
Of which befriending Elme shall ever strengthen
Your Subjects with a Soveraignty of power.   35

CROTOLON. Besides, most gracious Lord, the pith of
                              Oracles
Is to be then digested, when th' events
Expound their truth, not brought as soone to light
As utter'd; Truth is Child of Time, and herein
I finde no scruple,[(1)] rather cause of comfort,   40
With unity of kingdomes.

AMYCLAS.   May it prove so
For weale of this deare Nation.—Where is Ithocles?
Armostes, Crotolon, when this wither'd Vine
Of my fraile carkasse, on the funerall Pile
Is fir'd into its ashes, let that young man   45

ACT IV. SCENE III.
[1] *opening :* interpretation.

Be hedg'd about still with your cares and loves;
Much owe I to his worth, much to his service.
Let such as wait come in now.

ARMOSTES.   All attend here!

Enter ITHOCLES, CALANTHA, PROPHILUS, ORGILUS,
        EUPHRANEA, HEMOPHIL, *and* GRONEAS.

CALANTHA. Deare Sir, King, Father!

ITHOCLES.   O my royall Master!

AMYCLAS. Cleave not my heart, sweet Twins of my life's   50
                solace,
With your fore-judging feares : there is no Physicke
So cunningly restorative to cherish
The fall of Age, or call backe youth and vigor,
As your consents in duty : I will shake off
This languishing disease of time, to quicken   55
Fresh pleasures in these drooping houres of sadnesse.
Is faire Euphranea married yet to Prophilus?

CROTOLON. This morning, gracious Lord.

ORGILUS.   This very
                morning,
Which—with your Highnesse leave—you may observe
                too.
Our sister lookes (me thinks) mirthfull and sprightly;   60
As if her chaster fancy could already
Expound the riddle of her gaine in losing
A trifle; Maids know onely that they know not :
Pish! prethee,[1] blush not; 'tis but honest change
Of fashion in the garment, loose for streight,2   65
And so the modest maid is made a wife :
Shrewd businesse, is't not, sister?

EUPHRANEA.   You are pleasant.

AMYCLAS. We thanke thee, Orgilus; this mirth becomes
                thee :
But wherefore sits the Court in such a silence?
A wedding without Revels is not seemely.   70

CALANTHA. Your late indisposition, Sir, forbade it.

AMYCLAS. Be it thy charge, Calantha, to set forward

2 *streight :* tight.

The bridall sports, to which I will be present :
If not, at least consenting.—Mine owne Ithocles,
I have done little for thee yet.

ITHOCLES.   Y'have built me   75
To the full height I stand in.

CALANTHA. [*Aside.*]   Now or never.—
May I propose a suit?

AMYCLAS.   Demand and have it.

CALANTHA. Pray, Sir, give me this young man, and no
                              further
Account him yours then he deserves in all things
To be thought worthy mine; I will esteeme him   80
According to his merit.

AMYCLAS.   Still th'art my daughter,
Still grow'st upon my heart.—[*to* ITHOCLES.] Give me
                              thine hand.
Calantha, take thine owne; in noble actions
Thou'lt find him firme and absolute.—I would not
Have parted with thee, Ithocles, to any   85
But to a mistresse who is all what I am.

ITHOCLES. A change, great King, most wisht for, 'cause
                              the same.

CALANTHA. [*Aside to* ITHOCLES.] Th'art mine.—Have I
                              now kept my word?

ITHOCLES. [*Aside to* CALANTHA.]   Divinely.

ORGILUS. Rich fortunes,[2] guard to favour of a Prin-
                              cesse,
Rocke thee, brave man, in ever crowned plenty;   90
Y'are minion[3] of the time, be thankfull for it.
[*Aside.*] Ho, here's a swinge in Destiny.—Apparent,
The youth is up on tiptoe, yet may stumble.

AMYCLAS. On to your recreations; now convey me
Unto my bed-chamber : none on his forehead   95
Wear[3] a distempered looke.

OMNES.   The gods preserve 'ee.

CALANTHA. [*Aside to* ITHOCLES.] Sweet, be not from my
                              sight.

---

[3] *minion :* favorite.

ITHOCLES. [*Aside to* CALANTHA.] My whole felicity!
Exeunt. Carrying out of the King. ORGILUS *stayes*
ITHOCLES.

ORGILUS. Shall I be bold, my Lord?

ITHOCLES.   Thou canst not,
                Orgilus;
Call me thine owne, for Prophilus must henceforth
Be all thy sisters; friendship, though it cease not   100
In marriage, yet is oft at lesse command
Then when a single freedome can dispose it.

ORGILUS. Most right, my most good Lord, my most great
                Lord,
My gracious Princely Lord,—I might adde—royall.

ITHOCLES. Royall! A Subject royall?

ORGILUS.   Why not, pray, Sir?   105
The Soveraignty of Kingdomes in their nonage
Stoop'd to desert, not birth : there's as much merit
In clearenesse of affection as in puddle
Of generation : you have conquer'd Love
Even in the loveliest; if I greatly erre not,   110
The sonne of *Venus* hath bequeath'd his quiver
To Ithocles his manage, by whose arrowes
Calantha's brest is open'd.

ITHOCLES.   Can't be possible?

ORGILUS. I was my selfe a peece of suitor once,
And forward in preferment too, so forward   115
That, speaking truth, I may without offence, Sir,
Presume to whisper that my hopes, and—hark 'ee—
My certainty of marriage stood assured
With as firme footing—by your leave—as any's
Now at this very instant—but—

ITHOCLES.   'Tis granted :   120
And for a league of privacy betweene us,
Read o'er my bosome and pertake a secret;
The Princesse is contracted mine.

ORGILUS.   Still⁴—why not?
I now applaud her wisdome; when your kingdome

---

⁴ *Still :* Forever.

Stands seated in your will secure, and setled,   125
I dare pronounce you will be a just Monarch :
Greece must admire and tremble.
ITHOCLES.   Then the sweetnesse
Of so imparadis'd a comfort, Orgilus!
It is to banquet with the gods.
ORGILUS.   The glory
Of numerous children, potency of Nobles,   130
Bent knees, hearts pav'd to tread on.
ITHOCLES.   With a friendship
So deare, so fast as thine.
ORGILUS.   I am unfitting
For Office, but for service—
ITHOCLES.   Wee'll distinguish
Our fortunes meerely in the Title,—partners
In all respects else but the bed.
ORGILUS.   The bed?   135
Forefend it *Joves* owne Jealousie, till lastly
We slip downe in the common earth together;
And there our beds are equall, save some Monument
To shew this was the King, and this the Subject.
                                        Soft sad musicke.

List! What sad sounds are these?—extremely sad ones. 140
ITHOCLES. Sure, from Penthea's lodging.
ORGILUS.   Harke! A voyce too.
                    A Song [within].
Oh no more, no more, too late
    Sighes are spent; the burning Tapers
Of a life as chast as Fate,
    Pure as are unwritten papers,   145
        Are burnt out : no heat, no light
        Now remaines; 'tis ever night.
Love is dead; let lovers eyes
    Lock'd in endlesse dreames,
        Th' extremes of all extremes,   150
Ope no more, for now Love dyes,
        Now Love dyes, implying
        Loves Martyrs must be ever, ever dying.
ITHOCLES. Oh my misgiving heart!

ORGILUS.   A horrid stilnesse
Succeeds this deathfull ayre; let's know the reason :   155
Tread softly, there is mystery in mourning. *Exeunt.*

[ACTUS QUARTUS. SCAENA QUARTA.]

Enter CHRISTALLA *and* PHILEMA, *bringing in* PENTHEA
*in a chaire, vaild : two other servants placing two
chaires, one on the one side, and the other with
an Engine*[1] *on the other; the maids sit downe
at her feet mourning; the servants goe out;
meet them* ITHOCLES *and* ORGILUS.

SERVANT. [*Aside to* ORGILUS.] 'Tis done,—that on her
right hand.
ORGILUS. [*Aside.*]   Good. Begone.
                                        [*Exeunt* SERVANTS.]
ITHOCLES. Soft peace inrich this roome.
ORGILUS.   How   fares   the
Lady?
PHILEMA. Dead.
CHRISTALLA.   Dead.
PHILEMA.   Starv'd.
CHRISTALLA.   Starv'd.
ITHOCLES.   Me miserable!
ORGILUS.   Tell us
How parted she from life?
PHILEMA.   She call'd for musicke,
And begg'd some gentle voyce to tune a farewell   5
To life and griefes : Christalla touch'd the Lute,
I wept the funerall song.
CHRISTALLA.   Which scarce was ended
But her last breath seal'd up these hollow sounds,
"O cruell Ithocles, and injur'd Orgilus!"
So downe she drew her vaile, so dy'd.
ITHOCLES.   So dy'd!   10

ACT IV. SCENE IV.
[1] *Engine :* Mechanism.

ORGILUS. Up; you are messengers of death, goe from us;
   Here's woe enough to court without a prompter.
   Away; and, harke ye, till you see us next,
   No sillable that she is dead.—Away,
   Keepe a smooth brow.—

Exeunt PHILEMA and CHRISTALLA.

My Lord.

ITHOCLES.   Mine onely sister,   15
   Another is not left me.
ORGILUS.   Take that chayre,
   I'le seat me here in this : betweene us sits
   The object of our sorrowes; some few teares
   Wee'll part among us; I perhaps can mixe
   One lamentable story to prepare 'em.   20
   There, there, sit there, my Lord.
ITHOCLES.   Yes, as you please.

ITHOCLES sits downe, and is catcht in the Engine.

   What meanes this treachery?
ORGILUS.   Caught! you are caught,
   Young master : 'tis thy throne of Coronation,
   Thou foole of greatnesse! See, I take this vaile off;
   Survey a beauty wither'd by the flames   25
   Of an insulting[2] Phaeton,[1] her brother.
ITHOCLES. Thou mean'st to kill me basely.
ORGILUS.   I foreknew
   The last act of her life, and train'd[3] thee hither
   To sacrifice a Tyrant to a Turtle.[4]
   You dream't of kingdomes, did 'ee? How to bosome   30
   The delicacies of a youngling Princesse,
   How with this nod to grace that subtill Courtier,
   How with that frowne to make this Noble tremble,
   And so forth; whiles Penthea's grones, and tortures,
   Her agonies, her miseries, afflictions,   35
   Ne'er toucht upon your thought; as for my injuries,
   Alas! they were beneath your royall pitty;

---

2 insulting : overbearing,
  arrogant.

3 train'd : lured.
4 Turtle : Dove.

But yet they liv'd, thou proud man, to confound
                              thee :
Behold thy fate, this steele! [*He draws his dagger.*]
ITHOCLES.   Strike home; a courage
    As keene as thy revenge shall give it welcome :   40
    But prethee,[1] faint not; if the wound close up
    Tent[5] it with double force, and search it deeply.
    Thou look'st that I should whine and beg compassion,
    As loath to leave the vainnesse of my glories;
    A statelier resolution armes my confidence,   45
    To cozen[6] thee of honour; neither could I,
    With equall tryall of unequall fortune
    By hazard of a duell; 'twere a bravery[7]
    Too mighty for a slave intending murther :
    On to the Execution, and inherit   50
    A conflict with thy horrors.
ORGILUS.   By *Apollo,*
    Thou talk'st a goodly language! for requitall
    I will report thee to thy mistresse richly :
    And take this peace along; some few short minutes
    Determin'd, my resolves shall quickly follow   55
    Thy wrathfull ghost; then if we tug for mastery,
    Pentheas sacred eyes shall lend new courage.
    Give me thy hand; be healthfull in thy parting
    From lost mortality : thus, thus I free it.   *Kils him.*
ITHOCLES. Yet, yet I scorne to shrinke.
ORGILUS.   Keepe up thy   60
                spirit :
    I will be gentle even in blood; to linger
    Paine, which I strive to cure, were to be cruell.
                              [*He stabs him again.*]
ITHOCLES. Nimble in vengeance—I forgive thee; follow
    Safety; with best successe O may it prosper!
    Penthea, by thy side thy brother bleeds :   65
    The earnest[8] of his wrongs to thy forc'd faith;
    Thoughts of ambition, or delitious banquet,

---

[5] *Tent :* Probe.   [7] *bravery :* glory.
[6] *cozen :* cheat.   [8] *earnest :* payment.

With beauty, youth, and love, together perish
In my last breath, which on the sacred Altar
Of a long-look'd-for peace—now—moves—to heaven.   70
Moritur.[9]
ORGILUS. Farewell, faire spring of manhood; henceforth
welcome
Best expectation of a noble suffrance :
I'le locke the bodies safe, till what must follow
Shall be approv'd.[10] Sweet Twins, shine stars forever.
In vaine they build their hopes whose life is shame;
No monument lasts but a happy Name.
Exit ORGILUS.

ACTUS QUINTUS. SCAENA PRIMA.

Enter BASSANES *alone.*
BASSANES. *Athens,* to *Athens* I have sent, the Nursery
Of Greece for learning, and the Fount of knowledge;
For here in Sparta there's not left amongst us
One wise man to direct,—we're all turn'd madcaps :
'Tis said, *Apollo* is the god of herbs;   5
Then certainly he knowes the vertue of 'em :
To *Delphos* I have sent too[1]; if there can be
A helpe for nature, we are sure yet.
Enter ORGILUS.
ORGILUS.   Honour
Attend thy counsels ever.
BASSANES.   I beseech thee
With all my heart—let me goe from thee quietly;   10
I will not ought to doe with thee, of all men.
The doublers[1, 2] of a Hare, or, in a morning,
Salutes from a splay-footed witch, to drop
Three drops of blood at th' nose just, and no more,
Croaking of Ravens, or the screech of Owles,   15

---

[9] *Moritur :* He dies.
[10] *approv'd :* tested by
experience.

ACT V. SCENE i.
[1] *doublers :* doubling across
one's path.

Are not so boading mischiefe as thy crossing
My private meditations : shun me, prethee,[3]
And if I cannot love thee hartily,
I'le love thee as well as I can.

ORGILUS.   Noble Bassanes,
Mistake me not.

BASSANES.   Phew! then we shall be troubled;   20
Thou wert ordain'd my plague, heaven make me
                    thankfull;
And give me patience too, heaven, I beseech thee.

ORGILUS. Accept a league of amity; for henceforth
I vow by my best Genius,[2] in a sillable,
Never to speake vexation; I will study   25
Service and friendship with a zealous sorrow
For my past incivility towards 'ee.

BASSANES. Heydey! good words, good words! I must be-
                    leeve 'em
And be a Coxcombe[3] for my labor.

ORGILUS.   Use not
So hard a Language; your misdoubt is causelesse :   30
For instance, if you promise to put on
A constancy of patience, such a patience
As Chronicle or history ne'er mentioned,
As followes not example but shall stand
A wonder and a Theame for imitation,   35
The first, the *Index*[4] pointing to a second,
I will acquaint 'ee with an unmatch'd secret,
Whose knowledge to your griefes shall set a period.

BASSANES. Thou canst not, Orgilus, 'tis in the power
Of the gods onely; yet for satisfaction,   40
Because I note an earnest in thine utterance,
Unforc'd and naturally free, be resolute
The Virgin Bayes shall not withstand the lightning
With a more carelesse danger, than my constancy
The full of thy relation : could it move   45

[2] *Genius :* Attendant good   [4] *Index :* Printer's pointing
    angel.   hand.
[3] *Coxcombe :* Fool.

Distraction in a senselesse marble statue,
It should finde me a rocke : I doe expect now
Some truth of unheard moment.

ORGILUS.   To your patience
You must adde privacie, as strong in silence
As mysteries lock'd up in *Joves* owne bosome.   50

BASSANES. A skull hid in the earth a treble age
Shall sooner prate.

ORGILUS.   Lastly, to such direction
As the severity of a glorious *Action*
Deserves to lead your wisdome and your judgement,
You ought to yeeld obedience.

BASSANES.   With assurance   55
Of will and thankfulnesse.

ORGILUS.   With manly courage
Please then to follow me.

BASSANES.   Where e'er,—I feare not.
                              Exeunt omnes.

[ACTUS QUINTUS. SCAENA SECUNDA.]

Lowd musicke. Enter GRONEAS *and* HEMOPHIL
leading EUPHRANEA, CHRISTALLA *and* PHILEMA
leading PROPHILUS, NEARCHUS *supporting*
CALANTHA, CROTOLON *and* AMELUS. *Cease
loud Musicke; all make a stand.*

CALANTHA. We misse our servant Ithocles and Orgilus,
On whom attend they?

CROTOLON.   My sonne, gracious Princesse,
Whisper'd some new device, to which these Revels
Should be but usher : wherein I conceive
Lord Ithocles and he himselfe are Actors.   5

CALANTHA. A faire excuse for absence : as for Bassanes,
Delights to him are troublesome. Armostes
Is with the King?

CROTOLON.   He is.

CALANTHA.   On to the dance :

Deare Cozen, hand you the Bride; the Bridegroome
    must be
Intrusted to my Courtship : be not jealous,   10
Euphranea, I shall scarcely prove a temptresse.
Fall to our dance.
             Musicke.

NEARCHUS *dance with* EUPHRANEA, PROPHILUS *with*
  CALANTHA, CHRISTALLA *with* HEMOPHIL, PHILEMA
     with GRONEAS.
  Dance the first change, during which
    enter ARMOSTES.

ARMOSTES. *in* CALANTHA'S *eare.* The King your father's
     dead.

CALANTHA. To the other change.

ARMOSTES.   Is't possible?
   Dance againe. Enter BASSANES.

BASSANES. [*in* CALANTHA'S *ear.*]   O Madam!
  Penthea, poore Penthea's starv'd.

CALANTHA.   Beshrew thee.—
  Lead to the next.

BASSANES.   Amazement duls my senses.   15
   Dance againe. Enter ORGILUS.

ORGILUS. [*in* CALANTHA'S *ear.*] Brave Ithocles is murther'd, murther'd cruelly.

CALANTHA. How dull this musicke sounds! Strike up
    more sprightly;
  Our footings are not active like our heart,
  Which treads the nimbler measure.

ORGILUS.   I am thunder-strooke.
   Last change. Cease musicke.

CALANTHA. So,—let us breath a while. Hath not this   20
    motion
  Rais'd fresher colour on your cheeks?

NEARCHUS.   Sweet Princesse,
  A perfect purity of blood enamels
  The beauty of your white.

CALANTHA.   We all looke cheerfully :
  And, Cozen, 'tis, me thinks, a rare presumption

In any who prefer[1] our lawfull pleasures   25
Before their owne sowre censure, to interrupt
The custome of this Ceremony bluntly.
NEARCHUS. None dares, Lady.
CALANTHA. Yes, yes; some hollow voyce deliver'd to me
How that the King was dead.
ARMOSTES.   The King is dead: 30
That fatall newes was mine; for in mine armes
He breath'd his last, and with his Crowne bequeath'd
                           'ee
Your mothers wedding Ring, which here I tender.
CROTOLON. Most strange!
CALANTHA.   Peace crown his ashes: we are
                    queen then.
NEARCHUS. Long live Calantha, Sparta's Soveraigne   35
                    Queene!
OMNES. Long live the Queene!
CALANTHA.   What whispered Bassanes?
BASSANES. That my Penthea, miserable soule,
Was starv'd to death.
CALANTHA.   Shee's happy; she hath finish'd
A long and painefull progresse.—A third murmure
Pierc'd mine unwilling eares.
ORGILUS.   That Ithocles   40
Was murther'd—rather butcher'd, had not bravery
Of an undaunted spirit, conquering terror,
Proclaim'd his last Act triumph over ruine.
ARMOSTES. How! murther'd?
CALANTHA.   By whose hand?
ORGILUS.   By mine; this
                    weapon
Was instrument to my revenge: the reasons   45
Are just and knowne: quit him of these, and then
Never liv'd Gentleman of greater merit,
Hope, or abiliment to steere a kingdome.
CROTOLON. Fye! Orgilus.
EUPHRANEA.   Fye! brother.
CALANTHA.   You have done it.

BASSANES. How it was done let him report, the forfeit   50
  Of whose alleageance to our lawes doth covet
  Rigour of Justice; but that done it is
  Mine eyes have beene an evidence of credit
  Too sure to be convinc'd.[1] Armostes, rent not
  Thine Arteries with hearing the bare circumstances   55
  Of these calamities : thou'st lost a Nephew,
  A Neece, and I a wife : continue man still;
  Make me the patterne of digesting evils,
  Who can out-live my mighty ones, not shrinking
  At such a pressure as would sinke a soule   60
  Into what's most of death, the worst of horrors :
  But I have seal'd a covenant with sadnesse,
  And enter'd into bonds without condition
  To stand these tempests calmely; marke me, Nobles,
  I doe not shed a teare, not for Penthea!   65
  Excellent misery!
CALANTHA.   We begin our reigne
  With a first act of Justice : thy confession
  Unhappy Orgilus, doomes thee a sentence;
  But yet thy fathers, or thy sisters presence,
  Shall be excus'd : give, Crotolon, a blessing   70
  To thy lost sonne : Euphranea, take a farewell,
  And both be gone.
CROTOLON.   Confirme thee, noble sorrow,
  In worthy resolution.
EUPHRANEA.   Could my teares speake,
  My griefes were sleight.
ORGILUS.   All goodnesse[2] dwell amongst
                          yee!
  Enjoy my sister, Prophilus; my vengeance   75
  Aym'd never at thy prejudice.[2]
CALANTHA.   Now withdraw.
      Exeunt CROTOLON, PROPHILUS, *and* EUPHRANEA.
  Bloody relator of thy staines in blood,

ACT V. SCENE II.   [2] *at thy prejudice :* at your
[1] *convinc'd :* overcome.   injury.

For that thou hast reported him whose fortunes
And life by thee are both at once snatch'd from him
With honourable mention, make thy choyce   80
Of what death likes[3] thee best; there's all our bounty.
But to excuse delayes, let me, deare Cozen,
Intreat you and these Lords see execution
Instant before 'ee part.
NEARCHUS.   Your will commands us.
ORGILUS. One suit, just Queene, my last; vouchsafe your
                    clemency   85
That by no common hand I be divided
From this my humble frailty.
CALANTHA.   To their wisdomes
Who are to be spectators of thine end
I make the reference : those that are dead,
Are dead; had they not now dy'd, of necessity   90
They must have payd the debt they ow'd to nature
One time or other.—Use dispatch, my Lords,
Wee'll suddenly prepare our Coronation.
        Exeunt CALANTHA, PHILEMA, [*and*] CHRISTALLA.
ARMOSTES. 'Tis strange, these Tragedies should never
                    touch on
Her female pitty.
BASSANES.   She has a masculine spirit :   95
And wherefore should I pule, and like a girle
Put finger in the eye : let's be all toughnesse,
Without distinction betwixt sex and sex.
NEARCHUS. Now, Orgilus, thy choyce?
ORGILUS.   To bleed to death.
ARMOSTES. The Executioner?
ORGILUS.   My selfe,—no Surgeon.   100
I am well skill'd in letting blood : bind fast
This arme, that so the pipes may from their conduits
Convey a full streame : here's a skilfull Instrument.
                    [*He flourishes his dagger.*]
Onely I am a beggar to some charity

[3] *likes :* pleases.

To speed me in this Execution,   105
By lending th'other pricke to th' tother arme,
When this is bubling life out.
BASSANES.   I am for 'ee.
It most concernes my art, my care, my credit;
Quicke, fillet[4] both [his][3] armes.
ORGILUS.   Gramercy, friend-
                ship :
Such curtesies are reall which flow cheerefully   110
Without an expection of requitall.
Reach me a staffe in this hand : if a pronenesse
Or custome in my nature from my cradle
Had beene inclin'd to fierce and eager bloodshed,
A coward guilt, hid in a coward quaking,   115
Would have betray'd fame to ignoble flight
And vagabond pursuit of dreadfull[5] safety :
But looke upon my steddinesse and scorne not
The sicknesse of my fortune, which since Bassanes
Was husband to Penthea, had laine bed-rid.   120
We trifle time in words : thus I shew cunning
In opening of a veine too full, too lively.
                              [*He cuts a vein.*]
ARMOSTES. Desperate courage.
ORGILUS.   Honourable infamy.[4]
HEMOPHIL.[5] I tremble at the sight.
GRONEAS.   Would I were loose.
BASSANES. It sparkles like a lusty wine new broacht;   125
The vessell must be sound from which it issues;
Graspe hard this other sticke : I'le be as nimble.
But prethee,[6] looke not pale; have at 'ee,—stretch
                out
Thine arme with vigor and unshooke vertue.
                              [*He cuts a vein.*]
Good! O I envy not a Rivall fitted   130
To conquer in extremities; this pastime
Appeares majesticall : some high-tun'd poem

---

[4] *fillet :* bind.   [5] *dreadfull :* fearfull.

Hereafter shall deliver to posterity
The writers glory, and his subjects triumph.
How is't man? Droope not yet?

ORGILUS.   I feele no palsies :   135
On a paire royall doe I wait in death,—
My Soveraigne, as his Liegeman, on my Mistresse
As a devoted servant, and on Ithocles
As if no brave yet no unworthy enemy :
Nor did I use an engine to intrap   140
His life out of a slavish feare to combate
Youth, strength, or cunning,[6] but for that I durst not
Ingage the goodnesse of a cause on fortune,
By which his name might have out-fac'd my
                              vengeance.
Oh Tecnicus, inspir'd with *Phoebus* fire,   145
I call to mind thy Augury, 'twas perfect;
"Revenge proves its owne Executioner."
When feeble man is bending to his mother,
The dust 'a was first fram'd on, thus he totters.

BASSANES. Life's fountaine is dry'd up.

ORGILUS.   So falls the Standards   150
Of my prerogative in being a creature :
A mist hangs o'er mine eyes; the Sun's bright splendor
Is clouded in an everlasting shadow :
Welcome thou yce that sit'st about my heart,
No heat can ever thaw thee.   *Dyes.*

NEARCHUS.   Speech hath left him.   155

BASSANES. 'A has shooke hands with time : his funerall
                              urne
Shall be my charge : remove the bloodlesse bodie;
The Coronation must require attendance :
That past, my few dayes can be but one mourning.
                                        Exeunt.

---

[6] *cunning :* skill.

[ACTUS QUINTUS. SCAENA TERTIA.]

An altar covered with white. Two lights of Virgin wax
during which musicke of Recorders; enter foure bear-
ing ITHOCLES *on a hearse, or in a chaire, in a rich*
robe and a Crowne on his head; place him on
one side of the Altar; after him enter CALAN-
THA *in a white robe, and crown'd;* EUPHRA-
NEA, PHILEMA, [*and*] CHRISTALLA *in*
white; NEARCHUS, ARMOSTES, CROTO-
LON, PROPHILUS, AMELUS, BASSANES,
HEMOPHIL, *and* GRONEAS. CALAN-
THA *goes and kneeles before*
the Altar, the rest stand off,
the women kneeling be-
hind; cease Recorders
during her devotions.
Soft musicke. CA-
LANTHA *and the*
rest rise, doing
obeysance
to the
Altar.

CALANTHA. Our Orisons are heard, the gods are merci-
full :
Now tell me, you whose loyalties payes tribute
To us your lawfull Soveraigne, how unskilfull[1]
Your duties or obedience is, to render
Subjection to the Scepter of a Virgin,   5
Who have beene ever fortunate in Princes
Of masculine and stirring composition!
A woman has enough to governe wisely
Her owne demeanours, passions, and divisions.
A Nation warlike and inur'd to practice   10

ACT V. SCENE III.
[1] *unskilfull* : unwise.

Of policy and labour cannot brooke
A feminate authority : we therefore
Command your counsaile, how you may advise us
In choosing of a husband whose abilities
Can better guide this kingdome.

NEARCHUS.   Royall Lady,   15
Your law is in your will.

ARMOSTES.   We have seene tokens
Of constancy too lately to mistrust it.

CROTOLON. Yet, if your highnesse settle on a choice
By your owne judgement both allow'd and lik'd of,
Sparta may grow in power, and proceed   20
To an increasing height.

CALANTHA.   Hold you the same minde?

BASSANES. Alas, great mistris, reason is so clouded
With the thicke darkenesse of my infinite[1] woes
That I forecast nor dangers, hopes, or safety :
Give me some corner of the world to weare out   25
The remnant of the minutes I must number,
Where I may heare no sounds but sad complaints
Of Virgins who have lost contracted partners,
Of husbands howling that their wives were ravisht
By some untimely fate, of friends divided   30
By churlish opposition, or of fathers
Weeping upon their childrens slaughtered carcasses,
Or daughters groaning o'er their fathers hearses;
And I can dwell there, and with these keepe consort
As musicall as theirs : what can you looke for   35
From an old foolish, peevish, doting man
But crasinesse of age?

CALANTHA. Cozen of *Argos*,—

NEARCHUS.   Madam.

CALANTHA.   Were I presently
To choose you for my Lord, Ile open freely
What articles I would propose to treat on   40
Before our marriage.

NEARCHUS.   Name them, vertuous Lady.

CALANTHA. I would presume you would retaine the
                    royalty

Of Sparta in her owne bounds : then in *Argos*
Armostes might be Viceroy; in *Messene*
Might Crotolon beare sway, and Bassanes—   45
BASSANES. I, Queene? Alas, what I?
CALANTHA.   Be Sparta's Marshall :
  The multitudes of high imployments could not
  But set a peace to private griefes : these Gentlemen,
  Groneas and Hemophil,[2] with worthy pensions
  Should wait upon your person in your Chamber :   50
  I would bestow Christalla on Amelus,—
  Shee'll prove a constant wife,—and Philema
  Should into *Vesta's* Temple. [1]
BASSANES. [*Aside.*]   This is a Testament,
  It sounds not like conditions on a marriage.
NEARCHUS. All this should be perform'd.
CALANTHA.   Lastly, for   55
              Prophilus,
  He should be, Cozen, solemnly invested
  In all those honors, titles, and preferments
  Which his deare friend and my neglected husband
  Too short a time enjoy'd.
PROPHILUS.   I am unworthy
  To live in your remembrance.
EUPHRANEA.   Excellent Lady!   60
NEARCHUS. Madam, what meanes that word "neglected
                  husband"?
CALANTHA. Forgive me.
  [*To the body of* ITHOCLES.] Now I turne to thee, thou
                  shadow
  Of my contracted Lord. Beare witnesse all,
  I put my mother's[3] wedding Ring upon
  His finger; 'twas my fathers last bequest :   65
  Thus I new marry him whose wife I am;
  Death shall not separate us. O my Lords,
  I but deceiv'd your eyes with Anticke gesture,
  When one newes straight came hudling on another
  Of death, and death, and death,—still I danc'd   70
                  forward;
  But it strooke home, and here, and in an instant.

Be such meere women, who with shreeks and out-
                    cries
Can vow a present end to all their sorrowes,
Yet live to vow new pleasures, and out-live them.
They are the silent griefes which cut the hart-strings;   75
Let me dye smiling. (2)

NEARCHUS.   'Tis a truth too ominous.

CALANTHA. One kisse on these cold lips, my last. Cracke,
                    cracke!
Argos now's Sparta's King. Command the voyces
Which wait at th' Altar, now to sing the song
I fitted for my end.

NEARCHUS.   Sirs, the song.   80
                    A Song.

ALL.   Glories, pleasures, pomps, delights, and
                    ease,
                 Can but please
        [The] outward senses, when the mind[4]
        Is not untroubled,[5] or by peace refin'd.

1. [VOICE.] Crownes may flourish and decay,   85
        Beauties shine, but fade away.

2. [VOICE.] Youth may revell, yet it must
        Lye downe in a bed of dust:

3. [VOICE.] Earthly honors flow and wast,
        Time alone doth change and last.   90

ALL.   Sorrowes mingled with contents, prepare
                    Rest for care;
        Love onely reignes in death: though Art
        Can find no comfort for a broken heart.
                    [CALANTHA *falls and dies.*]

ARMOSTES. Looke to the Queene.

BASSANES.   Her heart is broke in-   95
                    deed.
O royall maid, would thou hadst mist this part;
Yet 'twas a brave one: I must weepe to see
Her smile in death.

ARMOSTES.   Wise Tecnicus, thus said he,
"When youth is ripe, and age from time doth part,
The livelesse Trunke shall wed the broken heart":   100

'Tis here fulfill'd.

NEARCHUS.   I am your King.

OMNES.   Long live
Nearchus King of Sparta!

NEARCHUS.   Her last will
Shall never be digrest from; wait in order
Upon these faithfull lovers, as becomes us.
The Counsels of the gods are never knowne,   105
Till men can call th' effects of them their owne.

                                    [*Exeunt.*]

THE EPILOGUE.

Where Noble Judgements, and cleare eyes are fix'd
To grace Endevour, there sits Truth not mix'd
With Ignorance : those censures may command
Beleefe, which *talke* not, till they *understand*.
Let some say *This was flat;* some *Here the Sceane*   5
Fell from its height; Another that the Meane
Was *ill observ'd,* in such a growing passion,
As it transcended either state or fashion :
Some *few* may cry, *'twas pretty well or so,*
But,—and there shrugge in silence; yet we know   10
Our writers ayme, was in the whole addrest
Well to deserve of *All,* but please the *Best.*
Which granted, by th' allowance of this straine,
The *Broken Heart* may be piec't up againe.

FINIS.

THE LADY OF PLEASURE

BY

JAMES SHIRLEY

THE
LADY OF
PLEASVRE.

A
COMEDIE,

As it vvas Acted by her Majesties Servants, at the private
Houſe in *Drury* Lane.

Written by *James Shirly.*

LONDON,
Printed by *Tho. Cotes,* for *Andrew Crooke,*
and *William Cooke.*
1637.

Persons of the Comedy.

LORD. [1]

SIR THOMAS BORNWELL.

SIR WILLIAM SENTLOVE. [1], (2)

MASTER ALEXANDER KICKSHAW.

MASTER JOHN LITTLEWORTH.

MASTER HAIRCUT.

MASTER FREDERICK, [*Nephew to* LADY BORNWELL].

STEWARD *to the* LADY ARETINA.

STEWARD *to the* LADY CELESTINA.

SECRETARY, [*to the* LORD].

SERVANTS, &c.

ARETINA, SIR THOMAS BORNWELLS *Lady.*

CELESTINA [LADY BELLAMOUR], *a young Widow.*

ISABELLA,
MARIANA, *her sister,* } [*Kinswomen of* CELESTINA].

MADAM DECOY.

    [GENTLEWOMAN *to* LADY CELESTINA.]

SCENE
THE STRAND, [LONDON].

TO THE RIGHT HONORABLE
RICHARD LORD LOVELACE[1] *of* HURLEY.

My Lord,

I Cannot want encouragement to present a Poeme to your Lordship, while you possesse so noble a breast, in which so many seedes of honour, to the example and glory of your Name obtain'd, before your yeares a happy maturity. This Comedy fortunate in the Scene, and one that may challenge a place in the first forme of the Authors compositions, most humbly addresseth it selfe to your honour; if it meete your gracious acceptance, and that you repent not to be a Patron, your Lordshipps will onely crownes the imagination, and for ever by this favour oblige,[2]

> My Lord
> The most humble Services
> of your Honourer,
> JAMES SHIRLY.

The First Act. [Scene i.]

Enter ARETINA *and her* STEWARD.

STEWARD. Be patient, Madam, you may have your
    pleasure.
ARETINA. Tis that I came to towne for, I wo'd not
  Endure againe the countrey conversation,
  To be the Lady of sixe shires! The men
  So neare the Primitive making, they retaine   5
  A sence of nothing but the earth, their braines
  And barren heads standing as much in want
  Of plowing as their ground. To heare a fellow
  Make himselfe merry—and his horse—with whisteling
  Sellingers round![1] To observe with what solemnitie   10
  They keepe their Wakes,[2] and throw for pewter
        Candlestickes!
  How they become the Morris! with[1] whose bells
  They ring all into Whitson Ales,[3] and sweate
  Through twenty Scarffes and Napkins, till the
        Hobbyhorse [1]
  Tire, and the maide Marrian, dissolv'd to a gelly,   15
  Be kept for spoone meate.[4]
STEWARD. These—with your pardon—are no Argument
  To make the country life appeare so hatefull,
  At least to your particular,[5] who enjoy'd
  A blessing in that calme, would you be pleasd   20
  To thinke so, and the pleasure of a kingdome;
  While your owne will commanded what should move
  Delights, your husbands love and power joyned
  To give your life more harmony; you liv'd there
  Secure and innocent, beloved of all,   25
  Praisd for your hospitality, and praid for;
  You might be envied, but malice knew

ACT I. SCENE I.

1 *round;* an old rural dance
  tune.
2 *Wakes :* Holidays, usually
  with bonfires.

3 *Whitson Ales :* June festival
  with morris dance.
4 *spoone meate :* soft food.
5 *your particular :* in your own
  case.

Not where you dwelt. I wo'd not prophecy
But leave to your owne apprehension
What may succeede your change.

ARETINA.   You doe imagine,   30
No doubt, you have talk'd wisely, and confuted
London past all defence; your Master should
Doe well to send you backe into the countrie,
With title of Superintendent Baylie.[6]

STEWARD. How, Madam?

ARETINA.   Even so, sir.

STEWARD.   I am a Gentleman,   35
Though now your servant.

ARETINA.   A country gentleman,
By your affection to converse with stuble;
His tenants will advance your wit, and plumpe it so
With beefe and bag-pudding.[7]

STEWARD.   You   may   say   your
                                pleasure,
It becomes not me dispute.

ARETINA.   Complaine to   40
The Lord of the soyle, your master.

STEWARD.   Y'are a woman
Of an ungovern'd passion, and I pity you.

                Enter SIR THOMAS BORNWELL.

BORNWELL. How, how?[2] Whats the matter?

STEWARD.   Nothing,
                        Sir.   [*Exit.*]

BORNWELL. Angry, sweet heart?

ARETINA.   I   am   angry   with   my
                        selfe,
To be so miserably restrained in things,   45
Wherein it doth concerne your love and honour
To see me satisfied.

BORNWELL.   In what, Aretina,
Dost thou accuse me? Have I not obeyd
All thy desires? Against mine owne opinion
Quitted the countrie, and removed the hope   50

[6] *Baylie :* Bailiff.   [7] *bag-pudding :* boiled sausage.

Of our returne, by sale[2] of that faire Lordship
We liv'd in? Chang'd a calme and retire[d][3] life
For this wild towne, composd of noise and charge.[8]
ARETINA. What charge more than is necessarie
For a Lady of my birth and education?   55
BORNWELL. I am not ignorant, how much Nobilitie
Flowes in your bloud, your kinsmen great and
                              powerful
I'th State; but with this lose not your memory
Of being my wife. I shall be studious,
Madam, to give the dignitie of your birth   60
All the best ornaments which become my fortune,
But would not flatter it, to ruine both,
And be the fable of the towne, to teach
Other men losse of wit by mine, emploid
To serve your vaste expences.
ARETINA.   Am I then   65
Brought in the ballance?[9] So, Sir.
BORNWELL.   Though you weigh
Me in a partiall scale my heart is honest,
And must take libertie to thinke you have
Obeyed no modest counsell to [a]ffect,[4]
Nay, study wayes of pride and costly ceremony;   70
Your change of gaudy furniture and pictures,
Of this Italian Master, and that Dutchmans;
Your mighty looking-glasses, like Artillery
Brought [home][5] on Engins; the superfluous plate,
Anticke and novell; vanities of tires;[10]   75
Fourescore pound suppers for my Lord your kinsman;
Banquets for tother Lady, aunt, and cozens;
And perfumes that exceede all; traine of servants
To stifle us at home and shew abroad
More motley than the French, or the Venetian,   80
About your Coach, whose rude Postillion
Must pester every narrow lane, till passengers[11]

---

[8] *charge* : expense.   [10] *tires* : headdresses.
[9] *ballance* : weighed in   [11] *passengers* : pedestrians.
   judgment.

And tradsmen curse your choaking up their stalls,
And common cries pursue your Ladiship
For hindring o' their market.

ARETINA.   Have you done, sir?   85

BORNWELL. I could accuse the gayetie of your wardrobe,
And prodigall embroderies, under which
Rich Sattens, Plushes, cloath of Silver, dare
Not shew their owne complexions; your jewells,
Able to burne out the Spectators eyes,   90
And shew like Bonfires[6] on you by the tapers.
Something might here be spar'd, [with safety][7] of
Your birth and honour, since the truest wealth
Shines from the soule, and drawes up just admirers.
I could urge something more :—

ARETINA.   Pray doe; I like   95
Your homilie of thrifte.

BORNWELL.   I could wish, Madam,
You would not game so much.

ARETINA.   A gamster too?

BORNWELL. But are not come to that repentance yet,
Should teach you skill enough to raise your profit;
You looke not through the subtiltie of Cards,   100
And mysteries of Dice; nor can you save
Charge with the boxe,[12] buy petticotes and purles,
And keepe your familie by the precious income;
Nor doe I wish you should,—my poorest servant
Shall not upbraid my tables, nor his hire   105
Purchasd beneath my honour. You make play
Not a Pastime but a tyrannie, and vexe
Your selfe and my estate by't.

ARETINA.   Good, proceed!

BORNWELL. Another game you have, which consumes
                        more
Your fame than purse; your revells in the night,   110
Your meetings cal'd the Ball,[3] to which appeare,
As to the Court of Pleasure, all your gallants
And Ladies thither bound by a Subpena

[12] *boxe :* box for dicing.

Of *Venus*, and small *Cupids* high displeasure;
Tis but the family of love[13, (4)] translated   115
Into more costly sinne; there was a play on't,[14]
And had the Poet not beene brib'd to a modest
Expression of your Anticke gambolls in't,
Some darkes had beene discovered, and the deeds too.
In time he may repent and make some blush,   120
To see the second part danc'd on the Stage;
My thoughts acquit you for dishonouring me
By any foule act, but the vertuous know,
Tis not enough to cleare our selves, but the
Suspitions of our shame.

ARETINA.   Have you concluded   125
Your lecture?

BORNWELL.   I ha' done, and howsoever
My language may[8] appeare to you, it carries
No other than my faire and just intent
To your delights, without curbe to their modest
And noble freedome.

ARETINA.   Ile not be so tedious   130
In my reply, but without arte or elegance,
Assure you, I keepe still my first opinion;
And though you vayle[9] your avaritious meaning
With hansome names of modesty, and thrift,
I finde you would intrench and wound the liberty   135
I was borne with. Were my desires unpriviledged
By example, while my judgement thought 'em fit,
You ought not to oppose; but when the practise
And tract of every honourable Lady
Authorise[(5)] me, I take it great injustice   140
To have my pleasures circumscribed and taught me.
A narrow-minded husband is a theefe
To his owne fame, and his preferment[15] too;
He shuts his parts[16] and fortunes from the world,

---

[13] *family of love*: religious sect   [15] *preferment*: advancement at
    suspected of free love.   court.
[14] *a play on't*: Shirley's *The   [16] *parts*: talents.
    Ball*.

While from the popular vote and knowledge, men   145
Rise to imployment in the state.
BORNWELL.   I have
No great ambition to buy preferment
At so deare rate.
ARETINA.   Nor I to sell my honour,
By living poore and sparingly; I was not
Bred in that ebbe of fortune, and my fate   150
Shall not compell me too't.
BORNWELL.   I know not, Madam,
But you pursue these wayes—
ARETINA.   What wayes?
BORNWELL. In the strict sence of honestie I dare
Make oath, they are Innocent.
ARETINA.   Do not divert,
By busie troubling of your braine, those thoughts   155
That should preserve em.
BORNWELL.   How was that?
ARETINA.   Tis English.
BORNWELL. But carries some unkinde sence.
                    Enter MADAM DECOY.
DECOY. Good morrow, my sweete Madam.
ARETINA.   Decoy, welcome!
This visite is a favour.
DECOY.   Alas, sweet Madam,
I cannot stay, I came but to present   160
My service to your Ladiship; I could not
Passe by your doore, but I must take the boldnesse
To tender my respects.
ARETINA.   You oblige me, Madam,
But I must not dispence so with your absence.
DECOY. Alas, the Coach, Madam, stayes for me at the   165
                    doore.
ARETINA. Thou sha't command mine; prethee, sweete
                    Decoy,—
DECOY. I wou'd waite on you Madam, but I have many
Visits to make this morning. I beseech—
ARETINA. So you will promise to dine with me.

DECOY.   I shall
  Present a guest.
ARETINA.   Why then, good morrow, Madam.   170
DECOY. A happy day shine on your Ladiship.   *Exit.*
                    Enter STEWARD.
ARETINA. What's your newes, sir?
STEWARD.   Madam, two gentlemen.
ARETINA. What gentlemen? Have they no names?
STEWARD.   They are
  The gentleman with his owne head of haire
  Whom you commended for his horsemanship   175
  In Hide Parke,(6) and becomming the saddle,
  The tother day.
ARETINA.   What circumstance is this
  To know him by?
STEWARD.   His name's at my tongues end,—
  He lik'd the fashion of your pearle chaine, Madam,
  And borrowed it for his Jeweller to take   180
  A coppie by it.
BORNWELL. [*Aside.*] What cheating gallant's this?
STEWARD. That never walkes without a Ladies buske,17
  And playes with fannes,—Master Alexander Kick-
                  shaw!—
  I thought I should remember him.
ARETINA.   What's the other?
STEWARD. What an unluckie memorie I have!   185
  The gallant that still danceth in the streete,
  And weares a grosse of Ribbon in his hat;
  That carries *Oringado*18 in his pocket,
  And Suger-plumbs, to sweeten his discourse;
  That studies complement,(7) defies all wit   190
  [In][10] blacke,(8) and censures playes that are not
                  bawdy,—
  Master John Littleworth.
ARETINA.   They are welcome, but

                                    18 *Oringado :* Candied orange-
17 *buske :* corset.   peel.

Pray entertaine them a small time, lest I
Be unprovided.
BORNWELL.   Did they aske for me?
STEWARD.   No, sir.
BORNWELL. It matters not, they must be welcome.   195
ARETINA. Fie! how's this haire disordered? Here's a curle
Straddle[s][11] most impiously; I must to my closet.
                                                        Exit.
BORNWELL. Waite on em, my Lady will returne agen.
                                        [*Exit* STEWARD.]
I have to such a height fulfill'd her humor,
All application's[19] dangerous; these gallants   200
Must be received or shee will fall into
A tempest, and the house be shooke with names
Of all her kindred. Tis a servitude
I may in time shake off.
Enter ALEXANDER [KICKSHAW] *and* LITTLEWORTH.
KICKSHAW.   ⎱
LITTLEWORTH.   ⎰ Save you, Sir Thomas!
BORNWELL.   Save you, gentle-   205
                        men.
KICKSHAW.[12] I kisse your hand.
BORNWELL.   What day[20] is it
                        abroad?
LITTLEWORTH. The morning rises from your Ladies eyes;
If she looke cleare, we take the happy omen
Of a faire day.
BORNWELL.   Sheele instantly appeare
To the discredit of your complement,   210
But you expresse your wit thus.
KICKSHAW.   And you—modestie,
Not to affect the praises of your owne.
BORNWELL. Leaving this subject, what game's now on
                        foote?
What exercise carries the generall vote

19 *application* : corrective.

20 *What day :* What kind of
day.

O' th' towne now? Nothing moves without your   215
        knowledge.

KICKSHAW. The cocking[(9)] now has all the noise; Ile
        have

A hundred peeces[21] of one battle. Oh!

These birds of *Mars!*

LITTLEWORTH.   *Venus* is *Mars* his bird too.

KICKSHAW. Why, and the pretty Doves are *Venusses,*

To show that kisses draw the Charriot.   220

LITTLEWORTH. I am for that skirmish.

BORNWELL.   When shall wee
        have

More Booths and Bag-pipes upon Bansted downes?[22]

No mighty race is expected?—But my Lady returnes.

        Enter ARETINA.

ARETINA. Faire morning to you, gentlemen!

You went not late to bed by your early visit.   225

You doe me honour.

KICKSHAW.   It becomes our service.

ARETINA. What newes abroade? You hold precious
        intelligence.

LITTLEWORTH. All tongues are so much busie with your
        praise

They have not time to frame other discourse.

Will[t][13] please you, Madam, tast a Sugerplum?   230

        [ARETINA *accepts the offer.*]

BORNWELL. What do's the Goldsmith thinke the Pearle
        is worth

You borrowed of my Lady?

KICKSHAW.   Tis a rich one.

BORNWELL. She has many other toyes whose fashion
        you

Will like extremely. You have no intention

To buy any of her Jewels?

KICKSHAW.   Understand me—   235

---

21 *peeces*: gold coin (*unite*)
    worth 22 shillings.

22 *Bansted downes*: place in
    Surrey.

BORNWELL. You had rather sell perhaps. But, leaving
                                    this,
  I hope you'le dine with us.

KICKSHAW.   I came a' purpose.

ARETINA. And where were you last night?

KICKSHAW.   I, Madam?
                                    Where
  I slept not; it had beene sin where so much
  Delight and beauty was to keepe me waking.   240
  There is a Lady, Madam, will be worth
  Your free societie; my conversation
  Ne'er[14] knew so elegant and brave a soule,
  With most incomparable flesh and bloud,—
  So spirited! so Courtly! speaks the Languages,   245
  Sings, Dances, playes o' th' Lute to admiration!
  Is faire and paints not, games too, keepes a table
  And talkes most witty Satyre, has a wit
  Of a cleane Mercury.

LITTLEWORTH.   Is shee married?

KICKSHAW.   No.

ARETINA. A Virgin?

KICKSHAW.   Neither.

LITTLEWORTH.   What, a widow? Something   250
  Of this wide commendation might have beene
  Excusd. This, such a prodigie?

KICKSHAW.   Repent
  Before I name her. Shee did never see
  Yet full sixteene, an age in the opinion
  Of wise men not contemptible; she has   255
  Mourned out her yeare too for the honest Knight
  That had compassion of her youth, and dy'd
  So timely. Such a widow is not common,
  And now she shines more fresh and tempting
  Then any naturall Virgin.

ARETINA.   What's her name?   260

KICKSHAW. Shee was Christened Celestina. By her hus-
                                    band
  The Lady Bellamour. This Ring was hers.

BORNWELL. You borrowed it to coppie out the Posie?[23]

KICKSHAW. Are they not pretty Rubies? 'Twas a grace
   She was pleasd to shew me, that I might have one   265
   Made of the same fashion, for I love
   All prettie formes.

ARETINA.   And is she glorious[(10)]?

KICKSHAW. She is full of Jewels, Madam, but I am
   Most taken with the bravery[24] of her minde,
   Although her garments have all grace and ornament.   270

ARETINA. You have beene high in praises.

KICKSHAW.   I come short,
   No flattery can reach her.

BORNWELL. [*Aside.*]   Now my Lady
   Is troubled, as she feared to be eclipsd;
   This newes will cost me somewhat.

ARETINA.   You deserve
   Her favour for this noble character.[25, (11)]   275

KICKSHAW. And I possesse it, by my starres benevolence!

ARETINA. You must bring us acquainted.

BORNWELL.   I pray doe, sir,
   I long to see her too. Madam, I have
   Thought upon't and corrected my opinion.
   Pursue what wayes of pleasure your desires   280
   Incline you too; not onely with my state,[26]
   But with my person I will follow you.
   I see the folly of my thrift, and will
   Repent in Sacke[27] and prodigalitie
   To your owne hearts content.

ARETINA.   But doe not mocke.   285

BORNWELL. Take me to your imbraces, gentlemen,
   And tutor me.

LITTLEWORTH. And will you kisse the Ladies?

BORNWELL. And sing and dance. I long to see this
            beauty;
   I would faine lose a hundred pounds at dice now;

---

[23] *Posie :* Verse inscription.

[24] *bravery :* splendor.

[25] *noble character :* literary
   idealization.

[26] *state :* estate.

[27] *Sacke :* pun on sack-cloth and
   sack (sherry).

Thou sha't have another gowne and petticote.   290
Tomorrow will you sell my running horses?
We have no Greeke wine in the house, I thinke,
Pray send one of our footemen to the Merchant,
And throw the hogsheads of March-beer[15] into
The kenell[28] to make roome for Sackes and Clarret!   295
What thinke you to be drunke yet before dinner?
We will have constant musicke and maintaine
Them and their Fidles in phantasticke liveries;
Ile tune my voyce to catches.[12] I must have
My dyning roome enlarg'd to invite Embassadors;   300
Weele feast the parish in the fields, and teach
The Military men new discipline,
Who shall charge all their new Artillerie
With Oringes and Lemonds, boy, to play
All dinner upon our capons.
KICKSHAW.   Hee's exalted!   305
BORNWELL. I will doe anything to please my Lady.
Let that suffice, and kisse oth' same condition.
I am converted, doe not you dispute
But patiently allow the miracle!
ARETINA. I am glad to heare you, sir, in so good tune.   310
                    Enter SERVANT.
SERVANT. Madam, the Painter.
ARETINA.   I am to sit this morning.
BORNWELL. Doe, while I give new directions to my
                    Steward.
KICKSHAW. With your favour, we'le waite on you; sit-
                    ting's but
A melancholy exercise without
Some company to discourse.
ARETINA.   It does conclude   315
A Ladies morning worke. We rise, make fine,
Sit for our Picture, and tis time to dine.
LITTLEWORTH. Praying's forgot?
KICKSHAW.   Tis out of fashion.
                                                          Exeunt.

---

[28] *kenell* : gutter, channel.

[FIRST ACT. SCENE II.]

Enter CELESTINA *and her* STEWARD.

CELESTINA. Fie, what an aire this roome has!

STEWARD.   Tis perfum'd.

CELESTINA. With some cheape stuffe. Is it your wise-
      domes thrift
  To infect my nostrils thus? Or is't to favour
  The Gout in your worships hand? You are afraid
  To exercise your pen in your account Booke?   5
  Or doe you doubt my credit to discharge
  Your bills.

STEWARD. Madam, I hope you have not found
  My dutie with the guilt of sloath or jealousie,
  Unapt to your command.

CELESTINA.   You can extenuate
  Your faults with language, sir, but I expect   10
  To be obeyed. What hangings have we here?

STEWARD. They are Arras,(1) Madam.

CELESTINA.   Impudence—I know't.
  I will have fresher and more rich, not wrought
  With faces that may scandalise a Christian,
  With Jewish stories stufft with Corne and Camells.[1]   15
  You had best wrap all my chambers in wild Irish,
  And make a nursery of Monsters here
  To fright the Ladies comes to visite me.

STEWARD. Madam, I hope—

CELESTINA.   I say I will have other,
  Good Master Steward, of a finer loome,   20
  Some silke and silver, if your worship please
  To let me be at so much cost; Ile have
  Stories to fit the seasons of the yeare,
  And change as often as I please.

ACT I. SCENE II.
[1] Dyce suggests the story of
Joseph and his brethren.

STEWARD.   You shall, Madam.

CELESTINA. I am bound to your consent, forsooth! And is   25
  My coach brought home?

STEWARD.   This morning I expect it.

CELESTINA. The inside, as I gave direction,
  Of crimson plush?

STEWARD.   Of crimson Camell plush.[2]

CELESTINA. Ten thousand mothes consum't! Shall I ride
                  through
  The streets in penance, wrapt up round in haire   30
                  cloath?
  Sel't to an Alderman, twill serve his wife
  To goe a-feasting to their country house,
  Or fetch a Merchants Nurse-child, and come home
  Laden with fruite and Cheese-cakes. I despise it!

STEWARD. The nailes adorne it, Madam, set in method   35
  And pretty formes.

CELESTINA.   But single guilt, I warrant.

STEWARD. No, Madam.

CELESTINA.   Another Solecisme! Oh fie!
  This fellow will bring me to a Consumption
  With fretting at his ignorance. Some Lady
  Had rather never pray than goe to Church in't.   40
  The nailes not double guilt? To market wo't?[3]
  Twill hackny out to Mile-end,[4] or convey
  Your citie tumblers to be drunke with Creame
  And Prunes at Islington.[5]

STEWARD.   Good Madam, heare me.

CELESTINA. Ile rather be beholding to my Aunt,   45
  The Countesse, for her mourning coach, then be
  Disparag'd so. Shall any juggling tradsman
  Be at charge to shooe his running horse with gold,[(2)]
  And shall my coach-nailes be but single guilt?

---

[2] *Camell plush :* Camel's hair.
[3] *wo't :* wilt thou?
[4] *Mile-end :* Popular resort of
  citizens near East London.

[5] Tumblers were prostitutes.
  The food was common in
  brothels.

How dare these knaves abuse me so?
STEWARD.   Vouchsafe   50
To heare me speake.
CELESTINA.   Is my Sedan yet finish'd?
And liveries for my men-Mules[6] according
As I gave charge.
STEWARD.   Yes, Madam, it is finish'd,
But without tilting plumes at the foure corners;
The scarlet's pure but not embroidered.   55
CELESTINA. What mischiefe were it to your conscience
Were my coach lin'd with tissue,[7] and my harnesse
Cover'd with needleworke? If my Sedan
Had all the story of the Prodigall
Embrodered with pearle?
STEWARD.   Alas, good Madam,   60
I know tis your owne cost. I am but your Steward
And wo'd discharge my duty the best way.
You have been pleasd to heare me; tis not for
My profit that I manage your estate
And save expence, but for your honour, Madam.   65
CELESTINA. How sir, my honour?
STEWARD.   Though you hear it not,
Mens tongues are liberall in[8] your character,
Since you began to live thus high. I know
Your fame is precious to you.
CELESTINA.   I were best
Make you my governor. Audacious Varlet!   70
How dare you interpose your doting counsell?
Mind your affaires with more obedience,
Or I shall ease you of an office, sir.
Must I be limited to please your honour?
Or for the vulgar breath confine my pleasures?   75
I will pursue 'em in what shapes I fancie,
Here[1] and abroad; my entertainements shall
Be oftner and more rich. Who shall controule me?

[6] men-Mules : men who carried the sedan-chair.

[7] tissue : usually of silver or gold thread.

[8] liberall in : malicious about.

I live i' th' Strand, whither[2] few Ladies come
To live and purchase[9] more than fame. I will   80
Be hospitable then, and spare no cost
That may engage all generous report
To trumpet forth my bounty and my braverie,
Till the Court envie and remove.[10] Ile have
My house the Academy of wits, who shall   85
Exalt with[3] rich Sacke and Sturgeon,
Write Panegyricks of my feasts, and praise
The method of my wittie superfluities.
The horses shall be taught, with frequent waiting
Upon my gates, to stop in their careere   90
Toward Charing-crosse, spight of the Coachmans
                        fury.
And not a tilter but shall strike his plume[11]
When he sailes by my window. My Balconie
Shall be the Courtiers Idoll, and more gaz'd at
Than all the Pageantry at Temple-barre[12]   95
By countrey Clients.

STEWARD.   Sure my Ladie's mad!
CELESTINA. Take that for your ill manners.
                                        [*She strikes him.*]
STEWARD.   Thanke you,
              Madam.
I would there were lesse quicksilver in your fingers.
                                                Exit.
CELESTINA. There's more than simple honesty in a serv-
              ant
Requir'd to his full dutie; none should dare   100
But with a looke, much lesse a sawcie language,
Checke at their Mistresse pleasure. I'me resolv'd
To pay for some delight, my estate will beare it,
Ile rein it shorter when I please.
                    Enter STEWARD.

---

9 *purchase :* acquire.   12 *Temple-barre;* boundary be-
10 *remove :* come to me.   tween the City and West-
11 *plume :* mounted men will   minster.
   doff their plumes.

STEWARD. A gentleman
    Desires to speake with your Ladiship.
CELESTINA. His name? 105
STEWARD. He saies you know him not, he seemes to be
    Of qualitie.[13]
CELESTINA. Admit him.   [*Exit* STEWARD.]
        Enter HAIRCUT.
        Sir, with me?
HAIRCUT. Madam, I know not how you may receive
    This boldnesse from me, but my faire intents
    Knowne will incline you to be charitable. 110
CELESTINA. No doubt, sir.
HAIRCUT. He must live obscurely, Madam,
    That hath not heard what vertues you possesse,
    And I, a poore admirer of your fame,
    Am come to kisse your hand.
CELESTINA. That all your businesse?
HAIRCUT. Though it were worth much travell, I have 115
                more
    In my ambition.
CELESTINA. Speake it freely, sir.
HAIRCUT. You are a widow.
CELESTINA. So.
HAIRCUT. And I a Bachelor.
CELESTINA. You come a-wooing, sir, and would perhaps
    Shew me a way to reconcile the[4] two.
HAIRCUT. And blesse my starres for such a happinesse. 120
CELESTINA. I like you, sir, the better, that you doe not
    Wander about, but shoote home to the meaning;
    Tis a confidence will make a man
    Know sooner what to trust to. But I never
    Saw you before, and I beleeve you come not 125
    With hope to finde me desperate upon marriage.
    If maides, out of their ignorance of what
    Men are, refuse these offers, widowes may,
    Out of their knowledge, be allow'd some coynesse;

---

[13] *Of qualitie :* Established as a
gentleman.

And yet I know not how much happinesse   130
A peremptorie answer may deprive me of.
You may be some young Lord, and though I see not
Your footmen and your groome, they may not be
Farre off in conference with your horse. Please you
To instruct me with your title, against which   135
I would not willingly offend.

HAIRCUT.   I am
A gentleman; my name is Haircut, madam.

CELESTINA. Sweet Master Haircut, are you a Courtier?

HAIRCUT. Yes.

CELESTINA.   I did thinke so by your confidence.
Not to detaine you, sir, with circumstance,   140
I was not so unhappy in my husband
But that tis possible I may be a wife
Agen; but I must tell you, he that winnes
My affection shall deserve me.

HAIRCUT.   I will hope,
If you can love, I sha' not present, Madam,   145
An object to displease you in my person;
And when time and your patience shall possesse you
With further knowledge of me, and the truth
Of my devotion, you will not repent
The offer of my service.

CELESTINA.   You say well.   150
How long doe you imagine you can love, sir?
Is it a Quotidian,14 or will it hold
But every other day?

HAIRCUT.   You are pleasant, Madam.

CELESTINA. Dost take you with a burning at the first,
Or with a cold fit? For you gentlemen   155
Have both your Summer and your Winter service.

HAIRCUT. I am ignorant what you meane, but I shall
                         never
Be cold in my affection to such beautie.

14 *Quotidian* : Recurrent fever,
    daily.

CELESTINA. And twill be somewhat long ere I be warme
       in't.
HAIRCUT. If you vouchsafe me so much honour, Madam, 160
 That I may waite on you sometimes, I sha' not
 Despaire to see a change.
CELESTINA.   But now I know
 Your minde, you shall not neede to tell it when
 You come agen; I shall remember it.
HAIRCUT. You make me fortunate.
       Enter STEWARD.
STEWARD.   Madam, your kins- 165
      women,
 The Lady Novice⁽³⁾ and her sister are
 New lighted from their coach.
CELESTINA.   I did expect 'em,
 They partly are my pupills; Ile attend 'em.
HAIRCUT. Madam, I have beene too great a trespasser
 Upon your patience; Ile take my leave. 170
 You have affaires, and I have some imployment
 Calls me to Court; I shall present agen
 A servant to you.   *Exit* HAIRCUT.
CELESTINA.   Sir, you may present,
 But not give fire, I hope.¹⁵ Now to the Ladies.
 This recreation's past, the next must be 175
 To read to them some Court Philosophie.
        Exeunt.

THE SECOND ACT. [SCÉNE I.]

   Enter SIR THOMAS BORNWELL.
[BORNWELL.] Tis a strange humour I have undertaken,
 To dance, and play,¹ and spend as fast as she does;
 But I am resolv'd, it may doe good upon her
 And fright her into thrift. Nay, Ile endeavour
 To make her jealous too; if this doe not 5

¹⁵ Changing the metaphor to   ACT II. SCENE I.
 "present arms."   ¹ *play :* gamble.

Allay her gamboling, shee's past a woman
And onely a miracle must tame her.
                    Enter STEWARD.
STEWARD. Tis Master Frederick, my Ladies nephew.
BORNWELL.   What of him?
STEWARD. Is come from the Universitie.
BORNWELL.   By whose directions?
STEWARD. It seemes, my Ladies.
BORNWELL.   Let me speake with him   10
     Before he see his Aunt.   [*Exit* STEWARD.]
                    I doe not like it.
     Enter MASTER FREDERICK [*in scholar's black*],
                    [*with* STEWARD.]
     Master Frederick, welcome! I expected not
     So soone your presence; what's the hasty cause?
FREDERICK. These letters from my Tutor will acquaint
                    you.
STEWARD. Welcome home, sweet Master Frederick!
FREDERICK.   Where's my Aunt?   15
STEWARD. Shee's busie about her painting in her closet,
     The Outlandish[2] man of Art is copying out
     Her countenance.
FREDERICK.   She is sitting for her picture?
STEWARD. Yes, sir, and when tis drawne[(1)] she will be
                    hang'd
     Next the French Cardinall in the dining roome;   20
     But when she heares you'r come, she will dismisse
     The Belgicke gentleman to entertaine
     Your worship.
FREDERICK.   Change of aire has made you witty.
                    [*Exit* STEWARD.]
BORNWELL. Your Tutor gives you a hansome character,
     Frederick, and is sorry your Aunts pleasure   25
     Commands you from your studies; but I hope
     You have no quarrell to the liberall arts.
     Learning is an addition[3] beyond
     Nobilitie of birth; honour of bloud

---

[2] *Outlandish* : Foreign.   [3] *addition* : title of honor.

Without the ornament of knowledge is   30
A glorious[4] ignorance.

FREDERICK. I never knew more sweet and happy houres
Than I emploid upon my bookes; I heard
A part of my Philosophy and was so   .
Delighted with the harmony of nature,   35
I could have wasted my whole life upon't.

BORNWELL. [*Aside.*] Tis pitty a rash indulgence should
                              corrupt
So faire a Genius.—Shee's here; Ile observe.

    Enter ARETINA, ALEXANDER [KICKSHAW],
        LITTLEWORTH, [*and*] STEWARD.

FREDERICK. My most lov'd Aunt!

ARETINA.   Support me, I shall
                    faint!

LITTLEWORTH. What ailes your Ladiship?

ARETINA.   Is· that Frederick   40
  In blacke.

KICKSHAW. Yes, Madam, but the doublet's Sattin.

ARETINA. The boy's undone!

FREDERICK.   Madam, you appeare troubled.

ARETINA. Have I not cause? Was not I trusted with
Thy education, boy, and have they sent thee
Home like a very scholler?

KICKSHAW.   Twas ill done,   45
Howe'er they usd him in the Universitie,
To send him to his friends thus.

FREDERICK.   Why, sir, blacke
(For tis the colour that offends your eyesight)
Is not within my reading any blemish;
Sables are no disgrace in Heraldry.   50

KICKSHAW. Tis comming from the Colledge thus, that
                    makes it
Dishonorable; while you ware it for
Your father, it was commendable; or were
Your Aunt dead, you might mourne and justifie.

ARETINA. What lucke[5] I did not send him into France! 55

---

[4] *glorious :* vainglorious.   [5] *lucke :* misfortune.

They would have given him generous(2) education,
Taught him another garbe, to weare his locke,[6]
And shape,[7] as gawdie as the Summer; how
To dance, and wagge his feather a la mode,
To complement, and cringe, to talke not modestly,   60
Like "I forsooth," and "no forsooth,"—to blush
And looke so like a Chaplaine! There he might
Have learned a brazen confidence, and observ'd
So well the custome of the countrey, that
He might by this time have invented fashions   65
For us, and beene a benefit to the Kingdome,
Preserv'd our Tailors in their wits, and sav'd
The charge of sending into forraine Courts
For pride and anticke[8] fashions. Observe
In what a posture he does hold his hat now.   70
FREDERICK. Madam, with your pardon, you have
                    practisd
Another dialect then was taught me when
I was commended to your care and breeding.
I understand not this; Latine or Greeke
Are more familiar to my apprehension,   75
Logicke was not so hard in my first lectures
As your strange language.
ARETINA.   Some strong waters! Oh!
LITTLEWORTH. Comfits will be as comfortable to your
                    stomacke, Madam.
                              [*He offers his box.*]
ARETINA. I feare hee's spoild for ever! He did name
Logicke, and may—for ought I know—be gone   80
So farre to understand it. I did alwayes
Suspect they would corrupt him in the Colledge.
Will your Greeke sawes and sentences discharge
The Mercer,[9] or is Latin a fit language
To court a mistresse in? Master Alexander,   85
If you have any charitie, let me

---

[6] *locke :* lovelock.   [9] *discharge the Mercer :* pay
[7] *shape :* clothing.   clothing bills.
[8] *anticke :* foolishly strange.

Commend him to your breeding. I suspect
I must employ my Doctor first, to purge
The Universitie that lies in's head;
It alters his complexion.[10]

KICKSHAW.   If you dare   90
Trust me to serve him.

ARETINA.   Master Littleworth,
Be you joynd in commission.

LITTLEWORTH.   I will teach him
Postures and rudiments.

ARETINA.   I have no patience
To see him in this shape, it turnes my stomacke.
When he has cast his Academicke skinne   95
He shall be yours; I am bound in conscience
To see him bred; his owne state shall maintaine
The charge, while hee's my Ward. Come hither, sir.

FREDERICK. What does my Aunt meane to doe with me?

STEWARD. To make you a fine gentleman, and translate   100
                    you
Out of your learned language, sir, into
The present Goth and Vandall, which is French.

BORNWELL. [*Aside.*] Into what mischiefe will this
                    humour ebbe?
Shee will undo the boy; I see him ruind.
My patience is not manly, but I must   105
Use stratagem to reduce her; open wayes
Give me no hope.   *Exit.*

STEWARD.   You shall be obey'd, Madam.
                    Exeunt [all but FREDERICK *and* STEWARD.]

FREDERICK. Master Steward, are you sure we doe not
                    dreame?
Was't not my Aunt you talkt to?

STEWARD.   One that loves you
Deare as her life. These cloathes doe not become you,   110
You must have better, sir,—

FREDERICK.   These are not old.

---

[10] *complexion :* personality.

STEWARD. More sutable to the towne and time; we keepe
    No Lent here, nor is't my Ladies pleasure you
    Should fast from any thing you have a minde to,
    Unlesse it be your learning, which she would have   115
        you
    Forget with all convenient speed that may be,
    For the credit of your noble family.
    The case is alter'd since we liv'd i' th' country;
    We doe not invite the poore o' th' parish
    To dinner, keepe a table for the tenants;   120
    Our kitchen does not smell of beefe, the sellar
    Defies the price of malt and hops; the footmen
    And coachdrivers may be drunke like gentlemen
    With wine, nor will three Fidlers upon holidayes
    With aid of Bagge pipes, that cald in the countrey   125
    To dance, and plough the hall up with their hob-
        nailes,
    Now make my Lady merry. Wee doe feed
    Like princes, and feast nothing but princes,
    And are these robes fit to be seene amongst 'em?
FREDERICK. My Lady keepes a court then! Is Sir   130
        Thomas
    Affected with[11] this state and cost?
STEWARD.   He was not,
    But is converted, and I hope you wo' not
    Persist in heresie, but take a course
    Of riot to content your friends; you shall
    Want nothing, if you can be proud and spend it   135
    For my Ladies honour. Here are a hundred
    Peeces, will serve you till you have new clothes;
    I will present you with a nag of mine,
    Poore tender[12] of my service; please you accept;
    My Ladies smile more than rewards me for it.   140
    I must provide fit servants to attend you,
    Monsieures for horse and foote.

---

[11] *Affected with :* Favorable towards.   [12] *tender :* token offering.

FREDERICK.   I shall submit,
If this be my Aunts pleasure, and be rul'd;
My eyes are open'd with this purse already,
And Sacke will helpe to inspire me. I must spend it?   145
STEWARD. What else, sir?
FREDERICK.   Ile begin with you, to incourage
You to have still a speciall care of me;
There is five peeces,—not for your nag.
STEWARD. No, sir, I hope it is not.
FREDERICK.   Buy a Beaver
For thy owne blocke;[13] I shall be ruld. Who does   150
Command the wineseller?
STEWARD.   Who command but you, sir?
FREDERICK. Ile try to drinke a health or two, my Aunts
Or any bodies, and if that foundation
Stagger me not too much, I will commence
In all the arts of London.
STEWARD.   If you finde, sir,   155
The operation of the wine, exalt
Your bloud to the desire of any femall
Delight, I know your Aunt wo' not deny
Any of her chambermaides to practise on;
She loves you but too well.
FREDERICK.   I know not how   160
I may be for that exercise. Farewell, *Aristotle!*
Prethee commend me to the Library
At Westminster[14]; my bones I bequeath thither,
And to the learned wormes that meane to visit 'em.
I will compose my selfe; I beginne to thinke   165
I have lost time indeed. Come, to the wineseller.
                                   [*Exeunt.*][1]

[SECOND ACT. SCENE ii.]

Enter CELESTINA, MARIANA, [*and*] ISABELLA.
MARIANA. But shall we not, Madam, expose our selves
To censure for this freedome.

13 *blocke :* head piece.   14 Westminster Abbey.

CELESTINA.   Let them answer
That dare mistake us. Shall we be so much
Cowards to be frighted from our pleasure,
Because men have malitious tongues, and shew   5
What miserable soules they have? No, cozen,
We hold our life and fortunes upon no
Mans charitie; if they dare shew so little
Discretion to traduce our fames, we will
Be guilty of so much wit to laugh at em.   10
ISABELLA. Tis a becomming fortitude.
CELESTINA.   My starres
Are yet kinde to me; for—in a happy minute
Be't spoke—I'me not in love, and men shall never
Make my heart leane with sighing, nor with teares
Draw on my eyes the infamie of spectacles.   15
Tis the chiefe principle to keepe your heart
Under your owne obedience; jeast, but love not.
I say my prayers, yet can weare good clothes,
And onely satisfie my tailor for em.
I wo' not lose my priviledge.   20
MARIANA. And yet they say your entertainments are,—
Give me your pardon, Madam,—to proclaime
Your selfe a widow, and to get a husband.
CELESTINA. As if a Lady of my yeares, some beautie
Left by her husband rich, that had mourn'd for him   25
A twelve moneth too, could live so obscure i' th'
                    towne
That gallants would not know her, and invite
Themselves without her chargeable proclamations!
Then we are worse than Citizens; no widow
Left wealthy can be thoroughly warme in mourning,   30
But some one noble bloud or lusty kindred
Claps in, with his gilt coach and Flandrian[1] trotters,
And hurries her away to be a Countesse.
Courtiers   have   spies,   and   great   ones   with
              charge[d][2, [1]] titles,

ACT II. SCENE II.   [2] *charged :* emblazoned with
[1] *Flandrian :* Flemish.   heraldry.

Cold in their owne estates, would warme themselves   35
At a rich city bonfire.[2]

ISABELLA.   Most true, Madam.

CELESTINA. No matter for corruption of the bloud,—
Some undone Courtier made her husband rich,[3]
And this new Lord receives it backe againe.
Admit it were my policie, and that   40
My entertainements pointed to acquaint me
With many sutors, that I might be safe
And make the best election, could you blame me?

MARIANA. Madam, tis wisdome.

CELESTINA.   But I should be
In my thoughts miserable to be fond   45
Of[4] leaving the sweet freedome I possesse,
And court my selfe into new marriage fetters;
I now observe mens severall[5] wits, and windings,
And can laugh at their follies.

MARIANA.   You have given
A most ingenious[6] satisfaction.   50

CELESTINA. One thing Ile tell you more, and this I give
                            you
Worthy your imitation from my practise;
You see me merry, full of song and dancing,
Pleasant in language, apt to all delights
That crowne a publike meeting; but you cannot   55
Accuse me of being prodigall of my favours
To any of my guests. I doe not summon,
By any winke, a gentleman to follow me
To my withdrawing chamber; I heare all
Their pleaes in Court, nor can they boast abroad   60
And doe me justice, after a salute[7]
They have much conversation with my lippe;
I hold the kissing of my hand a courtesie,
And he that loves me must, upon the strength

---

[3] The citizen had become rich   [5] *severall :* individual.
   by ruining a courtier.   [6] *ingenious :* ingenuous.
[4] *fond of :* foolishly disposed to.   [7] *salute :* kiss of greeting.

Of that, expect[8] till I renew his favour.   65
Some Ladies are so expensive in their graces
To those that honour 'em, and so prodigall,
That in a little time they have nothing but
The naked sinne left to reward their servants,[9]
Whereas a thrift in our rewards will keepe   70
Men long in their devotion, and preserve
Our selves in stocke, to encourage those that honour
                    us.[(1)]

ISABELLA. This is an art worthy a Ladies practise.

CELESTINA. It takes not from the freedome of our mirth,
But seemes to advance it, when we can possesse   75
Our pleasures with security of our honour;
And, that preservd, I welcome all the joyes
My fancy can let in. In this I have given
The copie of my minde, nor doe I blush
You understand it.

ISABELLA.   You have honord us.   80

        Enter CELESTINA'S GENTLEWOMAN.

GENTLEWOMAN. Madam, Sir William Sentlove's come to
                waite on you.

CELESTINA. There's one would be a client. Make excuse
For a few minuts.   [*Exit* GENTLEWOMAN.]

MARIANA.   One that comes a-wooing?

CELESTINA. Such a thing he would seeme, but in his
                guiltinesse
Of little land, his expectation is not   85
So valiant as it might be. He weares cloathes,
And feeds with noblemen; to some, I heare,
No better than a wanton emissarie
Or scout for *Venus* wild foule, which made tame,
He thinkes no shame to stand court centinell,   90
In hope of the reversion.[10, (2)]

MARIANA.   I have heard
That some of them are often my Lords tasters;
The first fruits they condition for,[11] and will

---

[8] *expect :* wait.   consent.
[9] *servants :* suitors.   [11] *condition for :* demand in the
[10] *reversion :* later possession by   bargain.

Exact as fees for the promotion.[12]

CELESTINA. Let them agree; there's no account shall lie   95
  For me among their trafficke.

                Enter GENTLEWOMAN.

GENTLEWOMAN.   Master Haircut, Madam,
  Is new come in, to tender you his service.

CELESTINA. Let him discourse a little with Sir William.

                Exit [GENTLEWOMAN.]

MARIANA. What is this gentleman, Master Haircut,
              Madam?

I note him very gallant, and much courted   100
  By gentlemen of qualitie.

CELESTINA.   I know not,
  More than a trim gay man; he has some great office,
  Sure, by his confident behaviour.
  He would be entertaind under the title
  Of servant to me, and I must confesse,   105
  He is the sweetest of all men that visite me.

ISABELLA. How meane you, Madam?

CELESTINA.   He is full of powder;
  He will save much in perfume for my chamber,
  Were he but constant here. Give 'em accesse.

Enter SIR WILLIAM SENTLOVE [*and*] MASTER HAIRCUT.

SENTLOVE. Madam, the humblest of your servants is   110
  Exalted to a happinesse, if you smile
  Upon my visit.

HAIRCUT.   I must begge your charitie
  Upon my rudenesse, Madam; I shall give
  That day up lost to any happinesse,
  When I forget to tender you my service.   115

CELESTINA. You practise Courtship,[13] gentlemen.

SENTLOVE.   But cannot
  Find where with more desert to exercise it.
  What Ladie's this, I pray?

CELESTINA.   A kinswoman
  Of mine, Sir William.

---

[12] Arranging a later affair with   [13] *Courtship :* Courtliness.
  Sir William.

SENTLOVE.   I am more her servant.

[SENTLOVE *talks apart with* ISABELLA.]

CELESTINA. You came from Court now, I presume.

HAIRCUT.   Tis, Madam,   120
    The sphere I move in, and my destinie
    Was kinde to place me there, where I enjoy
    All blessings that a mortall can possesse
    That lives not in your presence; and I should
    Fix my ambition, when you would vouchsafe   125
    Me so much honour, to accept from me
    An humble entertainment there.

CELESTINA.   But by
    What name shall I be knowne; in what degree
    Shall I be of kin[d]red[3] to you.

HAIRCUT.   How meane you,
    Madam?

CELESTINA. Perhaps you'le call me sister; I shall take   130
    it
    A speciall preferment; or it may be
    I may passe under title of your Mistresse,
    If I seeme rich and faire enough to engage
    Your confidence to owne me.

HAIRCUT.   I would hope—

CELESTINA. But tis not come to that yet. You will, sir,   135
    Excuse my mirth.

HAIRCUT.   Sweet Madam!

CELESTINA.   Shall I take
    Boldnesse to aske what place you hold in Court?
    Tis an uncivill curiositie,
    But you'le have mercie to a womans question.

HAIRCUT. My present condition, Madam, carries   140
    Honour and profit, though not to be nam'd
    With that employment I expect i' th' state,
    Which shall discharge the first maturitie
    Upon your knowledge; untill then I begge
    You allow a modest silence.

CELESTINA.   I am charmd, sir,   145
    And if you scape embassador, you cannot
    Reach a preferment wherein I'me against you.[3]

But where's Sir William Sentlove?

HAIRCUT.   Give him leave
  To follow his nose, Madam, while he hunts
  In view; hee'le soone be at a fault.[14]

CELESTINA.   You know him?   150

HAIRCUT. Know Sentlove? Not a page but can decipher
              him;
  The waitingwomen know him to a scruple;[(4)]
  Hee's cal'd the Blistermaker[15] of the towne.

CELESTINA. What's that?

[HAIRCUT.][4]   The laundry Ladies[(5)] can re-
      solve [16] you,
  And you may guesse; an arrant Epicure   155
  As this day lives, borne to a prettie wit,
  A Knight but no gentleman. I must
  Be plaine to you; your Ladiship may have
  Use of this knowledge, but conceale the author.
     [SENTLOVE *approaches as* HAIRCUT *retires.*]

SENTLOVE. I kisse your fairest hand.

MARIANA.   You make a dif-   160
      ference;
  Pray reconcile 'em to an equall whitenesse.

SENTLOVE. You wound my meaning, Lady.

CELESTINA.   Nay, Sir William
  Has the art of complement.

SENTLOVE.   Madam, you honor me
  'Bove my desert of language.

CELESTINA.   Will you please
  To enrich me with your knowledge of that gentle- 165
      man?

SENTLOVE. Doe you not know him, Madam?

CELESTINA.   What is he?

SENTLOVE. A Camphire[17] ball; you shall know more
      hereafter.
  He shall tell you himselfe, and save my character;

---

[14] *at a fault* : on a false trail,
   punning on "Scent-love."
[15] *Blistermaker* : Pander.

[16] *resolve* : convince by proof.
[17] *Camphire* : Camphor (used
   by barbers).

Till then,—you see hee's proud.

               [HAIRCUT *approaches.*]

CELESTINA.   One thing, gentlemen,
I observe in your behaviour, which is rare   170
In two that court one mistresse; you preserve
A noble friendship; there's no gum within
Your hearts, you cannot fret,[18] or shew envy
Of one anothers hope; some would not governe
Their passions with that temper.

SENTLOVE.   The whole world 175
Sha' not divorce our friendship. Master Haircut,
Would I had lives to serve him! He is lost
To goodnesse does not honour him.

HAIRCUT.   My knight!

CELESTINA. [*Aside.*] This is right playing at Court
             Shuttlecocke.

            Enter GENTLEWOMAN.

GENTLEWOMAN. Madam, there is a gentleman desires 180
To speake w'ee, one Sir Thomas Bornwell.

CELESTINA.   Bornwell?

GENTLEWOMAN. He sayes he is a stranger to your Ladi-
             ship.

SENTLOVE. I know him.

HAIRCUT.   Your neighbour, Madam.

SENTLOVE.   Husband to
The Lady that so revells in the Strand.

HAIRCUT. He has good parts, they say, but cannot helpe 185
His Ladies bias.

CELESTINA.   They have both much fame
I' th' towne for severall[19] merits. Pray admit him.

                 [*Exit* GENTLEWOMAN.]

HAIRCUT. [*Aside.*] What comes he for?

       Enter SIR THOMAS [BORNWELL.]

BORNWELL. Your pardon, noble Lady, that I have
Presum'd, a stranger to your knowledge.

              [*He kisses* CELESTINA.]

---

[18] Velvet was stiffened with   [19] *severall :* different.
    gum, causing rubs to show.

CELESTINA.   Sir,   190
   Your worth was here before you, and your person
   Cannot be here ingratefull.[20]
BORNWELL.   Tis the bounty
   Of your sweet disposition, Madam. Make me
   Your servant, Lady, by her faire example,
   To favour me.—   [ISABELLA *turns her lips away.*]
                I never knew one turne   195
   Her cheeke to a gentleman that came to kisse her
   But sh'ad a stinking breath. Your servant, gentlemen.
   Will Sentlove, how ist?
CELESTINA. [*Aside to* ISABELLA.] I am sorry, Coze,
   To accuse you; we in nothing more betray
   Our selves to censure of ridiculous pride,   200
   Then answering a faire salute too rudely.
   Oh it shewes ill upon a gentlewoman
   Not to returne the modest lip, if she
   Would have the world beleeve her breath is not
   Offensive.
BORNWELL. Madam, I have businesse   205
   With you.
SENTLOVE. [*Aside.*] His lookes are pleasant.
CELESTINA. [*Walking aside with* BORNWELL.] With me,
                sir?
BORNWELL. I heare you have an ex'lent wit, Madam;
   I see you're[5] faire.
CELESTINA.   The first is but report,
   And doe not trust your eyesight for the last,
   Cause I presume y'are mortall and may erre.   210
HAIRCUT. [*Aside.*] He is very gamesome.
BORNWELL.   Y'ave an ex'lent
          voyce;
   They say you catcht it from a dying Swan,—
   Which, joyn'd to the sweete harmony of your lute,
   You ravish all mankind.
CELESTINA.   Ravish mankind?
BORNWELL. With their consent.

[20] *ingratefull :* unpleasing.

CELESTINA.   It were the stranger   215
              rape,
    But there's the lesse inditement lies against it;
    And there is hope, your little honesties[21]
    Cannot be much the worse, for men doe rather
    Beleeve they had a maiden head, then put
    Themselves to th' racke of memory, how long   220
    Tis since they left the burden of their innocence.
BORNWELL. Why you are bitter, Madam!
CELESTINA.   So is physicke;[22]
    I doe not know your constitution.
BORNWELL. You shall, if please you, Madam.
CELESTINA.   Y'are too
              hasty;
    I must examine what certificate   225
    You have first, to preferre you.
BORNWELL.   Fine! Certificate?
CELESTINA. Under your Ladies hand and seale.
BORNWELL.   Go to,
    I see you are a wag.
CELESTINA.   But take heede, how
    You trust too't.
BORNWELL.   I can love you in my wedlocke,
    As well as that young gallant o' th' first haire,   230
    Or the knight Bachelor, and can returne
    As amorous delight to thy soft bosome.
CELESTINA. Your person and your language are both
              strangers.
BORNWELL. But may be more familiar; I have those
    That dare make affidavit for my body.   235
CELESTINA. D'ee meane your Surgeon?
BORNWELL.   My Surgeon, Madam?
    I know not how you value my abilities,
    But I dare undertake as much, to expresse
    My service to your Ladiship, and with
    As fierce ambition, fly to your commands,   240
    As the most valiant of these, lay siege to you.

[21] *honesties :* chastities.   [22] *physicke :* medicine.

CELESTINA. You dare not, sir.
BORNWELL.   How, Madam?
CELESTINA.   I will justifi't.
  You dare not marry me, and I imagine
  Some here, should I consent, would fetch a priest
  Out of the fire.
BORNWELL.   I have a wife indeede.   245
CELESTINA. And there's a statute not repeald, I take it.
BORNWELL. Y'are in the right; I must confesse y'ave
                    hit
  And bled me in a master veine.
CELESTINA.   You thinke
  I tooke you on the advantage; use your best
  Skill at defence, I'le come up to your valour   250
  And shew another worke you dare not doe;
  You dare not, sir, be vertuous.
BORNWELL.   I dare!
  By this faire hand, I dare! and aske a pardon
  If my rude words offend thy innocence,
  Which, in a forme so beautifull, would shine   255
  To force a blush in them suspected it,
  And from the rest draw wonder.
HAIRCUT. [*Aside to* ISABELLA.]   I like not
  Their secret parly; shall I interrupt em?
ISABELLA. By no means, sir.
SENTLOVE.   Sir Thomas was not wont
  To shew so much a Courtier.
MARIANA.   He cannot   260
  Be prejudiciall to you; suspect not
  Your owne deserts so much; hee's married.
BORNWELL. I have other businesse, Madam; you keepe
                    musicke,
  I came to try how you can dance.
CELESTINA.   You did?
  [*Aside.*] Ile trie his humour out of breath.—   265
  Although I boast no cunning, sir, in revells,
  If you desire to shew your art that way,
  I can waite on you.
BORNWELL.   You much honour me.

Nay, all must joyne to make a harmony.

> *They dance.*

BORNWELL. I have nothing now, Madam, but to be-   270
  seech,
  After a pardon for my boldnesse, you
  Would give occasion to pay my gratitude.
  I have a house will be much honourd
  If you vouchsafe your presence, and a wife
  Desires to present her selfe your servant.   275
  I Came with the ambition to invite you;
  Deny me not, your person you shall trust
  On faire securitie.

CELESTINA.   Sir, although I use not
  This freedome with a stranger, you shall have
  No cause to hold me obstinate.

BORNWELL.   You grace me.—   280
  Sir William Sentlove.—

HAIRCUT.   I must take my leave.
  You will excuse me, Madam. Court attendances—

CELESTINA. By any meanes.

BORNWELL.   Ladies, you will vouchsafe
  Your company?

ISABELLA. ⎱
MARIANA. ⎰ We waite upon you, sir.

> *Exeunt.*

THE THIRD ACT. [SCENE I.]

Table and Lookingglasse.
Enter LORD *unready.*[1] HAIRCUT *preparing his*
Periwigge.

LORD. What houre ist?

HAIRCUT.   Bout three a'clocke, my Lord.

LORD. Tis time to rise.

HAIRCUT.   Your Lordship went but late
  To bed last night.

LORD.   ·   Twas early in the morning.

SECRETARY. [*Within.*] Expect[1] a while, my Lord is busie.
Enter SECRETARY.
LORD. What's the matter?
SECRETARY.   Here is a Lady   5
    Desires accesse to you upon some affaires
    She saies may specially concerne your Lordship.
LORD. A Lady? What's[1] her name?
SECRETARY.   Madam Decoy.
LORD. Decoy? Prethee admit her.
Enter DECOY.
                            Have you businesse,
           Madam,
  With me?
DECOY. And such I hope as will not be   10
    Offensive to your Lordship.
LORD.   I pray speake it.
DECOY. I would desire your Lordships eare more private.
LORD. Waite i' th' next chamber till I call.
Exeunt [SECRETARY *and* HAIRCUT.]
                              Now, Madam.
DECOY. Although I am a stranger to your Lordship
    I wo'd not lose a faire occasion offer'd,   15
    To shew how much I honour, and would serve you.
LORD. Please you to give me the particular,
    That I may know the extent of my engagement;
    I am ignorant by what desert you should
    Be encouragd to have care of me.
DECOY.   My Lord,   20
    I will take boldnesse to be plaine; beside
    Your other excellent parts, you have much fame
    For your sweet inclination to our sexe.
LORD. How d'ee meane, Madam?
DECOY.   I' that way your Lord-
        ship
    Hath honorably practisd upon some   25
    Not to be nam'd; your noble constancie

Act III. Scene i.
[1] *Expect :* Wait.

To a mistresse hath deserv'd our generall vote,
And I—a part of woman kind—have thought
How to expresse my duty.

LORD.   In what, Madam?

DECOY. Be not so strange,[2] my Lord. I know the beauty   30
And pleasures of your eyes, that hansome creature
With whose faire life all your delight tooke leave,
And to whose memory you have paid too much
Sad tribute.

LORD.   What's all this?

DECOY.   This,—if your Lordship
Accept my service, in pure zeale to cure   35
Your melancholy, I could point where you might
Repaire your losse.

LORD.   Your Ladiship, I conceive,
Doth trafficke in flesh marchandize.

DECOY.   To men
Of honour like your selfe; I am well knowne
To some in court and come not with ambition   40
Now to supplant your officer.[3]

LORD.   What is
The Lady of pleasure(2) you preferre.

DECOY.   A Lady
Of birth and fortune, one upon whose vertue
I may presume, the Lady Aretina.

LORD. Wife to Sir Thomas Bornwell?

DECOY.   The same, sir.   45

LORD. Have you prepard her?

DECOY. Not for your Lordship, till I have found your
                              pulse;
I am acquainted with her disposition,
She has a very appliable nature.

LORD. And, Madam, when expect you to be whipt   50
For doing these fine favors?

DECOY.   How, my Lord?
Your Lordship does but jeast, I hope; you make
A difference betweene a Lady that

---

[2] *strange :* stand-offish.   [3] *officer :* pander.

Does honorable offices, and one
They call a bawd; your Lordship was not wont   55
To have such course opinion of our practise.
LORD. The Lady Aretina is my kinswoman.
DECOY. What if she be, my Lord? The nearer bloud
The dearer sympathie.
LORD.   Ile have thee carted.[4]
DECOY. Your Lordship wo' not so much staine your   60
                              honour
And education, to use a woman
Of my qualitie—
LORD.   Tis possible you may
Be sent off with an honorable convoy
Of Halberdeers.
DECOY.   Oh my good Lord!
LORD. Your Ladiship shall be no protection   65
If thou but stai'st three minutes.
DECOY.   I am gone.
When next you finde rebellion in your bloud,[5]
May all within ten mile o' th' court turne honest.[6]
                                                      Exit.

LORD. I doe not finde that pronenesse since the faire
Bella Maria died; my bloud is cold,   70
Nor is there beautie enough surviving
Tɔ highten me to wantonnesse.—Who waites?
              Enter HAIRCUT [*and* SECRETARY.]
And what said my Lady?
HAIRCUT. The silent language of her face, my Lord,
Was not so pleasant as it shewd upon   75
Her entrance.
LORD.   Would any man that meetes
This Lady take her for a bawde?
HAIRCUT.   She does
The trade an honor, credit to the profession.
We may in time see baldnesse, quarter noses,[(3)]

---

4 Whipping at a cart's tail was   experience bestial passion.
   a common punishment.   6 *honest :* virtuous.
5 *finde rebellion . . . bloud :*

And rotten legges[7] to take the wall[8] of footclothes. [4]   80
LORD. I ha' thought better, call the Lady backe;
    I wo' not lose this opportunitie.
    Bid her not feare; the favour is not common,
    And Ile reward it.   [*Exit* SECRETARY.]
                    I doe wonder much
    Will Sentlove was not here to-day.   85
HAIRCUT. I heard him say this morning, he would waite
    Upon your Lordship.—She is returnd, sir.
                Enter SECRETARY *and* DECOY.
SECRETARY. Madam, be confident, my Lord's not angry.
LORD. You returne welcome, Madam. You are better
    Read in your art, I hope, then to be frighted   90
    With any shape of anger, when you bring
    Such newes to gentlemen. Madam, you shall
    Soone understand how I accept the office.
DECOY. You are the first Lord, since I studied carriage,[9]
    That shew'd such infidelity and fury   95
    Upon so kind a message; every gentleman
    Will   shew   some   breeding,   but   if   one   right
                    honourable [5]
    Should not have noble bloud—
LORD.   You shall returne
    My complement in a letter to my Lady
    Aretina; favour me with a little patience.   100
    Shew her that chamber.
DECOY.   Ile attend your Lordship.
                    Exeunt [DECOY *and* HAIRCUT.]
LORD. Write.[2] "Madam, where your honour is in
    danger, my love must not be silent."[2]
                Enter SENTLOVE *and* KICKSHAW.
    Sentlove and Kickshaw!
KICKSHAW.   Your Lordship's busie.
LORD. Writing a letter; nay, it sha' not barre   105
    Any discourse.
            [*He moves between* SECRETARY *and the others.*]

---

[7] Caused by syphilis.   [9] *carriage :* manners.
[8] Taking social precedence.

SECRETARY. "Silent."

LORD. "Though I be no Physitian, I may prevent a feaver
in your bloud."
    And where have you spent the mornings conversa-   110
            tion?

SENTLOVE. Where you would have given the best
            Barbary
    In your stable to have met on honorable termes.

LORD. What new beautie? You acquaint your selves
    With none but wonders.

SENTLOVE.   Tis too low,—a miracle!

LORD. Twill require a strong faith.   115

SECRETARY. "Your bloud."

LORD. "If you be innocent, preserve your fame, least this
    Decoy Madam betray it to your repentance."
    By what name is she knowne?

SENTLOVE.   Aske Alexander,
    He knowes her.

KICKSHAW.   Whom?

SENTLOVE.   The Lady Celestina.   120

LORD. He has a vast knowledge of Ladies, 'las, poore
            Alexander!
    When dost thou meane thy body shall lie fallow?

KICKSHAW. When there is mercy in a petticote,
    I must turne pilgrime for some breath.

LORD.   I thinke
    Twere cooler travell—if you examine it—   125
    Upon the hoofe through *Spaine*.

SENTLOVE.   Through *Ethiopia*.

LORD. Nay, lesse laborious to serve a prentiship
    In *Peru*, and dig gold out of the mine,
    Though all the yeare were dogdayes. [6]

SECRETARY. "To repentance."   130

LORD. "In briefe, this Lady, could you fall from vertue,
    within my knowledge will not blush to be a Bawde."

SENTLOVE. But hang't, tis honorable journey worke;
    Thou art famous by't, and thy name's up.

KICKSHAW.   So, sir,
    Let me aske you a question, my deare knight.   135

Which is lesse servile,—to bring up the Pheasant,
And waite, or sit at table uncontrould
And carve to my owne appetite?
SENTLOVE.   No more;
     Th' art witty, as I am.—
SECRETARY.   "A bawd."
SENTLOVE.   How's that?
KICKSHAW. Oh you are famous by't, and your name's up,   140
                    sir.
LORD. "Be[3] wise, and reward my caution with timely
     care of your selfe, so I shall not repent to be knowne
     your lovinge[4] kinsman and servant."
     Gentlemen, the Lady Celestina,
     Is she so rare a thing?[3]
KICKSHAW.   If you'le have my   145
     Opinion, my Lord, I never saw
     So sweete, so faire, so rich a peece of nature.
LORD. Ile shew thee a fairer presently, to shame
     Thy eyes and judgement. Looke o' that.
                    [*He gives him a miniature.*]
                         So, Ile subscribe.
                    [*He signs the letter.*]
     Seale it; Ile excuse your pen for the direction.   150
KICKSHAW. Bella Marias picture; she was hansome.
SENTLOVE. But not to be compar'd—
LORD. Your patience, gentlemen, Ile returne instantly.
                                             Exit.
KICKSHAW. Whither is my Lord gone?
SECRETARY. To a Lady i' th' next Chamber.
SENTLOVE.   What is she?   155
SECRETARY. You shall pardon me, I am his Secretary.
SENTLOVE. I was wont to be of his counsell. A new
                    officer[10]
     And I not know't? I am resolvd to batter
     All other with the praise of Celestina.
     I must retaine him.
                    Enter LORD.

[10] *officer :* pander.

LORD.   Has not that object   160
   Convinc't your erring judgements.
KICKSHAW.   What! this picture?
LORD. Were but your thoughts as capable as mine
   Of her Idea,[7] you would wish no thought
   That were not active in her praise, above
   All worth and memory of her sexe.
SENTLOVE.   She was faire,   165
   I must confesse; but had your Lordship look'd
   With eyes more narrow and some lesse affection
   Upon her face,—
KICKSHAW. [*Returning the miniature.*] I doe not love the
                 copies
   Of any dead; they make me dreame of goblins.[8]
   Give me a living mistresse, with but halfe   170
   The beauty of Celestina. Come, my Lord,
   Tis pitty that a Lord of so much flesh
   Should waste upon a ghost, when they are living
   Can give you a more honourable consumption.
SENTLOVE. Why, doe you meane, my Lord, to live an   175
                 Infidell?
   Doe, and see what will come ont; observe[11] still
   And dote upon your vigills; build a chamber
   Within a rocke, a tombe among the wormes,
   Not farre off, where you may in proofe apocryphall
   Court em not devoure the pretty pile   180
   Of flesh your mistresse carried to the grave.
   There are no women in the world; all eyes
   And tongue and lippes are buried in her coffin.
LORD. Why doe you thinke your selves competent Judges
   Of beauty, gentlemen?
BOTH.   What should hinder us?   185
KICKSHAW. I have seene and tried as many as another
   With a mortall backe.
LORD.   Your eyes are bribd,
   And your hearts chain'd to some desires; you cannot
   Enjoy the freedome of a sence.

---

[11] *observe :* worship.

KICKSHAW.   Your Lordship
  Has a cleare eyesight, and can judge and penetrate.   190
LORD. I can, and give a perfect censure[12] of
  Each line and point, distinguish beautie from
  A thousand formes, which your corrupted optiks
  Would passe for naturall.
SENTLOVE.   I desire no other
  Judge should determine[13] us, and if your Lordship   195
  Dare venture but your eyes upon this Lady,
  Ile stand their justice, and be confident
  You shall give Celestina victorie,
  And triumph o'er[5] all beauties past and living.
KICKSHAW. I dare, my Lord, venture a sute of clothes,   200
  You will be o'ercome.
LORD.   You doe not know my for-
                          tit[ude.][6]
SENTLOVE. Nor frailtie; you dare not trust your selfe to
                          see her.
LORD. Thinke you so, gentlemen? I dare see this creature
  To make you know your errors, and the difference
  Of her, whose memory is my Saint. Not trust   205
  My sences? I dare see, and speake with her.
  Which holds the best acquaintance to prepare
  My visit to her?
SENTLOVE.   I will doo't, my Lord.
KICKSHAW. Shee is a Lady free in entertainements.
LORD. I would give this advantage to your cause,—   210
  Bid [her][7] appeare in all the ornaments
  Did ever waite on beautie, all the riches
  Pride can put on, and teach her face more charme
  Then ever Poet drest up *Venus* in;
  Bid her be all the graces and the queene   215
  Of love in one. Ile see her, Sentlove, and
  Bring off my heart, arm'd but [in] single[8] thought
  Of one that is dead, without a wound; and when
  I have made your follie prisoner, Ile laugh at you.

[12] *censure :* judgment.   [13] *determine :* judge for.

SENTLOVE. She shall expect you; trust to me for   220
    knowledge.
LORD. I'me for the present somewhere else engagd.
 Let me heare from you.   [*Exit.*]
SENTLOVE.   So! I am glad hee's yet
 So neere conversion.
KICKSHAW.   I am for Aretina.
SENTLOVE. No mention of my Lord.
KICKSHAW.   Prepare his Lady.
 Tis time he were reduc'd[14] to the old sport; 225
 One Lord like him more would undoe the court.
          [*Exeunt.*]

[THIRD ACT. SCENE II.]

 Enter ARETINA *with a letter* [*and*] DECOY.
DECOY. He is the ornament of your bloud, Madam;
 I am much bound to his Lordship.
ARETINA.   He gives you
 A noble character.
DECOY.   Tis his goodnesse, Madam.
ARETINA. [*Aside.*] I wanted such an engine; my Lord
    has
 Done me a curtesie to disclose her nature; 5
 I now know one to trust, and will employ her.
 [*To her.*] Touching my Lord, for reasons which I
    shall
 Offer to your Ladiship hereafter, I
 Desire you would be silent; but, to shew
 How much I dare be confident in your secrecie, 10
 I powre my bosome forth. I love a gentleman
 On whom there wo' not [need][1] much conjuration
 To meet.—Your eare.   [*She whispers.*]
DECOY.   I apprehend you, and I shall
 Be happy to be serviceable; I am sorry
 Your Ladiship did not know me before now. 15

14 *reduc'd :* led back.

I have done offices, and not a few
Of the nobilitie, but have done feates
Within my house, which is so convenient
For situation, and artfull chambers,—
Such pretty pictures to provoke the fancie!   20

          Enter LITTLEWORTH.

LITTLEWORTH. Madam, all pleasures languish in your
               absence.
ARETINA. Your pardon a few minutes, sir.

               [*She takes* DECOY *aside.*]
                        You must
Contrive it thus.   [*They whisper.*]
LITTLEWORTH.   I attend, and shall account it
Honour to waite on your returne.
ARETINA.   He may not
Have the least knowledge of my name, or person.   25
DECOY. I have practisd that already for some great ones,
And dare agen to satisfie you, Madam;
I have a thousand wayes to doe sweet offices.
LITTLEWORTH. If this Lady Aretina should be honest,
I ha' lost time. Shee's free as aire; I must   30
Have closer conference, and if I have art,
Make her affect[1] me in revenge.
DECOY.   This evening—
Leave me to manage things.
ARETINA.   You will oblige me.
DECOY. You shall commend my art, and thanke me after.
                            Exit.
ARETINA. I hope the revells are maintained within.   35
LITTLEWORTH. By Sir Thomas and his Mistris.
ARETINA.   How? His
         Mistris?
LITTLEWORTH. The Lady Celestina. I ne'er saw
Eyes shoote more amorous enterchange.
ARETINA.   Ist so?
LITTLEWORTH. He weares her favor with meere pride.
ARETINA.   Her favor?
LITTLEWORTH. A feather that he ravish'd from her fan,   40
And is so full of courtship, which she smiles on.

ARETINA. Tis well.

LITTLEWORTH.   And praises her beyond all poetry.

ARETINA. I'me glad he has so much wit.

LITTLEWORTH. [*Aside.*]   Not jealous!

ARETINA. [*Aside.*] This secures me; what would make
            other Ladies pale

With jealousie gives but a licence to my wandrings.   45

Let him now taxe me if he dare,—and yet

Her beauti's worth my envie, and I wish

Revenge upon it, not because he loves,

But that it shines above my owne.

            Enter ALEXANDER [KICKSHAW.]

KICKSHAW.   Deare Madam.

ARETINA. [*Aside.*] I have it.—You two gentlemen   50
            professe

Much service to me. If I have a way

To employ your wit and secrecie,—

BOTH.   You'le honour us.

ARETINA. You gave a high and worthy character
    Of Celestina.

KICKSHAW.   I remember, Madam.

ARETINA. Doe either of you love her?

KICKSHAW.   Not I, Madam.   55

LITTLEWORTH. I wod not if I might.

ARETINA.   Shee's now my guest,
    And by a tricke, invited by my husband
    To disgrace me. You gentlemen are held
    Wits of the towne, the Consulls that doe governe
    The Senate here, whose jeeres are all authenticke.   60
    The Tavernes and the Ordinaries(2) are
    Made academies where you come, and all
    Your sinnes and surfets made [the] times[2] example.
    Your very nods can quell a Theater,
    No speech or Poem good without your seale;   65
    You can protect scurrility, and publish.
    By your authority beleev'd, no rapture
    Ought to have honest meaning.

KICKSHAW.   Leave our characters.

LITTLEWORTH. And name the emploiment.

ARETINA.   You must
                         exercise
The strength of both your wits upon this Lady,   70
And talke her into humblenesse or anger,
Both which are equall—to my thought. If you
Dare undertake this slight thing for my sake,
My favour shall reward it; but be faithfull,
And seeme to let all spring from your owne freedome.   75

KICKSHAW. This all? We can defame her; if you please,
My friend shall call her whore or any thing,
And never be endangerd to a duell.

ARETINA.   How's that?

KICKSHAW. He can endure a cudgelling, and no man
Will fight after so faire a satisfaction;   80
But leave us to our Art, and doe not limit us.

ARETINA. They are here; begin not till I whisper you.

        Enter SIR THOMAS, CELESTINA, MARIANA, [*and*]
                      ISABELLA.

ARETINA. *Je vous prie, madame, d'excuser l'importunité
de mes affaires, qui m'ont fait offenser, par mon absence, une dame de laquelle j'ai reçu*[3] *tant d'obli-*   85
gation.[1]

CELESTINA. *Pardonnez-moi, madame; vous me faites*[4]
trop d'honneur.[2]

ARETINA. *C'est bien de la douceur de vôtre nature,*[5]
que vous tenez cette langage;[6] *mais j'espère que
mon mari*[6] *n'a pas manqué de vous entretenir en*   90
mon absence.[3]

CELESTINA. *En vérité, monsieur nous a fort obligé.*[4]

ACT III. SCENE II.   me too much honor.
[1] I beg you, madame, to excuse   [3] It is from the sweetness of
the press of my affairs, which   your nature that you phrase it
have made me offend, by my   thus; but I hope my husband
absence, a lady from whom I   has not failed to entertain you
have received so many kind-   in my absence.
nesses.   [4] In truth Monsieur has put me
[2] Pardon me, madam; you do   greatly in his debt.

ARETINA. *Il eût trop failli,*[7] *s'il n'eût tâché de tout son pouvoir à vous rendre toutes sortes de services.*[5]

CELESTINA. *C'est de sa bonté qu'il nous a tant favorisé.*[6]

ARETINA. *De la vôtre plutôt,*[8] *madame, qui vous fait donne d'interprétation si benigne a ses efforts.*[7]   95

CELESTINA. *Je vois*[9] *bien que la victoire sera toujours*[9] *à madame, et de langage*[10] *et de la courtoisie.*[8, 10]

ARETINA. *Vraiment,*[11] *madame, que jamais personne a plus désiré l'honneur de vôtre*[12] *compagnie*   100
que moi.[9, 12]

CELESTINA. *Laissons-en, je vous supplie, des compliments, et permettez à vôtre*[13] *servante de vous baiser les mains.*[10]

ARETINA. *Vous m'obligez trop.*[11]

BORNWELL. I have no more patience; let's be merry agen
In our owne language. Madam, our mirth cooles.   105
Our Nephew!

Enter FREDERICK [*drunk, with* STEWARD.]

ARETINA. Passion of my braine!

FREDERICK. Save you, gentlemen! Save you, Ladies!

ARETINA.   I am undone.

FREDERICK. I must salute, no matter at which end I
begin.

[*He kisses* CELESTINA.]

ARETINA. There's a complement!

CELESTINA.   Is this your nephew,
Madam?

---

[5] He has failed too much if he has not striven with all his might to render you every kind of service.

[6] Out of his generosity he has greatly favored me.

[7] Even more of your's, madame, which makes you give so kind an interpretation to his efforts.

[8] I see that the victory will always go to madame, both in language and in courtesy.

[9] It is true, madame, that no one ever desired the honor of your company more than I.

[10] Let's forget the compliments, I beg you, and permit your servant to kiss your hand.

[11] You put me under too great an obligation.

ARETINA. *Je vous prie, madame, d'excuser les habits*[14] 110
*et le rude comportement de mon cousin. Il est tout
fraîchement venu de l'université, où on l'a tout
gâté*[12, [15]]

CELESTINA. *Excusez-moi, madame, il est bien ac-
compli.*[13, [16]]

FREDERICK. This language should be French, by the
motions
Of your heads, and the mirth of your faces.

ARETINA.   I am dishonor'd. 115

FREDERICK. Tis one of the finest tongues for Ladies to
shew their
Teeth in. If you'le Latine I am for you, or Greeke it.
My tailor has not put me into French yet.
Mille basia, basia mille.[14]

CELESTINA. *Je ne vous entends*[17] *pas, monsieur.* 120
I understand you not, sir.

FREDERICK.   Why, so!
You and I then shall be in charity,
For though we should be abusive, we ha' the benefit
Not to understand one another : where's my Aunt?
I did heare musicke somewhere, and my braines, 125
Tun'd with a bottle of your capering claret,
Made haste to shew their dancing.

LITTLEWORTH.   Please you, Madam,
They are very comfortable.[15]

[Offering his candy-box to CELESTINA.]

STEWARD.   Alas, Madam!
How would you have me helpe it? I did use
All meanes I could, after he heard the musicke, 130
To make him drunke, in hope so to containe him;
But the wine made him lighter, and his head
Flew hither, ere I mist his heeles.

KICKSHAW. Nay, he spoke Latine to the Lady!

[12] I beg you, madam, to excuse
the dress and rude manner of
my relative. He has just come
from the university, where he
was completely corrupted.

[13] Excuse me, madame, he is
quite accomplished.

[14] A thousand kisses.

[15] *comfortable :* comforting.

ARETINA. Oh most unpardonable! Get him off   135
   Quickly, and discreetly, or if I live—
STEWARD. Tis not in my power; he sweares I am
   An absurd sober fellow; and if you keepe
   A servant in his house to crosse his humour,
   When the rich sword and belt comes home, hee'le kill   140
      him. [3]
ARETINA. What shall I doe? Try your skill, Master
      Littleworth.
LITTLEWORTH. He has ne'er a sword.—Sweet Master
      Frederick.
BORNWELL. Tis pitty, Madam, such a scion[18] should
   Be lost.—But you are clouded.
CELESTINA.   Not I, sir,
   I never found my selfe more cleare at heart.   145
BORNWELL. I could play with a feather. Your fan, Lady.
   Gentlemen, Aretina, ta, ra, ra, ra! Come, Madam.
FREDERICK. Why, my good tutor in election! [4]
   You might have beene a scholler.
LITTLEWORTH.   But I thanke
   My friends they brought me up a little better.   150
   Give me the towne wits that deliver jeasts
   Cleane from the bow, that whistle in the aire
   And cleave the pin[16] at twelvescore. Ladies doe
   But laugh at a gentleman that has any learning;
   Tis sinne enough to have your clothes suspected.   155
   Leave us, and I will find a time to instruct you.
   Come, here are sugar plumbes. Tis a good Frederick.
FREDERICK. Why, is not this my Aunts house in the
      Strand?
   The noble Rendevous? Who laughes at me?
   Go, I will root here, if I list, and talke   160
   Of Retoricke, Logicke, Latine, Greeke, or any thing,
   And understand 'em too! Who sayes the contrary?
   Yet—in a faire way—I contemne all learning,
   And will be ignorant as he, or he,
   Or any taffata, satten, scarlet, plush,   165

---

[16] *pin :* target center.

Tissue, or cloath a' bodkin[17] gentleman,
Whose manners are most gloriously infected.
Did you laugh at me, Lady?
CELESTINA.   Not I, sir!
But if I did shew mirth upon your question,
I hope you wod not beate me, little gentleman.   170
FREDERICK. How! "Little gentleman?" You dare not
                              say
These words to my new cloathes, and fighting sword.
ARETINA. Nephew Frederick!
FREDERICK.   "Little gentleman!"
[Tis][19] an affront both to my bloud and person;
I am a gentleman of as tall a birth   175
As any [boast][20] nobility. Though my clothes
Smell o' the lampe, my coate is honourable,—
Right honourable,—full of or and argent.[18]
A "little gentleman!"
BORNWELL.   Coze, you must be patient.
My Lady meant you no dishonour, and   180
You must remember shee's a woman.
FREDERICK. Is she a woman? That's another matter.
D'ee heare; my uncle tells me what you are.
CELESTINA. So, sir.
FREDERICK. You cald me "little gentleman."
CELESTINA.   I did sir.   185
FREDERICK. A little pinke[19] has made a lusty ship
Strike her topsaile; the Crow may beard the
                    Elephant;
A whelpe may tame the Tiger; spight of all
False decks[20] and murderers,[21] and a "little gentle-
                    man"
Be hard enough to grapple with your Ladiship,   190
Top and top gallant.—Will you goe drinke, uncle?
Tother inchanted bottle? You and I

---

[17] *cloath a' bodkin:* expensive   [20] *False decks:* Platform to
or brocaded cloth.   repel boarders.
[18] *full of . . . argent:* gold and [21] *murderers:* spread-shot
silver on his coat of arms.   cannon.
[19] *pinke:* sailing ship.

Will tiple and talke phylosophy.
BORNWELL.   Come, Nephew.
You will excuse a minutes absence, Madam.
Waite you on us.
STEWARD.   My duty, sir.
    Exeunt [BORNWELL, FREDERICK, *and* STEWARD.][21]
ARETINA.   Now, gentlemen.   195
KICKSHAW. Madam, I had rather you accuse my lan-
                        guage
For speaking truth, then vertue suffer in
My further silence; and it is my wonder
That you, whose noble carriage hath deserv'd
All honour and opinion, should now   200
Be guilty of illmanners.
CELESTINA.   What was that
You told me, sir?
LITTLEWORTH.   Doe you not blush, Madam,
To aske that question?
CELESTINA.   You amaze rather
My cheeke to palenesse. What [meane you][22] by
                        this?
I am not troubled with the hickup, gentlemen,—   205
You should bestow this fright upon me.[22]
LITTLEWORTH.   Then
Pride and ill memory goe together.
CELESTINA.   How, sir?
KICKSHAW. The gentleman on whom you exercise[d][23]
Your thin wit, was a nephew to the Lady
Whose guest you are; and though her modesty   210
Looke calme on the abuse of one so neare
Her bloud, the affront was impious.
LITTLEWORTH.   I am asham'd on't.
You an ingenious[23] Lady, and well mannered?
Ile teach a Beare as much civility.
CELESTINA. You may be master of the Colledge, sir,   215
For ought I know.

---

[22] "That" is understood at the   [23] *ingenious :* naturally
    head of the line.   honorable.

LITTLEWORTH.   What Colledge?

[CELESTINA.] [24]   Of the Beares.
Have you a plot upon me? D'ee possesse
Your wits, or know me, gentlemen.

                    Enter BORNWELL [*behind*].

BORNWELL.   How's this?

KICKSHAW. Know you? Yes, we doe know you to an
          atome.

LITTLEWORTH. Madam, we know what stuffe your soule   220
          is made on.

CELESTINA. But doe not barke so like a mastive, pray.—
Sure they are mad.—Let your braines stand awhile
And settle, gentlemen; you know not me;
What am I?

LITTLEWORTH. Th'art a puppet, a thing made
Of clothes and painting, and not halfe so hansome   225
As that which plaid *Susanna* in the faire.

CELESTINA. I heard you visited those canvas tragedies,—
One of their constant audience,—and so taken
With *Susan* that you wishd your selfe a rivall
With the two wicked elders.

KICKSHAW.   You thinke this   230
Is wit now! Come you are—

CELESTINA.   What, I beseech you?
Your character will be full of salt and satyre,
No doubt. What am I?

KICKSHAW.   Why, you are a woman—

CELESTINA. And that's at least a bow wide[(5)] of
          you[r][25] knowledge.

KICKSHAW. Wo'd be thought hansome, and might passe
                    i' th' country   235
Upon a market day, but miserably
Forfeit to pride and fashions, that if heaven
Were a new gowne, you'd not stay in't a fortnight.

CELESTINA. It must be miserably out of fashion then.
Have I no sinne but pride?

KICKSHAW.   Hast any vertue?   240
Or but a good face, to excuse that want?

CELESTINA. You prais'd it yesterday.

KICKSHAW.   That made you proud.

CELESTINA. More pride?

KICKSHAW.   You need not. To close up the
            praise,
I have seene a better countenance in a Sibill.[6]

CELESTINA. When you wore spectacles of sacke,[24] mis-   245
            tooke
The painted cloth, and kist it for your mistresse.

KICKSHAW. Let me aske you a question. How much
Have you consum'd[25] in expectation
That I would love you?

CELESTINA.   Why, I thinke as much
As you have paid away in honest debts   250
This seven yeare. Tis a pretty impudence,
But cannot make me angry.

LITTLEWORTH.   Is there any
Man that will cast away his limbes upon her?

KICKSHAW. You doe not sing so well as I imagind,
Nor dance; you reele in your coranto,[26] and pinch   255
Your petticoate too hard; y'ave no good eare
To th' musicke, and incline too much one shoulder,
As you were dancing on the rope and falling.
You speake abominable French, and make
A courtsey like a Dairie maide.—[*Aside.*] Not mad?   260

LITTLEWORTH. [*Aside.*] Doe we not sting her hansomely?

BORNWELL. [*Aside.*]   A conspiracie!

KICKSHAW. Your state[27] is not so much as tis reported,
When you conferre notes, all your husbands debts
And your owne reconcild;—but that's not it
Will so much spoile your marriage.

CELESTINA.   As what, sir?   265
Let me know all my faults.

KICKSHAW.   Some men doe whisper
You are not overhonest.[28]

---

[24] *wore spectacles of sacke :*
  saw through an alcoholic
  haze.

[25] *consum'd :* spent.

[26] *coranto :* a fast dance.

[27] *state :* estate, fortune.

[28] *overhonest :* particularly
  chaste.

CELESTINA.   All this shall not
  Move me to more than laughter, and some pittie,
  Because you have the shapes[29] of gentlemen;
  And though you have beene insolent upon me,   270
  I will engage no friend to kicke or cudgell you,
  To spoile your living and your limbes together.
  I leave that to diseases that offend you,
  And spare my curse,—poore silken Vermine!—and
  Hereafter shall distinguish Men from Monkies.   275
BORNWELL. [*Advancing.*] Brave soule!—You brace of
                horseleaches![30] I have heard
  Their barbarous language, Madam; y'are too merci-
                full.
  They shall be silent to your tongue; pray punish 'em.
CELESTINA. They are things not worth my character,[31]
                nor mention
  Of any cleane breath,—so lost in honesty   280
  They cannot satisfie for wrongs enough,
  Though they should steale out of the world at
                Tiburne.[32]
LITTLEWORTH. We are hang'd already.
CELESTINA. Yet I will talke a little to the pilchards.[33]
  You two—that have not twixt you both the hundred   285
  Part of a soule—course woollen witted fellowes
  Without a nap, with bodies made for burdens!
  You, that are onely stuffings for apparrell,
  As you were made but engines[34] for your Taylors
  To frame their clothes upon and get them custome,   290
  Untill men see you moove; yet, then you dare not,
  Out of your guilt of being the ignobler beast,
  But give a horse the wall, whom you excell
  Onely in dancing of the brawles,[35] because
  The horse was not taught the French way. Your two   295
                faces,

---

[29] *shapes :* clothing.   [33] *pilchards :* sardines; the term
[30] *horseleaches :* bloodsuckers.   suggested "pilferer."
[31] *character :* analysis.   [34] *engines :* instruments.
[32] *Tiburne :* place of hangings.   [35] *brawles :* French cotillion.

One fat like Christmas, tother leane like Candelmas,
And Prologue to a Lent, both bound together
Would figure *Janus,* and doe many cures
On Agues and the greene disease[7] by frighting;
But neither can, with all the characters[36]   300
And conjuring circles, charme a woman, though
Sh'ad fourescore yeares upon her, and but one
Tooth in her head, to love or thinke well of you;
And I were miserable to be at cost
To court such a complexion[37] as your malice   305
Did impudently insinuate. But I waste time
And staine my breath in talking to such tadpoles!
Goe home and wash your tongues in Barly water.
Drinke[38] cleane Tobacco, be not hot i' th' mouth,
And you may scape the Beadle;[8] so I leave you   310
To shame and your owne garters.[39]—Sir, I must
Entreate you, for my honour, doe not pennance em.
They are not worth your anger,—how[9] I shall
Acquit your Ladies silence.

BORNWELL.   Madam, I
Am sorry to suspect, and dare revenge.   315
CELESTINA. No cause of mine.
BORNWELL.   It must become me to
Attend you home.
CELESTINA.   You are noble.—Farewell, Mush-
                              roomes.[10]

　　　　　　　[*Exit* CELESTINA *with* BORNWELL.]

ARETINA. Is she gone?
LITTLEWORTH.   I thinke we peperd her.
KICKSHAW. I am glad tis over;
But I repent no service for you, Madam.   320
　　　　Enter SERVANT *with a letter* [*and jewel*].
To me? From whence?—A Jewell, a good preface!
Be happy the conclusion.   *He smiles upon't.*
ARETINA.   Some love letter.
LITTLEWORTH. He has a hundred Mistresses; you may

---

[36] *characters :* magic signs.   [38] *Drinke :* Smoke.
[37] *complexion :* disposition.   [39] To hang yourselves in.

Be charitable, Madam. I ha' none;
He surfets, and I fall away i' th' kidneys.[26]   325
KICKSHAW. Ile meet.   [*Exit* SERVANT.]
　　[*Aside.*] Tis some great Lady questionlesse, that has
　　Taken notice, and would satisfie her appetite.
ARETINA. Now, Master Alexander, you looke bright o'
　　　　　　　　the suddaine;
　　Another spirit's in your eye.
KICKSHAW.   Not mine, Madam,   330
　　Onely a summons to meete a friend.
ARETINA.   What friend?
LITTLEWORTH. By this Jewell, I know her not!
ARETINA. Tis a she-friend? Ile follow, gentlemen;
　　We may have a game at [Cent]40, [27] before you
　　　　　　　　goe.
KICKSHAW. I shall attend you, Madam.
LITTLEWORTH.   Tis our duty.   335
　　　　　　[*Exeunt* KICKSHAW *and* LITTLEWORTH.]
ARETINA. I blush while I converse with my owne
　　　　　　　　thoughts;
　　Some strange fate governes me, but I must on.
　　The wayes are cast already, and we thrive
　　When our sinne feares no eye nor perspective.(11)
　　　　　　　　　　　　　　　　　　Exit.

THE FOURTH ACT. [SCENE I.]

　　Enter two men leading ALEXANDER [KICKSHAW]
　　　　blinded, and goe off suddenly.
KICKSHAW. I am not hurt; my patience to obey em,
　　Not without feare to ha' my throat cut else,
　　Did me a curtesie. Whither ha' they brought me?
　　　　　　　[*He takes off the blindfold.*]
　　Tis devillish darke; the bottome of a well
　　At midnight, with but two starres on the top,   5

40 *Cent:* Card game in which
　　100 won.

Were broad day to this darknesse. I but thinke
How like a whirlewinde these rogues caught me up,
And smoothered my eyesight. Let me see;
These may be spirits and—for ought I know—
Have brought me hither over twenty steeples.   10
Pray heaven they were not Bayliefes, that's more
                  worth
My feare,—and this a prison; all my debts
Reeke in my nostrill, and my bones beginne
To ake with feare to be made dice; and yet
This is too calme and quiet for a prison.   15
What if the riddle prove I am robd? And yet
I did not feele em search me. How now! Musicke!
    Enter DECOY *like an old woman, with a light.*
And a light! What beldam's this? I cannot pray.—
What art?
DECOY.   A friend. Feare not, young man, I am
  No spirit.
KICKSHAW. Off!
DECOY.   Despise me not for age,   20
  Or this course outside, which I weare not out
  Of poverty; thy eyes be witnesse, tis
  No cave or beggars cell th'art brought too; let
  That gold speake here's no want, which thou maist
                spend,
  And finde a spring to tire even prodigality   25
  If thou beest wise.
KICKSHAW.   The devill was a coyner
  From the beginning, yet the gold lookes currant.
DECOY. Th'art still in wonder. Know I am Mistresse of
  This house, and of a fortune that shall serve
  And feed thee with delights; twas I sent for thee,   30
  The jewell and the letter came from me.
  It was my art, thus to contrive our meeting,
  Because I would not trust thee with my fame,
  Untill I found thee worth a womans honor.
KICKSHAW. [*Aside.*] Honour and fame? The devill   35
                meanes to have
  A care on's credit! Though she sent for me,

I hope she has another customer
To doe the tricke withall; I wod not turne
Familiar[1] to a witch.
DECOY.   What saist? Canst thou
    Dwell in my armes to-night? Shall we change[2]   40
            kisses,
And entertaine the silent houres with pleasure,
Such as old Time shall be delighted with,
And blame the too swifte motion of his wings
While we embrace?
KICKSHAW. [*Aside.*]   Embrace? She has had no teeth
    This twenty yeares, and the next violent cough   45
Brings up her tongue; it cannot possibly
Be sound at root. I doe not thinke but one
Strong sneeze upon her—and well meant—would make
Her quarters fall away; one kicke would blow
Her up like gunpowder, and loose all her limbs.   50
She is so cold, an *Incubus*[3] wod not heate her;
Her phlegme would quench a furnace, and her breath
    Would dampe a musket bullet.
DECOY.   Have you, sir,
    Considerd?
KICKSHAW.   What?
DECOY.   My proposition.
    Canst love?
KICKSHAW. I could have done. Whom doe you meane?   55
    I know you are pleas'd but to make sport.
DECOY.   Thou art not
    So dull of soule as thou appearst.
KICKSHAW. [*Aside.*]   This is
But some device; my granam has some tricke in't :—
    Yes, I can love.
DECOY.   But canst thou affect me?
KICKSHAW. Although to reverence so grave a matron   60
    Were an ambitious word in me, yet since

ACT IV. SCENE I.   [3] *Incubus:* Demon in male
[1] *Familiar :* Servant spirit.   form.
[2] *change :* exchange.

You give me boldnesse, I doe love you.
DECOY.   Then
   Thou art my owne.
KICKSHAW. [*Aside.*] Has she no cloven foote?
DECOY. And I am thine, and all that I command
   Thy servants; from this minute thou art happy,   65
   And fate in thee will crowne all my desires.
   I griev'd a proper⁴ man should be compeld
   To bring his body to the common market.
   My wealth shall make thee glorious, and—the more
   To encourage thee—howe'er this forme may fright   70
   Thy youthfull eyes, yet thou wo't find by light
   Of thy owne sense, for other light is banish'd
   My chamber, when our armes tie lovers knots
   And kisses seale the welcome of our lippes,
   I shall not there affright thee, nor seeme old,   75
   With riveld veines; my skin is smooth and softe
   As *Ermines*, with a spirit to meete thine,
   Active and equall to the queene of Loves
   When she did court *Adonis*.
KICKSHAW. [*Aside.*]   This doth more
   Confirme she is a devill, and I am   80
   Within his owne dominions; I must on
   Or else be torne a' peeces; I have heard
   These Succubi⁵ must not be crost.
DECOY.   We trifle
   Too precious time away; Ile shew you a prospect
   Of the next chamber, and then out the candle.   85
KICKSHAW. Have you no sacke i' th' house? I would goe
                     arm'd
   Upon this breach.
DECOY.   It sha' not need.
KICKSHAW.   One word
   Mother; have not you beene a Cat in your dayes?
DECOY. I am glad you are so merry, sir. You observe
   That bed?

                              ⁵ *Succubi*: Demons in female
⁴ *proper*: well formed.   form.

KICKSHAW. A very brave one.

DECOY.   When you are   90
  Disrob'd, you can come thither in the darke.
  You sha' not stay for me; come, as you wish
  For happinesse.   *Exit.*

KICKSHAW.   I am preferd, if I
  Be modest and obey. She cannot have
  The heart to doe me harme, and[6] she were *Hecate*[(1)]   95
  Herselfe. I will have a strong faith, and thinke,
  I march upon a Mistris, the lesse evill.
  If I scape fire now, I defie the devill.

[FOURTH ACT. SCENE II.]

Enter FREDERICK [*fashionably dressed*],
        LITTLEWORTH, [*and*] STEWARD.

FREDERICK. And how d'ee like me now?

STEWARD.   Most excellent.

FREDERICK. Your opinion, Master Littleworth.

LITTLEWORTH.   Your French tailor
  Has made you a perfect gentleman; I may
  Converse now with you, and preserve my credit.
  D'ee find no alteration in your body   5
  With these new clothes?

FREDERICK.   My body altered? No.

LITTLEWORTH. You are not yet in fashion then; that must
  Have a new motion, garbe,[1] and posture too,
  Or all your pride is cast away. It is not
  The cut of your apparrell makes a gallant,   10
  But the geometricall wearing of your clothes.

STEWARD. Master Littleworth tells you right; you weare
                        your hat
  Too like a citizen.

LITTLEWORTH.   Tis like a Midwife;
  Place it with best advantage of your haire.

                                ACT IV. SCENE II.
  [6] *and :* if.   [1] *garbe :* manner.

Is halfe your feather[1] molted? This does make   15
No shew; it should spread over like a Canopy;
Your hot-reind[2] Monsieur weares it for a shade
And cooler to his backe. Your doublet must
Be more unbutton'd hereabouts; you'le not
Be a sloven else; a foule shirt is no blemish;   20
You must be confident, and outface cleane linnen!
Your doublet and your breeches must be allow'd
No private meeting here; your cloak's too long,
It reaches to your buttocke and doth smell
Too much of Spanish gravitie. The fashion   25
Is to weare nothing but a Cape, a coate
May be allowed a covering for one elbow;
And some, to avoid the trouble, choose to walke
In quirpo[3] thus.
STEWARD. [*Aside.*] Your coat and cloak's a-brushing
   In Long-lane, Lumbard.[4]
FREDERICK.   But what if it raine?   30
LITTLEWORTH. Your belt about your shoulder is suf-
                           ficient
To keepe off any storme; beside, a reede[2]
But wav'd discreetly, has so many pores,
It suckes up all the raine that falls about one.
With this defence, when other men have beene   35
Wet to the skin through all their cloakes, I have
Defied a tempest and walk'd by the Tavernes
Drie as a bone.
STEWARD. [*Aside.*] Because he had no money
   To call for wine.
FREDERICK.   Why, you doe walke enchanted!
Have you such pretty charmes in towne? But stay,   40
Who must I have to attend me?
LITTLEWORTH.   Is not that
   Yet thought upon?
STEWARD.   I have laid out[5] for servants.

---

2 *hot-reind* : lusty.
3 *quirpo* : with exposed body
   (*cuerpo*).

4 *Lumbard* : street of pawn
   shops.
5 *laid out* : spent money **for.**

LITTLEWORTH. They are every where.

STEWARD.   I cannot yet be
          furnish'd
   With such as I would put into his hands.

FREDERICK. Of what condition must they be, and how   45
   Many in number, sir?

LITTLEWORTH.   Beside your fencing,
   Your singing, dancing, riding, and French master,
   Two may serve domesticke to be constant waiters
   Upon a gentleman,—a foole, a pimpe.

STEWARD. For these two officers I have enquird,   50
   And I am promisd a convenient whiskin.⁶
   I could save charges, and employ the Pye Wench
   That carries her intelligence in whitepots,⁷
   Or tis but taking order with the woman
   That holds the ballads; she could fit him with   55
   A concubin to any tune; but I
   Have a designe to place a fellow with him
   That has read all Sir *Pandarus* workes, a Trojan⁸
   That lies conceal'd, and is acquainted with
   Both citty and suburbian fripperies,⁹   60
   Can fetch em with a spell at midnight to him,
   And warrant which are for his turne; can, for
   A neede, supply the Surgeon too.

FREDERICK.   I like
   Thy providence—such a one deserves
   A livery twice a yeare.   65

STEWARD. It sha' not need; a cast suite of your worships
   Will serve; he'le find a cloke to cover it
   Out of his share with those he brings to bed to you.

FREDERICK. But must I call this fellow Pimpe?

LITTLEWORTH.   It is
   Not necessary; or *Jacke*, or *Harry*,   70
   Or what hee's knowne abroad by, will sound better,
   That men may thinke he is a Christian.

---

⁶ *whiskin :* pander.   ⁸ *Trojan :* merry-maker.
⁷ *whitepots :* dishes of milk,   ⁹ *fripperies :* prostitutes.
   eggs, and pot cheese.

FREDERICK. But heare you, Master Littleworth, is there
                             not
   A method and degrees of title in
   Men of this art?
LITTLEWORTH.   According to the honour   75
   Of men that do employ em. An Emperour
   May give this office to a Duke, a King
   May have his Viceroy to negotiate for him,
   A Duke may use a Lord, the Lord a Knight,
   A Knight may trust a gentleman; and when   80
   They are abroad and merry, gentlemen
   May pimpe to one another.
FREDERICK.   Good, good fellowship!
   But for the foole now, that should waite on me,
   And breake me jeasts!
LITTLEWORTH.   A foole is necessary.
STEWARD. By any meanes.
FREDERICK.   But which of these two   85
                          servants
   Must now take place?
LITTLEWORTH.   That question, Master Frederick,
   The schoole of Heraldry should conclude upon;
   But if my judgement may be heard, the foole
   Is your first man, and it is knowne a point
   Of state to have a foole.
STEWARD.   But, sir, the other   90
   Is held the finer servant; his employments
   Are full of trust, his person cleane and nimble;
   And none so soone can leape[10] into preferment,
   Where fooles are poore.
LITTLEWORTH.   Not all, there's story[11] for't.
   Princes have beene no wiser than they should be;   95
   Would any noble man that were no foole
   Spend all in hope of the Philosophers stone,
   To buy new Lordships in another countrey?
   Would Knights build Colledges, or gentlemen

---

[10] *leape* : play on term for the   [11] *story* : example in history.
sexual act.

Of good estates, challenge the field and fight   100
Because a whore wo' not be honest?[12] Come,
Fooles are a family over all the world;
We doe affect[13] one naturally; indeede
The foole is Leiger[14] with us.

STEWARD.   Then the Pimpe
Is extraordinary.

FREDERICK.   Doe not you fall out   105
About their places.—Here's my noble Aunt!

Enter ARETINA.

LITTLEWORTH. How doe you like your nephew, Madam,
                              now?

ARETINA. Well! Turne about, Frederick. Very well!

[FREDERICK].[1] Am I not now a proper gentleman?
The vertue of rich clothes! Now could I take   110
The wall of *Julius Cesar,* affront
Great *Pompeys* upper lip, and defie the Senate.
Nay, I can be as proud as your owne heart, Madam;
You may take that for your comfort; I put on
That vertue with my clothes, and I doubt not   115
But in a little time, I shall be impudent
As any Page or Players boy. I am
Beholding to this gentlemans good discipline,
But I shall doe him credit in my practise;
Your Steward has some pretty notions too   120
In morall mischiefe.

ARETINA.   Your desert in this
Exceedes all other service, and shall bind me
Both to acknowledge and reward.

LITTLEWORTH.   Sweet Madam!
Thinke me but worth your favour, I wo'd creepe
Upon my knees to honour you; and for every   125
Minute you lend to my reward, Ile pay
A yeare of serviceable tribute.

ARETINA.   You
Can complement.

---

12 *honest :* chaste.   14 *Leiger :* Resident ambassador.
13 *affect :* feel affection for.

LITTLEWORTH. [*Aside.*] Thus still she puts me off.
   Unlesse I speake the downe-right word, she'le never
   Understand me; a man would thinke that creeping   130
   Upon one's knees were English to a Lady.
      Enter ALEXANDER [KICKSHAW, *gaudily attired*].
KICKSHAW. How ist, Jacke? Pleasures attend you,
            Madam.
   How does my plant of honour?
ARETINA.   Who is this?
KICKSHAW. Tis Alexander.
ARETINA.   Rich and glorious!
LITTLEWORTH. Tis Alexander the great!
KICKSHAW.   And my *Buceph-*   135
        alus[3]
   Waites at the doore.
ARETINA.   Your case[15] is alterd, sir.
KICKSHAW. I cannot helpe these things; the Fates will
        have it,
   Tis not my land does this.
LITTLEWORTH.   But thou hast a plough
   That brings it in.
ARETINA.   Now he lookes brave and lovely.
FREDERICK. Welcome, my gallant Macedonian.   140
KICKSHAW. Madam, you gave your Nephew for my
        pupil.
   I read[16] but in a taverne; if you'le honour us,
   The Beare[4] at the bridge foote[17] shall entertaine
        you.
   A drawer is my *Ganimed,*[5] he shall skinke[18]
   Briske *Nectar* to us; we will onely have   145
   A dozen Partridge in a dish, as many Phesants,
   Quailes, Cockes, and Godwits[19] shall come marching
        up
   Like the train'd band;[20] a fort[21] of Sturgeon

---

[15] Play on sense of "costume."
[16] *read :* lecture.
[17] A tavern in Southwark near
    London Bridge.
[18] *skinke :* pour.
[19] *Godwits :* Snipes.
[20] *band :* militia.
[21] *fort :* pastry.

Shall give most bold defiance to an army,
And triumph o'er the table.

ARETINA.   Sir, it will   150
But dull the appetite to heare more, and mine
Must be excusd; another time I may
Be your guest.

KICKSHAW.   Tis growne in fashion now with Ladies.
When you please Ile attend you.—Littleworth.
Come, Frederick.

FREDERICK.   Wee'le have musicke, I love noise.   155
We will outroare the Thames and shake the bridge,
                    boy.

                    Exit [FREDERICK *and* KICKSHAW.]

LITTLEWORTH. Madam, I kisse your hand. Wod you wod
                    thinke
Of youre poore servant; flesh and bloud is fraile,
And troublesome to carry without helpe.

ARETINA. A coach will easily convey it, or   160
You may take water at Strand Bridge.

LITTLEWORTH.   But I
Have taken fire.

ARETINA.   The Thames will coole—

LITTLEWORTH. But never quench my heart; your charitie
Can onely doe that!

ARETINA.   I will keepe it cold
Of purpose.

LITTLEWORTH. Now you blesse me, and I dare   165
Be drunke in expectation!   [*Exit.*]

ARETINA.   I am confident
He knowes me not, and I were worse than mad
To be my owne betrayer.—Here's my husband.

                    Enter BORNWELL.

BORNWELL. Why, how now, Aretina? What, alone?
The mystery of this solitude? My house   170
Turne desart o' th' sudaine? All the gamsters
Blowne up? Why is the musicke put to silence?
Or ha' their instruments caught a cold, since we
Gave 'em the last heate? I must know thy ground
Of Melancholy.

ARETINA.   You are merry, as   175
  You came from kissing Celestina.
BORNWELL.   I
  Feele her yet warme upon my lip; she is
  Most excellent company. I did not thinke
  There was that sweetnesse in her sexe; I must
  Acknowledge twas thy cure to disinchant me   180
  From a dull husband to an active lover.
  With such a Lady, I could spend more yeeres
  Than since my birth my glasse hath run soft minutes,
  And yet be young; her presence has a spell
  To keepe off age; she has an eye would strike   185
  Fire through an adamant.
ARETINA.   I have heard as much
  Bestow'd upon a dull fac'd chambermaid,
  Whom love and wit would thus commend. True
               beauty
  Is mock'd when we compare thus, it selfe being
  Above what can be fetch'd[22] to make it lovely.   190
  Or, could our thoughts reach some thing to declare
  The glories of a face, or bodies elegance,
  That touches but our sense; when[23] beauty spreads
  Over the soule, and calls up understanding
  To looke, when thence is offer'd, and admire.   195
  In both I must acknowledge Celestina
  Most excellently faire, faire above all
  The beauties I ha' seene, and one most worthy
  Mans love and wonder.
BORNWELL.   Doe you speake, Aretina,
  This with a pure sence to commend, or ist   200
  The mockery of my praise?
ARETINA.   Although it shame
  My selfe, I must be just, and give her all
  The excellency of women; and were I
  A man.
BORNWELL. What then?

---

[22] *fetch'd* : brought in for com-   [23] *when* : while, on the other
    parison; far-fetched.   hand.

ARETINA.   I know not with what losse
I should attempt her love; she is a peece   205
So angellically moving, I should thinke
Frailty excusd to dote upon her forme,
And almost vertue to be wicked with her.   *Exit.*
BORNWELL. What   should   this   meane?   This   is   no
                              jealousie,
Or she beleeves I counterfeit. I feele   210
Something within me, like a heate, to give
Her cause, would Celestina but consent.
What a fraile thing is man! It is not worth
Our glory to be chaste, while we deny
Mirth and converse with women. He is good   215
That dares the tempter, yet corrects his bloud.   *Exit.*

[FOURTH ACT. SCENE III.]

[*Enter*] CELESTINA, MARIANA, [*and*] ISABELLA.
CELESTINA. I have told you all my knowledge; since he
                              is pleasd
To invite himselfe, he shall be entertaind,
And you shall be my witnesses.
MARIANA.   Who comes with him.
CELESTINA. Sir William Sentlove, that prepard me for
The honourable encounter; I expect   5
His Lordship every minute.
                    Enter SENTLOVE.
SENTLOVE.   My Lord is come.
CELESTINA. He has honord me.
                    Enter LORD [*and*] HAIRCUT.
SENTLOVE.   My Lord, your periwig is
                              awry!
LORD. You, sir.—
                    While HAIRCUT *is busie about his haire,*
                         SENTLOVE *goes to* CELESTINA.
SENTLOVE.   You may guesse at the gentleman that's
                              with him.
It is his Barbar, Madam, d'ee observe?

And your Ladiship want a shaver.

HAIRCUT.   She is here, sir.—   10
I am betraid.—Sentlove, your plot. I may
Have opportunity to be reveng'd.   *Exit.*

SENTLOVE. She in the midst.

LORD.   She's faire, I must confesse;
But does she keepe this distance out of state?[1]

CELESTINA. Though I am poore in language to expresse   15
How much your Lordship honors me, my heart
Is rich and proud in such a guest. I shall
Be out of love with every aire abroad,
And for his grace done my unworthy house,
Be a fond prisoner, become anchorite,   20
And spend my houres in prayer, to reward
The blessing, and the bounty of this presence.

LORD. Though you could turne each place you move in
                        to
A temple, rather than a wall should hide
So rich a beauty from the world, it were   25
Lesse want to lose our piety and your prayer.
A throne were fitter to present you to
Our wonder, whence your eyes, more worth than all
They looke on, should chaine every heart a prisoner.

SENTLOVE. Twas pretty well come off.

LORD.   By your example   30
I shall know how to complement; in this
You more confirme my welcome.   [*He kisses her.*]

CELESTINA.   I shall love
My lippes the better, if their silent language
Perswade your Lordship but to thinke so truely.

LORD. You make me smile, Madam.

CELESTINA.   I hope you came not   35
With feare that any sadnesse here should shake
One blossome from your eye; I should be miserable
To present any object should displease you.

LORD. You doe not, Madam.

Act IV. Scene iii.
[1] *state :* social protocol.

CELESTINA.   As I should account
   It no lesse sorrow, if your Lordship should   40
   Lay too severe a censure on my freedome,
   I wo' not court a Prince against his justice,
   Nor bribe him with a smile to thinke me honest.
   Pardon, my Lord, this boldnesse, and the mirth
   That may flow from me; I beleeve my father   45
   Thought of no winding sheete when he begot me.
LORD. She has a merry soule.—It will become
   Me aske your pardon, Madam, for my rude
   Approach, so much a stranger to your knowledge.
CELESTINA. Not, my Lord, so much stranger to my   50
        knowledge;
   Though I have but seene your person a-farre off,
   I am acquainted with your character,
   Which I have heard so often, I can speake it.
LORD. You shall doe me an honor.
CELESTINA.   If your Lordship will
   Be patient.
LORD.   And glad to heare my faults.   55
CELESTINA. That as your conscience can agree upon em.
   However, if your Lordship give me priviledge,
   Ile tell you what's the opinion of the world.
LORD. You cannot please me better.
CELESTINA.   Y'are a Lord
   Borne with as much nobilitie as would,   60
   Divided, serve to make ten noble men
   Without a Herald; but with so much spirit
   And height of soule, as well might furnish twenty.
   You are learnd, a thing not compatible now
   With native honour, and are master of   65
   A language that doth chaine all [eares],[1] and
        charme
   All hearts where you perswade; a wit so flowing
   And prudence to correct it, that all men
   Beleeve they onely meete in you, which, with
   A spacious memory, make up the full wonders.   70
   To these—you have [showne][2] valour, and upon
   A noble cause, know how to use a sword

To honors best advantage, though you wear[3] none.
You are as bountifull as the showers that fall
Into the Springs greene bosome; as you were   75
Created Lord of Fortune, not her steward;
So constant to the cause in which you make
Your selfe an advocate, you dare all dangers,
And men had rather you should be their friend,
Than justice or the bench bound up together.   80
LORD. But did you heare all this?
CELESTINA.   And more, my Lord.
LORD. Pray let me have it, Madam.
CELESTINA. To all these vertues, there is added one,
    (Your Lordship will remember when I name it,
    I speake but what I gather from the voyce   85
    Of others)—it is growne to a full fame
    That you have lov'd a woman.
LORD.   But one, Madam?
CELESTINA. Yes, many. Give me leave to smile, my Lord;
    I shall not neede to interpret in what sence,—
    But you have shewd your selfe right honorable,   90
    And for your love to Ladies have deserv'd,—
    If their vote might prevaile,—a marble statue.
    I make no comment on the peoples text;
    My Lord, I should be sorry to offend.
LORD. You cannot, Madam, these are things we owe   95
    To nature for.
CELESTINA.   And honest men will pay
    Their debts.
LORD.   If they be able, or compound.[2]
CELESTINA. She had a hard heart, would be unmercifull
    And not give day[3] to men so promising;
    But you ow'd women nothing.
LORD.   Yes, I am   100
    Still in their debt, and I must owe them love;
    It was part of my character.
CELESTINA.   With your Lordships
    Pardon, I onely said, you had a fame

---

2 *compound* : make a settlement.   3 Of grace.

For loving women; but of late, men say,
You have against the imperiall lawes of love   105
Restraind the active flowings of your bloud,
And with a Mistris buried all that is
Hop'd for in loves succession, as all beauty
Had died with her, and left the world benighted!
In this you more dishonor all our sexe   110
Than you did grace a part, when every where
Love tempts your eye to admire a glorious harvest,
And every where as full blowne eares submit
Their golden heads, the laden trees bow downe
Their willing fruit, and court your amorous tasting.   115

LORD. I see men would dissect me to a fibre;
But doe you beleeve this?

CELESTINA.   It is my wonder,
I must confesse, a man of nobler earth
Then goes to vulgar composition,
Borne and bred high, so unconfind, so rich   120
In fortunes, and so read in all that summe
Up humane knowledge, to feed gloriously
And live at court, (the onely spheare wherein
True beauty moves, natures most wealthy garden,
Where every blossome is more worth than all   125
The *Hesperian* fruite by jealous Dragon watch'd,
Where all delights doe circle appetite,
And pleasures multiply by being tasted,)
Should be so lost with thought of one turne[d][4]
                              ashes.
There's nothing left, my Lord, that can excuse you,   130
Unlesse you pleade what I am asham'd to prompt
Your wisedome to!

LORD.   What's that?

CELESTINA.   That you have plaid
The Surgeon with your selfe.

LORD.   And am made Eunuch?

CELESTINA. It were much pitty.

LORD.   Trouble not your selfe;
I could convince your feares with demonstration   135
That I am man enough, but knew not where,

Untill this meeting, beauty dwelt. The court
You talk'd of must be where the queene of love is,
Which moves but with your person; in your eye
Her glory shines, and onely at that flame   140
Her wanton boy doth light his quickning torch.

CELESTINA. Nay, now you complement; I would it did
My Lord, for your owne sake.

LORD.   You would be kind,
And love me, then?

CELESTINA.   My Lord, I should be loving
Where I found worth to invite it, and should cherish   145
A constant man.

LORD.   Then you should me, Madam.

CELESTINA. But is the ice about your heart fallen off?
Can you returne to doe what love commands?
Cupid, thou shalt have instant sacrifice,
And I dare be the Priest!

LORD.   Your hand, your lip.   150
                  [*He kisses her.*]
Now I am proofe gainst all temptation.

CELESTINA. Your meaning, my good Lord?

LORD.   I, that have
         strength
Against thy voyce and beauty, after this
May dare the charmes of womankind.—Thou art,
Bella Maria, unprophaned yet;   155
This Magicke has no power upon my bloud.
Farewell, Madam. If you durst be the example
Of chaste as well as faire, thou wert a brave[4] one.

CELESTINA. I hope your Lordship meanes not this for
         earnest.
Be pleasd to grace a banquet.

LORD.   Pardon, Madam.   160
Will Sentlove, follow; I must laugh at you.

CELESTINA. My Lord, I must beseech you stay, for
         honour,
For her whose memory you love best.

---

[4] *brave :* glorious.

LORD.   Your pleasure.
CELESTINA. And by that vertue you have now profest,
I charge you to beleeve me too! I can   165
Now glory that you have beene worth my triall,
Which I beseech you pardon. Had not you
So valiantly recoverd in this conflict,
You had beene my triumph, without hope of more
Than my just scorne upon your wanton flame.   170
Nor will I thinke these noble thoughts grew first
From melancholy, for some femall losse,
As the phantasticke world beleeves, but from
Truth, and your love of Innocence, which shine
So bright in the two royall luminaries[5, (1)]   175
At Court, you cannot lose your way to chastitie.
Proceede, and speake of me as honour guides you.
                                              Exit LORD.
I am almost tir'd.—Come, Ladies, weele beguile
Dull time, and take the aire annother while.   *Exeunt.*

FIFTH ACT. [SCENE I.]

Enter ARETINA *and* SERVANT [*with a money-bag*].
ARETINA. But hath Sir Thomas lost five hundred pounds
   Already?
SERVANT.   And five hundred more he borrow'd.
   The Dice are notable devourers, Madam;
   They make no more of peeces than of pebbles,
   But thrust their heapes together to engender.   5
   "Two hundred more the Caster!" cries this gentleman.
   "I am w'ee." "I ha' that to nothing, sir," the Caster
   Agen. Tis covered, and the table too
   With summes that frighted[1] me. Here one sneakes
                     out
   And with a Martyrs patience smiles upon   10
   His moneyes Executioner, the Dice,
   Commands a pipe of good Tobacco and

─────────────
[5] Charles I and Henrietta Maria.

I' th' smoke on't, vanishes. Another makes
The bones vault o'er his head, sweares that ill
    throwing
Has put his shoulder out of joynt, calls for   15
A bone setter. That lookes to th' boxe, to bid
His master send him some more hundred pounds,
Which lost, he takes tobacco, and is quiet.
Here a strong arme throwes in, and in, with which
He brusheth all the table, payes the Rookes[1]   20
That went their smelts[2] a-peece upon his hand,
Yet sweares he has not drawne a stake this seven
    yeare.
But I was bid make haste; my master may
Lose this five hundred pounds ere I come thither.
              Exit.

ARETINA. If we both waste so fast, we shall soone finde 25
Our state[3] is not immortall; some thing in
His other wayes appeare not well already.
Enter SIR THOMAS [BORNWELL, *and* SERVANTS *with*
    money-bags].
BORNWELL. Yee Tortoises! why make you no more haste?
Go pay to th' master of the house that money,
And tell the noble gamsters I have another   30
Superfluous thousand pound; at night Ile visit em.
D'ee heare?
SERVANTS.   Yes, and please you.
BORNWELL.   Doo't, ye drudges.
        [*Exit* SERVANTS.]
Ta, ra, ra!—Aretina!
ARETINA.   You have a pleasant humor, sir.
BORNWELL. What, should a gentleman be sad?
ARETINA.   You have
    lost—
BORNWELL. A transitory summe, as good that way 35
As another.

Act V. Scene i.
[1] *payes the Rookes :* wins everything and pays the fools.
[2] *went their smelts :* bet half-
 guineas.
[3] *state :* financial estate.

ARETINA. Doe you not vexe within for't?

BORNWELL. I had rather lose a thousand more, than one
  Sad thought come neere my heart for't. Vexe for
                    trash?
  Although it goe from other men like drops
  Of their life bloud, we lose with the alacrity   40
  Wee drinke a cup of sacke or kisse a Mistris.
  No money is considerable with a gamster;
  They have soules more spacious than Kings. Did two
  Gamsters divide the Empire of the world,
  They'd make one throw for't all; and he that lost   45
  Be no more melancholy then to have plai'd for
  A mornings draught. Vexe a rich soule for dirt,
  The quiet of whose every thought is worth
  A Province?

ARETINA.   But when Dice have consumd all,
  Your patience will not pawne for as much more.   50

BORNWELL. Hang pawning! Sell outright, and the feare's
                    over.

ARETINA. Say you so? I'le have another coach to-morrow
  If there be rich above ground.

BORNWELL.   I forgot
  To bid the fellow aske my Jeweller,
  Whether the chaine of Diamonds be made up;   55
  I will present it to my Lady Bellamour,
  Faire Celestina.

ARETINA.   This gowne I have worne
  Six dayes already; it lookes dull, Ile give it
  My waiting woman, and have one of cloth
  Of gold enbrodered; shooes and pantables⁴   60
  Will show well of the same.

BORNWELL.   I have invited
  A covey of Ladies and as many gentlemen
  To-morrow to the *Italian* Ordinary.⁵
  I shall have rarities and regallias⁶
  To pay for, Madam,—musicke, wanton songs,   65

---

⁴ *pantables* : slippers.   ⁶ *regallias* : delicacies.
⁵ *Ordinary* : Eating place.

And tunes of silken petticotes to dance to.
ARETINA. And to-morrow have I invited halfe the Court
  To dine here. What misfortune tis, your company
  And ours should be devided! After dinner
  I entertaine 'em with a play.
BORNWELL.   By that time   70
  Your play inclines to the Epilogue, shall we
  Quit our *Italian* host, and whirle in coaches
  To the [Dutch][2] Magazine of sawce, the Stillyard,[7]
  Where deale and backragge,[8] and what strange wine
           else
  They dare but give a name too in the reckoning   75
  Shall flow into our roome, and drowne Westphalias,[9]
  Tongues and Anchoavis, like some little towne
  Endangered by a sluce, through whose fierce ebbe
  We wade and wash our selves into a boate,
  And bid our Coachmen drive their leather tenements   80
  By land, while we saile home with a fresh tide
  To some new randevous.
ARETINA.   If you have not
  Pointed the place, pray bring your Ladies hither;
  I meane to have a Ball to-morrow night,
  And a rich banquet for 'em, where we'le dance   85
  Till morning rise and blush to interrupt us.
BORNWELL. Have you no Ladies i' th' next roome, to
        advance
  A present mirth? What a dull house you governe!
  Farewell, a wife's no company.—Aretina,
  I've summ'd up my estate, and find we may have   90
  A month good yet.
ARETINA.   What meane you?
BORNWELL.   And Ide rather
  Be Lord one moneth of pleasures, to the height
  And rapture of our senses, than be yeares
  Consuming what we have in foolish temperance,
  Live in the darke, and no fame waite upon us.   95

[7] *Stillyard* : Steelyard, enclave   [8] *backragge* : Rhine wines.
  of German merchants.   [9] *Westphalias* : Hams.

I will live so, posterity shall stand
At gaze when I am mentioned.
ARETINA.   A month good?
And what shall be done then?
BORNWELL.   Ile over Sea,
    And traile a pike. With watching, marching, lying
    In trenches, with enduring cold and hunger,   100
    And taking here and there a musketshot,
    I can earne every weeke foure shillings, Madam;
    And if the bullets favour me to snatch
    Any superfluous limbe, when I returne,
    With good friends, I despaire not to be enrold   105
    Poore Knight of Windsore;[10] for your course, Madam,
    No doubt you may doe well. Your friends are great,
    Or if your poverty and their pride cannot
    Agree, you neede not trouble much invention
    To find a trade to live by; there are customers.   110
    Farewell, be frolicke, Madam! If I live
    I will feast all my senses, and not fall
    Lesse than a *Phaeton*[(1)] from my throne of Pleasure,
    Though my estate flame like the world about me.
                                                  Exit.

ARETINA. Tis very pretty!
                    Enter DECOY.
                    Madam Decoy!
DECOY.   What, melancholy   115
    After so sweet a nights worke? Have not I
    Shew'd my selfe Mistris of my art?
ARETINA.   A Lady.
DECOY. That title makes the credit of the act
    A story higher; y'ave not seene him yet?
    I wonder what hee'le say.
ARETINA.   He's here.
        Enter ALEXANDER [KICKSHAW] *and* FREDERICK.
KICKSHAW.   Beare up,   120

[10] *Poore Knight of Windsore :* a
    royal charity.

My little *Mirmidan.*(2) Does not Jacke Littleworth
Follow?
FREDERICK. Follow? He fell into the Thames
    At landing.
KICKSHAW.   The devill shall dive for him
    Ere I endanger my silke stockings for him.
    Let the Watermen alone; they have drags and   125
                engins.
    When he has drunke his Julip,(3) I shall laugh
    To see him come in pickeld the next tide.
FREDERICK. Hee'le never sinke, he has such a corke
                braine.
KICKSHAW. Let him be hang'd or drown'd, all's one to me;
    Yet he deserves to die by water, cannot   130
    Beare his wine credibly.
FREDERICK.   Is not this my Aunt?
KICKSHAW. And another hansome Lady; I must know
                her.
                [*He goes to* DECOY.]
FREDERICK. My bloud is rampant too, I must court some
                body,
    As good my Aunt as any other body.
ARETINA. Where have you beene, cozen?
FREDERICK.   •   At the bridge, 135
    At the Beares foote,(4) where our first health began
    To the faire Aretina, whose sweet company
    Was wished by all. We could not get a lay,
    A Tumbler, a Device, a *bona roba*—
    For any money; drawers were growne dull;   140
    We wanted our true firkes[11] and our vagaries.
    When were you in drinke, Aunt?
ARETINA.   How?
FREDERICK.   Do not Ladies
    Play the good fellowes too? There's no true mirth
    Without 'em. I have now such tickling fancies!
    That Doctour of the chaire of wit has read   145
    A precious lecture, how I should behave

[11] *firkes :* whims, fancies.

My selfe to Ladies, as now, for example.
ARETINA. Would you practise upon me?
FREDERICK.   I first salute you.
                                   [*He kisses her.*]
You have a soft hand, Madam; are you so
All over?
ARETINA.   Nephew!
FREDERICK.   Nay, you should but smile;   150
And then agen I kisse you, and thus draw
Off your white glove, and start[12] to see your hand
More excellently white. I grace my owne
Lip with this touch, and turning gently thus,
Prepare you for my skill in Palmistry,   155
Which out of curiosity no Lady
But easily applies too.[13] The first line
I looke[3] with most ambition to find out
Is *Venus* girdle, a faire semicircle
Enclosing both the mount of *Sol* and *Saturne*.   160
If that appeare, she's for my turne, a Lady
Whom nature has prepar'd for the careere;
And *Cupid* at my elbow, I put forward.
You have this very line, Aunt.
ARETINA.   The boy's franticke!
FREDERICK. You have a Couch or Palate;[4] I can shut   165
The Chamber doore.[5] Enrich a stranger, when
Your Nephew's comming into play?
ARETINA.   No more!
FREDERICK. Are you so coy to your owne flesh and
                    bloud?
KICKSHAW. Here, take your playfellow; I talke of sport,
And she would have me marry her.
FREDERICK.   Here's Littleworth.   170
              Enter LITTLEWORTH *wet.*
Why, how now, Tutour?
LITTLEWORTH.   I ha' beene fishing.
FREDERICK. And what ha' you caught?

---

[12] *start :* express wonder.   [13] *applies too :* complies with.

LITTLEWORTH.   My belly full of
        water.
KICKSHAW. Ha, ha! Where's thy rapier?
LITTLEWORTH.   My rapier's[6]
        drown'd,
  And I am little better; I was up bi' th' heeles,
  And out came a tun of water, beside wine.   175
KICKSHAW. 'T has made thee sober.
LITTLEWORTH.   Would you have me
        drunk
With Water?
ARETINA. I hope your fire is quenched by this time.
FREDERICK. It is not now, as when your worship "walkd
  By all the tavernes," Jacke, "drie as a bone."
KICKSHAW. You had store of fish under water, Jacke.   180
LITTLEWORTH. It has made a poore John[14] of me.
FREDERICK. I doe not thinke but if we cast an angle
  Into his belly, we might find some Pilchards.[15]
LITTLEWORTH. And boild, by this time.—Deere Madam,
        a bed.
KICKSHAW. Carry but the water Spaniel to a grasseplot   185
  Where he may roule himselfe; let him but shake
  His eares twice in the Sunne, and you may grind him
  Into a posset.[16]
FREDERICK.   Come, thou shalt to my bed,
  Poore pickerell.
DECOY.   Alas, sweete gentleman.
LITTLEWORTH. I have ill lucke and[17] I should smell by
        this time,   190
  I am but new tane, I am sure.—Sweet gentlewoman.
DECOY. Your servant.
LITTLEWORTH.   Pray doe not plucke off my skin;
  It is so wet, unlesse you have good eyes
  You'le hardly know it from a shirt.

14 *poore John* : salted herring.
15 *Pilchards* : sardines.
16 *posset* : drink of curdled wine
  and milk.
17 *and* : if.

DECOY.   Feare nothing.
                    Exeunt [all but ARETINA *and* KICKSHAW.]
ARETINA. [*Aside.*] He has sacke enough, and I may find
                    his humor.   195
KICKSHAW. And how ist with your Ladiship? You looke
    Without a sunshine in your face.
ARETINA.   You are glorious
    In mind and habit.
KICKSHAW.   Ends of gold and silver!
ARETINA. Your other clothes were not so rich. Who was
    Your tailor, sir?
KICKSHAW.   They were made for me long since.   200
    They have knowne but two bright dayes upon my
                    backe;
    I had a humor, Madam, to lay things by.
    They will serve two dayes more; I thinke I ha' gold
                    enough
    To goe to th' Mercer. Ile now allow my selfe
    A suite a weeke as this, with necessary   205
    Dependances, Beaver, silke stockings, garters,
    And roses[18] in their due conformitie.
    Bootes are forbid a cleane[19] legge but to ride in.
    My linnen every morning comes in new;
    The old goes too great bellies.[20]
ARETINA.   You are charitable.   210
KICKSHAW. I may dine w'ee sometime, or at the Court,
    To meete good company, not for the table.
    My Clarke o' th' Kitchin's here, a witty Epicure,
    A spirit, that to please me with what's rare
    Can flie a hundred mile a day to market,   215
    And make me Lord of Fish and Foule. I shall
    Forget there is a butcher; and to make
    My footman[7] nimble, he shall feede on nothing
    But wings of wildfoule.
ARETINA.   These wayes are costly.
KICKSHAW. Therefore Ile have it so. I ha' sprung a mine.   220

---

[18] On the shoes.   [20] *great bellies :* pregnant
[19] *cleane :* well shaped.   women.

ARETINA. You make me wonder, sir, to see this change
  Of fortune; your revenew was not late
  So plentifull.
KICKSHAW.   Hang durty land and Lordships!
  I wo' not change one lodging I ha' got
  For the Chamber of London.[21]
ARETINA.   Strange, of such a sudden   225
  To rise to this estate; no fortunate hand
  At dice could lift you up so, for tis since
  Last night; yesterday you were no such Monarke.
KICKSHAW. There be more games then dice.
ARETINA.   It cannot be
  A Mistris, though your person is worth love;   230
  None possibly are rich enough to feed
  As you have cast the method of your riots.
  A Princesse, after all her Jewels, must
  Be forc'd to sell her provinces.
KICKSHAW.   Now you talke
  Of Jewels, what doe you thinke of this?
ARETINA.   A rich one.   235
KICKSHAW. You'le honour me to wear't. This other toy
  I had from you, this chaine I borrowed of you,
  A friend had it in keeping.
              [*He gives her the chain and the jewel.*]
                        If your Ladiship
  Want any summe, you know your friend and Alex-
                ander.
ARETINA. Dare you trust my security?
KICKSHAW.   There's gold;   240
  I shall have more to-morrow.
ARETINA.   You astonish me.
  Who can supply these?
KICKSHAW.   A deare friend I have.
  She promisd we should meete agen i' th' morning.
ARETINA. Not that I wish to know
  More of your happinesse then I have already   245

21 Capital city of London.

Heart to congratulate,—be pleasd to lay
My wonder.

KICKSHAW. Tis a secret.

ARETINA.   Which Ile die
Ere Ile betray.

KICKSHAW.   You have alwayes wish'd me well;
But you shall sweare not to reveale the partie.

ARETINA. Ile lose the benefit of my tongue.

KICKSHAW.   Nor be   250
Afraid at what I say. What thinke you first
Of an old Witch, a strange ill-favor'd hag,
That for my company last night, has wrought
This cure upon my fortune? I doe sweat
To thinke upon her name.

ARETINA.   How, sir, a Witch?   255

KICKSHAW. I would not fright your Ladiship too much
At first, but Witches are a-kin to Spirits.
The truth is—nay, if you looke pale already,
I ha' done.

ARETINA.   Sir, I beseech you!

KICKSHAW.   If you have
But courage then to know the truth, Ile tell you   260
In one word; my chiefe friend is the devill.

ARETINA. What devill? How I tremble!

KICKSHAW.   Have a Heart!
Twas a shee-divell too, a most insatiate
Abominable devill with a taile
Thus long.

ARETINA.   Goodnesse defend me, did you see her?   265

KICKSHAW. No, twas i' th' darke, but she appeard first to
                              me
I' th' likenesse of a [Beldam][8], and was brought
I know not how, nor whither, by two Goblins,
More hooded than a Hawke.

ARETINA.   But would you venter
Upon a devill?

KICKSHAW.   I, for meanes.

ARETINA. [*Aside.*]   How blacke   270
An impudence is this!—But are you sure

It was the devill you enjoy'd.
KICKSHAW.   Say nothing.
  I did the best to please her, but as sure
  As you live, twas a Helcat.
ARETINA.   D'ee not quake?
KICKSHAW. I found my selfe [in] the very [roome] i' th'
                    morning,[9]   275
  Where two of her familiars had left me.
                    Enter SERVANT.
SERVANT. My Lord is come to visite you.
KICKSHAW.   No words,
  As you respect my safety. I ha' told tales
  Out of the devills schoole; if it be knowne,
  I lose a friend. Tis now about the time   280
  I promis'd her to meete agen; at my
  Returne Ile tell you wonders. Not a word.   *Exit.*
                    [ARETINA *goes to a mirror.*]
ARETINA. Tis a false glasse; sure I am more deform'd.
  What have I done? My soule is miserable.
                    Enter LORD.
LORD. I sent you a letter, Madam.
ARETINA.   You exprest   285
  Your noble care of me, my Lord.
                    Enter BORNWELL [*and*] CELESTINA.
BORNWELL.   Your Lordship
  Does me an honour.
LORD.   Madam, I am glad
  To see you here. I meant to have kist your hand
  Ere my returne to Court.
CELESTINA.   Sir Thomas has
  Prevaild to bring me, to his trouble, hither.   290
LORD. You doe him grace.
BORNWELL.   Why, what's the matter, Madam?
  Your eyes are tuning *Lachrimae.*[22]
ARETINA.   As you
  Doe hope for heaven, withdraw, and give me but

----

22 *Lachrimae :* Tears, a song by
   John Dowland.

The patience of ten minutes!

BORNWELL.   Wonderfull!
I wo' not heare you above that proportion.—   295
Shee talkes of heaven. Come, where must we to
                    counsell?

ARETINA. You shall conclude me when you please.

                                                  Exit.

BORNWELL.   I follow.

LORD. [*Aside.*] What alteration is this? I, that so late
Stood the temptation of her eye and voyce,
Boasted a heart 'bove all licentious flame,   300
At second veiw turne renegade, and thinke
I was too superstitious and full
Of phlegme, not to reward her amorous Courtship
With manly freedome.

CELESTINA. [*to* BORNWELL.] I obey you, sir.

BORNWELL. Ile waite upon your Lordship presently.   305

                                                  [*Exit.*]

LORD. [*Aside.*] She could not want a cunning to seeme
                    honest
When I neglected her. I am resolv'd.—
You still looke pleasant, Madam.

CELESTINA.   I have cause,
My Lord, the rather for your presence, which
Hath power to charme all trouble in my thoughts.   310

LORD. I must translate that complement and owe
All that is cheerefull in my selfe to these
All-quickning smiles; and rather than such bright
Eyes should repent their influence upon me,
I would release the aspects,[23] and quit the bountie   315
Of all the other starres. Did you not thinke me
A strange and melancholy gentleman
To use you so unkindly.

CELESTINA.   Me, my Lord?

LORD. I hope you made no loude complaint; I wo'd not
Be tride by a Jury of Ladies.

CELESTINA.   For what, my Lord?   320

---

[23] *aspects :* heavenly influence.

LORD. I did not meete that noble entertainment
  You were late pleasd to shew me.
CELESTINA.   I observd
  No such defect in your Lordship, but a brave
  And noble fortitude.
LORD.   A noble folly!
  I bring repentance for't; I know you have,   325
  Madam, a gentle faith, and wo' not ruine
  What you have built to honour you.
CELESTINA.   What's that?
LORD. If you can love Ile tell your Ladiship.
CELESTINA. I have a stubborne soule else.
LORD.   You are all
  Composd of harmony.
CELESTINA.   What love d'ee meane?   330
LORD. That which doth perfect both. Madam, you have
              heard
  I can be constant, and if you consent
  To grace it so, there is a spacious dwelling
  Prepar'd within my heart for such a Mistresse.
CELESTINA. Your Mistris, my good Lord?
LORD.   Why, my good 335
          Lady,
  Your sexe doth hold it no dishonour
  To become Mistris to a noble servant
  In the now court Platonicke[5] way. Consider
  Who tis that pleades to you; my birth and present
  Value can be no staine to your embrace.   340
  But these are shadowes when my love appeares,
  Which shall in his first miracle returne
  Me in my bloome of youth, and thee a Virgin,
  When I, within some new *Elisium*
  Of purpose made and meant for us, shall be   345
  In every thing *Adonis*, but in his
  Contempt of love, and court thee from a *Daphne*
  Hid in the cold rinde of a bashfull tree,[24]

[24] Daphne was turned into a
  bay laurel tree.

With such warme language, and delight, till thou
Leape from that bayes into the queene of love,   350
And pay my conquest with composing garlands
Of thy owne mirtle for me.[25]

CELESTINA.   What's all this?

LORD. Consent to be my Mistris, Celestina,
And we will have it Spring-time all the yeare,
Upon whose invitations, when we walke,   355
The windes shall play soft descant[26] to our feete,
And breathe rich odors to repure the aire.
Greene bowers on every side shall tempt our stay,
And Violets stoope to have us treade upon em.
The red rose shall grow pale, being neere thy cheeke,   360
And the white blush, o'ercome with such a forehead.
Here laid, and measuring with our selves some banke,
A thousand birds shall from the woods repaire,
And place themselves so cunningly behinde
The leaves of every tree, that while they pay   365
[Us][10] tribute of their songs, thou sha't imagine
The very trees beare musicke, and sweet voyces
Doe grow in every arbour. Here can we
Embrace and kisse, tell tales, and kisse agen,
And none but heaven our rivall.[6]

CELESTINA.   When we are   370
Weary of these, what if we shift our Paradise?
And through a grove of tall and even pine,
Descend into a Valley that shall shame
All the delights of *Tempe,* upon whose
Greene plush the graces shall be cald to dance   375
To please us, and maintaine their Fairy revells,
To the harmonious murmurs of a streame
That gently falls upon a rocke of pearle.
Here doth the Nimph, forsaken Eccho, dwell,
To whom we'le tell the story of our love,   380
Till at our surfet and her want of joy,
We breake her heart with envy. Not farre off

[25] Myrtle was sacred to Venus.

[26] *soft descant :* harmonious variations.

A grove shall call us to a wanton river,
To see a dying Swan give up the ghost,
The fishes shooting up their teares in bubbles   385
That they must lose the Genius[27] of their waves,—
And such love-linsey-woolsey,[28]—to no purpose.
LORD. You chide me hansomely! Pray tell me how
    You like this language.   [*He embraces her.*]
CELESTINA.   Good my Lord, forbeare.
LORD. You neede not flie out of this circle, Madam.   390
    These widowes are so[11] full of circumstance!
    Ile undertake, in this time I ha' courted
    Your Ladiship for the toy, to ha' broken ten,
    Nay, twenty colts,—Virgins, I meane,—and taught em
    The amble, or what pace I most affected.   395
CELESTINA. Y'are not, my Lord, agen the Lord I thought
                     you,
    And I must tell you now, you doe forget
    Your selfe and me.
LORD.   You'le not be angry, Madam?
CELESTINA. Nor rude,—though gay men have a privi-
              ledge,—
    It shall appeare.—There is a man, my Lord,   400
    Within my acquaintance, rich in worldly fortunes,
    But cannot boast any descent of bloud,
    Would buy a coate of armes.
LORD.   He may, and legges
    Booted and spurr'd, to ride into the countrey.
CELESTINA. But these will want antiquitie, my Lord,   405
    The seale of honour. What's a coate cut out
    But yesterday to make a man a gentleman?
    Your family, as old as the first vertue
    That merited an Escutcheon, doth owe[29]
    A glorious coat of armes. If you will sell now   410
    All that your name doth challenge in that ensigne,

---

[27] The Swan, generative spirit of the water.

[28] *love-linsey-woolsey* : low grade imitation of love.

[29] *owe* : own.

Ile helpe you to a chapman,[30] that shall pay
And powre downe wealth enough for't.

LORD.   Sell my armes?
I cannot, Madam.

CELESTINA.   Give but your consent.
You know not how the state may be enclind   415
To dispensation; we may prevaile
Upon the Heralds office afterward.

LORD. Ile sooner give these armes to th' hangmans axe,
My head, my heart, to twenty executions
Than sell one atome from my name!

CELESTINA.   Change that,[31]   420
And answer him would buy my honour from me;
Honour, that is not worne upon a flagge
Or pennon, that, without the owners dangers,
An enemy may ravish and beare from me,
But that which growes and withers with my soule,   425
Beside the bodies staine. Think, thinke, my Lord!
To what you would unworthily betray me,
If you would not, for price of gold or pleasure,
(If that be more your idoll), lose the glory
And painted honour of your house.—I ha' done.   430

LORD. Enough to rectifie a Satyres[12], (7) bloud.
Obscure my blushes here.

Enter SENTLOVE *and* HAIRCUT.

HAIRCUT.   Or this or fight with me.
It shall be no exception[32] that I waite
Upon my Lord. I am a gentleman;
You may be lesse and be a Knight. The office   435
I doe my Lord is honest, sir; how many
Such you have beene guilty of, heaven knowes.

SENTLOVE. Tis no feare of your sword, but that I wod
                              not
Breake the good lawes established against duells.

---

[30] *chapman :* merchant.   this.
[31] Consider my comparable   [32] *exception :* breach of the
    position; exchange that for   code.

HAIRCUT. Off with your periwig, and stand bare!
[SENTLOVE *hesitates and* HAIRCUT *snatches off his*
periwig.]
LORD. [*to* CELESTINA.]   From this   440
Minute Ile be a servant to thy goodnesse.
A Mistris in the wanton sence is common;
Ile honor you with chaste thoughts, and call you so.
CELESTINA. Ile study to be worth your faire opinion.
LORD. Sentlove, your head was usd to a covering   445
Beside a hat; when went the haire away?
SENTLOVE. I laid a wager, my Lord, with Haircut,
Who thinkes I shall catch cold, that Ile stand bare
This halfe houre.
HAIRCUT.   Pardon my ambition,
Madam, I told you truth; I am a gentleman,   450
And cannot feare that name is drown'd in my
Relation to my Lord.
CELESTINA.   I dare not thinke so.
HAIRCUT. From henceforth call my service duty,
Madam.
That Pigges head[33] that betraid me to your mirth
Is doing penance for't.
SENTLOVE.   Why may not I,   455
My Lord, begin a fashion of no haire.
CELESTINA. Doe you sweat, Sir William?
SENTLOVE.   Not with store
of nightcaps.
Enter ARETINA [*and*] BORNWELL.
ARETINA. Heaven has dissolv'd the clouds that hung
upon
My eyes, and if you can with mercy meet
A penitent, I throw my owne will off,   460
And now in all things obey yours,—my nephew
Send backe agen to th' colledge, and my selfe
To what place you'le confine me.
BORNWELL.   Dearer now

[33] *Pigges head:* closely shorn
head.

Than ever to my bosome, thou sha't please
Me best to live at thy owne choice. I did   465
But fright thee with a noise of my expences;
The summes are safe, and we have wealth enough,
If yet we use it nobly.—My Lord—Madam,
Pray honour [us] to-night.[13]

ARETINA.   I begge your presence,
And pardon.

BORNWELL.   I know not how my Aretina   470
May be disposd to-morrow for the country.

CELESTINA. You must not goe, before you both have
                                  done
Me honour to accept an entertainment
Where I have power; on those termes I'me your guest.

BORNWELL. You grace us, Madam.

ARETINA. [*Aside.*]   Already   475
I feele a cure upon my soule, and promise
My after life to vertue. Pardon, heaven,
My shame yet hid from the worlds eye.

                    Enter DECOY.

DECOY.   Sweet Madam!

ARETINA. Not for the world be seene here. [*Aside.*] We
                            are lost,
Ile visite you at home;—   [*Exit* DECOY.]
                            but not to practise   480
What she expects; my counsell may recover her.

                Enter ALEXANDER [KICKSHAW].

KICKSHAW. Where's Madam?
[*Aside to* ARETINA.]   Pray lend me a little money;
My spirit has deceiv'd me; *Proserpine*
Has broke her word.

ARETINA. [*Aside.*]   Do you expect to find
The devill true to you?

KICKSHAW. [*Aside.*]   Not too loud.

ARETINA. [*Aside.*]   Ile voyce it   485
Louder, to all the world, your horrid sinne,
Unlesse you promise me religiously
To purge your foule bloud by repentance, sir.

KICKSHAW. [*Aside.*] Then I'me undone.

ARETINA. [*Aside.*]   Not while I have
                                power
To encourage you to vertue; Ile endeavour
To find you out some nobler way at Court
To thrive in.
KICKSHAW. [*Aside.*] Doo't, and Ile forsake the devill,
And bring my flesh to obedience; you shall steere
                                me.—
My Lord,—your servant.
LORD.   You are brave agen.
KICKSHAW. [*to* CELESTINA.] Madam, your pardon.
BORNWELL.   Your
                  offence requires
Humility.
KICKSHAW. Low as my heart.—Sir Thomas,
Ile sup with you, a part of satisfaction.
BORNWELL. Our pleasures coole. Musicke! And when our
                                Ladies
Are tired with active motion, to give
Them rest, in some new rapture to advance
Full mirth, our soules shall leape into a dance.
                                            Exeunt.

                        FINIS.

VARIANTS

VARIANTS

In order to simplify notation, brackets inserted in the text have not been repeated in the variants. Punctuation is repeated only where significant. Variations of spelling in titles and speech headings are not recorded. The frequent errors in placement and names of characters in stage directions are not recorded unless (as in the case of *The Revenger's Tragedy*) they are of special interest. All works and editions referred to in short form are given in full at the end of the volume.

THE CHANGELING

The text was made from Xerox prints of the Folger Library copy of the 1653 Quarto.

        Q   Quarto of 1653 (Folger).
        B   Edition of Bawcutt.

DRAMATIS PERSONAE:

  DRAMATIS] Drammatis *Q.*
  BEATRICE-JOANNA] Beatrice *Q.*

THE SCENE:

  Alicant] Allegant *Q.*

ACT I. SCENE I.

  [1] Enter Beatrice, Diaphanta, and Servants, Joanna. *Q.*
  [2] of] or *Q. Emendation of Dilke followed by B, Dyce, and Bullen.*
  [3] sound *Q B. All other modern editions emend to "found."*
  [4] What might] And what might *Q. Emendation of Dilke followed by B.*
  [5] Ingrediant] Ingredian *Q*
  [6] Iulan] Julan *Q. Emendation of Dyce followed by B.*
  [7] Alicant] Alligant *Q.*

Act I. Scene II.

[1] *The words of Pedro are printed as verse in Q.*

[2] *Printed as verse in Q.*

[3] you I'le make] you make Q] you I make B. *This edition follows the emendation of Dyce.*

[4] *Printed as verse in Q.*

[5] *Printed as verse in Q.*

Act II. Scene I.

[1] in his passions Q. *Omitted by Dilke, Dyce, and B. This edition follows Baskervill in returning to Q.*

[2] w'are Q. *B notes an uncorrected state of Q reading* we are.

Act II. Scene II.

[1] lock'd] lock Q.

[2] you're] your Q.

[3] ne'er] ne're Q. *The words "never," "ever," and their compounds have been regularized.*

[4] *Printed with numerals in Q as part of the next line.*

[5] Faugh] vauh Q.

[6] for't now] for't, now Q.

[7] Puh Q] Push B.

Act III. Scene III.

[1] Enter franciscus] Enter Loll : Franciscus. Q.

[2] sings] sing Q *at end of foregoing line.*

[3] Aunt] Ant Q.

[4] she Q] he B. *B follows the emendation of Dyce.*

[5] neerest Q] the nearest B. *B follows the emendation of Dilke.*

Act III. Scene IV.

[1] have kept unsold] have Q] have slept at ease B *following Dilke.*

[2] off] of Q.

[3] it not] it Q. *Only Baskervill follows Q.*

[4] may you] may Q. *Emendation of Dyce and B.*

Act IV. Scene I.

[1] One who's] One both Q] One that's B. *This edition follows Dilke and Dyce.*

[2] by him] by by him Q.

[3] vials] viols Q.

[4] down] dow *Q.*
[5] sleight] slight *Q. Emendation of Baskervill and B.*

Act IV. Scene ii.

[1] unexpectedly] unexepectedly *Q.*
[2] An] One *Q B. Emendation of Dyce and Bullen.*
[3] tho] thou *Q.*
[4] Keeps] Keep *Q. Emendation of Dyce and B.*

Act IV. Scene iii.

[1] weighting] waiting *Q B. Dilke suggests "new or waning."
Dyce and Bullen emend to "waning."*
[2] have made] have have made *Q.*
[3] Why] We *Q. Emendation of B and all modern editions.*
[4] rises] rise *Q.*
[5] he] she *Q. Emendation of B and all modern editions.*
[6] streets *Q*] straits *B following Dyce and Bullen.*
[7] throw] throuw *Q.*
[8] What do] What? Do *Q. Emendation of all modern editions.*

Act V. Scene i.

[1] an] a *Q. Emendation of Dilke and B.*
[2] thank *Q*] thank'd *B and all other modern editions. Q is not
grammatical, but it is colloquial and readily understandable.*
[3] Phosphorus] Bosphorus *Q.*
[4] a-fire] of fire *Q B.*

Act V. Scene ii.

[1] touch him] touch *Q. Emendation of Dilke and B.*
[2] neer] ne're *Q*] near *B following Dyce and Bullen. Dilke
thought the word was "ne'er."*
[3] wifes] wives *Q.*

Act V. Scene iii.

[1] for your sake] (for your sake) *Q.*
[2] It] I *Q. Emendation of Dilke and B. Baskervill returns to Q.*
[3] pander] pandor *Q.*
[4] sewer] shewer *Q. Emendation of all modern editions.*
[5] hang *Q*] hung *B following Dyce and Bullen. Dilke pre-
serves Q.*
[6] thence *Q B. Baskervill also returns to Q, but Dilke and
Dyce emended to "hence."*

THE REVENGER'S TRAGEDY

The text was made from Xerox prints of the Folger Library copy of the 1607 edition of the play, which has the alternate 1608 title page. See Greg's *Bibliography,* 253 A. Both issues were made up of sheets from the same edition. I have also checked certain readings with the Harvard copy, which has the 1607 title page.

Q   Quarto of 1607–1608 (Folger).
N   Edition of Allardyce Nicoll.

Act I. Scene i.

[1] showst] shoust Q.
[2] e'er] ere Q. *The words "ever," "never," "over," and their compounds have been normalized throughout.*
[3] Enter his] Enter her Q] Enter his N.
[4] to] too Q.
[5] GRATIANA] Moth. Q *throughout.*
[6] Court] Cour Q.

Act I. Scene ii.

[1] seare] searce Q] seare N.
[2] their] therr Q. off] of Q.
[3] YOUNGEST SON] Iuni. Q *throughout.*
[4] me] my Q N. ceast Q N. *J. C. Collins emends to* "'sess'd" *and is followed by J. A. Symonds.*
[5] Pox on't] Pax ont Q.
[6] meate, and sleepe] meate and sleepe Q.
[7] 'tis] 'tus Q.
[8] *Printed as prose in Q.*
[9] shrewd] shrowd Q.
[10] SPURIO] Spi. Q.
[11] rose] rise Q.

Act I. Scene iii.

[1] *Printed as prose in Q.*
[2] Foole Q N. *J. C. Collins emends to* "'Sfoote" *and is followed by J. A. Symonds.*
[3] *Printed as prose in Q.*
[4] my] me Q.
[5] *Printed as prose in Q.*
[6] blood] good Q N. *Emendation of J. C. Collins.*

Act I. Scene iv.

[1] antonio] L. Ant. *Q throughout.*

Act II. Scene i.

[1] *Printed as prose in Q.*
[2] own] one *Q.*
[3] *second* in't] it *Q.*
[4] *Printed as prose in Q.*
[5] *second* fooles] foole *Q.*
[6] Madam] Mad-man *Q.*
[7] others] other *Q.*
[8] *Printed as prose in Q.*

Act II. Scene ii.

[1] *Printed as prose in Q.*
[2] *Printed as prose in Q.*
[3] *Printed as prose in Q.*
[4] *The words of Vindice are printed as prose in Q.*
[5] *Printed as prose in Q.*

Act II. Scene iii.

[1] words] word *Q.*
[2] vindice and hippolito flee] dissemble a flight *Q.*
[3] *Printed as prose in Q.*
[4] —Rise] Which, rise *Q N.*

Act III. Scene i.

[1] he *Q. Perhaps an error for "ye."*
[2] Blest] Blast *Q.*
[3] off] of *Q.*

Act III. Scene iv.

[1] Enter in prison Iunior Brother *Q.*
[2] *Printed as prose in Q.*

Act III. Scene v.

[1] I easily (to] (I easily to *Q.*
[2] its] it *Q.*
[3] *Printed as prose in Q.*
[4] Slobbering] Flobbering *Q N.*
[5] Banquets] Banquests *Q.*

Act III. Scene vi.

[1] woo] woe *Q*.

Act IV. Scene i.

[1] the] thee *Q*.
[2] The Nobles enter] *printed in Q as part of foregoing speech.*
[3] rid] rod *Q*.

Act IV. Scene ii.

[1] Duke's] Duke *Q*.
[2] lussurioso] Hip. *Q*.
[3] fine] fiue *Q*] fine *N*.
[4] We] Me *Q*] We *N*.
[5] *Printed as prose in Q.*

Act IV. Scene iii.

[1] their] there *Q*.

Act IV. Scene iv.

[1] Parent] Parents *Q*.
[2] seld] sild *Q*.
[3] The Dukes] Dukes *Q*.
[4] child] held *Q*. *Emendation of Collins, Symonds, and N.*
[5] Be] Buy *Q N. Emendation of Collins and Symonds.*

Act V. Scene i.

[1] slay] slaine *Q N*.
[2] nake] make *Q*. *N notes a corrected state of Q reading* nake.
[3] *second* all *Q N*.
[4] have at the] have the *Q N*.
[5] *Printed as prose in Q.*

Act V. Scene iii.

[1] wear] were *Q*.
[2] most near, it] most it *Q N. Emendation of Symonds.*
[3] supervacuo] Spur. *Q N*.
[4] make] wake *Q*] make *N*.
[5] Sbloud] Sloud *Q*.
[6] to] two *Q*.
[7] murdrers] murders *Q*.

THE BROKEN HEART

The text was made from Xerox prints of the Folger Library copy of the 1633 Quarto.

Q   Quarto of 1633 (Folger).
GD   Edition of Gifford and Dyce.
B   Edition of Baskervill, Heltzel, and Nethercot.

EPISTLE DEDICATORY:

[1] entertainment] entertaiment Q.
[2] professed] professe Q GD. *The Q reading may be a conditional verb.*

SPEAKERS NAMES:

[1] HEMOPHIL] LEMOPHIL Q.

ACT I. SCENE I.

[1] holy union Q. *Some copies of Q omit* holy. *See GD B.*

ACT I. SCENE II.

[1] altogether Q] all together GD B.
[2] Feathers] Fathers Q.
[3] Exeunt] exeunt omnes Q.

ACT I. SCENE III.

[1] puzles] pusles Q.

ACT II. SCENE I.

[1] their] the Q. *Emendation of GD B.*
[2] sirrah] sirrha Q.
[3] GRAUSIS] Gransis Q. *The name is consistently misspelled in Q.*
[4] Porpises] Porpiseis Q.
[5] sinnes Q] saints GD.

ACT II. SCENE II.

[1] Prethee] Prethe Q.

ACT II. SCENE III.

[1] Nature Q] nature once GD B.
[2] argue little skill] argue skill Q. *Emendation of GD B.*

[3] Prethee] Prethe *Q*.

[4] The holiest Artars, Virgin teares (like *Q*.

[5] On Vesta's odours) sprinkled dewes to feed 'em, *Q*. *These two lines are arranged by GD thus:*

As sweetly scented as the incense smoking
On Vesta's altars,_____
_____ the holiest odours, virgin's tears,
_____ sprinkled, like dews, to feed them.

B follows Q. The emendation of the present text was suggested by Oliphant Smeaton.

[6] I'le] I'e *Q*.

[7] rheumes] rhemes *Q*.

[8] *GD and B assign the words of this speech from* then let us to the end *to Penthea.*

Act III. Scene i.

[1] heart] hearts *Q. Emendation of GD. B follows Q.*

[2] or] of *Q. Emendation of GD B.*

[3] Your] You *Q. Emendation of GD.*

Act III. Scene ii.

[1] heard] hard *Q*.

[2] The untroubled of Country toyle, drinkes streames *Q. Emendation of GD B.*

[3] Which *Q*] While *GD*] Whiles *B*.

[4] or tie] or *Q*] or nearness *GD B. Emendation of Weber followed by GD B.*

[5] silent] sinlent *Q. Perhaps the correct reading is "sinless."*

[6] cry 'a Jealousie] jealousy decry *GD*.

Act III. Scene iii.

[1] grave] graves *Q. Emendation of GD. B follows Q.*

[2] prethee] prethe *Q*.

Act III. Scene iv.

[1] wish] with *Q. Emendation of GD B.*

Act III. Scene v.

[1] *Centered above this line Q has* Calantha, Penthea.

[2] PENTHEA *is omitted from Q.*

[3] prethee] prethe *Q*.

[4] that? *Q*] that jewel? *GD*.

[5] revell in Elizium] revell Elizium *Q. Emendation of GD.*

ACT IV. SCENE I.

[1] stands] stand *Q*. *Emendation of GD. B follows Q.*
[2] be deny'd] beny'd *Q*. *Emendation of GD.*
[3] prethee] prethe *Q*.
[4] merit] myrit *Q*.
[5] Which less rash] Which rash *Q*. *Emendation of GD.*
[6] muzled] musled *Q*.

ACT IV. SCENE II.

[1] largenesse *Q*. *Weber emended to "largess," which is adopted by Hazelton Spencer.*
[2] been] bee *Q*.
[3] roof] root *Q*. *Emendation of GD B.*
[4] appear'd Impostors] appear'd, Impostors *Q*] appear'd imposture *GD*.
[5] Sun] Swan *Q*. *Emendation of GD, adopted from Weber.*
[6] bawdy *Q*] bandy *GD*.
[7] too] to *Q*.
[8] PENTHEA *is omitted from Q.*
[9] prethee] prethe *Q*.
[10] augury *Q*. *Weber emends to "angry," which is adopted by Hazelton Spencer.*

ACT IV. SCENE III.

[1] prethee] prethe *Q*.
[2] fortunes, guard to] fortuness guard to *Q*] fortunes guard, the *GD*.
[3] Wear] Were *Q*.

ACT IV. SCENE IV.

[1] prethee] prethe *Q*.

ACT V. SCENE I.

[1] too] to *Q*.
[2] doublers *Q*] doubles *GD B.*
[3] prethee] prethe *Q*.

ACT V. SCENE II.

[1] prefer] prefers *Q*. *Emendation of GD. B follows Q.*
[2] goodnesse] goddesse *Q*. *Emendation of GD B.*
[3] his] this *Q*. *Emendation of GD B.*

[4] Org. Honourable infamy. *Q. GD give these words to Near-chus, and are followed by Hazelton Spencer.*

[5] HEMOPHIL] Lem. *Q.*

[6] prethee] prethe *Q.*

ACT V. SCENE III.

[1] infinite] infinites *Q. Emendation of GD.*

[2] Hemophil] Lemophil *Q.*

[3] mother's] mother *Q. B notes that the Q reading is probably an old genitive.*

[4] *A space in Q indicates the loss of a word.*

[5] Is not untroubled *Q*] Is or untroubled *GD*] Is untroubled *B. Hazelton Spencer also follows Q.*

Q has FINIS *under the concluding speech of Nearchus on K 4ʳ. The Epilogue is on K 4ᵛ.*

THE LADY OF PLEASURE

The text was made from Xerox prints of the Folger Library copy of the 1637 Quarto.

Q   Quarto of 1637 (Folger).
GD   Edition of Gifford and Dyce.
B   Edition of Baskervill, Heltzel, and Nethercot.

PERSONS OF THE COMEDY:

[1] SENTLOVE Q] SCENTLOVE *GD B and all modern editions.*

ACT I. SCENE I.

[1] with] whith Q.
[2] How, how? Q] How now? *GD B.*
[3] retired] retire Q.
[4] affect] effect Q B.
[5] home] whom Q. *Emendation of GD B.*
[6] Bonfires] Bonefires Q.
[7] with safety] which safely Q. *Emendation of GD B.*
[8] may] my Q.
[9] vayle] vay'le Q.
[10] In] On Q B.
[11] Straddles] Straddle Q. *Emendation of GD B.*
[12] *Q consistently has* Alexander *in stage directions and* Al. *in speech headings for Kickshaw.*
[13] Willt] Will Q.
[14] Ne'er] Nere Q. *The words "never," "ever," and their compounds have been regularized throughout.*
[15] March-beer] March-beare Q.

ACT I. SCENE II.

[1] Here] Her Q.
[2] whither] whether Q.
[3] Exalt with Q] Exalt their genius with *GD B.*
[4] the] thee Q.

ACT II. SCENE I.

[1] Exeunt] Exit Q.

ACT II. SCENE II.

[1] charged] charge Q] large *GD B.*
[2] bonfire] bonefire Q.

[3] kindred] kinred Q.
[4] HAIRCUT] Is. Q. *Emendation of GD B.*
[5] you're] your Q.

ACT III. SCENE I.

[1] What's] What Q.
[2] *Printed as verse in Q.*
[3] *Printed as verse in Q.*
[4] lovinge] lovings Q.
[5] o'er] ors Q.
[6] fortitude] fortit Q.
[7] her] him Q. *Emendation of GD B.*
[8] but in single] but single Q] but with a single GD B.

ACT III. SCENE II.

[1] wo' not need] woo'not meet Q. *Emendation of GD B.*
[2] made the times] made times Q. *Emendation of GD.*
[3] reçu] receu Q.
[4] faites] faictez Q.
[5] vôtre nature] vostre naturel Q.
[6] cette langage] Ceste language Q. mari] mary Q.
[7] failli, s'il n'eût] failly, s'il n'eust Q.
[8] vôtre plutôt] vostre plustot Q.
[9] vois] voy Q. toujours] toutsjours Q.
[10] langage] language Q. courtoisie] courtesie Q.
[11] Vraiment] Vrayement Q.
[12] vôtre] vostre Q. moi] moy Q.
[13] vôtre] vostre Q.
[14] habits] habitz Q.
[15] gâté] gastè Q.
[16] accompli] accomply Q.
[17] entends] entende Q.
[18] scion] syen Q.
[19] Tis] This Q.
[20] boast] least Q. *Emendation of GD B.*
[21] Ex. all but Cel. & Alex. & Little. Q.
[22] meane you] you meane Q.
[23] exercised] exercise Q.
[24] Cel. *is omitted from Q on this line but appears on the next.*
[25] your] you Q.
[26] kidneys] kidnyes Q.
[27] Cent] Sant Q.

ACT IV. SCENE II.

[1] FREDERICK] Are. Q.

ACT IV. SCENE III.

[1] eares] yeares Q. *Emendation of GD B.*
[2] showne] knowne Q] known B] join'd valour *GD.*
[3] wear] were Q.
[4] one turned] one, turne Q] one, turn B.

ACT V. SCENE I.

[1] frighted] frighed Q.
[2] Dutch] Douch Q.
[3] looke] tooke Q. *Emendation of GD B.*
[4] Palate] Palater Q.
[5] doore] dooee Q.
[6] rapier's] rapier's is Q.
[7] footman] footmen Q.
[8] Beldam] Bedlam Q. *Emendation of GD.*
[9] I found my selfe the very same in i'th morning, Q. *Emendation of GD B.*
[10] Us] As Q. *Emendation of GD B.*
[11] are so] so are Q B. *Emendation of GD.*
[12] Satyres] Satires Q.
[13] honour us to-night] honour to night Q. *Emendation of GD B.*

NOTES

NOTES

THE CHANGELING

TITLE. The term "changeling" referred primarily to the deformed or sub-normal child which the fairies left as substitute for a normal child they stole. Therefore, it came to mean "idiot" or "mentally inferior person," as Antonio pretends to be, although he is never called "changeling" within the text of the play. It could also mean "any inferior substitute or untrustworthy person," especially a weak woman. By analogy, then, Beatrice, Diaphanta, and Deflores are all "changelings."

DRAMATIS PERSONAE.

(1) ALIBIUS. The name means "being in another place," and the character is offstage most of the time, allowing for his essential role of jealous husband.

THE SCENE.

(2) *Alicant.* The Spanish Valencian seaport of Alicante.

ACT I. SCENE I.

(1) *home back.* As Dilke and Bawcutt note, the idea is that through marriage one regains paradise, underlining the irony of the love affair begun in church and leading to unusual degradation.

(2) *buy.* A more familiar instance of a witch selling a wind occurs at the opening of I. iii. in *Macbeth.* Bawcutt also cites Webster and Rowley's *A Cure for a Cuckold,* IV. ii. 97 : "The winds which Lapland Witches sell to men."

(3) *chang'd your orizons.* Referring to the prayers of the foregoing line. Note also the suggestion that Alsemero is another changeling in his "religion."

(4) *Valentia.* Valencia, the native place of Alsemero. Cf. line 168.

(5) *first sight.* The beginning of a line of metaphor central to

the play. Beatrice states it more fully at 73 ff. The eyes are easily deceived by appearances.

(6) *five dayes past.* The time during which Beatrice has been betrothed to Alonzo.

(7) *Basilisk.* See T. H. White, *The Bestiary, A Book of Beasts* (New York, 1960), pp. 168 ff.

(8) *poppy.* Mandragora or opium as a sedative.

(9) *discover.* Reveal, by taking off his clothes.

(10) *change.* Suggesting that Beatrice too is a changeling.

(11) *call me so.* Her father used to call her "My best love."

(12) *Iulan.* Pronounced as three syllables. Bawcutt notes that Rowley may have read in a commentary on the *Aeneid* that the name Iulus Ascanius (*Aeneid*, I, 267) was derived from the Greek word meaning "first growth of beard." If the phrase were not commonly understood, however, such erudition would be pointless. Iulus would simply be an image of the young hero.

(13) *Saint Jaques.* St. James the Greater, whose shrine is at Compostella. He is the patron saint of Spain.

(14) *Gibralter.* The Dutch defeated the Spanish in a sea fight on April 25, 1607. A truce was signed at The Hague two years later; "the late League" of line 186.

(15) Alsemero is like Romeo in following a fate to an evil end. The "murderers," however, are not aimed at him.

(16) *Serpent.* Ambiguous in the context. It may be her evil love or Deflores. There would be little point in her dropping her glove deliberately at this time. More likely, she is disturbed by the proximity of Deflores and the increasing desire to have Alsemero.

(17) *Now.* Glossed by Bawcutt as meaning "although." But the fact that Deflores has long known of her hatred for him may be irrelevant. In a comic mood, Deflores is simply pretending to discover it for the first time.

ACT I. SCENE II.

(1) *ring.* Bawcutt cites the parallel in Middleton's *Family of Love*, V. iii. 418–421 : "be it proclaimed to all that are jealous, to wear their wife's ring still on their fingers, as best for their security, and the only charm against cuckoldry." See the edition of Bullen, III, 118.

(2) *thrift.* Profit from his profession, also mixed with worries (*care*).

(3) *Visitants.* Those who came to Bethlehem Hospital (Bedlam) to enjoy the display of madmen.

(4) *like an Idiot.* A picture of what Antonio may have looked like occurs in J. J. Elson's edition of *The Wits, or Sport upon Sport* (Ithaca and London, 1932).

(5) *Tonie.* The name became synonymous with fool or madman. The *NED* credits the usage to the Antonio of this play.

(6) *no beast.* Aristotle observed that laughter distinguishes man from beast.

(7) *at first sight.* One of the ways in which the sub-plot parodies the main plot. Lollio, however, is not aware of the accuracy of his vision.

(8) *wind him up.* Apparently a windlass image related to the earlier uses of *raise.*

(9) *push-pin.* A common game of pushing one pin across another, but suggesting Antonio's interest in Isabella.

(10) Lollio makes Alibius stand between him and Antonio.

(11) *we three.* The inscription on a picture of two fools, implying that the viewer is the third. Cf. *Twelfth Night,* II. iii.

(12) *rope.* Bawcutt notes that the word refers to "rope of onions" as well as the hangman's rope.

(13) *her.* M. W. Sampson notes that "her" is stage-Welsh for "my." The Welsh were proverbially mad about cheese.

ACT II. SCENE I.

(1) *eyes.* Continuing the irony of Beatrice's forced sense of value.

(2) *Diamond.* Precious gems like diamonds and carbuncles were thought to give their own light and have magic powers.

(3) Compare lines 89 ff of this scene and V. iii. 154 ff.

(4) *Garden Bull.* Referring to Paris Garden on the Bankside near the Globe Theatre, in which bulls and bears were baited.

(5) *keep the night.* Beatrice is too disturbed to intend any precise meaning, such as her refusing to consummate an unwanted marriage. She probably means she will do everything she can to prevent the marriage. The dramatist may be thinking of her later preparations for the wedding night with the man she does want to marry.

(6) *in his passions.* Bawcutt, Dilke, and Dyce omit this phrase from Q because it cannot be explained. The explanation, however, seems to me simply the emphasis on the word *his.* Tomazo is pointing out that Alonzo's sexual union with Beatrice will be—in her imagination—her lover's passions.

Act II. Scene ii.

(1) *dangerous.* The danger is that Beatrice will suspect Diaphanta of interest in Alsemero.

(2) *poyson to't.* That is, if Alonzo knew of the kiss he would wish it poisoned.

(3) *strike off.* The metaphor may be one of striking off fetters, as Bawcutt suggests, but I prefer one of eliminating an item from a list of debts.

(4) *cause.* Bawcutt notes the "scholastic tag, 'remove the cause and the effect ceases.' "

(5) *the law.* Probably referring to the laws against duelling.

(6) *Perfect.* That is, "complete." The Latin sense is more obvious here than in the *perfection* of I. i. 12.

(7) Ironically, Beatrice traps herself here by a pretended change.

(8) *Angels food.* The biblical "manna." Psalm LXXVIII, 25.

Act III. Scene i.

(1) The movements between II. ii. and III. i. combined with III. ii. are notable. A double change of scene is apparently indicated by twice exiting at one door and entering at another. A simpler instance occurs in *The Revenger's Tragedy* between II. ii. and II. iii.

Act III. Scene ii.

(1) Bawcutt observes that the idea of cutting off the finger with the ring is not in the source. Since the ring is Beatrice's token to Alonzo, their inescapable union, despite her change, seems to be symbolized.

Act III. Scene iii.

(1) These lines suggest Lollio's sexual interest in Isabella from the start.

(2) *proper.* Handsome, as a gentleman's should be.

(3) *understanding.* A joking insult to the members of the audience standing under the foot of the stage.

(4) *shooting a bolt.* Playing on the proverb : "a fool's bolt is soon shot."

(5) *Spider.* It was believed that a spider in a drink made it poisonous. Compare the use of the idea in *The Winter's Tale*, II. i. 39 ff.

(6) *Titania.* Probably taken from Shakespeare's *Midsummer-Night's Dream,* although Oberon is the popular king of the fairies in folklore.

(7) *Diomed.* The king of Bistonia in Thrace who fed his horses with human flesh. Hercules, in his eighth labor, killed him and fed his body to the horses, making them tame.

(8) *Bucephalus.* The horse of Alexander, which only he could ride. Franciscus invites Lollio to mount him.

(9) *Esculapius.* The Greek god of medicine.

(10) *Tiresias.* The blind prophet of Thebes. Having changed into a woman, he discovered that the sexual act was more pleasurable to women than men. For revealing the fact Juno struck him blind. Ovid, *Metamorphoses,* III.

(11) *big-bellied.* A metaphor for the full moon (*Luna*). The evil aspect of the triple moon goddess was Hecate.

(12) *Licanthropi.* A kind of madness in which the victim imagined himself to be a wolf. A familiar instance is that of Ferdinand in *The Duchess of Malfi,* V. ii. The dog and bush referred to belong traditionally to the man in the moon.

(13) *Orlando.* The crazed hero of Ariosto's *Orlando Furioso.* The adjective *left-handed* may mean "substitute."

(14) *parlous.* Witty, sharp, and shrewd, suggesting "dangerous."

(15) *hell.* A term from the game of barley-brake for a space through which couples had to run and were caught by a pair or pairs within the space.

(16) *Lipsius.* The scholar Justus Lipsius (1547–1606) whose work came to represent the curt or Senecan style of prose.

(16) *Ars Amandi.* The Art of Love; probably an allusion to the work of Ovid.

(17) *Do you.* A proper form of the imperative. Cf. *Look you* in line 181.

(18) *fear enough.* Isabella makes a moral point here which reflects on the bestiality of Beatrice and Deflores.

(19) *Lacedemonian.* M. W. Sampson suggests a play on "laced mutton," a term for a prostitute. It may be related to "merry Greek."

(20) Isabella parodies the violence of Beatrice.

(21) *Lawyers Haven.* Bawcutt cites a popular collection of jests in which a lawyer leaves a bequest to Bedlam because he got all his wealth from madmen.

Act III. Scene iv.

(1) *eye.* The eye of Alonzo. The eye symbolized both reason and lust.

(2) *refulgent.* Breaking forth in a shining blaze.

(3) *capcase.* A hat-box.

(4) Beatrice seems to be offering Deflores a paper draught.

(5) A combination of ironic puns on the play's title.

Act IV. Scene i.

(1) *Stage direction : accident.* Simply "occurrence," or "event."

(2) *Secrets in Nature.* The title of a work (*De Arcanis Naturae*) by Antonius Mizaldus, a French scholar (1520–1528). See the long note in Bawcutt's edition. Dyce and Sampson have found the pregnancy and virginity tests in another work by Mizaldus, but not in the *De Arcanis.* Such fabulous tests go back to Pliny's *Natural History.* In Middleton's *Hengist, King of Kent* the heroine is forced to conceal the loss of her virginity in a test which assumes that a virgin can cure an epileptic fit. (II. iii. 248 ff).

(3) Bullen suggests an allusion to the trial for divorce brought by the Countess of Essex in 1613. Charging that her marriage was not consummated, she was examined by a selected group of women.

(4) *portion.* Dowry.

Act IV. Scene ii.

(1) *Briamata.* In Reynold's story, the name of a country house.

(2) *sins and vices.* The common emendation is "chins and noses." The error can be explained by assuming common misreading of a badly written Tudor secretary hand, but I am not convinced that the error is there. Deflores is witty enough to be punning : as their faces turn witch-like their vices become devilish.

(3) *puts me on.* Incites me.

(4) Bawcutt suggests that the scene overheard is probably III. iv.

(5) *obscurely.* Hidden in darkness, and probably veiled.

Act IV. Scene iii.

(1) *weighting.* The adjective describes the increasingly full moon which portends madness. Cf. III. iii. 77.

(2) *Knight of the Sun.* Hero of a popular romance published in nine parts from 1578 to 1601, translated from a Spanish work. *Scorpio* was the sign governing the sexual parts of the body. The

middle Region suggests the "waist" and serves for Hamlet's jest with Rosencrantz and Guildenstern about Fortune's "privates." (II. ii).

(3) *peesles.* The whips, with Lollio's characteristic play on sexual meanings.

(4) *trunck.* Not a reference to horns, but a compliment to the virility of the old man.

(5) *wax.* Icarus, *son of Cretan Dedalus* constructed wings with wax, which melted, causing his death.

(6) *Clue.* The thread which Ariadne gave to Theseus as a guide through the labyrinth of Minos.

(7) *Endymion.* The young man with whom the Moon fell in love.

(8) *Fox-skin.* Purely metaphorical for "deception," since a bestial garb would not suit Antonio's other appearances or this one.

(9) *Latona.* Leto, mother of Apollo and Artemis.

(10) *deserve it.* If Lollio is thinking of Antonio or Franciscus as victim of a legal maneuver by which Alibius would get control of an estate as guardian, the joke would be finally on Alibius, since neither of the "fools" is "incurable."

Act V. Scene i.

(1) *first fruits.* A similar usage occurs in *The Lady of Pleasure*, II. ii. 93.

(2) *frailty.* Common human nature.

(3) *well said.* Cf. IV. iii. 209.

(4) *Mine.* Bawcutt suggests that the "close calls" may be having passed the virginity tests and having deceived Alsemero.

(5) *that?* Surely not the body of Diaphanta. Vermandero is exclaiming, "What's that you say?"

Act V. Scene ii.

(1) *hard bested.* Hard put to it; in a difficult position. From "bestead."

Act V. Scene iii.

(1) *adultery.* By arguing that Beatrice belongs to his dead brother, Tomazo can accuse Beatrice and Alsemero of adultery.

(2) *rib.* A fine use of the biblical account of the creation of Eve. Genesis II. 21 ff.

(3) *Meteor.* An evil omen. Meteors were bred out of impurities, according to Elizabethan "science." The stars were eternal and pure.

(4) *barly-break.* See the note on III. iii., 162, Note (15). The couples in the game were not supposed to let go of each others' hands.

(5) *circumscribes.* Includes within its bounds.

(6) *token.* Apparently, at line 139 Deflores wounds himself as a sign of his love for Beatrice.

(7) *thence.* From the bodies. The *black fugitives* are the spirits of Beatrice and Deflores.

(8) *Your.* He is addressing Tomazo.

THE REVENGER'S TRAGEDY

Dramatis Personae.

(1) LUSSURIOSO. Related to the older meaning of "luxury," which was "lechery."

(2) SUPERVACUO. Although his name means "Over-foolish," he challenges his "ambitious" brother for the throne and has to be killed.

(3) DONDOLO. Allardyce Nicoll notes that the name is taken from Marston's *Parasitaster, or The Fawn.*

(4) GRATIANA. Her name means "Grace." The fact is only temporarily ironic, since she does repent.

Act I. Scene i.

(1) *luxur.* Compare Lussurioso.

(2) *Quit-rent.* Nicoll explains: "a rent paid by a free-holder for services which might be required of him. Here Vengeance is made the free-holding 'tenant' to tragedy." However, it seems to be "murder" who is the tenant and "vengeance" the quit-rent. Perhaps the service "murder" wishes to escape is "punishment." Or, there is a confusion of "vengeance" with "murder."

(3) *three-pilde.* The finest quality velvet.

(4) *Dutchesse skirt.* The implications of this remark for the character of Hippolito are completely ignored in the rest of the play. In typical Elizabethan style, the concept of "motivated personality" is subordinated to dramatic structure and moral theme.

(5) *occasion.* See Erwin Panofsky, *Studies in Iconology* (New York, 1939), plate XXI.

(6) *French Moale.* Nicoll notes the phrase to be a translation of "taupe."

(7) Vindice seems to be saying that in moral matters, Castiza and Gratiana are incorruptible; but being women, they will easily accept explanations of most affairs.

Act I. Scene ii.

(1) *for-head.* An important image of the play, combining allusions to honor, cuckoldry and impudence. Compare also lines 33, 107, and I. iii. 8.

(2) *boweld.* In the process of embalming, corpses were disembowelled.

(3) *sonne-in-law*. That is, treat him as if he were your own, and ignore the law.

(4) *ceast*. Nicoll suggests the sense of "left, or let off." It could also be simply "stopped in that sport."

(5) *woman*. Compare I. i. 114.

(6) *Hatted-dame*. Ladies of noble rank did not wear hats.

(7) Nicoll explains this passage admirably. The fellow was so tall that on horseback he could peep into windows left open. Men preferred him on foot and asked him to dismount. His head also knocked against the tavern signs and barber-basin signs.

(8) *beggar*. Based on the proverb: "set a beggar on horseback and he'll ride a gallop." But the Duchess is thinking of sex rather than politics. See Tilley, B 238.

ACT I. SCENE III.

(1) *Grace the bawde*. A reference to an actual woman has been suspected, but she remains undiscovered.

(2) *Verge*. Playing on the sense of "the limits of the royal court" ruled by the rod (*virga*), with perhaps another play on "beyond virginity."

(3) *Time*. Tourneur's sense of present evils is almost apocalyptic, but the theme was common from classical literature. The *"Maide in the old time"* of line 13 is a version of *nuda Antiquitas*, or *Veritas*, as J. C. Collins notes. See also Erwin Panofsky, *Studies in Iconology* (New York, 1939), pp. 151 ff., on the innocence associated with nakedness.

(4) *blanckes*. G. B. Harrison may be correct in glossing the word as "tickets in a lottery that bear no prizes."

(5) *Scrivener*. A legal secretary who draws up agreements.

(6) *drunckards*. The dramatist is particularly revolted with the sin of drunkenness.

(7) *enter*. To take possession of, as a devil. One of the several allusions to deviltry which make the play more characteristic of earlier moralities than Jacobean melodrama.

(8) *waxt lines*. Letters sealed for secrecy.

(9) *Phaenix*. For an interesting discussion of this "real" or fabulous creature see T. H. White, *The Bestiary, A Book of Beasts* (New York, 1960), pp. 125 ff.

(10) *winde up*. G. B. Harrison suggests a windlass metaphor. Nicoll notes that "good fellow" was a cant word for "criminal" or "thief."

(11) *travayld.* With the usual connotation of "experienced in evil."

Act I. Scene iv.

(1) *Stage directions: Discovering.* Uncovering, revealing.
(2) No source for this Latin proverb has been found.
(3) From Seneca's *Hippolytus,* line 607, "Curae leves loquntur, ingentes stupent." Compare Penthea's line : "They are the silent griefes which cut the hart-strings." *The Broken Heart,* V. iii. 75.
(4) *saver.* Nicoll notes that this term is common to various games.

Act II. Scene. i.

(1) *limits.* Compare the note for I. iii. 17.
(2) *Angells.* Gold coins worth ten shillings.
(3) *Enter.* Combining the senses of devil-possession and sexual union. See also line 136.
(4) *mother.* Playing on the sense of "hysteria." Compare line 241.
(5) *charge.* Expense, in the sense of "living overhead." Perhaps there is a play on "care."
(6) *fore-head.* See the note for I. ii. 4.
(7) Inferiors removed their hats in the presence of their lords, who might allow them to "cover." Castiza's followers will not have to "uncover" to others but leave their hats at home on the staghorn racks. There is again the play on cuckoldry.
(8) *fore-tops.* Compare the thematic uses of *fore-head.*
(9) *brooke it.* Endure it. We cannot endure such a loss.
(10) Another use of the devil-possession metaphor.

Act II. Scene ii.

(1) The sense is : "I'll call you a knave to your face and make a fool of you behind your back."
(2) *travell.* Again with the sense of "experience in evil."
(3) *Knit.* Probably in the sense of "conceive a child."
(4) *drab.* A mistress.
(5) *fees.* What follows is a burlesque of Jacobean monopolies.
(6) *lessen not.* Based on Exodus XX. 12 : "Honour thy father and thy mother : that thy dayes may bee long upon the land, which the Lord thy God giveth thee." Another allusion occurs at IV. iv. 9.
(7) *beneficiall perjury.* By the doctrine of equivocation one could morally lie under oath for a good cause.

(8) *fees.* For "phease" or "pheaze," meaning "hangings" or "tatters."

Act II. Scene iii.

(1) The movement between this and the fore-going scene indicates that the location has been changed. Meanwhile, the Duke and Duchess are probably displayed in bed.

Act III. Scene iii.

(1) *die black.* G. B. Harrison notes the instance in Nashe's *Jack Wilton* of a blasphemer's corpse turning black. See R. B. McKerrow's edition of Nashe, II, 326.

Act III. Scene iv.

(1) *signe.* G. B. Harrison notes that bleeding had to be done under favorable astrological conditions. The *Buckminster Almanac* for 1598 named those of Aries, Libra, Sagittarius, or Pisces.

Act III. Scene v.

(1) *for-head.* A striking development in the imagery.
(2) *White divill.* In the common sense of "hypocrite."
(3) *Brooke.* Vindice's pun may be based on the metaphor of the King as fountain of honor and life.

Act III. Scene vi.

(1) *modell.* Plan.
(2) *sirrah.* I assume that the officer is being threatened.

Act IV. Scene i.

(1) *yron-age.* Ironage or fetters. One thinks also of the dramatist's view of the present Age of Iron.

Act IV. Scene ii.

(1) *Secretary.* Another league-with-the-devil metaphor.
(2) *change tongue.* Vindice's earlier words printed in the quarto as prose are easily relined as verse. The form of prose is best reserved for the rustic idiom which begins in this scene.
(3) *Anno Quadragesimo secundo.* The forty-second year.
(4) *Anno sextagesimo tertio.* The sixty-third year.
(5) *winde.* Probably a hunting metaphor: "drive him down wind by letting him scent you."
(6) *worst.* Emphasizing the play's strong view of drink.
(7) *substantiall.* Solid and unchanging in nature.

ACT IV. SCENE III.

(1) *this or these.* Referring to kisses or gestures of affection, not to people.

ACT IV. SCENE IV.

(1) *Quarled.* There is a metaphor here of the mother's milk curdling and becoming poisonous.

(2) *Cut not.* Compare the note for II. ii. 97.

(3) *fore-head.* Related to the "impudence" theme.

(4) *did not.* Castiza means : "I did not speak the truth when I spoke of becoming the Duke's mistress."

ACT V. SCENE I.

(1) *eight returnes.* G. B. Harrison notes that this phrase implies no detailed legal knowledge. Any common almanac could offer it. A "return" was an officer's report on the execution of a writ or court order.

(2) *dyes drunke.* Again relating drunkenness to unusual damnation.

(3) Allardyce Nicoll gives this speech to Ambitioso, assuming that it is out of character for Supervacuo and that a mistake has been made. But there is no error here. Rather, it is at V. iii. 56, where the compositor misread "Super." as "Spur." Otherwise, there is no way of explaining what happens to the Dukedom and Supervacuo's right to it.

ACT V. SCENE II.

(1) *Winde up.* This may be a windlass metaphor or a cross-bow figure.

(2) *drunke downe.* Implying a punishment for their sin.

ACT V. SCENE III.

(1) *star.* The star is a comet, and as such would be ominous to princes. "When beggars die there are no comets seen." *Julius Caesar*, II. ii.

(2) This line makes Vindice's revenge perfect, before he makes the error of confession. In orthodox fashion, the right of vengeance reverts to the Lord, as was foreshadowed all along.

THE BROKEN HEART

Epistle Dedicatory.

(1) LORD CRAVEN. William, Lord Craven (1606–1697) was made a baron in 1627 and earl in 1664. In 1632 he aided the Queen of Bohemia in the Palatinate and devoted his life to her service.

The Sceane.

(1) H. J. Oliver comments (p. 59) : "not so much the Sparta of history as that of Sidney's *Arcadia*." Ford's Spartans arrive in the ornate coaches known as caroches.

Prologue.

(1) *A Truth.* The truth could have been the relation of Sir Philip Sidney to his Stella, the unhappy Lady Rich. See Stuart P. Sherman, "Stella and the *Broken Heart*," *PMLA,* XXIV (1909), 274–285.

Act I. Scene i.

(1) *brauch't.* Steeped.
(2) *Hymenean.* Hymen was the god of marriage.
(3) *Aconite.* Wolf's bane or monk's hood. In myth, the poison made by Hecate from the foam of Cerberus when Hercules brought him up from Hades. See H. J. Rose, *A Handbook of Greek Mythology* (London, 1933), pp. 215–216. Shakespeare uses the form "Aconitum" in *Henry IV Part II*, IV. iv. 48.
(4) *Vesta's sacred fires.* The Roman hearth cult attended by virgins. When, in V. iii, Calantha sends Philema to the Temple of Vesta, she seems to be thinking of it as an English nunnery. Vestal candidates were between the ages of six and ten.

Act I. Scene ii.

(1) *Messene.* The province or district state rather than the town.
(2) *Pephon.* A Laconian city bordering on Messenia.
(3) *Chaplet.* A wreath for the victor's brow, of laurel.
(4) *provinciall garland.* Gifford notes that it was an honor given to the general who had added a province to the empire of Rome. Neither here nor in the phrase "provincial roses" is there any connection with Provence.
(5) *Vulcan.* The husband of Venus who trapped her in the act of adultery with Mars.

(6) *Kennell*. Here used in the sense of "dog shelter" or "lair of a fox." More commonly, the word is used in the sense of "gutter."

(7) *dog*. Smeaton observes that this is an allusion to clipping poodles so as to leave tufts.

(8) *Corncutters*. Not reapers but foot-surgeons.

Act I. Scene iii.

(1) *fore-dooming*. That is, pre-judging the fate of Orgilus as an evil one.

(2) *Oratory*. A study or lecture hall.

(3) Orgilus puts on an antic disposition like that of Hamlet or Malevole the Malcontent.

(4) *absurd*. Gifford observes that this term was used when an opponent drew false conclusions from one's premises in scholastic debate.

(5) *speculations*. Observations of the heavens, particularly.

(6) *accidents*. That is, not substances, in Aristotelian philosophy.

(7) *mushrome*. Not in the more common sense of "upstart" but of a lowly person who lives mostly in the dark.

Act II. Scene i.

(1) *lick'd*. From the common belief that bear whelps were licked into shape by their mothers.

(2) *springall*. As the term implies, a youth. Shakespeare does not use the term, but Smeaton cites its use in Spenser's *Faerie Queene*, V. v. 6.

(3) *Eare-wrig*. The term derives its sense from an insect that penetrates into the ear.

(4) *ride*. This may be an allusion to the Vice riding on the Devil's back.

(5) *horne*. The cornucopia, a symbol of prosperity, but here with the implication of cuckoldry many times over.

(6) *chopping*. Large and vigorous, a "whopper."

(7) *collops*. Strips of flesh.

(8) *tympany*. A swelling or tumor, often associated with pride or jealousy.

Act II. Scene ii.

(1) *vipers*. For an early account of this natural habit see T. H. White, *The Bestiary, A Book of Beasts* (New York, 1960), p. 170.

(2) *schoole-tradition*. For a similar attitude towards medieval scholasticism compare *The Revenger's Tragedy*, III. iv. 64, where

subtle verbal distinctions are attacked as dunce-ish (from Duns Scotus).

ACT II. SCENE III.

(1) *Schoole.* Another allusion to medieval philosophy. Cf. II. ii. 11.

(2) *reall.* Pronounced as two syllables.

(3) *equall.* In the sense of equally consenting, as expressed at II. ii. 100.

(4) *Genius.* Here used in the sense of good angel.

(5) *Aches.* Pronounced like the plural of the letter "h," "aitches."

(6) *excellentest.* A double superlative. For similar instances in Ben Jonson see A. C. Partridge, *The Accidence of Ben Jonson's Plays, Masques and Entertainments* (Cambridge, 1953), pp. 116–117.

ACT III. SCENE I.

(1) *reall.* Here and at line 50 again pronounced as two syllables.

(2) *moderators.* The sense seems to combine that of "ruler" and "umpire." The term was used for the controllers of academic debate at Cambridge, and for elected officers in the Presbyterian Church.

(3) *Delphos.* Ford combines, as does Shakespeare, the place Delphi on the slopes of Parnassus with the island of Delos, birthplace of Apollo and Artemis.

ACT III. SCENE II.

(1) *Stage directions : severall stands.* In separate positions.

(2) *discovered.* Revealed by withdrawing a curtain from a previously prepared area of the stage.

(3) *art.* From her position as an artificial wife and forced lover. Compare line 206.

(4) *Touch-hole.* The hole in the breech of a firing arm by which it is set off. A good term for a bawd.

(5) *Pandora's box.* For the history of this symbolic object see Dora and Erwin Panofsky, *Pandora's Box* (New York, 1956).

(6) *Art.* The art of pretending or acting a role.

ACT III. SCENE IV.

(1) *Borrow of Nature.* The appeal to nature over established authority.

ACT IV. SCENE I.

(1) *Ixion.* A standard image of presumption. Compare Marston's use in *The Malcontent*, II. i. 4.

(2) *beauty.* The Platonic argument that the power of beauty abrogates all laws and customs.

(3) *mortall.* Synonymous with *deadly* in the next line, but the emphasis is on the verb *prove* between them.

ACT IV. SCENE II.

(1) *garland of good-will.* The title of a collection of popular songs (1604).

(2) *Quintescence.* The fifth element beyond the basic four of earth, air, fire, and water, the object of the Alchemists' search.

(3) This passage seems to have a relation to T. S. Eliot's *Burnt Norton*: "Footfalls echo in the memory / Down the passage which we did not take / Towards the door we never opened / Into the rose-garden."

(4) *Amethist.* This gem was believed to prevent intoxication.

(5) *Lord ascendant.* An astrological term for the star ruling the eastern quarter of the heavens.

ACT IV. SCENE III.

(1) *scruple.* A small point to trouble the conscience.

ACT IV. SCENE IV.

(1) *Phaeton.* A more than usually good use of the classical allusion. He was the son of Helios, and not being able to control his father's chariot he scorched the earth, until Zeus struck him down with a thunderbolt.

ACT V. SCENE III.

(1) See the note for I. i. 98, footnote (4).

(2) An English version of Seneca's *Hippolytus*, line 607: "Curae leves loquntur, ingentes stupent." See *The Revenger's Tragedy*, I. iv. 23.

Concluding note: Charles Lamb, in his *Specimens of English Dramatic Poets Who Lived About the Time of Shakespeare* (London, 1808), remarked: "I do not know where to find in any Play a catastrophe so grand, so solemn, and so surprising as this." Of Ford's genius he said: "Ford was of the first order of Poets. He sought for sublimity, not by parcels in metaphors or visible images, but directly where she has her full residence in the heart of man; in the actions and sufferings of the greatest mind." See E. V. Lucas, ed., *The Works of Charles and Mary Lamb* (7 vols., London, 1903–1905), IV, 218, 610–611.

Title. Two passages in the play (I. i. 109–119; III. i. 39–42) indicate the phrase implied professional immorality. Aretina's comic reformation is therefore the major action of the play.

PERSONS OF THE COMEDY.

(1) LORD. The Lord is an earl, as the mode of address "right honourable" implies. See III. i. 97.

(2) SENTLOVE. The preferred modern spelling is "Scentlove." However, this character both "scents" love for courtiers and "is sent" love by them when they tire of their women. The quarto consistently omits the "c." See II. ii. 88 ff.

DEDICATION.

(1) LORD LOVELACE. Sir Richard Lovelace (1568–1634) was created Lord Lovelace of Hurley, Berkshire, in 1627. He was a distant relative of the poet Richard Lovelace, whose family long resided in Kent.

(2) *oblige.* Perhaps an "s" has been lost on the end of the verb.

ACT I. SCENE I.

(1) *Hobbyhorse.* In the Morris Dance a male dancer impersonated a horse. Maid Marian, Robin Hood's sweetheart, was another participant.

(2) *sale.* Compare Vindice's ironic tirade in *The Revenger's Tragedy,* II. i. 210 ff.

(3) *the Ball.* The context of this passage suggests an allusion to censorship of Shirley's play *The Ball,* which revealed immoralities in the new practice of subscription dances. See A. H. Nason, *James Shirley,* pp. 230 ff.

(4) *family of love.* The name of a religious sect of Anabaptist origins and suspected of lewd practices. Also the title of a play by Middleton. See the headnote in Bullen's Middleton, III, 3–5.

(5) *Authorise.* The word was accented on the second syllable.

(6) *Hide Parke.* The subject or locale of a realistic comedy by Shirley licenced in 1632. See A. H. Nason, *James Shirley,* pp. 227 ff.

(7) *complement.* Shirley's first play, licenced in 1625, was titled *Love Tricks, or The School of Compliment.* It included a satirical scene of teaching the art by book.

(8) *In blacke.* Printed works of the seventeenth century were frequently presented as treasuries of wit. The term "wit" was nar-

rowing from its earlier sense of "wisdom" or "intelligence" towards "sophisticated verbalism."

(9) *cocking*. Cockfights.

(10) *glorious*. The adjective here probably has a double sense of "splendid" and "vainglorious."

(11) *character*. The name of a literary genre popular in the seventeenth century, derived from the Theophrastan tradition of satire but including ideal types.

(12) *catches*. Part songs sung as rounds.

Act I. Scene II.

(1) *Arras*. Wall hangings with a woven picture-story and convenient for hidden actions and spying. Compare Vindice's comic monopoly in *The Revenger's Tragedy*, II. ii. 72 ff.

(2) *with gold*. In *Hyde Park*, IV. iii, Venture sings a song about horses including one called Toby with golden shoes.

(3) *Novice*. A candidate for membership in a religious house.

Act II. Scene I.

(1) *drawne*. A play on the legal sense of a criminal's being hanged, drawn, and quartered.

(2) *generous*. The adjective retains a Latinate sense of "breeding and spirit."

Act II. Scene II.

(1) Celestina's moral position shrewdly combines the possibilities of Platonic courtship and advantageous marriage.

(2) These lines indicate that Sentlove receives as well as procures women. Panders such as he feed (*are . . . tasters*) at the courtiers' tables; while the lords demand the *first fruits*.

(3) Celestina seems to mean that she would not be interested in a man of rank under that of ambassador.

(4) *scruple*. Literally, one twenty-fourth of an ounce. Compare *The Malcontent*, II. iv. 12.

(5) *laundry Ladies*. They were proverbially of immoral character.

Act III. Scene I.

(1) *Stage direction: unready*. Not completely dressed.

(2) *Lady of pleasure*. Here used in the sense of whore or prostitute.

(3) *noses*. Sir William Davenant—for one—lost the bridge of his nose through venereal disease.

(4) *footclothes.* They were a sign of social precedence because they were a luxury, protecting the rider from mud and dirt by hanging down the side of the horse. They were also frequently of expensive quality.

(5) *right honourable.* The mode of addressing an earl.

(6) *dogdayes.* The hottest part of the summer ruled by the Dog-star Sirius.

(7) *Idea.* The term was common in Elizabethan sonnet sequences, indicating that Henrietta Maria's cult was nothing new to English aristocracy.

(8) *goblins.* Ironically, Kickshaw comes to serve—so he believes —the Devil himself.

ACT III. SCENE II.

(1) *affect.* Used here in a much stronger sense than at II. i. 131, namely, "to feel passion for."

(2) *Ordinaries.* Common eating places.

(3) *Compare line 172.*

(4) *in election.* In discrimination and taste.

(5) *bow wide.* That is, a bow shot wide.

(6) *Sibill.* The sibyls were prophetic hags. Compare T. S. Eliot's epigraph to *The Waste Land,* I.

(7) *greene disease.* For a discussion of this much diagnosed ailment, see R. F. Fleissner, "Falstaff's Green Sickness Unto Death," *Shakespeare Quarterly,* XII (1961), 47–55, especially 48, 49, and notes.

(8) *Beadle.* The officer who would arrest him for debt, as he fears in IV. i.

(9) *how.* Compressed form for "which is how."

(10) *Mushroomes.* The term implied the sense of "upstart," and "questionable character" because the plant grows in darkness, out of the face of the sun (king).

(11) *perspective.* A magnifying glass or telescope.

ACT IV. SCENE I.

(1) *Hecate.* The evil aspect of the moon goddess.

ACT IV. SCENE II.

(1) *feather.* On his hat. For an earlier allusion to the style see *The Malcontent,* Induction, 44; and V. iii. 40–41.

(2) *reede.* This bit of fancy about using a reed as a cloak is related to a colloquialism. As Gifford explains it, "a staff was an-

ciently called a Dunkirk, or a Plymouth cloak." See his edition of Massinger (4 vols., III, 494). Littleworth's idea gains comic impact from our learning earlier (III. ii. 79) that he can "endure a cudgelling."

(3) *Bucephalus.* The horse of Alexander the Great. Compare *The Changeling*, III. iii. 55, and note (8).

(4) *Beare.* Gifford notes: "This tavern is frequently mentioned by our old dramatists. The bridge meant was, in Shirley's time, called the Strand-bridge; it crossed (as Pennant says) the Strand, nearly opposite the present Catherine-street, where the collected waters from the high grounds were discharged into the Thames." See the Gifford and Dyce edition of Shirley (1833), IV, 72.

(5) *Ganimed.* The cup-bearer and paramour of Zeus.

ACT IV. SCENE III.

(1) *luminaries.* See the introductory discussion of Ford and Shirley.

ACT V. SCENE I.

(1) *Phaeton.* The standard image of glittering failure. Compare *The Broken Heart*, IV. iv. 26, and note (1).

(2) *Mirmidan.* Myrmidon, the name of the soldiers of Achilles who were famed for loyalty and ruthlessness.

(3) *Julip.* A sweetened drink containing medicine.

(4) *Beares foote.* As Gifford notes, this is probably an intentional blunder.

(5) *Platonicke way.* Since the Lord is testing Celestina, he is employing a common abuse of the term.

(6) A late version of "Come live with me and be my love," by Marlowe, to which Ralegh wrote a reply in Celestina's mood and which Donne also varied.

(7) *Satyres.* Being made up of a human trunk on the body of a goat, a satyr was extremely lecherous.

SELECTED BIBLIOGRAPHY

SELECTED BIBLIOGRAPHY

This list of works includes those given earlier in short form. The additional titles are limited to those of primary importance, either for the study of the period or the individual authors.

The following standard abbreviations for periodicals have been used :

CL.	Comparative Literature.
EIC.	Essays in Criticism (Oxford).
ELH.	Journal of English Literary History.
ES.	English Studies.
JEGP.	Journal of English and Germanic Philology.
MLN.	Modern Language Notes.
MLQ.	Modern Language Quarterly.
MLR.	Modern Language Review.
MP.	Modern Philology.
N&Q.	Notes and Queries.
PBSA.	Papers of the Bibliographical Society of America.
PMLA.	Publications of the Modern Language Association of America.
PQ.	Philological Quarterly (Iowa City).
RES.	Review of English Studies.
RMS.	Renaissance and Modern Studies (University of Nottingham).
SP.	Studies in Philology.
SR.	Sewanee Review.
TSE.	Tulane Studies in English.

I. BASIC GUIDES

Adams, J. Q., ed. *The Dramatic Records of Sir Henry Herbert.* New Haven, 1917.

Bentley, G. E. *The Jacobean and Caroline Stage.* 5 vols. Oxford, 1941–1956.

Chambers, E. K. *The Elizabethan Stage*. 4 vols. Oxford, 1923.

Greg, W. W. *A Bibliography of the English Printed Drama to the Restoration*. 4 vols. London, 1939–1959.

Harbage, A. *Annals of English Drama 975–1700*. Philadelphia and London, 1940.

Murray, J. A. H., *et al. The Oxford English Dictionary, Being a Corrected Re-Issue . . . of A New English Dictionary*. 13 vols. Oxford, 1933.

Nungezer, Edwin. *A Dictionary of Actors and of Other Persons Associated with the Public Representation of Plays in England Before 1642*. New Haven, 1929.

Parrott, T. M., and R. H. Ball. *A Short View of Elizabethan Drama*. New York, 1943.

Tilley, M. P. *A Dictionary of the Proverbs in England in the Sixteenth and Seventeenth Centuries*. Ann Arbor, 1950.

Ward, A. W. *A History of English Dramatic Literature to the Death of Queen Anne*. 3 vols. London, 1899.

II. COLLECTIONS

Baskervill, C. R., V. B. Heltzel, and A. H. Nethercot, eds. *Elizabethan and Stuart Plays*. New York, 1949.

Brooke, C. F. T., and N. B. Paradise, eds. *English Drama 1580–1642*. New York, 1933.

Dilke, C. W., ed. *Old English Plays. Being a Selection from the Early Dramatic Writers*. 6 vols. London, 1814–1815.

Jacobs, J., ed. *The Fables of Aesop as First Printed by William Caxton in 1484 with Those of Avian, Alfonso and Poggio*. 2 vols. London, 1889.

Rimbault, E. F., ed. *The Miscellaneous Works in Prose and Verse of Sir Thomas Overbury, Knt*. London, 1856.

Spencer, H., ed. *Elizabethan Plays*. Boston, 1933.

III. THEATRE

Campbell, L. B. *Scenes and Machines on the English Stage during the Renaissance*. Cambridge, 1923.

Hodges, C. W. *The Globe Restored, A Study of the Elizabethan Theatre*. London, 1953.

Linthicum, M. C. *Costume in the Drama of Shakespeare and His Contemporaries*. Oxford, 1936.

Reynolds, G. F. *The Staging of Elizabethan Plays at the Red Bull Theater 1605–1625.* New York and London, 1940.

Small, R. A. *The Stage-Quarrel between Ben Jonson and the So-Called Poetasters.* Breslau, 1899.

Sharpe, R. B. *The Real War of the Theaters : Shakespeare's Fellows in Rivalry with the Admiral's Men, 1594–1603 : Repertories, Devices, and Types.* Boston and London, 1935.

Wallace, C. W. *The Children of the Chapel at Blackfriars 1597–1603.* Lincoln, 1908.

IV. STUDIES AND CRITICISM

Bennett, J. W., O. Cargill, and V. Hall, Jr., eds. *Studies in the English Renaissance Drama.* New York, 1959.

Bethell, S. L. *The Cultural Revolution of the Seventeenth Century.* London, 1951.

Boas, F. S. *An Introduction to Stuart Drama.* Oxford, 1946.

Bowers, F. T. *Elizabethan Revenge Tragedy 1587–1642.* Princeton, 1940.

Bradbrook, M. C. *Themes and Conventions of Elizabethan Tragedy.* Cambridge, 1935.

—— *The Growth and Structure of Elizabethan Comedy.* London, 1955.

Brown, J. R., and B. Harris, eds. *Jacobean Theatre.* London and New York, 1960.

Bush, D. *Mythology and the Renaissance Tradition in English Poetry.* Minneapolis and London, 1932.

—— *English Literature in the Earlier Seventeenth Century 1600–1660.* Oxford, 1945.

Campbell, O. J. *Comicall Satyre and Shakespeare's Troilus and Cressida.* San Marino, 1938.

Clark, W. S. *The Early Irish Stage : the Beginnings to 1720.* Oxford, 1955.

Cunliffe, J. W. *The Influence of Seneca on Elizabethan Tragedy, An Essay.* London, 1893.

Doran, M. *Endeavors of Art : A Study of Form in Elizabethan Drama.* Madison, 1954.

Ellis-Fermor, U. M. *The Jacobean Drama, An Interpretation.* London, 1936.

Eliot, T. S. *Elizabethan Essays.* London, 1934.

Farnham, W. *The Medieval Heritage of Elizabethan Tragedy.* Berkeley, 1936.

Gagen, J. E. *The New Woman. Her Emergence in English Drama 1600–1730*. New York, 1954.

Harbage, A. *Thomas Killigrew, Cavalier Dramatist 1612–1683*. Philadelphia and London, 1930.

—— *Cavalier Drama. An Historical and Critical Supplement to the Study of the Elizabethan and Restoration Stage*. New York, 1936.

—— *Shakespeare and the Rival Traditions*. New York, 1952.

Herrick, M. T. *Tragicomedy : Its Origin and Development in Italy, France, and England*. Urbana, 1955.

Jewkes, W. T. *Act Division in Elizabethan and Jacobean Plays 1583–1616*. Hamden, 1958.

Lewis, C. S. *English Literature in the Sixteenth Century Excluding Drama*. Oxford, 1954.

Lucas, F. L. *Seneca and Elizabethan Tragedy*. Cambridge, 1922.

Ornstein, R. *The Moral Vision of Jacobean Tragedy*. Madison, 1960.

Panofsky, D., and E. *Pandora's Box*. New York, 1956.

Panofsky, E. *Studies in Iconology. Humanistic Themes in the Art of the Renaissance*. New York, 1939.

Prior, M. E. *The Language of Tragedy*. New York, 1947.

Reed, R. *Bedlam on the Jacobean Stage*. Cambridge, Mass., 1952.

Russell, H. K. "Tudor and Stuart Dramatizations of the Doctrines of Natural and Moral Philosophy," *SP*, XXXI (1934), 1–27.

Spencer, T. *Death and Elizabethan Tragedy, A Study of Convention and Opinion in the Elizabethan Drama*. Cambridge, Mass., 1936.

Swinburne, A. C. *The Age of Shakespeare*. New York and London, 1908.

Symons, A. *Studies in the Elizabethan Drama*. New York, 1919.

Wells, H. W. *Elizabethan and Jacobean Playwrights*. New York, 1939.

White, T. H. *The Bestiary. A Book of Beasts. Being a Translation from A Latin Bestiary of the Twelfth Century*. New York, 1954, 1960.

Wilson, F. P. *Elizabethan and Jacobean*. Oxford, 1945.

V. THOMAS MIDDLETON

Tannenbaum, S. A. *Thomas Middleton: A Concise Bibliography.* New York, 1940.

EDITIONS

Bald, R. C., ed. *A Game at Chesse by Thomas Middleton.* Cambridge, 1929.
——— *Honourable Entertainments by Thomas Middleton.* Oxford, 1953.
Bawcutt, N. W., ed. *The Changeling.* London, 1958.
Bullen, A. H., ed. *The Works of Thomas Middleton.* 8 vols. London, 1885–1886.
Dilke, C. W., ed. [See vol. IV of this edition as described in Section II. COLLECTIONS.]
Dyce, A., ed. *The Works of Thomas Middleton.* 5 vols. London, 1840.
Ellis, H., ed. *Thomas Middleton.* 2 vols. London, 1887–1890. (Introduction by A. C. Swinburne.)
Sampson, M. W., ed. *Thomas Middleton.* New York, 1915.

STUDIES

Bald, R. C. "The Sources of Middleton's City Comedies," *JEGP*, XXXIII (1934), 373–387.
——— "The Chronology of Middleton's Plays," *MLR*, XXXII (1937), 33–43.
Barker, R. H. *Thomas Middleton.* New York, 1958.
Bradford, G. "The Women of Middleton and Webster," *SR*, XXIX (1921), 14–29.
Bullock, H. B. "Thomas Middleton and the Fashion in Playmaking," *PMLA*, XLII (1927), 766–776.
Christian, M. G. "An Autobiographical Note by Thomas Middleton," *N&Q*, CLXXV (1938), 259–260.
——— "A Sidelight on the Family History of Thomas Middleton," *SP*, XLIV (1947), 490–496.
Dunkel, D. W. *The Dramatic Technique of Thomas Middleton in His Comedies of London Life.* Chicago, 1925.
Eccles, M. "Middleton's Birth and Education," *RES*, VII (1931), 431–441.
Eliot, T. S. "Thomas Middleton," *Elizabethan Essays*, London, 1934.

Fisher, M. "Notes on the Sources of Some Incidents in Middleton's London Plays," *RES*, XV (1939), 283–293.

Hibbard, G. R. "The Tragedies of Thomas Middleton and the Decadence of the Drama," *RMS*, I (1957), 35–64.

Holtzknecht, K. J. "The Dramatic Structure of *The Changeling*." *Renaissance Papers*, ed. A. H. Gilbert. Durham, 1954.

Jump, J. D. "Middleton's Tragedies." *The Age of Shakespeare: The Pelican Guide to English Literature*, Vol. II, ed. Boris Ford. Baltimore, 1962.

Power, W. "Middleton's Way with Names," *N&Q*, n.s. VII (1960), 26–29; 56–60; 95–98; 136–140; 175–179.

Price, G. R. "The Quartos of *The Spanish Gypsy* and Their Relation to *The Changeling*," *PBSA*, LII (1958), 111–125.

Ribner, I. "Middleton's *Women Beware Women*: Poetic Imagery and the Moral Vision," *TSE*, IX (1959), 19–33.

Ricks, C. "The Moral and Poetical Structure of *The Changeling*," *EIC*, X (1960), 290–306.

Schoenbaum, S. *Middleton's Tragedies, A Critical Study*, New York, 1955.

—— "Middleton's Tragicomedies," *MP*, LIV (1956), 7–19.

—— "A New Middleton Record," *MLR*, LV (1960), 82–84.

Sykes, H. D. "Thomas Middleton's Early Non-Dramatic Work," *N&Q*, CXLVIII (1925), 435–438.

Wiggin, P. G. *An Inquiry into the Authorship of the Middleton-Rowley Plays*. Cambridge, Mass., 1897. (*Radcliffe College Monographs No. 9.*)

VI. WILLIAM ROWLEY

Dunkel, W. D. "Did Not Rowley Merely Revise Middleton?" *PMLA*, XLVIII (1933), 799–805.

Mathews, E. G. "The Murdered Substitute Tale," *MLQ*, VI (1945), 187–195.

Morris, E. C. "On the Date and Composition of *The Old Law*," *PMLA*, XVII (1902), 1–70.

Robb, D. M. "The Canon of William Rowley's Plays," *MLR*, XLV (1950), 129–141.

VII. CYRIL TOURNEUR

EDITIONS

Collins, J. C., ed. *The Plays and Poems of Cyril Tourneur*. 2 vols. London, 1878.

Fluchère, H., ed. *La Tragédie du Vengeur, par Cyril Tourneur*. Paris, 1960.

Harrison, G. B., ed. *The Revenger's Tragedy*. London, 1934.

Nicoll, A., ed. *The Works of Cyril Tourneur*. London, 1930.

Symonds, J. A., ed. *Webster and Tourneur*. London, 1893.

STUDIES

Bawcutt, N. W. *"The Revenger's Tragedy* and the Medici Family," *N&Q*, n.s. IV (1957), 192–193.

Ekeblad, I-S. "An Approach to Tourneur's Imagery," *MLR*, LIV (1959), 489–498.

―――― "On the Authorship of *The Revenger's Tragedy*," *ES*, XLI (1960), 225–240.

Hamilton, A. C. "Spenser and Tourneur's *Transformed Metamorphosis*," *RES*, VIII (1957), 126–136.

Hunter, G. K. "A Source for *The Revenger's Tragedy*," *RES*, X (1959), 181–182.

Leech, C. *"The Atheist's Tragedy* as a Dramatic Comment on Chapman's Bussy Plays," *JEGP*, LII (1953), 525–530.

Lisca, P. *"The Revenger's Tragedy*: A Study in Irony," *PQ*, XXXVIII (1959), 242–251.

Ornstein, R. "The Ethical Design of *The Revenger's Tragedy*," *ELH*, XXI (1954), 81–93.

Peter, J. *"The Revenger's Tragedy* Reconsidered," *EIC*, VI (1956), 131–143; 485–486.

Salingar, L. G. "Tourneur and the Tragedy of Revenge." *The Age of Shakespeare: The Pelican Guide to English Literature*, Vol. II, ed. Boris Ford. Baltimore, 1962.

Schoenbaum, S. *"The Revenger's Tragedy*: Jacobean Dance of Death," *MLQ*, XV (1954), 201–207.

Tomlinson, T. B. "The Morality of Revenge: Tourneur's Critics," *EIC*, X (1960), 134–147.

VIII. JOHN FORD

Tannenbaum, S. A. *John Ford: A Concise Bibliography.* New York, 1941.

EDITIONS

De Vocht, H., ed. *John Ford's Dramatic Works Reprinted from the Original Quartos.* Louvain, 1927.

Ellis, H., ed. *John Ford.* London, 1888.

Gifford, W., and A. Dyce., eds. *The Works of John Ford.* 3 vols. London, 1869, 1895.

Scollard, C., ed. *The Broken Heart.* New York, 1895.

Smeaton, O., ed. *The Broken Heart.* London, 1906.

STUDIES

Anderson, D. K. "Kingship in Ford's *Perkin Warbeck*," *ELH*, XXVII (1960), 177–193.

——— "The Heart and the Banquet: Imagery in Ford's *'Tis Pity* and *The Broken Heart*," *Studies in English Literature 1500–1900*, II (1962), 209–217.

Bacon, W. A. "The Literary Reputation of John Ford," *HLQ*, XI (1948), 181–199.

Blayney, G. L. "Convention, Plot, and Structure in *The Broken Heart*," *MP*, LVI (1958), 1–9.

Carsaniga, G. M. "The Truth in John Ford's *The Broken Heart*," *CL*, X (1958), 344–348.

Davril, R. *Le Drame de John Ford.* Paris, 1954.

Ewing, B. S. *Burtonian Melancholy in the Plays of John Ford.* Princeton, 1940.

Harbage, A. "Elizabethan-Restoration Palimpsest," *MLR*, XXXV (1940), 287–319.

Howarth, R. G. "John Ford," *N&Q*, n.s. IV (1957), 241.

Kaufmann, R. J. "Ford's Tragic Perspective," *Texas Studies in Literature and Language*, I (1960), 522–537.

Leech, C. *John Ford and the Drama of His Time.* London, 1957.

Oliver, H. J. *The Problem of John Ford.* Melbourne, 1955.

Parrott, T. M. "A Note on Ford," *MLN*, LVIII (1943), 247–253.

Sargeaunt, M. J. *John Ford.* Oxford, 1935.

Sensabaugh, G. F. *The Tragic Muse of John Ford.* Stanford and London, 1944.

Sherman, S. P. *Ford's Debt to His Predecessors and Contemporaries, And His Contribution to the Decadence of the Drama.* Harvard University, 1906. (Unpublished Dissertation.)

——— "Stella and *The Broken Heart,*" *PMLA*, XXIV (1909), 274–285.

Ure, P. "The 'Deformed Mistress' Theme and the Platonic Convention," *N&Q*, CXCIII (1948), 269–270.

——— "Cult and Initiates in *Love's Sacrifice,*" *MLQ*, XI (1950), 298–306.

——— "Marriage and the Domestic Drama in Heywood and Ford," *ES*, XXXII (1951), 200–216.

IX. JAMES SHIRLEY

Tannenbaum, S. A. *James Shirley: A Concise Bibliography.* New York, 1946.

EDITIONS

Armstrong, R. L., ed. *The Poems of James Shirley.* New York, 1941.

Ellis, H., ed. *James Shirley.* London, 1888. (Introduction by Edmund Gosse.)

Gifford, W., and A. Dyce, eds. *The Dramatic Works and Poems of James Shirley.* 6 vols. London, 1833.

STUDIES

Baugh, A. C. "Some New Facts about Shirley," *MLR*, XVII (1922), 228–235.

——— "Further Facts about James Shirley," *RES*, VII (1931), 62–66.

Feil, J. P. "James Shirley's Years of Service," *RES*, VIII (1957), 413–416.

Forsythe, R. S. *The Relations of Shirley's Plays to the Elizabethan Drama.* New York, 1914.

Gregory, G. M. *Two Studies in James Shirley.* Durham, 1935.

Harbage, A. "Shirley's *The Wedding* and the Marriage of Sir Kenelm Digby," *PQ*, XVI (1937), 35–40.

——— "The Authorship of the Dramatic Arcadia," *MP*, XXXV (1938), 233–237.

Lynch, K. M. *The Social Mode of Restoration Comedy.* New York, 1926.

MacMullan, H. "The Source of Shirley's *St. Patrick for Ireland*," *PMLA*, XLVIII (1933), 806–814.

Miles, T. "Place Realism in a Group of Caroline Plays," *RES*, XVIII (1942), 428–440.

Morillo, M. " 'Frier Sherley' : James Shirley and *Mercurius Britanicus*," *N&Q*, n.s. VII (1960), 338–339.

Nason, A. H. *James Shirley, Dramatist.* New York, 1915.

Parlin, H. T. *A Study in Shirley's Comedies of London Life.* Austin, 1914.

Radtke, S. J. *James Shirley : His Catholic Philosophy of Life.* Washington, D. C., 1929.

Reed, R. A. "James Shirley and the Sentimental Comedy," *Anglia*, LXXIII (1955), 149–170.

Sensabaugh, G. F. "Platonic Love in *The Lady of Pleasure*." *A Tribute to George Coffin Taylor*, ed. A. Williams. Chapel Hill, 1952.

Stevenson, A. H. "Shirley's Years in Ireland," *RES*, XX (1944), 19–28.